Conflict and Gender

Conflict and Gender

Edited by

Anita Taylor

George Mason University

Judi Beinstein Miller

Oberlin College

HAMPTON PRESS, INC
CRESSKILL, NEW JERSEY

Printed in the United States of America

Library of Congress Cataloging-in-Publication Data

Conflict and gender / edited by Anita Taylor, Judi Beinstein Miller.
     p.   cm. -- (The Hampton Press communication series)
    Includes bibliographical references and indexes.
    ISBN 1-881303-80-2. -- ISBN 1-881303-81-0 (pbk.)
    1. Interpersonal conflict. 2. Conflict (Psychology) 3. Conflict management. 4. Men--Psychology. 5. Women--Psychology. 6. Sex differences (Psychology) I. Taylor, Anita, 1935- . II. Miller, Judi Beinstein. III. Series.
BF637.I48C63
303.6'9--dc20   94-28474
                                                        CIP

Hampton Press, Inc.
23 Broadway
Cresskill, NJ 07626

Contents

Acknowledgments

The majority of the chapters in this book are substantially rewritten research first presented in a conference on Gender and Conflict held at George Mason University in January 1991. The editors invited some additional chapters and established a general framework. Our purpose has extended beyond getting important research into the public forum to raising questions about previous scholarship in conflict. We hope to provoke more sensitivity to the role of gender in conflict and thus to generate new research reflecting that sensitivity.

As always, the editors and authors owe widespread thanks. Colleagues in the Institute for Conflict Analysis and Resolution at George Mason University made helpful comments on the manuscripts, especially Mary Clark and Maire Dugan. Editor Don Cegala helped focus and organize the editors' framework perspectives. Reviewers Derek Scheerhorn and Trisha Jones helped us select and improve chapters to be used. Family members, especially Ed Miller, provided encouragement and support for taking the time necessary. The editors here acknowledge the patience and cooperativeness of all authors through the many months required to achieve publication. And finally, also as always, any remaining errors are the responsibility of the authors and editors.

Introduction:
The Necessity of Seeing
Gender in Conflict

Anita Taylor
George Mason University

Judi Beinstein Miller
Oberlin College

Since the 1970s, conflict studies and feminist studies have benefited greatly from a convergence of interest by widely different people, including practitioners, theorists, and researchers. The academic study of conflict, conflict management, and conflict resolution has grown, and applications of conflict resolution strategies have become integral to legal, corporate, and bureaucratic structures and widespread in personal and interpersonal problem solving. Concurrently, the 20th-century women's movement brought major challenges to social and political organizations and changes in personal lives, at least in developed Western cultures. Yet, curiously, these developments have remained largely separate from each other. Although many, if not most, practitioners of interpersonal conflict management are women, most of those involved in the academic study of conflict and its resolution are not. Although much, if not most, of the application of conflict resolution

1

involves situations in which gender is an explicit or implicit element, little conflict resolution theory explicitly addresses issues of gender. This book grew from these curious ironies.

The idea that feminism and gender studies could contribute to theories of conflict resolution gave rise to a 1991 interdisciplinary conference about gender and conflict at George Mason University. Conferees examined how conflict resolution theories might incorporate gender and how perspectives of gender might influence understandings of conflict. They analyzed previous research about gender and conflict and presented original studies that addressed gender difference and its consequences. Their work included organizational and interpersonal contexts of conflict and drew specific attention to violence in conflicts between men and women.

This book, like the conference, covers different forms and contexts of conflict and includes chapters about theory and chapters about research. Taken as a whole, this book raises more questions than it answers and poses problems for which we have no definitive solutions. Yet, its questions and problems are of such consequence that we believe it important to stimulate dialogue that might lead to answers and solutions. Our concerns, which are generated by feminist thinking, converge on a single point: Too much theory, research, and practice of conflict management and conflict resolution fails to contextualize the conflict being addressed. As a result, our understandings of conflict are often incomplete, as are our attempts at resolving conflict.

Any conflict takes place within a context and is influenced by that context. Such a statement is a truism. Social and political structures as well as cultural beliefs and values affect individual perception, thought, feeling, and interactions. This, too, is widely acknowledged. Yet, too much research about conflict and conflict resolution processes fails to address such contextual considerations. Similarly, too much theory generalizes from specific conflict situations when such generalization may not be warranted, and too much application fails to adjust recommendations according to variations in context.

We are convinced that conflicts can be neither understood nor resolved without consideration of their contexts, both small and large, contemporary and historical. In patriarchal societies such as ours, gender and power are important characteristics of contexts in which status relations and values are negotiated. Disagreements over who is right and what is right are therefore influenced by gender and power as they are socially situated and culturally maintained. Domestic quarrels and public debates have this in common, that greater value is placed on the agendas of more highly valued participants. Hence such disputes are typically swayed by male agendas because cultures have historically imparted greater value to male than to female agendas.[1] Thus, gender influences conflict in ways not often obvious to surface examination. Gender shapes conflict issues as well as conflict management processes. And particularly in the public domain, where greater power is typically accorded to men than to women, conflict becomes a male prerogative. Yet, gender difference in the public domain—that is, male dominance in defining conflict issues, prescribing management procedures, and establishing decisional criteria—cannot be understood by sex difference because this asymmetry is a consequence of culturally transmitted, patriarchal beliefs rather than of genes.

The chapters that follow analyze conflicts as a function of contexts. The chapters in Part I address particularly visible and damaging conflicts in which the victimization of women is related to their low status, relative to men, and to the trivialization or denial of their concerns. The positions of wife, child, and secretary (whose attributes are culturally equated) entail vulnerability for their occupants, because the lesser status and trivialization associated with these positions impede social protection. Because such associations are longstanding parts of our culture, they are difficult to change and are generative of continued victimization. We ask what a feminist perspective can bring to theory, research, and practice in these kinds of conflicts.

Chapters in Part II examine the everyday, smaller contexts of conflict to demonstrate that conflict participants, due to their gender and power, are expected to manage conflict differently. These chapters also point to contextual factors beyond gender that make a difference in the conduct of conflict. Such factors as relationships among conflict parties, the physical setting of conflict, seriousness of offense, and attributions for conflict can both override and interact with influences of gender. Consequently, it becomes clear that conflicts between managers and subordinates, husbands and wives, and co-workers or competitors are best understood as involving a complex set of contextual factors. Here we again raise the question of what a feminist perspective can contribute.

Finally, the chapters in Part III return attention to the broader, historical context in which gender and power have come to influence conflict. Here, the very definition of power in conflict is questioned as being an historically male construction. Similarly, human needs that are thought to be served by conflict resolution are questioned as being male defined and potentially blind to differences of gender. Finally, we see how historical constructions of the male and female role may have

---

[1]By historical, we refer as is traditional in Western culture, to the times characterized by written records, typically beginning with the Greeks. Some intriguing records suggest that some "prehistorical" cultures may have been relatively free from the hierarchal social arrangements imposed by patriarchal cultures.

equipped men and women differently to understand the conflicts of others and negotiate their resolutions. We discuss the implications of applying a feminist critique to interim uses of alternative dispute resolution practices and point out the radical changes in thinking needed to resolve rather than manage conflicts.

Each chapter in this book addresses some aspect of context and its interaction with conflict processes, although many share the general tendency of conflict research to explore all ramifications of those contextual frameworks incompletely. Together, the chapters illustrate why contexts such as social structures and historical traditions, in both their macro and micro dimensions, are required to understand fully what occurs in conflict situations. In this introductory chapter, we outline three specific propositions that if carefully attended to would aid the contextualization of conflict in conflict resolution theory, research and practice.

Our first proposition is that it is inappropriate to study social issues (including conflict) without considering the impact of gender. It is inappropriate because gender is one factor that pervades all aspects and levels of conflict. Gender carries expectations for conflict behavior and for rights and responsibilities in conflict negotiations. As such, it connects social context to specific conflicts while influencing conflict processes directly. But the pervasiveness of gender makes its influence, like the air one breathes, too often unseen. Gender becomes a kind of subtext or buried premise that then supports other axiomatic conclusions. That invisibility is nowhere more important than in the paradigms on which Western science and philosophy are based, paradigms shared by mainstream conflict theorists and practitioners alike.

Mainstream theorists and practitioners have seldom recognized the gender bias inherent in their worldview, or have not perceived many phenomena as effects of male dominance, even when they questioned the tenets of logical positivism (e.g., Burton, 1990a; Clark, 1990b & 1991). Feminist scientists, however, have identified gender bias throughout Western thought and science (Bleier, 1984, 1988; Eichler, 1987; Harding, 1987a, 1987b; Haraway, 1988; Hrdy, 1988 Keller, 1985).[2] They have identified bias in locations ranging from the selection of research questions and populations (e.g., focusing on studying heart disease in men, or concentrating research resources on "public" policy issues) to the premises that inform data interpretation (e.g., interpreting a tendency of women to dislike competitive situations as "fear of success"). Keller (1985), Eisler (1987), and others have shown how masculine perspectives have pervaded Western thought since Plato, elevating the need for linear

---

[2]Such a statement should not be taken to "exempt" other philosophical and scientific traditions from gender bias. It is only to limit the conclusion to the particular science critiqued.

thinking, rationality, and objectivity to axiomatic status. The premise that "man" is a competitive animal, for example, is widely accepted and underlies much of social science, lay and public philosophy, and interpersonal interaction. These kinds of observations lead us to the conclusion that gender must be included in studies of conflict. To exclude it is to ignore or misunderstand a central element in human behavior. Although gender will not be equally salient in all conflicts, it will be involved in some way if the social and political structure in which the conflict occurs is patriarchal.

Several chapters in this book raise this point specifically. Those by Stephens, Sandole-Staroste, and Febbraro and Chrisjohn, in particular, show how conflict theorists operate from implicit perceptual screens that ignore the impact of gender. They show that relationships between masculinity and dominant ways of thinking are rarely understood or explicitly stated because gender is rarely foregrounded in discussions of conflict resolution or dispute management. Such silence is inappropriate because it permits unstated gender beliefs to influence models of conflict and conflict resolution without examination of the underlying assumptions. As a result, many of our chapters show, gender bias in models of conflict and conflict resolution remains hidden and, to the extent that practice reflects theory, so does bias in conflict resolution practices.

In contrast to its background position in mainstream theory and research, gender occupies center stage in feminist theories, which argue that no phenomena can be properly understood without a consideration of gender. Gender organizes social life, social structure, and social beliefs (Money & Ehrhardt, 1972) and, according to gender schema theory (Bem, 1981, 1985, 1987), gender also organizes the way we process information about the world and hence influences communication in and about conflict. The term schema refers to a network of associations that organize or guide perception.[3] Schemata include expectations or beliefs about things that go together, for example, attributes of friends versus enemies or, in the case of gender, what goes along with being female or male. Just as people infer attributes about a person from knowledge of a variety of characteristics (e.g., race, nationality, age), so does (presumed) knowledge of a person's sex evoke attributions about a person. Just as we use some attributes (e.g., spends time with me) to assign persons to a relationship category, we use other attributes (e.g., is nurturant or aggressive) to assess their femininity and masculinity.

The network of associations that constitute a schema not only enables interpretation, judgment, and prediction in situations in which

---

[3]Throughout this discussion of gender, we rely heavily on the writings of cognitive psychologist and others (e.g., Lakoff, 1987) whose ideas are derived in large part from cognitive psychology.

information is unavailable or ambiguous, it also guides categorization and assignment of meaning to the objects of our senses. The associations are not random collections of expectations but rather are born out of regularities in experience, which are culture-bound. Dimensions of experience that matter in a culture are thereby reproduced in the schematic knowledge of its members. Gender schemata, although quite different from one culture to another, are fundamental schemata for humans. Girls and boys in most societies learn to make gender distinctions early in life and continue to elaborate their networks of gender associations because everyone around them makes these distinctions.

The research of Sandra Bem (1985, 1987) shows how we come to see the world more or less through gender-colored glasses, depending on how well socialized, or in her words how sex-typed, we are. The better we have internalized cultural expectations about gender, including their application to our self-concepts, the more we understand the world, including ourselves, in gendered terms. Our culture makes the distinction between male and female relevant to nearly all aspects of life, with nearly all aspects becoming gendered, including places, events, objects, and behavior. Consequently, the more gender-schematic is our information processing, the greater is our readiness to associate and remember places, events, objects, and behavior on the basis of gender.

Bem and others (Bem, 1981, 1985) have provided convincing evidence for the organizing influence of gender schemata by comparing the information processing of sex-typed and nonsex-typed individuals. The subjects in her experiments first rate themselves on a series of traits (the Bem Sex Role Inventory) that are used to categorize them as sex-typed or nonsex-typed and various aspects of information processing and memory are then compared among these groups of subjects. For example, in one experiment subjects were shown slides of words that had been previously judged to be masculine, feminine, or neuter and told that their memory for these words would later be tested. The recall of sex-typed subjects was expected to manifest an organization by gender to a greater extent than the recall of other subjects. Bem expected and found that sex-typed subjects recalled clusters of same-gender words to a greater extent than nonsex-typed subjects did, presumably because remembering one schema-related item enhanced retrieval of another with which it was associated. In another experiment (Bem, 1985), subjects listened to a recorded discussion between three males and three females, whose pictures were projected on a screen as they spoke. Afterward, the subjects were asked to match each statement in the discussion with one or another of the photographs. Bem expected that sex-typed subjects would confuse statements by same-sex discussants more often than would nonsex-typed subjects because of their tendency to sort people on the basis of gender. Here, as in other experiments, she found evidence that sex-typed individuals were particularly inclined to organize information on the basis of gender.

Another source of evidence for the pervasive influence of gender comes from language. Although the extent to which language influences perceptions remains controversial (Bing, 1992; Bloom, 1981), it is clear that how people use language reflects how they perceive the world (Lakoff, 1987). Thus, it is significant that language reflects extensive gendering, both in the specific symbols used and in their organization (Miller & Swift, 1991; Penelope, 1990; Spender, 1985). Phenomena that are irrelevant to sex (e.g., cars, ships, nations, tools) are extensively gendered. Cohn (1987), in an analysis of language used by defense consultants to discuss deterrence, war, and nuclear weapons, provides one powerful example. Masculine-centered sexual imagery pervades this language—for example, "getting more bang for the buck," "losing your stuff by disarming," and in talk about erector launches, patting the missile, and deep penetration. Successful detonation of the first nuclear bomb was announced, in in-house communications, as the birth of a baby boy. The specific situation discussed by Cohn reflects a general characteristic of our language: It "embodies" a gendered view of reality. Chapters in this book that also call attention to language use and conflict include those by Febbraro and Chrisjohn, Robinson, Gourley, and Dewhurst and Wall.

Needless to say, when we use language to think, we think with its connotations. Because language, although highly variable from one culture to another, is deeply gendered, it necessitates careful consideration of a second proposition: Gender should not be studied by studying sex—which has been so widely done. We find it troubling to develop this point because it raises questions to which no one—including us and the other authors in this book—has even tentatively satisfactory answers. The difficulty of finding answers, however, must not deter attention to such an important question—as has been the case with most research about conflict.

Most scholars recognize that gender (as distinguished from biological sex) is a social construction, and much feminist research and theory has concentrated on examining the nature of gender (e.g., Bem, 1987; Deaux & Major, 1990; Hess & Ferree, 1987; Kessler & McKenna, 1978). But, most social scientific research about gender, including almost all research that relates gender to conflict, does not reflect its socially constructed nature. Instead, most researchers, including most writing in this volume, use the term *gender* when what they have actually measured is whether a person is considered (or whether they report themselves) to be male or female—which in most cases corresponds to the person's biological sex. Yet, unless one assumes that what is meant by sex and what is meant by gender are in fact equivalent, we cannot know whether or not what has been measured is gender. Even in common discourse, most people recognize some differences between what they think of as biological sex and the category of gender, regardless of what words they use. They make distinctions that have more to do with being masculine or feminine, or with how men and women are supposed to behave, think, and/or feel than with whether those people are male or female.

In short, the terms *sex* and *gender* are not equivalent and should not be used that way by scholars. Not only does equivalent usage lead to confounding of concepts, it raises other important questions about the phenomena we think we are studying. We do not mean that these questions invalidate previous research, but we do suggest that conclusions based on this research be reexamined. Moreover, we believe the ways in which gender influences human relations should be kept foregrounded in any discussion of conflict resolution and in any discussion involving gender.

Sometimes research and theory explicitly reflect the recognition that gender is a social construction; often they do not. In either case, implicit assumptions about gender should not remain unstated or unexamined. These assumptions are that there are two, and only two, genders, operationalized as man and woman; and that these two genders are invariable. These assumptions are made because gender is seen as inextricably related to two, and only two, invariable biological categories, male and female. Many scholars, including some writing in this volume, recognize that gender is not clearly demarked, but they operate on unstated assumptions that biological categories are. Thus, although they recognize that gender may be a variable construction, they conceive a person's sex to be discrete. But, because no good way of operationalizing the idea of gender has been conceived, scholars generally do so by "measuring" sex identifications. In writing, however, they nonetheless use the term *gender* to refer to what has been measured.[4]

The difficulty with such a convention should be obvious: Concepts recognized as different (sex and gender) are not defined differently (either conceptually or operationally) and in fact are confounded both in measurement and reporting. It is widely believed that sex and gender correlate highly, and such a belief may be warranted. But even without precise measurements we know sex and gender do not correlate perfectly, and without a clear operationalization of gender (Spence, 1984), we have no way to assess the degree of confidence we can have in any conclusions about gender differences or similarities when they are measured by sex identifications.

Scholarship based on humanistic methods is only slightly less

---

[4]Keashley's discussion of how she uses the terms sex and gender is related to this issue.

"guilty" of confounding sex and gender than that based on scientific methods. We have great sympathy with the arguments of many feminist scholars that humanistic methods are especially useful for gender research due to their focus on the complexities of individual experience. But humanistic writing is rarely freer than social scientific writing from the overarching confounding of sex and gender. Moreover, few scholars, regardless of discipline or method, have any clear concept of gender as other than an identity based on invariable, bipolar biological "realities." Few can say what it is that creates a sense of being male and female. Although all may recognize that the two "kinds" of gender are defined in relationship to each other, almost no one operationalizes that relationship in defining the concept. Many feminist scholars argue that a component of hierarchy exists between the (two) genders (Kramarae, 1989), but as we argue here, identifying and operationalizing that hierarchy has rarely been done.

Such thinking transfers buried assumptions about sex to gender without ever questioning the transfer, much less the original assumption (Fausto-Sterling, 1985; Kessler & McKenna, 1978). Having assumed two discrete, mutually exclusive sexes, we further assume that once identified, sex is unchanging. Although scholars (and most others) recognize that neither of these assumptions applies without qualification to gender, most thinking and research continues to be built around two discrete, mutually exclusive, and unchanging genders. Research about psychological gender may be an exception to such a conclusion, but even then a person's gender is thought to change only in relatively superficial ways (e.g., men may become more feminine as they age; Hyde, Krajnick, & Skuldt-Niederberger, 1991).

Several writers (Devor, 1989; Fausto-Sterling, 1985; Kessler & McKenna, 1978) have shown that even the biological dichotomy between male and female humans is not as clear as assumed. Unless one defines a male as any individual with a Y chromosome and a female as anyone without a Y chromosome, the male and female categories are not mutually exclusive, regardless of whether the criterion is hormones or any of the sex markers including secondary sex characteristics. For example, men and women share the same hormones, although in different quantities, and there is great variation among both men and women in how much of each hormone an individual has, which in turn changes for each person with time and environmental influences. In the absence of biotechnological developments that science fiction may foreshadow, men cannot birth babies nor can women inseminate men; but neither can all women birth babies, nor all men inseminate women. More significantly, many people with the "wrong" chromosomes develop female gender identities and some people with no Y chromosomes develop male gender identities. Although modern surgical techniques and modern media have permitted wider awareness of such "anomalies," such inconsistencies are not new phenomena. Nor have they been created by "modern" civilization. Some cultures have legitimated gender identities that were inconsistent with external genitalia; others have attributed special status to persons who possessed biological manifestations of both sexes.

Why then does our research about gender so rarely exhibit the appropriate caution in its generalizations? One (not the only) reason is that we do not see our conceptualization of gender as problematic. We may recognize that masculinity and femininity vary by degree, but we rarely extend that conception to our understanding of gender. If we recognize femininity and masculinity as being different from female and male, we may operationalize them as continuous variables and add the qualification, "psychological" gender (Bem, 1974, 1979; Spence & Helmreich, 1978, 1979). Even then, we rarely see gender as influenced by situation, and we do not construe it as defined in part by relationships. Rather, we treat it as an identity that is discrete (two, invariable, mutually exclusive categories) and seldom think of doing research that conceptualizes it any other way.

From our perspective, gender is behavior and schematic processing of behavior more than it is a "thing." Gender attributions are made by each person in everyday life, without testing their biological basis. In ways most of us never consider, each of us is always "doing" gender—and drawing conclusions about it. In that way, each person is a gender researcher (Kessler & McKenna, 1978). Almost never does any of us meet another without deciding what gender she or he is. And, without ever noticing, we use verbal and nonverbal communication to cue those around us to the gender identity we wish them to perceive, noticing those efforts only when they fail. Yet, the processes by which we make these gender decisions remain virtually unknown. Although some intriguing possibilities have been posed (Devor, 1989; Kessler & McKenna, 1978), little research explores these possibilities. Such research is essential for scholarship to illuminate adequately the nature of gender and the implications of gender difference.

Research about what leads to gender attributions can improve understanding of more than gender. It can be, for example, fundamental to developing theories about conflict and its management or resolution—for, inevitably, conflicts involve people who carry into all situations their gender schema, which guide their behavior in and communication about the situations. Attributions of gender involve far more than a simple decision of whether individuals are male or female. Those attributions inevitably entail implications about appropriate behavior and what behaviors mean.

In essence, what we argue about gender here is similar to what

Febbraro and Chrisjohn say about conflict in Part III. A conceptual clarification is required.[5] We need a conceptualization flexible enough to
allow for more than two genders, for malleable gender behavior, and for
change in what counts culturally as genderlike.[6] Women of color and
some feminist scholars (Davis, 1981; hooks, 1981, 1984, 1989; Hull, Scott,
& Smith, 1982; Joseph & Lewis, 1981; Spelman, 1988) have pushed current feminist thinking a long way toward that goal, a point we discuss
later. Feminists have largely recognized that no unifying "essence"
unites all women and that we must accommodate differences among
women if our thinking and research are to be accurate and useful.
Similar recognitions need to inform conflict research. We cannot usefully
continue the practice of measuring gender by sex.

The third proposition we believe necessary for adequate understanding of conflict and conflict resolution concerns power in conflict.
Specifically, attention must be paid to the nature of power in conflict, the
relationships of power to conflict, and the place of power in conflict, in
each case as power is modified by gender. This proposition is not quite
so problematic for conflict theory as our second because most conflict
theory examines power. What feminist thinking contributes is a recognition of the ways in which gender and power merge. To develop this
idea, we expand on points developed in this book by Febbraro and
Chrisjohn and Chataway and Kolb and on ideas about violence in Part I.

Foremost among these points is the need to reconceptualize
what we mean by power itself. Power in Western culture has been conceived of as the ability to control—whether the control is exerted on
other people, the environment, or oneself. It is, as such, integral to maintaining order in a hierarchal social structure. Rarely recognized, however, is the link between such an understanding and the construal of hierarchy as essential to social structure. Control in a hierarchy inevitably
involves a person or entity in a position to dominate those less powerful,

---

[5]We should make clear that ours is not the only, nor the first, call for reconceptualization. The original Kessler and McKenna work could be read in such a way,
and many others have made similar points, including Bem herself (1987). See,
for example, Morawski (1987). But insofar as few such results are yet visible, the
argument is still fresh.

[6]Especially useful in recognizing the variability of the phenomena of gender are
the distinctions Kessler and McKenna (1978) make among gender assignment
(what infants are labeled at birth), gender identity (what one calls oneself), gender role, and gender attribution (what gender other people decide a person is).
Notably, each of these groupings uses dichotomous categorization but does not
rely on and is not consistent with the supposedly clear biological dichotomy. We
feel the need to add an additional point: Gender identity has at least two facets,
which are not invariable as they are much influenced by situation. Two aspects
of gender identity are how one identifies oneself to oneself and how one identifies oneself to others.

whether that ability is exercised or simply accepted by those who are dominated. To conceive power as control might not be necessary in egalitarian systems.

Here again is a manifestation of the deeply buried assumptions that tie gender to conflict in usually unseen ways. Conceivably, hierarchy does not require a gender component. But in practice, most hierarchical systems that we know are patriarchal.[7] And in a patriarchy, gender is linked to power because the dominant entity is always male or identified with male, a conclusion demonstrated clearly by many feminist writers (e.g., Daly, 1978; deBeauvoir, 1952; Eisler, 1987; MacKinnon, 1987).

Schaef (1981) has proposed an alternative conception of power, one that is essentially feminist. Instead of construing power as power over others, she describes "power to" or "power with," which is the ability to empower oneself and others. These two concepts differ in important ways. The traditional conception of power as the ability to control (usually others) is of a limited entity. Any increase in power by the person or group being controlled involves a reduction in amount of power held by the controller. In contrast, the empowerment conception of power does not conceive of power as limited. Instead, in an empowerment construction power is unlimited and to empower generates increases in ones own power as well as those of other. This type of power not only does not require hierarchy or dominance, but is in fact thwarted by hierarchy and destroyed by dominance. This alternative conception of the nature of power is central to feminist thinking because equality is at the heart of feminism. Feminism rejects constructions of relationships between people that elevate one above the other and permit the domination of one by the other. Chapters in this book that raise questions about the relationships among gender, power, and conflict include those by Stephens, Sandole-Staroste, Febbraro and Chrisjohn and Chataway and Kolb. Chapters that illustrate the dynamics of "control over" in situations of abuse and harassment include those by Robinson, Shevlin, Gourley and Miller & Sotorin.

Clearly, whether one employs a power over or power with conception affects how power is seen in relation to conflict. Feminist analysis makes two points about power, both suggested by the chapters in this volume. The first (not a new idea to conflict theory) is that power asymmetry itself leads to conflict and thwarts its resolution. Control and domination thwart achievement of autonomy, which according to some schol-

---

[7]Matrilineal social structures rarely refute this conclusion. Although familial ties and descent may associate with female, power structures in most such cultures reflect strong gender components that privilege males. Most important to recognize is that dichotomous categorization of cultures into hierarchical or not is as inappropriate as is dichotomous categorization of gender.

ars (e.g., Burton, 1990a), is a basic human need. When any basic need remains unmet, individuals will search vigorously for ways to meet it. Being dominated is not a need satisfying way of living, and if the "history" of human cultures demonstrates anything, it is that the dominated must be controlled through actual or threatened coercion. Such a dynamic in large part explains why the history of hierarchically structured cultures is a history of forceful control of the dominated portions of the populace by successive elites (Clark, 1989; Eisler, 1987). It also explains why that same history includes few examples of conflicts, even those ostensibly ended by wars, that have actually been resolved. Coercion as a means of conflict control is antithetical to the actual resolution of conflicts.

A second point made by feminist analyses of power and conflict is newer to conflict theory: Hierarchy is strongly linked to patriarchy. Patriarchy, a hierarchical system of social structure that elevates males and that which is male identified, involves a concomitant devaluation of the feminine—females and female identified values, behaviors, or objects. In a patriarchy, people must be controlled through dominance, backed by force if necessary, and control is exercised by male or male-identified dominators.[8] Thus, values that perpetuate the hierarchy and the system of control are identified with males and become masculine values. Values that are less useful in perpetuating hierarchy and control are identified with females and become feminine values. Among these feminine values are those essential to maintaining the species itself (Clark, 1990a), but in a patriarchal culture they are not valued equally with masculine values. Moreover, enculturation processes insure that these devalued feminine characteristics are not distributed at random through the population, but found more among women than men. The chapters by Robinson, Gourley, Euwema and van de Vliert, and Miller and Sotorin in this book illustrate devaluation of the feminine and some of its results.

Particularly important to remember when applying feminist ideas to an analysis of conflict is that the gendering of conflict through conceptions of power is not limited to situations of conflict between women and men. Patriarchal arrangements place whatever is defined as feminine in devalued (hence disadvantaged) positions. Thus, in patriarchy women are disadvantaged because they are less valued and/or less powerful than men.

The role of hierarchy in patriarchy is particularly complicated because it is influenced by other elements as well. Race and class inequalities also characterize many relationships and may be as salient or more salient to patriarchal power as gender. Gender in such cases remains important, but it is modified by race, class, or both. The experience of

---

[8]See Daly (1978) for discussion of female dominators who are male identified in Western and non-Western cultures alike.

gender is then qualitatively different from race to race or class to class. Males ordinarily retain higher rank within the race or class, but the hierarchy distinguishes among them by race and class. Equally significant, although less often obvious, is the disadvantage of female-identified males. In a patriarchy, males within a class or race group retain their higher rank only when they embody masculine characteristics. Those who noticeably embody the feminine violate cultural prescriptions and may become the most disadvantaged of all. In modern U.S. culture, for example, it is possible—even desirable—for men to show sensitivity and to be caring toward their families. But, should they demonstrate female-identified qualities without sufficient balance of the traditionally masculine ones, they become among the most vilified people within the culture.

Feminist analysis raises the question of whether the use of power in conflict can ever be functional for resolving the conflict as opposed to managing it. Some conflict resolution theorists have noted how approaches to eliminating conflict have usually employed power and have ultimately resolved few conflicts (Burton, 1990b; Burton & Dukes, 1990). Our question is this: What would be the impact of bringing a feminist conception of power into conflict resolution theory and practice? Several of our authors address efforts to do so, especially Gourley, Stephens, and Shevlin. The same question should be posed by all who practice or theorize about conflict resolution.

Clearly, conflict theory needs to identify means of empowering the disadvantaged as well as the advantaged. Some efforts at doing so have been made. More important is the need to learn how to transform existing patriarchal systems (Clark, 1990b, 1991) because significant empowerment of disadvantaged groups will not be possible as long as power is conceived as limited and divisible rather than unlimited and generative. The conception of "power over" (coercive power) collides with outcomes of autonomy and equality for all parties.

This analysis of power and its place in conflict exposes the deeply radical nature of a feminist critique. As we argue in the concluding section of this book, conflicts among unequals—inevitable as long as humans strive for autonomy—cannot be resolved in a hierarchy. This feminist analysis is consistent with ideas about engaging conflict constructively that are common in communication and conflict studies. In emphasizing that individual and relationship growth can occur through the constructive handling of conflict, both feminist analysis and relational communication theory eschew the power over construction normally implied in the discourse about conflict. Feminist analysis goes further in that it links constructions of power and equality with gender and, we add, of necessity includes an understanding of the complexity of gender. Finally, we invite our readers to consider the implications of having the parties involved in conflicts—be they "ordinary" humans in personal relationships, supervisors in work relationships, "leaders" in governments, teachers in classrooms, mediators in disputes, or scholars in research academies—not only recognize the feminist conception of power but also share its absolute dedication to equality.

REFERENCES

Bem, S. (1974). The measurement of psychological androgyny. *Journal of Consulting and Clinical Psychology, 42,* 155-162.

Bem, S.L. (1979). Theory and measurement of androgyny: A reply to the Pedhazur-Tetenbaum and Locksley-Colten critiques. *Journal of Personality and Social Psychology, 37,* 1047-54.

Bem, S.L. (1981). Gender schema theory: A cognitive account of sex typing. *Psychological Review, 88,* 354-364.

Bem, S.L. (1985). Androgyny and gender schema theory: A conceptual and empirical integration. In T.B. Sonderegger (Ed.), *Nebraska symposium on motivation, 1984: Psychology and gender* (pp. 179-226). Lincoln: University of Nebraska Press.

Bem, S.L. (1987). Gender schema theory and the romantic tradition. In P. Shaver & C. Hendrick (Eds.), *Sex and gender* (pp. 251-271). Newbury Park, CA: Sage.

Bing, J. (1992). Penguins can't fly and women don't count. *Women and Language, 15* (2) 11-14.

Bleier, R. (1984). *Science and gender: A critique of biology and its theories on women.* New York: Pergamon Press.

Bleier, R. (Ed.). (1988). *Feminist approaches to science.* New York: Pergamon Press.

Bloom, A.H. (1981). *The linguistic shaping of thought: A study in the impact of language on thinking in China and the West.* Hillsdale, NJ: Erlbaum.

Burton, J. (Ed.). (1990a). *Conflict: Human needs theory.* New York: St. Martin's Press.

Burton, J. (1990b). *Conflict: Resolution and provention.* New York: St. Martin's Press.

Burton, J., & Dukes, F. (1990). *Conflict: Practices in management, settlement and resolution.* New York: St. Martin's Press.

Clark, M.E. (1989). *Ariadne's thread.* New York: St. Martin's Press.

Clark, M.E. (1990a). Meaningful social bonding as a universal human need. In J.W. Burton (Ed.), *Conflict: Human needs theory* (pp. 34-59). New York: St. Martin's Press.

Clark, M.E. (1990b, November). *Rethinking the 'rational' society: A plea for some broad-based philosophizing.* Paper presented at 10th Annual Lilly Conference on College Teaching, Miami University, Oxford, OH.

Clark, M.E. (1991). *On "science" and "nature"—"human nature."* Paper presented at Annual Conference of Council on Peace Research and Education, Fairfax, VA.

Cohn, C. (1987). Sex and death in the rational world of defense intellectuals. *Signs, 12,* 687-718.

Daly, M. (1978). *Gyn/ecology, the metaethics of radical feminism.* Boston: Beacon Press.

Davis, A. (1981). *Women, race and class.* New York: Random House.

Deaux, K., & Major, B. (1990). A. social-psychological model of gender. In D.L. Rhode (Ed.), *Theoretical perspectives on sexual difference* (pp. 239-254). New Haven, CT: Yale University Press.

deBeauvoir, S. (1952). *The second sex.* New York: Alfred A. Knopf.

Devor, H. (1989). *Gender blending: Confronting the limits of duality.* Bloomington: Indiana University Press.

Eichler, M. (1988). *Nonsexist research methods: A practical guide.* Boston: Allen & Unwin.

Eisler, R. (1987). *The chalice & the blade: Our history, our future.* New York: Harper & Row.

Epstein, C.F. (1988). *Deceptive distinctions: Sex, gender, and the social order.* New Haven, CT: Yale University Press.

Fausto-Sterling, A. (1985). Myths of gender: Biological theories about women and men. New York: Basic Books.

Haraway, D. (1988). Primatology is politics by other means. In R. Bleier (Ed.), *Science and gender: A critique of biology and its theories on women* (pp. 77-118). New York: Pergamon Press.

Harding, S. (Ed.). (1987a). *Feminism and methodology.* Bloomington: Indiana University Press.

Harding, S. (1987b). The instability of the analytical categories of feminist theory. In S. Harding & J. F. O'Barr (Eds.), *Sex and scientific inquiry* (pp. 283-302). Chicago: University. of Chicago Press.

Hess, B.B., & Ferree, M.M. (1987). Introduction. In B.B. Hess & M.M. Ferree (Ed.), *Analyzing gender: A handbook of social science research* (pp. 9-31). Newbury Park, CA: Sage.

hooks, b. (1981). *Ain't I a woman: Black women and feminism.* Boston: South End Press.

hooks, b. (1984). *Feminist theory: From margin to center.* Boston: South End Press.

hooks, b. (1989). *Talking back: Thinking feminist, thinking black.* Boston: South End Press.

Hrdy, S.B. (1988). Empathy, polyandry, and the myth of the coy female. In R. Bleier (Ed.), *Science and gender: A critique of biology and its theories on women* (pp. 199-146). New York: Pergamon Press.

Hull, G.T., Scott, P.B., & Smith, B. (1982). *All the women are white, all the blacks are men, but some of us are brave: Black women's studies.* New York: The Feminist Press.

Hyde, J.S, Krajnick, M., & Skuldt-Niederberger, K. (1991). Androgyny across the life span: A replication and longitudinal follow-up.

Developmental Psychology 27, 516-519.

Joseph, G.I., & Lewis, J. (1981). *Common differences: Conflicts in black and white feminist perspectives*. Boston: South End Press.

Keller, E.F. (1985). *Reflections on gender and science*. New Haven, CT: Yale University Press.

Kessler, S.J., & McKenna, W. (1978). *Gender: An ethnomethodological approach*. Chicago: University of Chicago Press.

Kramarae, C. (1989). Redefining gender, class and race. In C.L. Lont & S.A. Friedley (Eds.), *Beyond boundaries: Sex and gender diversity in communication* (pp. 317-330). Fairfax, VA: George Mason University Press.

Lakoff, G. (1987). *Women, fire, and dangerous things*. Chicago: University of Chicago Press.

MacKinnon, C.A. (1987). *Feminism unmodified: Discourses on life and law*. Cambridge, MA: Harvard University Press.

Miller, C. & Swift, K. (1991). *Words and women updated*. New York: Harper Collins Publishers.

Money, J., & Ehrhardt, A. (1972). *Man and woman/boy and girl*. Baltimore: Johns Hopkins Press.

Morawski, J.G. (1987). The troubled quest for masculinity, femininity, and androgyny. In P. Shaver & C. Hendrick (Eds.), *Sex and gender* (pp. 44-69). Newbury Park, CA: Sage.

Penelope, J. (1990). *Speaking freely: Unlearning the lies of the fathers' tongues*. New York: Pergamon Press.

Schaef, A.W. (1981). *Women's reality: An emerging female system in a white male society*. New York: Harper & Row.

Spelman, E.V. (1988). *Inessential woman: Problems of exclusions in feminist thought*. Boston: Beacon Press.

Spence, J.T. (1984). Masculinity, femininity, and gender-related traits: A conceptual analysis and critique of current research. In B.A. Maher & W.B. Maher (Eds.), *Progress in experimental personality research* (Vol. XIII, pp. 1-97). New York: Academic Press.

Spence, J.T., & Helmreich, R.L. (1978). *Masculinity and femininity: Their psychology dimension, correlates and antecedents*. Austin: University of Texas Press.

Spence, J.T., & Helmreich, R.L. (1979). The many faces of androgyny: A reply to Locksley and Colten. *Journal of Personality and Social Psychology, 37*, 1038.

Spender, D. (1985). *Man made language* (2nd ed.). London: Routledge & Kegan Paul.

Introduction to Part I

The four chapters of Part I discuss the conflicts involving gender that have the most obvious negative consequences: harassment, physical abuse and sexual abuse. In Chapter 1, "Denial and Patriarchy: The Relationship Between Patriarchy and Abuse of Women," Victor Robinson shows how cultural beliefs encourage silence about the abuse of women and children and how social attitudes aid justifications for abuse. Patriarchal beliefs enable separate, hierarchical spheres of influence for women and men and maintain gender-based asymmetries in power. The public sphere, the dominant one, which includes violence, is accorded to men, whereas the private sphere, which includes responsibility for sexuality, is accorded to women. Because a patriarchy highly values access to power and ability to control others, men are positioned to acquire power over others, especially women. Yet, the threat of violence in maintaining hierarchy creates contradictions that require denial and justification. People learn to be deferential and loyal, to ignore the occurrence of violence, and to accept its justifications. In these ways victims of abuse get blamed and the denial of abuse becomes institutionalized.

Jerri Shevlin's Chapter, "Wife Abuse: Its Magnitude and One Jurisdiction's Response," estimates the prevalence of male assaults on women in heterosexual, intimate relationships. Using surveys conducted since 1975, she argues that the scope of abuse, particularly in marital relationships, has been promoted historically by differences in the legal treatment of private and public conflicts. The legal system has been reluctant to charge or prosecute offenders in family conflicts, despite victims' rights to protection under the law, which increases the likelihood of marital abuse. She believes solutions depend on the legal system making abuse costly, for example, by pro-arrest policies and vigorous prosecution. Shevlin illustrates these points using the history of legal nonintervention in Virginia and recent legislative attempts to address inequities. She generates an agenda of research questions with reference to one county's efforts in using such policies.

Charity Gourley, in Chapter 3, "Mediator Differences in Perception of Abuse: A Gender Problem?", shows how less obvious cases of abuse can be mishandled in mediation. She reviews the literature on gender differences in the mediation of family disputes and draws on it to suggest that male and female mediators may interpret and respond to these disputes differently. She offers suggestions for screening disputants and training mediators in ways that might increase fairness of mediation and satisfaction with its outcomes. Her observations emphasize the importance of balancing power among disputants to provide them with equal opportunities in mediation.

In the final chapter, "Gender and Ambivalence: Ambivalence as a Site of Conflict in the Secretarial Position," David Miller and Patricia Sotirin trace sexual harassment and other demeaning treatments of women to ambiguities and contradictions in the feminine role. They use, as exemplar, the traditionally defined and embodied role of the secretary. They argue that women have been, historically, both trusted and suspected and that this ambivalence is reproduced in organizational positions gendered feminine, such as secretary. The secretary is invaluable yet devalued. Indispensable for interpersonal caretaking in the organization, she marks status of those she serves. Yet, the technical expertise she provides can be replaced by service pools and machinery. Because a secretary's demeanor and appearance, availability, and flexibility are taken as indicators of sexuality as well as professional competence, the boundaries of her services must be continually negotiated. In a context of ambiguous and contradictory role expectations, boundaries often are overstepped. In this context, filled with ambiguities and contradictions, secretaries often fail to recognize or report incidents of sexual harassment. The secretary's involvement in reproducing the problem echoes the processes whereby people deny the abuse that Robinson discusses.

All four chapters illustrate the importance of seeing conflicts in their contexts and of looking at gender and power in conflict situations.

All highlight the complex interrelations among these three factors, as well as the difficulty of appropriately conceptualizing gender as other than an invariable, bipolar construct. Each author discusses gender as a phenomenon acknowledged to be socially constructed, but still falls back on categories of female and male. To achieve the goals we have articulated for dealing with gender in conflict requires accounting for variations over time, as well as impacts of other variables such as race and class.

These chapters clarify two additional implications of the failure to make gender an explicit component of conflict analysis and resolution. They show how ambiguity complicates the function of gender in conflict and how the separation of public and private spheres required by a patriarchy disadvantages females and what is considered female.

The ambiguities described in these chapters are problematic. As Robinson points out, women are not only the primary objects of male violence, they are often devalued as "damaged goods" because of it. Robinson and Shevlin both indicate how laypeople, academics, and social service providers often blame such women for their own victimization. Service providers concentrate on treating the battered more than punishing the batterer, whereas scholars and others spend more effort trying to understand why she doesn't leave than asking why do men beat women and children?

Robinson's analysis and Shevlin's case study afford insight into how ambiguity fosters denial, thereby making it possible for individuals to ignore the consequences of their behavior and their responsibility for it. Ambiguity also enables patriarchal structures to permit, condone, and even at times encourage such violence. The observations of Robinson and Shevlin are consonant with those of Gourley who notes the ambivalence of many mediators, mediation trainers, and scholars of conflict resolution on how to deal with violent men. For Miller and Sotorin, the contradictory expectations that lead to the sexual harassment of secretaries grow from the ambiguities of the role.

These chapters also directly or indirectly show how the role segregation associated with modern "developed" cultures separates life into public and private spheres.[1] The public sphere is male identified and largely controlled by men; the private sphere is female identified and largely controlled by the public sphere. As a result, men and masculine values dominate the culture and identify which issues, including domestic ones, deserve public attention and resources. The Shevlin case study as well as Robinson's analysis of responses to violence by men

---

[1]Belief in the possibility of such a separation is one of those axiomatic gender biases in modern Western thought. That such a separation is even possible is arguable, but until feminist critics questioned the conclusion, it was rare to hear any doubts expressed that it is.

against women illustrate the dichotomy between public and private spheres and how the public sphere commands the most attention and resources. Gourley demonstrates that even mediation, which by its nature would seem feminine, is guided by masculine perspectives. Miller and Sotorin's analysis of embedded sexuality in the secretary's role illustrates the complex interplay of dominance and gender and of the public and private spheres.

Although none of these chapters explicitly addresses economics, we think it is important to note how a patriarchal cultural system genders a market-based economic system, which further disadvantages females and whatever is identified with females. Production in the public sphere has economic value; production in the private sphere does not, even though it is is essential to perpetuate the entire system. This work, which Marx defined as production for use, should be recognized as gendered. Ferguson's (1989) naming such work "reproductive labor" highlights both how production for use is gendered and how it provides the foundation for patriarchal cultures.[2] Production for use is devalued whether it is done in public or private, and it is primarily the domain of women, thus it is feminized. This gendering of the economic system is particularly evident in the devaluing of men who do women's work. Most U. S. adults interpret the term *house husband*, for example, as pejorative. Occupations that require men to perform feminized work are renamed. When men must do clerical work, they are called clerks, administrative assistants, or office managers—almost never secretaries. Gendering of the economic system is built on elevating a male identified value to the level of a "norm" or "given," as in the axiom of rational "man" who is competitive by nature and seeks personal gain by "his" choices.

Robinson, Shevlin, and Gourley each show the ultimate consequences of living in a gendered economic system that exacerbates social inequities. In situations among intimates in which men are violent, economics can constrain women's liberty. A woman may not feel any freer to leave a violent husband than do dependent children. When women do have paid employment outside the home, it is most likely in female-identified and dominated work roles with lower pay than male-identified and dominated work. Women in the United States in 1992 still earned median incomes, for example, amounting to little more than two-thirds of men's (Nasar, 1992). "Women's work" is both unpaid and underpaid. Even women who do paid employment outside the home on a full-time basis still assume the primary burden of the reproductive

---

[2]Ferguson's use of this term clearly identifies the role of production for use in sustaining a culture and refers to a much broader concept than biological reproduction. Without all of the activities considered "women's work" and done without pay, cultures would not be maintained or reproduced through time.

labor (Hochschild, 1989), working more hours and investing more emotional capital than men in sustaining the family unit. Gourley describes this imbalanced investment by women in custody and support mediations. Miller and Sotorin describe another imbalance, this one affecting secretaries whose harassment by male supervisors is at least partially sustained by masculine economic privilege. People, of course, sometimes harass those perceived as equals, but it occurs much less often than harassment of people considered less valuable and known to have fewer economic alternatives to their current employment.

The chapters in Part I demonstrate how patriarchy and a competitive economic system interact to disadvantage women in conflict. They show the importance of keeping the macro context in mind even when examining the most micro of interpersonal interactions. These chapters also show how gender relates to what is ignored, denied, or devalued and how the gendering of roles, values, and behaviors impacts conflict processes. Perhaps most importantly, these chapters raise a question to which we often return: Is it possible to resolve conflicts between unequals? And they raise a corollary issue: the necessity of knowing how to manage conflict until true equality can be achieved.

REFERENCES

Ferguson, A. (1989). *Blood at the root: Motherhood, sexuality & male dominance*. London: Pandora Press.

Hochschild, A. (1989). *The second shift: Working parents and the revolution at home*. London: Pandora Press.

Nasar, S. (1992, October 18). Women's progress stalled? Just not so. *New York Times*, Sec. 3: p. 1, 10.

1

Denial and Patriarchy: The Relationship Between Patriarchy and Abuse of Women

Victor Robinson
George Mason University

The physical and sexual abuse of children, wife battering, rape, and other forms of woman abuse all share at least two characteristics: (a) the perpetrators in these acts are, in the overwhelming majority of cases, men, and (b) these forms of abuse are all accompanied by a consistent pattern of denial. Denial is found in the victims, the perpetrators, and in the immediate circle of family and friends. It is also found in institutional recognition and response to the problem (or lack thereof) and in social awareness in general.

Individuals who commit armed robbery, who engage in assaults in barroom brawls, or who burglarize homes generally do not construct the kinds of elaborate excuses and justifications that one finds in the cases of abusers. Victims of those crimes do not wake up one day to realize that they had been victimized 20 years earlier as is sometimes the case with incest survivors and survivors of other forms of child abuse. Family, friends, and the legal system do not pretend the crimes were not committed and avoid exercising their responsibility to intervene. Nor is our society particularly shy about researching and publishing incidence figures for those crimes. The astounding extent of personal denial in the physical and sexual abuse of women and children and the consistent pattern of denial through all levels of society suggest that more is at work here than a simple psychological reaction to trauma. This chapter examines the sociological forces that reinforce personal denial in crimes of abuse against women and children.

DENIAL

I want to emphasize that *denial* in this chapter does not refer to hiding the facts of a crime to prevent criminal prosecution. The use of the term *denial* does not mean to imply that those who deny are consciously aware of the misdirection. Nor do I limit the definition of *denial* to a simple unconscious protective psychological reaction to trauma. This chapter looks at denial in a wider social and political context. Denial, for the purposes of this chapter, refers to the refusal or inability to recognize, acknowledge, or accept phenomena whose reality or implications one wishes to avoid.

In the following pages, I am particularly concerned with what might be labeled *cultural denial*. Cultural learning builds the framework within which we comprehend the world. However, the assumptions, attitudes, and beliefs built into that framework also create blind spots. An avid belief in free market capitalism may lead an individual to devalue or deny the suffering of those on the margins of economic survival. A singleminded focus on environmental protection may lead an individual to devalue or deny the economic suffering that may result from stringent environmental regulation. These examples are fairly obvious. But when a set of particular cultural assumptions is widely held and deeply embedded in social and institutional structures, it becomes increasingly difficult to "step outside" of the cultural framework to recognize what is hidden or obscured by it. This phenomenon, the tendency of cultural beliefs and assumptions to direct our attention away from certain facets of our social interaction, is what I refer to as *social* or *cultural denial*.

In this chapter I freely move between different levels of analysis examining the phenomenon of denial at the individual and the group and institutional level. The pervasiveness of the theme of denial throughout the literature on the abuse of women and children suggests an underlying framework of cultural belief and institutional structure that supports and encourages denial. The purpose of combining these different units of analysis is to reveal the consistent pattern of denial throughout the dominant U.S. culture and to identify denial in the abuse of women and children as a cultural, not simply an individual, phenomenon.

FORMS OF DENIAL IN CHILD AND WOMAN ABUSE

In my reading of the abuse literature I discern five categories of denial in child and woman abuse:

1. Denial that the act happened.
2. Denial that what happened was criminal.
3. Denial that what happened caused significant harm.
4. Denial of intention or control.
5. Denial of responsibility, victim-blaming.

All five forms of denial can be seen operating at both the individual and the social level.

Denial That the Act Happened

This form of denial is most dramatic in cases of incest, sexual abuse of children by outsiders, and other forms of physical abuse of children. Blume (1990) says that, in her experience as a therapist working with incest survivors, fewer than half the women who were sexually molested as children remember the trauma in adulthood and that almost none of her clients identified childhood sexual abuse as the cause of their problems. Blume says that often "incest survivors do not know that the abuse has even occurred! Even if asked, they say—quite sincerely—No, nothing happened" (p. xiii). Some may know that something happened but be unable to remember exactly what. Blume believes that "this surprising phenomenon is the rule, not the exception, of the post-incest experience." (p. xiii). The anxiety associated with secrecy and the emotional energy required to maintain the secret are arguably the sources of many of the most debilitating effects of child sexual abuse.

Clearly, the psychological defense mechanism of suppressing trauma is at work here. There is also strong evidence of sociological factors reinforcing the psychological denial. Children who report sexual abuse are often ignored or not believed. Adult survivors of incest who confront their families meet the same denial and disbelief. Authorities are reluctant to diagnose sexual abuse or to intervene when it comes to their attention.

This form of denial is also evident as a societal phenomenon. Few statistical studies are available about the incidence of child sexual abuse. What statistics are available are not publicized. When statistics are publicized they do not seem to impact social awareness.

Russell (cited in Caputi & Russell, 1990) conducted a survey in

San Francisco in which 44% of women reported being victimized by rape or attempted rape and 38% by child sexual abuse. The survey also found that 16% of the women reported being victims of incestuous abuse and 14% reported being raped by their husbands. Blume (1990) refers to studies that find between 25% and 40% of women nationally report being sexually abused in childhood.

These are astounding statistics. Due to personal psychological denial, even these figures probably do not adequately reflect the extent of sexual abuse in our culture. If any typical medical disease were so prevalent there would be a public outcry and millions allocated for research. Instead the epidemic continues virtually unnoticed.

Social myths reinforce this form of denial. People may acknowledge that certain crimes happen but they distance themselves from them; "it doesn't happen to people like me." One such prevalent myth suggests that child sexual abuse (and other forms of abuse) happens only within certain cultures, certain communities, or among certain social classes. It is never "our" culture, community, or social class. This idea, that certain communities are more susceptible to abuse, is, at best, only weakly supported by current research (see Gelles & Cornell, 1990). A second myth is the idea that abuse only happens within dysfunctional families. Again, the unspoken assumption is that "our" family is not dysfunctional.

Similar social myths disguise the perpetrators of abuse. Most of us may think, "no one I know would commit such a crime." Yet Russell's survey found that 88% of rape victims knew their attackers (cited in Warshaw, 1988). Still, as Warshaw points out, the prevalent myth about rape is of a stranger who jumps "out of the bushes at an unsuspecting female, brandishing a weapon and assaulting her" (p. 14).

A dramatic illustration of the power of social denial to blind us to the extent of abuse of women and children in our culture is a little-publicized story in the development of Freudian theory. Hall and Lloyd (1989) relate that Freud found many of his female patients reporting that they had been victims of sexual abuse and he began to link their symptoms to childhood sexual trauma. However, upon publication, these ideas were heavily criticized. Subsequently, Freud insisted that these descriptions of childhood sexual abuse were really only incestuous fantasies. Of his patients' descriptions of childhood sexual abuse, Freud later wrote "there can be no doubt of the imaginary nature of the accusation or of the motive that has led to it . . . these separated scenes of seduction had never taken place and they were only fantasies which my patients made up" (cited in Hall & Lloyd, 1989, p. 6).

Denial That What Happened was Criminal

Legal authorities traditionally consider what happens within the family to be outside legal jurisdiction (see Shevlin, this volume). The typical response of law enforcement to a report of wife battering is to defuse the immediate situation and discourage further legal action. In research conducted by Walker (1989), only 10% of battered women called the police for help. Most of the women who did call for help later stated that the police were no help at all and, in fact, "after the batterer saw that nothing had been done to stop him, he often continued his abuse with renewed violence" (p. 62).

Official inaction continues to be policy in many communities, despite the fact that " [a] study, funded by the Police Foundation in Minneapolis in 1981 and 1982, showed that arrest is the most effective police response for reducing further battering" (Walker, 1989, p. 61).

The situation is slowly changing with more and more jurisdictions adopting pro-arrest policies. However, the legal system seems to have found a new approach to ducking family issues by mandating alternative forms of dispute resolution in family-related matters.

Institutional values reflect, but also influence, individual attitudes. If courts are reluctant to prosecute, the message to the victim and the perpetrator is that the act is not criminal. In a study of unincarcerated rapists (noncontrol subjects reported via questionnaires or interviews that they had used force or threat of force to obtain or try to obtain sexual intercourse or sex with a woman), Lisak and Roth (1990) found that none of the unincarcerated rapists labeled their acts as rape or labeled themselves as rapists.

Victims may also be reluctant to characterize the aggressor's actions as criminal. A survey conducted by *Ms.* magazine on college campuses (Warshaw, 1988) found that, of women who described being victims of sexual assaults that met the legal definition of rape, only 27% labeled the assault as "rape."

Denial That What Happened Caused Significant Harm

This form of denial is especially prevalent in cases of wife battering. In a series of in-depth interviews with batterers, Ptacek (1988) found that men often claimed that women exaggerated the severity of the violence. Several men minimized the effects of their violence by suggesting that women bruise more easily than men.

This form of denial is also used to justify sexual abuse. Butler (1979) relates the case of Margaret, a woman who suspected her husband was engaging in incestuous behavior with their 5-year-old daughter:

> Margaret spoke with her husband's sister, a good friend who lived nearby. The sister assured her there was no need to worry about it, that it was "no big thing." She told Margaret that, in their family at least, such behavior was "natural" and went on to state that when she, her younger sister, and Ted were young, and until Ted passed through adolescence, they all had sexual contact with each other. That was "just the way it was" in their family. (p. 123)

In contrast to the views of Margaret's in-laws, evidence clearly shows that child sexual abuse can cause significant harm. Women who were sexually molested as children are prone to depression. They also may have difficulty with self-esteem, inappropriate sexual responses, and difficulties with trust. They may also have addictions or be suicidal as well as suffering other ailments associated with other forms of child abuse (see Blume, 1990; Peters, 1988).

Victims may also try to trivialize the effects of trauma. This often takes the form of suppressing their emotional response as a means of coping. Warshaw (1988) describes a phase during the act of rape in which the woman dissociates herself from what is happening. Warshaw describes this as "a protective reaction that helps the victim survive the experience by not feeling it completely" (p. 56). However, this coping mechanism may lead to a long-term blocking of the emotional response as is illustrated in the comments of one of Warshaw's (1988) subjects: "Those feelings—anger, rage, and guilt—remained suppressed and buried for nearly 16 years. But then, just this year, the lid flew off, and suddenly I was experiencing all those horrible emotions and fears" (p. 70).

Denial of Intention or Control

Denial of intention or control is a form of denial often used by perpetrators. Ptacek (1988) found 94% of the wife batterers he interviewed excused their battering behavior by asserting a loss of control. They attributed their lack of control to use of alcohol or other drugs, as a response to frustration, or simply as a an unexplained loss of control. Typical comments included:

> When I got violent, it was not because I really wanted to get violent. It was just because it was like an outburst of rage.

> I was a real jerk for almost a year. And anything would set me off. Anything. I was like uncontrollably violent. (p. 143)

The idea that a man who is sexually aroused cannot control his actions is a social myth that supports the denial of responsibility in cases of rape. Warshaw (1988) points out that a man's penis is frequently portrayed as a creature with a mind of its own. It may even be given its own name. Thus, the man is absolved of responsibility for the presumably independent actions of his penis.

Denial of control is institutionally sanctioned in the insanity defense in criminal trials. Early researchers aided this defense in cases of abuse by labeling men who abuse as deviant, mentally defective, alcoholic, psychotic, or psychopathic (Mayer, 1985). The tables are turned as these men are portrayed as victims themselves. Diagnoses of psychological or psychiatric problems absolve them of responsibility for their actions.

A related form of denial is mother-blaming. Many studies of child abuse and even wife abuse find fault with the mother. Typical is Mayer's description published in 1985 under the heading "Profile of the Incestuous Triad":

> Sometimes the mother covertly encourages incestuous abuse by setting up her daughter to be a victim of the father. Motivations for such a mother's behavior vary. She may have been a victim of incest and, due to unresolved anger, unconsciously wants her daughters to encounter the same abuse. On other occasions, a mother who wants to avoid sexual contact with her spouse subtly encourages her daughter to become a surrogate sexual partner for the father. (p. 15)

I do not argue against the possibility of such behavior by a mother. But I do dispute the implication that the abuser is to any extent absolved of responsibility because of a mother's behavior.

Denial of Responsibility: Victim-Blaming

Victim-blaming, another way of denying the responsibility of the perpetrator, is so prevalent it deserves discussion by itself. Victim-blaming occurs at all levels of analysis. Perpetrators blame victims, family and friends blame victims, victims blame victims, and society at large blames victims.

Victim-blaming in cases of rape is still widely accepted. One still hears of cases in which judges acquit rapists simply because the victim dressed or behaved provocatively. Past sexual history of the victim, "provocative" behavior by the victim, or simply the fact that the victim was voluntarily in the company of the attacker are all considered mitigating circumstances and evidence of consent by the victim. Hence, the legal system, perpetrators, families, boyfriends and husbands, and often the victim herself see her sharing in or shouldering most of the blame.

In cases of wife battering, the fact that a woman remained in the marriage can be damning evidence. Perpetrators, victims, family, and friends often suggest the wife brought the abuse on herself. In Ptacek's (1988) study, 78% of wife batterers justified their behavior by the wife's failure to fulfill the obligations of a good wife. The "failures" ranged from talking back and not being deferential to not being available for sex and not being a good cook.

Child molesters use this form of denial when they suggest that the child seduced them. Butler (1979) cites a typical case:

> Another aggressor, who abused his niece, insisted to his arresting officers that every time he came to visit his sister, the victim, then only ten years old, would behave in an explicitly seductive way toward him: "She was always wriggling around, shaking her butt right up at me. I knew what she wanted. Now she turns around and hollers rape. But I knew what signals she was giving me." (pp. 82-83)

Adults who physically assault children often use the child's behavior to justify the violence. Gelles and Cornell (1990) tell of a parent who says he did not usually use a strap and that he did not believe in hitting the head or the face. The parent goes on, however, to say he "slapped her in her face a couple of times because she was sassing. That she needed" (p. 40).

Researchers have been complicit in this form of denial. One, writing about wife battering, says:

> In a similar way, we see the husband's aggressive behavior as filling masochistic needs of the wife and to be necessary for the wife's (and the couple's) equilibrium. . . . Such wives as the one we have described in the case above, aggressive, efficient, masculine and sexually frigid, were the rule in our group. . . . The periods of violent behavior by the husband served to release him momentarily from his anxiety about his ineffectiveness as a man, while, at the same time, giving his wife apparent masochistic gratification and helping probably to deal with the guilt arising from the intense hostility expressed in her controlling castrating behavior. (Snell, Rosenwald, & Robey, 1964, pp. 110-111)

These justifications, in large part, reflect prevailing social views. About battered women, the question "Why did she stay?" is far more common than "Why is he violent?" Such social attitudes reinforce the victims' own soul-searching for a rational cause for their victimization: "I must have been in the wrong place" or "If I hadn't said this or done this, it wouldn't have happened." Outsiders also want to fault the victim, perhaps to deny the possibility that it could happen to them as well. Incidence statistics prove that rape, battering, and child abuse can happen to anybody, without regard to race, culture, or class. The only "appropriate" victims are those without power. Victim-blaming is the most heart wrenching and debilitating form of denial.

The framework I have presented is more than just a typology of conflict behaviors and responses. It is a pattern both explained and predicted by feminist analysis, a perspective without which efforts to understand abuse and denial are doomed to failure. To develop that conclusion, I move now to show how a feminist perspective illumines denial of abuse as an expected result of a patriarchal culture.

DENIAL OF ABUSE: AN OUTCOME OF PATRIARCHY

The Patriarchal Model

Patriarchy is characterized by two primary phenomena. The first is hierarchical social structures enforced by patterns of dominance. Hierarchy necessarily involves relations of superiority and inferiority among its parts. Ideological justifications for hierarchy propose the necessity of role differentiation for social organization and suggest that hierarchical power is limited to serving the needs and purposes of the institution. But as French (1985) points out, superiority in a hierarchy tends to become absolute, and "one's superior is superior in every way . . . his utterances are law, his caprices rules of nature . . . the cardinal rule is not to offend him" (pp. 302-303).

In socializing members of the culture into hierarchical structures, patriarchal societies place great emphasis on the importance of power to maintain control. Hierarchy requires preparation for subordinate roles as well. French describes three forms of obedience required as "membership dues" for belonging to a hierarchy. The first involves the correct attitude, "a delicate balance between servility and pride"; the second is loyalty, a loyalty that places the institution (and one's superiors in the institution) above oneself; the third is conformity, although "those who demand or offer" conformity call it "fitting in" (pp. 309-310).

The second key element in a patriarchy is the separation of the world into masculine and feminine spheres of influence. This separation arguably is what turns hierarchy into patriarchy. Males are traditionally trained for the public sphere, to exercise power and control over the environment and other human beings. Females are traditionally trained for the private sphere, to support and nurture. Masculinity is associated with power, control, rationality, and action in the world. Femininity is associated with nurturing, caring, emotion, sexuality, and the private world of relationships and family. The dichotomy extends across many qualities. Anything associated with a state of nature: Food, sexuality, emotion, and nature itself is "feminine." Rationality, power, and control are "masculine." Further, power and control are elevated as the highest values, and "feminine" qualities are relegated to secondary status.

Inherent in the positive valuation of power over others is the glorification of violence. Violence is intimately connected to the concept of masculinity. Because masculine qualities are associated with men, violence becomes the province of men. In a patriarchy, the willingness to use violence is a virtue for men and an essential quality for entrance into manhood.

Power and Control in Hierarchy

The highest values in a hierarchy are access to power and the ability to control others. Those with power are allowed, indeed expected, to exercise it. This is clearly reflected in the role of the state. Government is expected to control what is considered unacceptable deviations from social roles and is given legal right to use violence to enforce that control. Lawbreakers may be shot by police if they resist arrest. "Lawless" nations, those that can be portrayed as having broken the rules of international behavior, may be invaded by more powerful nations.

This pattern of hierarchical control coupled with the sanction of violent enforcement is replicated throughout all levels of a hierarchical society. Children and women traditionally have the least power within a hierarchical family structure. Adult males are expected to maintain control and discipline in the family. Some violence is generally accepted in the process.

Many parents suggest that some violence is necessary in disciplining children. The question becomes: How much violence may be used to maintain control? This provides perpetrators of violence with room to negotiate over significant harm, responsibility, and criminality.

In the cases presented by Athens in *The Creation of Dangerous Violent Criminals* (1989), adults give violence a critical role in training children for survival. Athens describes an essential step in the development of individuals who go on to commit heinous violent crimes as "violent coaching." In violent coaching, an individual who claims the right to instruct a child how to behave in conflictual situations teaches the child not to try to pacify, ignore, or run from protagonists but to physically attack them. If the child does not behave as instructed, the child is threatened with ridicule and sometimes actual physical harm from the coach.

Violent coaching is based on the "premise that the world is inhabited by many mean and nasty people . . . and the novice must be properly prepared to deal with these people when he meets them" (p. 47). Proper preparation includes coaching for and by means of violence. In such a world-view, the physical abuse of children is perceived not only to not cause significant harm but, in fact, to be a positive good, a valuable childrearing method. Insofar as this world-view is shared, to a greater or lesser extent, by the culture at large, is it any wonder that the legal system, family, friends, and neighbors are reluctant to interfere in violent childrearing?

The idea that the violent exercise of power is acceptable in one's first exposure to hierarchy, the family, becomes extended to the culture at large. The use of some violence in controlling children is widely accepted in educational institutions, especially in institutions that deal with "uncontrollable" children such as juvenile homes and detention centers. It is a very small step to extend this concept further to adults perceived as weaker, that is, as being lower on the hierarchical scale. In a patriarchal system, women become "appropriate victims" of the exercise of power as do the economically disadvantaged who are openly subjected to the coercive power of the state. Individuals and society as a whole are trained from the very beginning to accept the violent exercise of power by those in control as appropriate and, in fact, sometimes obligatory.

The importance of violence and the threat of violence in maintaining a hierarchy creates powerful contradictions that require the use of denial. To maintain the legitimacy of using force, it must be claimed in certain situations that violence does not cause significant harm. But human beings are detrimentally affected (even beyond purely physical harm) by violence. As Jaffe, Wolfe, and Wilson point out in *Children of Battered Women* (1990), simply witnessing violence can have severe emotional effects. Also, under a hierarchy, the line between criminal and noncriminal violence becomes obscured. Although physical and sexual abuse is criminal by the letter of the law, perpetrators of violent abuse may be surprised to be brought into court for what seems to them, in the context of their cultural training, to be justifiable behavior. Finally, because hierarchy teaches that the hierarchy must be maintained, by violence if necessary, the argument that victims of abuse have brought violence on themselves becomes logical. The child who does not follow the rules, the wife who is not properly deferential, the woman who walks down a dark street at night or dresses provocatively, is simply "asking for it."

Only in the context of hierarchy, a context in which the exercise of power and control are valued above the rights and needs of certain human beings, does violence become "logical." Hierarchy, therefore, sanctions and legitimizes the forms of denial just discussed.

To maintain hierarchy requires three things of those on its lower rungs: deference, loyalty, and conformity. Each acts to reinforce denial. Those who are not properly deferential subject themselves, within the context of hierarchy, to the exercise of power. As one of Ptacek's (1988) wife-battering subjects said:

> I think a lot of it had to do with my frustration of not being able to handle children. You know, they'd tell me to shut up. "You're not going to tell me to shut up." And then [my wife] would tell me, you know, "Let me handle this." I said, "I'm the man of the house." Then we'd start arguing. That's basically how they used to happen. (p. 148)

The rules governing subordination in a hierarchy are not only a source of denial for the perpetrator; victims are also trained for hierarchy, to know what is required of them. If a person in power, a superior, who by the rules of hierarchy is always right, exercises power, it must be because the subordinate failed to fulfill hierarchical obligations. The subordinate was not properly deferential, properly loyal, or properly conforming. Victimization then becomes the result of one's own failings. Hence, the victim often devalues or denies the violence rather than make her or his own failings public.

Even when the subordinate perceives that the superior is behaving inappropriately, training for hierarchy places further constraints on making this fact public. First there is loyalty, loyalty not just to the perpetrator but to the institution. One does not "air the family's dirty laundry in public." Victims of family abuse not only often feel that they must have done something to cause the abuse but may also feel that they cannot betray the family by revealing the abuse. The application of the family homily extends to hierarchical structures throughout society. Whistle blowers may be praised in the occasional editorial but are likely to face difficulty finding employment in any other hierarchy. Oliver North may have committed illegal acts but became a hero by protecting his commander in chief.

Hierarchy also requires conformity. Wanting to fit in means not revealing that you differ in some way, for example that you were abused as a child, or that you were raped. The effects of this training for conformity illustrate the interaction between societal and individual denial. As long as we continue to believe that acts of physical and sexual abuse are rare, that they are deviant acts, victims will be unwilling to admit to their "deviance." As long as individuals keep quiet about their victimization, a culture may continue to believe that such acts are rare.

Patriarchy: Making Hierarchy of Genders

Patriarchy divides the world into masculine and feminine spheres. How does this division affect the phenomenon of denial? First, sexuality is hidden. One does not talk about sex in polite company. Sex is "dirty." The victim of sexual abuse has been made unclean and is stigmatized by the act, even when not assigned responsibility for what happened. This provides good reasons for the victim to deny that it happened and for family and friends to assist in the cover-up. It can even be construed as "for the victim's own good."

Second, patriarchy places sexuality in the "female" sphere and hence absolves men of responsibility for sexual acts. Patriarchy perpetuates the myth that men cannot control their sexuality because women, associated with the natural and sensual, subvert a male's rationality and destroy his ability to control himself. Thus, victims of rape may blame themselves for somehow encouraging sexual contact or for not discouraging it enough. They may prefer believing they were not raped to acknowledging personal failure to keep the situation under control. A "virile" man is expected to always try to finagle sex; it is up to the "proper" female to say no. If a man forces a woman to have sex against her will, it must be because she encouraged it or was not forceful enough in her protestations. In the words of a father who began molesting his daughter when she was 6: "I would always tell her, anytime you want to stop what we're doing, you just tell me. She never did. Never came right out and said she didn't like it and that I should stop" (Butler, 1979, p. 74).

Patriarchy: Hierarchy in the Family

The paradoxes of patriarchal hierarchy extend to family relationships. The notion that the family is in the private sphere and the province of women places undue responsibility for family dysfunction on the mother. Mothers of children who are physically or sexually abused often are troubled by guilt. They see the abuse in the family as a personal failure. They are encouraged to deny that the abuse is occurring and, even if the abuse is undeniable, to refuse to acknowledge it publicly. Their fears of publicly acknowledging abuse are well founded because mothers often become a target of blame for the abuse. As noted, mothers are even blamed when they themselves are abused.

Children clearly have less power than their parents. Further, because of the division of the world under patriarchy, women also are usually in less powerful positions than male mates, even in the domain that is "theirs." In a patriarchal social system, women traditionally are not trained to operate in powerful positions in the public sphere. This fact, combined with discrimination and other institutional and social constraints, restricts their ability to earn salaries that support independence. The results are some very real practical reasons for not revealing family dysfunction. Breaking up the family can be an economic disaster for mother and children. Enduring abuse within the family can be seen as the lesser of two evils.

Women's dependency even in "their" sphere, the family, is not just economic. Patriarchy induces strong psychological dependencies as well. Who will believe a child's word against a parent's? What weight has a wife's word against a husband's? Males are trained to negotiate in the public sphere, to deal with lawyers and with authorities. Females are trained to operate in the private sphere. They may be isolated from outside contacts. In abusive homes this isolation tends to be especially intense.

Patriarchy: Gender in the Public Sphere

These gender-oriented psychological dependencies extend outside the family, in part, as a continuation of those which exist within the family. Butler (1979) compared the relationship between prostitutes and pimps to the relationship between daughters and abusive fathers. She notes that "a pimp is protected in many of the same ways that an incestuous father is" (p. 35). A prostitute often will not testify against a pimp. The pimp, no matter how abusive, is often the only protection a prostitute has. Butler believes that pimps recognize prostitutes' needs and they give them "the feeling of belonging they may never have received from their families" (p. 35).

Women may feel disadvantaged in the public sphere. In a study of sexual harassment in the military, The New York Times (Schmitt, 1990) reported that women were twice as likely as men to mention fear of reprisals or the belief that nothing would be done as reasons for not reporting harassment.

Psychological dependency may be reinforced by a rational assessment of male privilege as a fundamental cultural value. Gelles and Cornell (1990) provide two illustrations of such privilege:

> When asked why the U.S. Senate was not holding hearings on wife abuse, as it did for child abuse, a senator replied that eliminating wife abuse "would take all the fun out of marriage." A district court judge in an eastern city, after hearing a wife present her case against her husband's violence, leaned over the bench and smiled at the husband and said, "If I were you, I would have hit her too." (p. 65)

In such an atmosphere, denial may seem the only practical method of coping with abuse.

LEVELS OF DENIAL IN PROSCRIBED ACTS UNDER PATRIARCHY.

This analysis of the relationship between patriarchy and denial in personal abuse suggests a hypothesis about the relationship between the strength of denial and elements of patriarchy: The strength of denial depends on two factors, the gender of the act and the hierarchical context of the act. It is likely that interaction between the two factors strengthens denial in certain cases.

The relationships among denial, gender, and hierarchy apply beyond the physical and sexual abuse of women and children to all nominally proscribed acts within a patriarchy. In fact, the applicability of this hypothesis can be more clearly seen by placing these acts of personal abuse in a wider context. Physical and sexual abuse of women and children are characterized by a higher degree of denial than other proscribed acts because of their hierarchical and gendered attributes.

Denial operates more strongly at all levels in the act of incest than, for instance, wife battering. Wife battering in turn is characterized by a higher degree of denial than, for instance, physical assault in a barroom brawl. For the purposes of discussion I offer the following list of abusive acts in the order of decreasing levels of denial:

1. incest,
2. physical abuse of children within the family,
3. wife battering,
4. sexual abuse of children in other institutions,
5. physical abuse of children in other institutions,
6. sexual abuse of children by strangers,
7. acquaintance rape, and
8. stranger rape.

Although testing might demonstrate that contiguous groups differ little in degrees of denial, my hypothesis is that a continuum of denial similar to this one will emerge.

Gender of the Act

An act may be assigned a gender based on the patriarchal distinction between masculine and feminine worlds. Acts associated with masculine attributes such as the exercise of power or control over others or the environment may be called masculine acts. Actions associated with nurturing, sexuality, or open displays of emotion may be thought of as feminine.

Sexual acts seem more likely to invoke high levels of denial than acts of pure physical coercion. Rape is more likely to involve denial than a physical nonsexual assault. Incest is much more likely to inspire denial than the physical abuse of children. Spousal rape is barely considered a crime, whereas wife battering is becoming more openly subject to public legal action. Crimes of passion, emotional crimes, inspire more denial than, for instance, crimes of avarice. A man who commits assault in a burglary is less likely to invoke cultural justifications for the act than a man who commits assault in a fit of jealous rage.

The gender of the act is also tied into the gender of the actors. Male homosexual rape seems to inspire more denial than heterosexual rape. I suspect that there is more at work here than simple homophobia. Male homosexual rape is more likely to be gendered as a "female" act because both perpetrator and victim, in that they are having sexual relations with a man, are in feminine roles. My impression is that homosexual assault by a woman would be less likely to inspire denial than homosexual assault by a man. Because reported acts of homosexual abuse are rare, it is relatively difficult to test this idea.

Hierarchical Context

The hierarchical context has two dimensions. One is the strength and rigidity of the hierarchical structure in the context in which the act takes place. In a military institution, for instance, roles are well defined. Everyone knows who is superior and who is subordinate. The dominance relationship applies to almost all facets of the members' lives. Because acts within such a hierarchy are considered private, they are not subject to outsider scrutiny, and denial of abuse is high. The second dimension of hierarchical context involves the relationship between the perpetrator and the victim. In those cases in which the victim and perpetrator are on equal levels in the hierarchy, denial will be relatively less potent. When a proscribed act directly involves an authority relationship, denial will be stronger.

The first dimension can be illustrated by the difference between child abuse within the family and child abuse within educational institutions. Although the power relationship between children and adults within educational institutions is similar to the power relationship between children and parents within a family, the scope of hierarchical involvement is less within educational institutions. Schools are usually assigned control over children's lives for the purposes of education. Control over children's lives within the family is considered fairly absolute. Abuse of children in school will result in a far larger outcry than abuse of children within the family. Outsiders and authorities are more likely to intervene in the former situation than the latter. What is seen as abuse in schools often will not be considered abuse if done within the family. This is further illustrated by examining a halfway point between the two situations. Private schools often have more authority over children's lives than public schools. They may assume authority over children's moral as well as intellectual development. In such institutions a greater degree of tolerance is sometimes given in the use of violence toward children. Whether legal authorities even have a right to intervene, especially when the abuse takes place within a religiously oriented school, is debated.

The second dimension of hierarchical involvement can be illustrated within the context of the family. The physical or sexual abuse of a sibling by a sibling is less likely to result in the same level of denial than an equal degree of abuse of a child by a parent. Steinmetz (cited in Gelles & Cornell, 1990), for instance, in a study of sibling conflict, found parents willing to freely discuss sibling violence in their home because they did not view their children's behavior as abusive.

To take an example from outside the family, sexual relations between co-workers will be an open subject of office gossip. Sexual relations between a superior and a subordinate in the workplace, because it involves an abuse of hierarchy, is more subject to denial. Gossip will be more covert than overt, and it is likely that the corporate hierarchy will intervene if the abuse threatens to become public.

Both dimensions of hierarchy are illustrated in the reports of sexual harassment in the military that have recently surfaced in the media. The Washington Post (Moore, 1990), for instance, reported that in an 18-month period there were at least six rapes of female students or recruits at the Orlando Naval Training Center. None of the accused were prosecuted. The military's response was typically tight-lipped, and it was made clear that this was a matter to be dealt with within the context of the hierarchy:

> "I've looked at the numbers," said Vice Adm. Michael Boorda, the Navy's personnel chief. "They certainly are not pleasing. But the problem is not being ignored. The training is being done and the people are aware of the problem . . . " (p. A1)

Looking at the numbers rather than looking at the effects on individuals is itself a patriarchal form of denial.

CONCLUSIONS AND IMPLICATIONS

Denial on the part of perpetrators and institutions is functional in preserving patriarchal structures. Denial of the extent of abuses of power within hierarchical structures maintains the legitimacy of systems of power and control as appropriate methods of social organization. The gendering of proscribed acts obscures the extent of the power differential between men and women and perpetuates the gender dichotomies that pervade all levels of the culture.

Denial on the part of victims can also be seen as functional. Psychological denial is clearly a means of coping with trauma. Blume (1990) describes a child's responses to sexual abuse as cognitive adaptations. She says that the resulting emotional difficulties "are not deficits, but normal, natural reactions to abnormal situations" (p. 75). Public denial of personal abuse can also be seen as functional for the individual in the context of a patriarchy. A woman who denies abuse rather than leave an abusive husband may be making a rational decision in a culture in which she is forced to depend on her husband for economic survival. Similarly, a victim of rape or other form of sexual harassment may find denial a superior alternative to facing institutional indifference and the possibility of institutional revictimization.

However, the costs of denial are high. Kelly (1988) points out that forgetting allows abused women time to gather strength before coping with their experience of abuse. However, for some women, forgetting left them with no way to understand how the experience had affected their feelings, behavior and attitudes. Kelly describes one woman who, with no memory of her abuse, had become convinced that she was mad, and she tried to commit suicide numerous times.

Denial by victims is a temporary coping mechanism, not a solution. It does not stop the abuse, and the denial itself may cause further damage. As Blume says of incest survivors: "The survivor's responses . . . are natural and even meritorious, given the reality of her early life . . . But what has saved her may also cripple her" (p. 76).

The model we have been discussing points toward two essentials for breaking through personal denial. First, remove the victims from the hierarchical structure in which they are being abused. Battered women must have a haven, an alternative to the abusive home. Abused children must be removed from the abusive family. The preservation of hierarchy, privacy of the family for instance, should be a secondary consideration when clear and serious abuse is taking place. As long as the victims remain within the hierarchy, the social reinforcement of denial will continue. Second, shift the emphasis from the gender aspects of the abuse. Rape is not a sexual act, it is an act of violence. Outside of a patriarchy, the sexual component might not have the same negative associations it does within our culture. However, within a patriarchy, the sexual nature of some forms of abuse becomes an added stigma and reinforces denial. Within a patriarchy sexual abuse is primarily an exercise of power.

Although breaking through personal denial is an essential first step in treating the survivors of abuse, breaking through social denial is the essential first step in preventing abuse. No social problem can be adequately addressed until it is recognized. A male teacher in Boulder, MT was recently convicted of sexually molesting four elementary school children. The teacher had been removed from his teaching job in 1959 after allegations of molestation. He found a teaching job 20 miles away the next year and, in 1965, returned to the school he had left. The fathers of two of the abused children were in the courtroom. They both said that they had also been victims of the teacher when they were children. The sheriff's deputy who had investigated the complaint admitted that he had also been a victim 25 years earlier. ("Montana teacher," 1990, p. B5). Ignoring social problems perpetuates them.

There is rarely any mention of the phenomenon of denial in the traditional conflict literature. Similarly, the role of patriarchal structures in perpetuating abuse is also rarely noted. Denial may play important roles in obscuring the effects of an overt conflict; in avoidance, which may allow conflict behavior to become habitual; and in blocking attempts to address and resolve a conflict. It may also play an important role in obscuring the causes of conflicts. These effects are readily apparent in conflicts that manifest themselves in personal physical and sexual abuse.

When I began reading the literature on abuse, I was shocked by the statistics on the incidence of abuse of women and children. I had never before understood the prevalence of this personal abuse. Recognizing that the sources of our societal and personal denial are rooted deeply in the patriarchal values of our culture demanded of me a wholesale change of consciousness. A deeper scientific understanding of the social and cultural roots of denial is necessary if we are to adequately address these issues.

REFERENCES

Athens, L. (1989). *The creation of dangerous violent criminals.* London: Routledge.

Blume, E.S. (1990). *Secret survivors: Uncovering incest and its after effects in women.* New York: Wiley.

Butler, S. (1979). *Conspiracy of silence: The trauma of incest.* New York: Bantam Books

Caputi, J., & Russell, D.E.H. (1990, September/October). "Femicide": Speaking the unspeakable. *Ms*, pp. 34-37

French, M. (1985). *Beyond power: On women, men and morals.* New York: Ballantine Books.

Gelles, R.J., & Cornell, C.P. (1990). *Intimate violence in families.* Newbury Park, CA: Sage.

Hall, L., & Lloyd, S. (1989). *Surviving child sexual abuse.* New York: The Falmer Press.

Jaffe, P.G., Wolfe, D.A., & Wilson, S.K. (1990). *Children of battered women.* Newbury Park, CA: Sage.

Kelly, L. (1988). How women define their experiences of violence. In K. Yllo & M. Bograd (Eds.), *Feminist perspectives on wife abuse* (pp. 114-132). Newbury Park, CA: Sage.

Lisak, D., & Roth, S. (1990). Motives and psychodynamics of self-reported, unincarcerated rapists. *American Journal of Orthopsychiatry, 60*(2), 268-280.

Mayer, A. (1985). *Sexual abuse.* Holmes Beach, FL: Learning Publications.

Montana teacher, 63, molested male pupils over 2 generations (1990, November 14). *The Washington Times*, p. B4.

Moore, M. (1990, October 22). Navy failed to prosecute in 6 rapes. *The Washington Post*, p. A1.

Peters, S.D. (1988). Child sexual abuse and later psychological problems. In G.E. Wyatt & G.J. Powell (Eds.), *Lasting effects of child sexual abuse* (pp. 101-117). Newbury Park, CA: Sage.

Ptacek, J. (1988). Why do men batter their wives? In K. Yllo & M. Bograd (Eds.), *Feminist perspectives on wife abuse.* Newbury Park, CA: Sage.

Schmitt, E. (1990, September 12). 2 out of 3 women in military study report sexual harassment incidents. *The New York Times*, p. A22.

Snell, J., Rosenwald, R.J., & Robey, A. (1964). The wifebeater's wife: A study of family interaction. *Archives of General Psychiatry, 11*, 107-112.

Walker, L.E. (1989). *Terrifying love: Why battered women kill and how society responds.* New York: Harper & Row.

Warshaw, R. (1988). *I never called it rape.* New York: Harper & Row.

2

Wife Abuse: Its Magnitude and One Jurisdiction's Response

Jerri Schneider Shevlin

The most basic purpose of government is to protect its citizens. It does so by establishing laws to serve as ethical standards or norms and police forces and court systems to ensure that these guidelines are followed. The inviolability of the person has traditionally been one such norm of U.S. society and, consequently, all states have strictures regulating the use of violent physical actions against any person. It follows logically then that physical violence against women is against the law and that women, as citizens, are entitled to full protection of the law.

Yet, in the United States, it has been estimated that "fifty percent of all women will be battering victims at some point in their lives" (Walker, 1979, p. xv); that violence occurs in 50% of all marriages (Straus, 1978); that 8% of all married women are raped by their husbands (Russell, 1990); and that one in four college women are victims of rape or attempted rape (Warshaw, 1988). And, although in these cases the assaulters are known, it is unlikely that the assaults will be reported, much less prosecuted. According to one study, arrests were made in "only 1% of the cases involving assaults on wives" (Kantor & Straus, 1990, p. 484). Another study claims only one half of 1% of the cases reported to the police actually went to trial (Gelles & Cornell, 1990).

Assault is a crime in the United States; a man beating his wife is committing assault and thereby breaking a law for which he should be punished. Similarly, rape is against the law. Historically, however, relationship violence, especially a husband's violence against his wife, is handled differently than public or stranger violence.

Ascertaining the magnitude of the male violence against women in intimate relationships is hampered by: (a) the difficulty in "naming the phenomenon"; (b) the lack of common definitions of rape, assault, wife battery, and so on, across jurisdictions or among agencies in the same jurisdiction; (c) the absence of accurate and standardized measurement; and (d) underreporting. Disagreement as to the cause of male abuse of women and the failure of the legal system to consistently apply existing laws without regard to gender or marital status hamper resolution of the problem. This chapter explores these issues and then examines one specific jurisdiction's attempt to solve the problem.

DIMENSIONS OF MALE VIOLENCE AGAINST WOMEN

This analysis is limited to assault of a wife or female intimate partner by a man. *Assault* is any act of physical violence. (Threats of violence, verbal abuse, harassment, stalking, and psychological manipulation are forms of assault and can be defined as violence, but they are beyond the scope of this chapter.) The legal system generally differentiates degree of assault by severity of injury. Thus, if the skin is not broken, a simple assault (misdemeanor) is determined to have occurred; if the skin is broken or a weapon has been used to force compliance, it is defined as an aggravated assault (felony; *Black's Law Dictionary*, 1979). The severity of punishment is legally tied to this differentiation. Rape has been traditionally defined as "unlawful sexual intercourse with a female without her consent" (*Black's Law Dictionary*, 1979, p. 1988). For purposes of this chapter this definition will suffice with the exclusion of the word "unlawful." This exclusion is necessary because it is central to the issue of wife rape.

No single word describes the phenomenon of male abuse of women in intimate relationships. The term *domestic violence* has been commonly adopted as a "catch all" for all acts of violence committed by one family member on another. Wife abuse excludes women in other types of relationship violence. Spousal assault not only excludes unmarried women but also serves to obscure what many consider to be a gender issue by creating a genderless category. Martin (1976) used the term *battered wives* for lack of a better way to indicate intimacy regardless of marital status. Margolin, Sibner, and Gleberman (1988) alter this slightly to *battered women*, which they define as "women who have experienced physically injurious behavior at the hands of men with whom they once had, or were continuing to have, an intimate relationship" (p. 93).

The term *assaulted women* is used in this chapter to convey the illegality of physical violence and the gender of the victim. When possible, I use *wife assault* to indicate marital status. *Spousal assault* is used to denote violence committed by either husband or wife.

Violence within the family and in any intimate relationship is perpetrated by women as well as men. Societal constraints against aggression by women, imbalances of economic power, disparities in physical size, and so forth, lead to a disproportionate amount of violence by men against women. Males not only commit the "most dangerous and injurious forms of violence" (Straus, Gelles, & Steinmetz, 1980, p. 43), but they repeat violent acts more frequently than women (Straus et al., 1980). Accordingly, the focus of this chapter is male violence against women in intimate relationships. Enforcement of laws against all acts of physical violence without regard to gender will also serve to protect male victims of physical violence.

Magnitude of the Problem in the United States

A count of the number of reported rapes and murders that occur each year is kept by various agencies, but authorities acknowledge that rape is often underreported. Accurate statistics of the magnitude of male assaults on their female intimate partners are virtually impossible to compile because many, if not most, cases go unreported and because no effective method of compiling data from public health, social service, and law enforcement agencies has been developed.

The Federal Bureau of Investigation (FBI) compiles a count of all officially reported and documented cases of rape and murder on a yearly basis. In the case of murder, although the count is believed to be accurate, over 2,000 murders reported to the FBI do not include the gender of the victim; in the case of rape, FBI figures are believed to be "unrealistically low" (Marcus, 1990, p. A9). By Uniform Crime Reporting definition, the victims of forcible rape are always females. In recording assaults, the FBI does not specifically track male assaults on their intimate female partners.

In addition to the compilation of actual statistics, randomly selected samples are used as a basis for estimating the extent of rape in the general population. One such study is the National Crime Survey (NCS) that is compiled annually by the U.S. Department of Justice through sample interviews. Data is collected using two survey instruments, a Basic Screen Questionnaire and a Crime Incident Report, which then become the basis for estimating the extent of certain crimes. The Department of Justice's report for 1988 is the first NCS report to provide a supplemental analysis of family violence. Prior to that, obtaining data specifically related to domestic violence required additional research of their data banks. One report of NCS data was issued that dealt specifically with violence against women (Langan & Innes, 1986). The National Family Violence Survey (NFVS) of 1975 was the first major survey of incidence conducted to estimate the extent of spousal violence in the general population. Surveys of specific populations have also been used to measure the frequency or number of people affected by a particular problem, for example, the *Ms.* magazine survey reported by Warshaw (1988). All those involved in compiling such data acknowledge difficulties in doing so, but the statistics in Table 2.1 underscore the significance of the problem.

The major surveys shown in Table 2.1, however, do not use the same definitions of domestic violence. The NFVS defines violence as "an act which has the high potential for injuring the person being hit" and "measured violence in the family by asking about the means used to resolve conflicts of interest among family members" (Straus et al., 1980, pp. 22, 26). The NCS operative definition of domestic violence for the years 1978-1982 was "any rape, robbery, aggravated assault, or simple

Table 2.1. Crimes Against Women

	Murder	Rape	Wife Assault
Actual Statistics			
FBI 1991	4,693	106,593[*]	Not compiled
Random Samples			
National Crime Survey			
1988		127,370	241,860
1991		173,310	197,327**
1978-1982 (as reported by			
Langen & Innes, 1986)			2.1 million yearly
National Family Violence Survey			
1975 (2,143 married persons)			121 wives per 1,000
National Family Violence Resurvey			
1985 (6,002 households)			113 wives per 1,000
Surveys of Specific Populations			
Ms. Magazine (6,100 college students)		25%	
Russell—1970s (930 women)			
Stranger		38	
Acquaintance (14% by husband			
or ex-husband)		285	

*includes attempted rape.
**based on slightly less than 2 million out of an estimated 5 million assaults in 1991.

assault committed against a married, divorced, or separated woman by a relative or other person well known to the victim" (cited in Langan & Innes, 1986, p. 2). The 1988 NCR statistics released in the U.S. Department of Justice 1990 report defines family violence as any "crime committed by a relative" (p. 126). The NFVSs do not include marital rape or other sexual assault, and none of these surveys includes murder.

Additionally, these surveys do not measure the same populations. Langan and Innes' (1986) report on the National Crime Surveys for the years 1978-1982 dealt with women as victims of domestic violence. The 1988 NCS Report categorized assaults against spouses or ex-spouses and does not analyze the data by gender. The NFVS of 1975 was limited to "intact families"—couples who were currently married (Straus et al., 1980, p. 26)—whereas the 1985 resurvey included over samples of African-American and Hispanic households, recently divorced or separated individuals, and single parents who were currently living with a child under age 18 (Straus & Gelles, 1990).

Given then that these surveys were using different definitions of domestic violence and measuring different populations, they tell us different things about the magnitude of domestic violence. The first NFVS found that 3,800 husbands per 100,000 used physical violence against their wives in the year surveyed (Straus et al., 1980). Or, restated, 8% of the husbands responding admitted to committing an act of violence against their wives in a given year. The resurvey indicated that "1 woman in 22 was a victim of abusive violence during the 12-month period prior to the interview" (Gelles & Cornell, 1990, p. 69). To facilitate comparison of the results of the studies, Straus and Gelles (1990) adjusted the resurvey information to eliminate cases that were peculiar to the second study. Thus, over samples, unmarried individuals and new categories of violence that were not contained in the 1975 survey were excluded. The adjustment showed that husband-to-wife "overall violence" was 121 per 1,000 couples in 1975 and 113 per 1,000 couples in 1985. They project the last figure to estimate that there are 1.6 million "severely assaulted wives each year" (p. 127).

Although this roughly coincides with the Langen and Innes (1986) report on NCS statistics for the years 1978-1982, which estimated 2.1 million women per year were victims of domestic violence (including unmarried women), it is a far cry from FBI estimates that 197,327 *spousal* assaults occurred in 1991 (U.S. Department of Justice, FBI, 1991).

Nonempirical estimates from two experts are much higher. In testimony before the Civil Rights Commission in 1978, Straus reported a yearly incidence rate of "approximately 1.78 million wives beaten by their husbands" but warned "the true incidence rate for any use of violence in a marriage is probably closer to 50 to 60 percent of all couples" than the lower figures representing "women willing to describe violent acts in a mass interview survey" (pp. 467-68). Walker (1979) estimated that half of all women are assaulted at some point in their lives.

These widely differing estimates are at best confusing and at worst serve to delay resolution of the problem while we try to determine how many women are actually being assaulted by their intimate male partners. Even the extremely low estimate (241,327) based on the NCS forms the basis for Justice Department calculations that family violence accounted for "8% of all violent crimes including 13% of all completed crime" (U.S. Department of Justice, 1990, p. 126). Further, the Justice Department report states that women were 3.7 times more likely to be victims of family violence than men and that more than half of the "violent crimes occurring between relatives involved the spouse or the ex-spouse of the victim" (U.S. Department of Justice, 1990, p. 126).

Number Using Criminal Justice System

The second National Crime Report states that 48% of the incidents of domestic violence against women discovered in the survey were not reported to the police (Langan & Innes, 1986). Gelles and Cornell (1990) report "that fewer than 3% of the victims of minor violence" (p. 81) called the police and only 14% of the victims of "beatings, choking and other forms of severe violence" (p. 81) called the police. Kantor and Straus (1990) note the "NFVS data revealed only 6.7% of all husband-to-wife assaults are reported to police" (p. 476). Marital rape is virtually unreported. Stanko (1988) claims that Russell's figures indicate a "rape incidence 24 times that reported by the FBI Uniform Crime reports" (p. 80).

Underreporting

These surveys all indicate the number of women being assaulted by intimate partners or dates and acquaintances is staggering. But, as Stanko (1988) points out, violence against women, which "more often involves intimates" (p. 78) is the type of crime "most likely to be underreported to both the police and crime survey researchers" (p. 82). The Koss study (reported in Warshaw's book, 1988) indicated that 42% of the women who claimed they were raped told no one about their assaults, and only 5% of them reported their rape to the police.

Underreporting of domestic violence seems to occur for two interrelated sets of reasons: the victims' perspectives of the violence and social pressures that make it difficult for the victim to get help. Often the victim feels the dispute is private and doubts the police would take the matter seriously enough to do anything about it (Stanko, 1988). Gelles and Cornell (1990) claim that victims often "view the violence as appropriate" (p. 66) and "are reluctant to blame their partners for the violence" (p. 67), instead blaming themselves for provoking the violence. Kelly (1988) notes that 60% of the women in her study "did not initially define their experiences as a form of sexual violence" (p. 119). Langan and Innes state that the NCS information indicated that the most common reason (48%) given for not reporting was that "the women considered the crime a private or personal matter" (p. 3). They also note that fear of reprisal was the reason given by 12% of the women for not reporting. Warshaw (1988) notes that women raped by dates or acquaintances either did not call the attack *rape* or kept silent because they "did not want to undergo police or medical scrutiny" fearing "the police won't believe their stories, will blame them, or not consider the episode rape" (p. 62).

Warshaw's conclusions demonstrate how social pressures reduce reporting. Stanko (1988) argues that traditional viewing of "the public realm [as] predominately men's domain" (p. 76) and "women's traditional domain, the private sphere of the home" (p. 77) creates a public-private dichotomy that spills over into criminology. Thus, what constitutes *real crime* is that which happens in public and *private violence* is virtually ignored (Stanko, 1988). The result of this public-private dichotomy is that women are effectively silenced if they are assaulted by an intimate partner.

Thus, the low reporting of assault that occurs in private settings is not surprising. In a study on attitudes about domestic violence, Sigler (1989) found that although respondents believed that any act of a man hitting a woman was "always spouse abuse 80 to 87.7 percent of the time" (p. 95), only 6.7% responded that they would always report such an act to the police. Victims merely reflect society's view that acts of violence in a marriage or other intimate relationship and forced sex between spouses or friends are not crimes and, therefore, not subject to protection under the law.

Causes as the Basis for Solutions

Not all men use physical violence against women. Why some men do has been a major research question. Four explanations are most often proffered: psychopathological, sociological or societal structure, social learning, and feminist.

Psychopathological explanations locate cause primarily within the personality or individual characteristics of the abuser or the abused. This model holds that individual intrapsychic, psychological, or biological abnormalities are the cause of violence.

Sociological or social structure explanations view battering behavior as resulting from factors within the social structure. Thus, personal problems are seen "to arise from social antecedents . . . such as conflict, unemployment, isolation, unwanted pregnancy, and stress" (Gelles & Cornell, 1990, p. 112). These structural stress factors, when coupled with the cultural approval of force and violence in the home, are held to lead to violence.

Social learning explanations of the cause of male abuse of women are based on Bandura's (1973) social learning model that aggression is not innate but rather a learned behavior. This model includes four processes that influence whether one will engage in modeled behavior: attentional, retentional, motor reproduction, and motivational. In other words, if we attend to what we see, remember what was observed, are able to repeat what we saw, and the modeled behavior results in outcomes that are positive, we are likely to perform specific behavioral acts. Thus, men learn to be violent by watching or experiencing violence as children. Such behavior is reinforced by trial-and-error experiences whereby some benefit is gained from violent acts. Ganley (1981) notes one such benefit: "intense and mounting pressure and physiological tension" that often precedes violent episodes is followed by a "reduction in physical tension and physiological arousal" (p. 22). This sudden transition from unpleasant tension to relaxation and a sense of physical well-being then serves as what Ganley (1981) calls a "powerful reinforcer" (p. 23).

Feminists argue a fourth explanation of male violence against women—that of male entitlement flowing from the concept of patriarchy. Among the earliest writers to focus on male entitlement as the structural cause of wife abuse are Martin (1976) and Dobash and Dobash (1979). Martin claims the "economic and social structure of our present society depend upon the degradation, subjugation, and exploitation of women" (p. xv). The Dobashes state that the patriarchal (male-dominated) social order and family structure give husbands legitimate authority over their wives and the "legal and moral obligation to manage and control her behavior" (p. 74).

These theories of cause form the underpinnings for solutions. Those who believe that individual pathology is the cause look to incarceration, alcohol or drug treatment, and/or individual or group therapy as cures; sociologists to societal change; anger-based theorists to anger and stress reduction training; and feminists to criminalization and programs altering male consciousness about power and control issues.

Although any of these solutions might help some of the men, none will help them all. Blaming individual psychological characteristics disregards interactive processes and the role of society in the shaping of individual behavior as well as the structures in society that create conflict. Individual therapeutic measures can at best be only a partial solution—rarely will they prevent violence because they are invoked most often after violence has occurred. And, as Adams (1988) cautions, "it is naive to assume that counseling alone will be effective. Legal sanctions against battering are essential and counseling programs must not simply help men to circumvent the legal consequences of their past or continued violence" (p. 196).

French (1985) claims social control ultimately depends on the individual's "sense of autonomy, communal responsibility, and personal responsibility" (p. 405), not on the legal-judicial system. Yet, French also notes, "wife beating does not cease in societies in which law gives man total control over women" (p. 535). Dobash and Dobash (1988) state that solutions to the problem require "rejecting the violence unequivocally rather than setting limits on it by excusing it or rejecting only its most severe and public forms" (p. 66) and further state the "alternative to wife beating" must include "an ongoing confrontation with patriarchal forms of domination and control and a struggle for the development of egalitarian relations between women and men" (p. 67).

Gelles and Cornell's (1990) solution is to "increase the degree of social control over families, raise the costs of violence and reduce the rewards" (p. 121). One program working to implement such a solution is the Duluth Domestic Abuse Intervention Project. According to Pence and Shepard (1988), the project shifted from an emphasis on "the abnormalities of and within the batterer, the relationship, or the victim" (p. 285) to viewing wife assault as a crime "which must be responded to in an effective manner by the police and the courts imposing increasingly harsh penalties and restrictions on the abuser" (p. 285). Thus, although the psychiatric approach is not totally rejected:

> The goal of the Domestic Abuse Intervention Project is to protect battered women by bringing an end to the violence. Four objectives of the intervention process were implemented to achieve this goal:
>
> 1. to bring cases into the courts for resolution and to reduce the screening out of cases by police, prosecutors, judges, and other court personnel
>
> 2. to impose and enforce legal sanctions and to provide rehabilitation services to the assailant to deter him from committing further acts of violence
>
> 3. to provide safe emergency housing, education, and legal advocacy for women who are assaulted
>
> 4. to prevent assailants from either getting lost in or manipulating the judicial system by coordinating interagency information flow and monitoring each agency's adherence to agreed-upon policies and procedures. (pp. 285-286)

It seems clear then that no matter which cause is attributed to the assault of women, any solution must start with protecting assaulted women. This requires recognizing all physical assault as a crime regardless of the relationship of the parties. Thus, compelling equality of law and its enforcement is the first step to ending the physical abuse of women by their intimate partners.

THE LEGAL SYSTEM IN VIRGINIA

Thomas Jefferson saw the purpose of government as the protection of the individual's right to life, liberty, and the pursuit of happiness. Jefferson may or may not have meant to include women in his definition of the "individual," but the 14th Amendment to the Constitution prohibits any state from denying equal protection of its laws to anyone in its state. The primary way government protects the individual is by establishing laws and police forces and court systems to ensure that the laws are followed. Because in the United States laws that regulate individual behavior generally have been left to the individual states to enact, an examination of one jurisdiction's response to wife abuse as a case can be instructive.

The Virginia General Assembly (composed of a senate and a house of delegates whose members are elected by the general population) is responsible for establishing laws and has statutory control of the jurisdiction, practice, and procedure of the juvenile and domestic relations district courts. Each individual county establishes its own police force. Virginia has strictures regulating the use of violent physical actions against individuals that include prohibitions against assault, rape, and murder. Historically, however, the application of these laws depended on the victim not being married to the assailant.

Historical View of Wife Abuse

Much of the law in Virginia is based on English common law. (In this respect, Virginia law is similar to laws elsewhere in the United States.) The sources cited as the basis of the martial rape exclusion and, indeed, as the basis for nonresponse to abuse of women, are extrajudicial statements by Sir Matthew Hale and Sir William Blackstone. Hale, who lived in 17th-century England, wrote that "the husband cannot be guilty of a rape committed by himself upon his lawful wife, for by their mutual matrimonial consent and contract the wife hath given herself in this kind unto her husband, which she cannot retract" (cited in Salveson, 1986, p. 369). Over 100 years later, Blackstone wrote that, "the husband

and wife are one person in law, and the husband is that one" (cited in French, 1985, p. 194). Blackstone is also attributed with the assertion that "husbands had the right to 'physically chastise' an errant wife provided that the stick was no thicker than his thumb—thus the 'rule of thumb' was born" (cited in Gelles & Cornell, 1990, p. 28).

Although these views were supposedly discredited long ago, the marital rape exclusion was in effect until 1986. A 1976 Metropolitan Washington Council of Governments report on rape does not refer in any way to marital rape, and a 1977 law school text on domestic relations in Virginia by Phelps, a William and Mary law professor, contained no reference at all to marital rape or wife abuse. In 1979, a book detailing women's rights in Virginia informed the readers that "a husband is legally incapable of raping his wife" (Virginia Law Women, 1979, p. 80).

Wife abuse has been traditionally included in the common law offense of assault (unlawful touching), which is a misdemeanor, without regard to the severity of injury inflicted. In misdemeanor cases, police could arrest only if they actually saw the assault. Physical cruelty was grounds for divorce, but any woman who left the family home also left herself open to a charge of desertion. Thus, in general, the legal system was unwilling to charge and/or prosecute offenders, so the burden of prosecution was left up to the victim. This led to the charge that "failure to treat violence against women as a crime must be understood as a structural aspect of the criminal justice system" (Ptacek, 1988, p. 155). The law actually serves as a structure supporting the continuation of male violence against women.

This history (similar to all states in the United States) largely explains the low reporting of spousal assault, especially sexual assault. Victims merely reflect the structure's view that acts of violence in a marriage are not crimes and, therefore, no protection can be expected from the law (Dutton, 1988). This view began to change, however, in the 1960s when women began to meet to discuss women's issues. Their discussions led to the discovery that violence in the family was a common problem. Consequently, "women, who had believed that they were the only ones being beaten and that they deserved or precipitated their own victimization, discovered that there were many others with similar experiences and feelings" (Straus et al., 1980, p. 11). This new understanding brought crimes against women into the public eye and led to demands that the legal system be made more responsive to women.

Efforts to Change the System

The General Assembly's response to these demands was to create new statutes defining spousal abuse and to add provisions to existing statutes to specifically deal with spousal sexual assault. Consequently, any act of spousal abuse was determined to fall under the jurisdiction of the Juvenile & Domestic Relations (J&DR) Court and was defined as "any act of violence, including any forceful detention, which results in physical injury or places one in reasonable apprehension of serious bodily injury and which is committed by a person against such person's spouse, notwithstanding that such persons are separated and living apart" (Va. Code Ann. §16.1-228, Supp. 1991).

The changes effected by the General Assembly resulted in a situation in which spousal violence was differentiated from stranger or other relationship violence by statute.

Table 2.2 summarizes statutes in the Code of Virginia 1950 Annotated, as updated, that are applicable to the problem.

In cases in which a family member is charged with a felony, the J&DR Court's jurisdiction is limited to determining probable cause. Upon such a determination, the case is referred to the Circuit Court for hearing (Va. Code Ann. §16.1-244.J, Supp. 1991).

In addition to the statutes listed in Table 2.2, in 1984, a bill was passed giving the J&DR Court the right to issue preliminary protective orders to protect victims of spousal assault during the period following an alleged assault and the time the case could be heard. Unfortunately, protective orders could only be obtained during the court's regular working hours. The statute was amended in 1988 to allow the victim possession of the family residence to the "exclusion of the allegedly abusing spouse" or requiring the charged party to provide housing for the victim (Va. Code Ann. §16.1-253.1, 1988).

Violence that occurred between individuals living together but who were unmarried (boyfriend/girlfriend, roommates, homosexual relationships), did not fall under the jurisdiction of the J&DR Court, and victims of physical violence in those relationships could not obtain a preliminary protective order.

Figure 2.1 depicts the effects of these statues.

Task force.

In September 1990, the Virginia Attorney General appointed a Task Force on Domestic Violence. The Task Force's attention was directed to three major areas: "immediate intervention by law enforcement officers; reporting by law enforcement, medical personnel and others; and education" (Terry, 1991, p. 2). The Task Force produced two major legislative proposals to the General Assembly that passed into law effective July 1991.

One creates a habitual offender category whereby "a third or subsequent conviction for assault and battery against a family or house-

Table 2.2. Code of Virginia 1950 Annotated Statutes

Offense	Marital Status	Action	Court with Jurisdiction	Penalty
Simple assault	None Married	Touching w/o consent	Gen.Dis.Ct. J&DR Court	Class 1 misdemeanor up to 12 mos. and/or $1,000 fine
Aggravated Assault §18.2-61	None	Shoot, stab, cut, wound w/intent to maim, disfigure, disable or kill	Circuit Court	Class 3 felony 5 to 20 years
	Married		J&DR Court	
Rape §18.2-61	None	Forced sexual intercourse (penetration req'd)	Circuit Court	5 yrs. to life -State Prison
§18.2-61(B,C,D)	Married	Must be separated or accompanied by serious injury - 10-day limit rpt.	J&DR Court	Sentence can be suspended upon completion of counseling or therapy
Marital Sexual Assault §18.2-67.2:1	Married	Forced sexual intercourse and/or other sex acts - 10-day limit rpt.	J&DR Court	1 to 20 in St. prison or 12 mos. jail and/or fine up to $1,000
Sexual battery §18.2-67.4	None	Forced "sexual abuse" (nonconsensual touching)	Circuit Court	Class 1 misdemeanor
Aggravated sexual battery §18.2-67.3	None	No penetration. bodily injury, underage victim or dangerous weapon used	Circuit Court	1 to 20 yrs.

*In a non-jury trial the court can also defer judgment in lieu of counseling or therapy. If such treatment is successfully completed, charges can be dismissed (Va. Code Ann. §18.2-67.2:1.D [1988]).

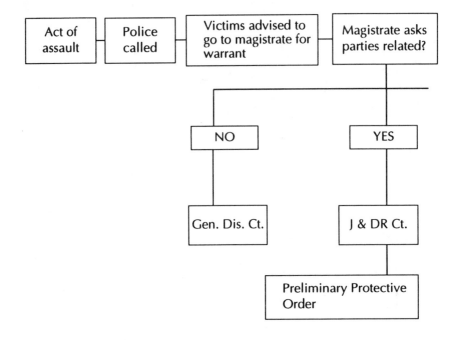

Figure 2.1. Effects of statutes

hold member" arising from at least three incidents occurring on separate dates during a 10-year period would be treated as a Class 6 felony (Va. Code Ann. §18.2-57.2, Supp. 1991). The current penalty for a Class 6 felony is 1 to 5 years in the penitentiary or 1 year in jail and/or a $2,500 fine. This new statute defines *family or household member* as:

> (i) the defendant spouse, whether or not he or she resides in the same home with the defendant, (ii) the defendant's former spouse, whether or not he or she resides in the same home with the defendant, (iii) the defendant's parents and children, brothers and sisters, grandparents and grandchildren who reside in the same home with the defendant, (iv) the defendant's mother-in-law, father-in-law, brothers-in-law and sisters-in-law who reside in the same home with the defendant, or (v) any person who has a child in common with the defendant, whether or not the defendant and that person have been married or have resided together at any time. (Va. Code Ann. §18.2-57.2.C, Supp. 1991)

The second new law grants police in the state the power to arrest without first obtaining a warrant in cases in which they believe an assault has occurred against a "family member" (Va. Code Ann. §19.2-81.3, Supp. 1991); extends the right of court-issued protective orders to former spouses and persons who have a child in common (Va. Code Ann. §16.1-253.3, Supp. 1991); and increases the penalty for violating protective orders (Va. Code Ann. §16.1-253.2, Supp. 1991). Police are also given the right to issue a "stay away" order to certain family members if the investigating officer believes there is a danger of further violence. Under this order the abuser has to "vacate the premises for 24 hours or be charged with a Class 1 misdemeanor" (Va. Code Ann §16.1-253.4, Supp. 1991).

The second round of Task Force efforts (passed by the General Assembly into law effective July 1, 1992) extends the jurisdiction of the J&DR Court to include criminal offenses to nonmarried partners who are residing together at the time of an assault as well as unmarried partners, and/or their children, who have lived together within the 12-month period preceding an act of assault. Also included are the relationship categories of stepparents, stepchildren, sons-in-law, and daughters-in-law if they reside in the same house as the defendant (Va. Code Ann. §18.2-57.2, Supp. 1992). Other legislative changes allow judges or magistrates to issue Emergency Protective Orders at the request of police officers (Va. Code Ann. §16-253.4, Supp. 1992) and extend Protective Order eligibility to include the same relationship categories just listed. Additionally, police officers are given the authority to serve protective orders (Va. Code Ann. §15.1-138, Supp. 1992).

Evaluation

Statute changes.

The statutes created by the General Assembly in 1986 still fail to provide married women with protection against sexual assault by their husbands. A married women cannot charge her husband with rape unless they are separated with the clear intent of divorcing, or she suffers serious physical injury. This, in effect, claims that rape in and of itself is not a serious injury. A married victim is also required to report the crime within 10 days, which is not required of other rape victims. If a woman meets these criteria, her case is heard in a J&DR Court rather than a criminal court, and the sentence can range from therapy or counseling to 20 years in the state penitentiary. This differentiation based on marital status suggests that rape by an estranged spouse is somehow less serious than sexual assault by a stranger and that spousal rape is a marital dispute. Technically, a husband can still not be charged with *rape* if he is living with his wife. He can be charged with marital sexual assault but, again, the penalties are not the same as in the case of stranger assaults. Salveson (1986) minces no words when he charges "acceptance of the spousal rape exclusion makes Virginia an accomplice in these crimes against nature and morality" (p. 383).

The new laws that resulted from the Task Force's efforts have created the legal basis to protect women from their intimate partners and have closed the loopholes as they have been discovered. Preliminary protective orders can be requested 24 hours a day. On the other hand, although police in the state are now able to arrest someone without a warrant when they believe an assault against a family or household member has occurred, they cannot do so in incidents of assault against anyone (including an intimate) who does not fall within the legal definition of a family or household member. In the case of an assault on a person who falls outside the new relationship definitions, the victim must still go to a magistrate to have a warrant issued.

Most individual acts of violence against another are chargeable with the same offense (if not under the same statute in Virginia), but, as reflected in Figure 2.1, determination of court jurisdiction is still based on the relationships of the parties. All offenses involving family members, including ex-spouses, are assigned to the J&DR Court. The only category excluded by the new statutes is boyfriend/girlfriend relationships in which the couple is not cohabiting. All criminal charges in the J&DR Court are prosecuted by the Commonwealth Attorney's Office, as they are in the General District and Circuit Courts, and in all cases attorneys are provided by the Commonwealth if the plaintiff does not have the means to hire one.

The General Assembly's intent in assigning all relationship assaults to J&DR Court is to allow the court to use its discretion to order counseling or therapy and later "discharge the accused" if the court finds such action will promote maintenance of the family unit" (Va. Code Ann. §19.2-218.1, 1988). The Fairfax County J&DR Court makes frequent use of such alternate sentencing (a treatment program for male batterers), but no system has been established to determine its effectiveness. Although a more detailed evaluation appears later in this chapter following discussion of the Fairfax County J&DR Court, it is important to note here that not all counties or J&DR Court jurisdictions in the Commonwealth of Virginia have programs for male batterers. Thus, one has to question what alternative sentencing is being used in those areas.

Magistrates.

The Magistrate System, as is shown in the next section, plays an important role in enforcing laws against domestic violence. The system was created by the General Assembly in 1974 to replace the Justice of the Peace system. Magistrates are empowered to issue summons or warrants of arrest based on "probable cause upon which to believe that a criminal offense has been committed, and that the person arrested has committed such an offense" (Va. Code Ann. §19.2-82, Supp. 1991). Magistrates are appointed and supervised by the Chief Judge of the Circuit Court and serve a term of four years. They need not be attorneys.

FAIRFAX COUNTY, VIRGINIA

Fairfax County Domestic Violence Coalition

In response to the growing awareness of domestic violence as a problem, the Fairfax County Domestic Violence Coalition(Coalition) was established in 1982. Committee members represent various social services departments operating in the county ranging from the police and the J&DR Court to private and public agencies. Its "primary purpose is to coordinate services and increase public awareness of both legal remedies and various services to families experiencing violence/abuse in the home" (Domestic Violence Coalition, personal communication, March 20, 1990).

The Coalition found that in Fairfax County, as in other jurisdictions, the magnitude of domestic violence (including male abuse of women in intimate relationships) could not be measured because the agencies involved were not keeping a count. Therefore, the Coalition sponsored a needs assessment of domestic violence victims turning to social service agencies. Other activities of the Coalition have included lobbying for a pro-arrest policy; getting pamphlets relating to domestic violence translated into several other languages; and preparing a handbook of county services available to victims of domestic violence that is extensively used by the J&DR Court, the police, and other social service agencies to educate victims on their legal rights and the resources available to them.

Magnitude of the Problem in Fairfax County

Domestic assault.

In preparing the Needs Assessment for the Coalition, its authors defined domestic violence as "any purposely inflicted injury or potential injury by one family member on another. Family includes persons who are or have been domiciled together or parented a child together" (Slaght, Zaucha, & Sheffield, 1990, p. 2).

Slaght et al. identified 10 entry points into the service system: the police, Magistrates, J&DR Court, shelters, social services, hospitals, telephone hotline (VAN), counseling programs (A Men's Program or the

Women's Center), private physicians, clergy, and attorneys. Data was available from only six of the entry points as the magistrates did not submit data and no way to access physicians, clergy, or attorneys was found. The researchers concluded, therefore, that the data they were able to collect was "inconclusive regarding the size of the problem of domestic violence" (p. 15). They were able to support only the figures found in Table 2.3 regarding domestic violence.

Estimates of spousal assault.

As noted earlier, Gelles and Straus found that 16% of the homes they surveyed were affected by spousal assault. If 16% of the homes in Fairfax County (270,634 in 1988 when the survey was conducted) are experiencing violence between spouses, more than 43,000 homes would be affected. This calculation is supported by the fact that the total number of assaults reported to the police during the survey period was 2,247 (5% of 43,000), which falls within the Gelles and Straus estimate of the percentage of women who actually report domestic assaults to the police.

Rape and murder.

The Fairfax County Police report that there were 95 rapes in 1990 and 72 rapes in 1991 (Fairfax County Police Dept., personal communication, August 27, 1991 & January 25, 1993). These figures do not include reported rapes that the police determined were unfounded. During fiscal year (FY) 1991 (July 1, 1990-June 30, 1991), the Victim Assistance Network (VAN) hotline reported 647 calls related to sexual assault (A. Van Rysin, personal communication, January 28, 1993). Although these calls did not include marital rape (which VAN categorizes under domestic violence),

Table 2.3. Fairfax County Domestic Violence Figures

Agency	Annual No. Served
Police	2,247
JDRC [J&DR Court]	860
Hospitals	400
Shelters	74
Social Services	755
Mental Health	
Men's Program	67
VAN	588
Total	4,991

they did include calls from victims who might not fall within the legal definition of rape, as well as calls from victims who might be reporting rapes that occurred in past years or in areas outside the county.

The police also reported that seven women were murdered in Fairfax County in 1991, six of which were related to domestic violence. During 1992, only three women were murdered in Fairfax County, but two of them were murder/suicides committed by their "intimate" partner, and one remains unsolved (Fairfax County Police Public Relations, personal communication, January 28, 1993).

Efforts to Address the Problem

The J&DR court. The range of legal resolutions available to the J&DR Court in Fairfax County for assault charges are as follows:

1. *Nolle prosequi*—no prosecution. Right to recharge is preserved for a 12-month period if the defendant is rearrested.
2. Dismissal
3. *Nolle prosequi* with peace bond for 1 year—sometimes the accused is required to attend A Men's Program
4. Diversion disposition—case is continued for 12 months and is dismissed if there are no further complaints of violence and if man successfully completes A Men's Program (this is for first time offenders only when no bodily injury results from the assault)
5. Guilty plea—anyone with prior assault convictions—no trial, defendant goes straight to sentencing
6. Trial—If the defendant pleads guilty or is found guilty at his trial, he can be ordered to A Men's Program with his sentence to be suspended if he successfully completes the program and is not charged with further violence.

The police.

One year prior to enactment of state laws authorizing police to arrest without a warrant, the Fairfax County Police Department instituted a pro-arrest policy with the intent of bringing police reaction to domestic violence to the same level as their response to stranger violence. The new policy states:

> Domestic violence is a crime that differs from other crimes because of the intimate relationship between the victim and the accused. Notwithstanding that difference, officers shall respond to domestic violence incidents as they would respond to any crime and take

appropriate action to arrest and pursue criminal remedies whenever sufficient probable cause exists. As with victims of all other crimes, officers shall ensure that victims are provided with all necessary assistance and are informed of services available to victims of domestic violence. (Fairfax County Police Department, 1990, p. 1)

The new policy was set out in a procedural directive distributed to the Command Staff by the chief of police. Commanders were instructed to ensure that all personnel were trained in the directive and would "comply with all requirements enumerated therein" (J.E. Granfield, personal communication, June 28, 1990). During the first year of the new policy, all new police recruits received 2 hours of instruction on domestic violence while at the police academy that included mediation training, which the police consider to be the preferred "technique" to achieve "long-term results" (Fairfax County Police Department, 1990, p. 5). During 1991, this training was increased to 8 hours.

Dispatchers inform police officers of the nature of any call on which they are sent including domestic violence calls. "DOMDIS" indicates a nonviolent criminal offense, with "DOMVIO" identifying use of physical force. Domestic violence calls include all "covered relationships," which are defined as "persons related by blood or marriage; persons who are biological parents of the same child; and *current or former sexual or intimate partners*" [emphasis added] (Fairfax County Police Department, 1990, p. 1).

Commonwealth attorney's office.

The Commonwealth Attorney's Office in Fairfax County consists of the Commonwealth Attorney (an elected position), a Deputy Commonwealth Attorney, and 17 assistants. In announcing the pro-arrest policy, the then chief of police cited the Commonwealth Attorney's "strongly expressed" support and noted that the Assistant Commonwealth Attorneys had been directed to vigorously prosecute such cases (J.E. Granfield, personal communication, November 15, 1990). This is frequently called a "no-drop" policy in which the Commonwealth exercises its right to prosecute despite the will of the victim. (A representative from this office joined the Coalition in 1992.)

A men's program.

The only intervention program offered to male assaulters of women in Fairfax County is A Men's Program; a 24-week program with the goal of eliminating violent behavior. The program is free and offers both psychoeducational self-help support groups for abusive men as well as couples' conflict resolution groups. Each men's group is co-facilitated by volunteers (one male and one female) and offers a mixture of anger management, cognitive restructuring around power and control issues, role expectations, and communication styles and skills.

Men are screened out if they have a language deficiency or are determined to have untreated alcohol or drug abuse problems or are a danger to the group members, the facilitators, or themselves. The number of men assessed has gone from 121 in FY 1989 to 254 in FY 1992, and the number of group participants, which hovered around 100 in any given year, rose to 161 in FY 1991.

Since the institution of the pro-arrest policy, J&DR Court judges frequently refer males who plead guilty to wife assault charges to A Men's Program as an alternative sentencing procedure, which is reflected in the increase of men in the program by court mandate from 19 in FY 1989 to 120 in FY 1992. Although General District Court judges have the same option, to date they have not ordered anyone into the program.

Shelters.

Fairfax County has seven shelters; two provide services exclusively for battered women and their children. The other shelters estimate that only "one to five percent of the women who use these shelters do so as a result of domestic violence" (Slaght et al., 1990, p. 11). During FY 1988-1989, 168 women and 201 children received services at the two women's shelters. A recent impact statement (1990) released by one of these shelters notes that in addition to providing "safe shelter and crisis counseling to an average of 300 clients (which includes 100 women and 200 children) per year" they counsel "approximately 1,200 women by phone per year" (p. 1).

Victim assistance network.

VAN offers countywide services for victims of domestic violence and sexual assault through support groups. The goal of the sexual assault groups is to assist the survivor of sexual assault in her understanding of what has happened to her and how her reactions are shared by fellow victims of assault. The goal of the domestic violence groups is to help assaulted women clarify their needs and protect themselves and their children.

Evaluation of Fairfax County Policies

Police.

The new pro-arrest policy has resulted in more arrests. The Fairfax Police report a 53% increase in arrests in the 18-month period following implementation of the pro-arrest policy in July 1990, compared to the 18-month period immediately preceding implementation of the policy. Nevertheless, during the first 3 months that the new policy was in effect, then Fairfax County Chief Granfield reported that "1,274 domestic violence cases ha[d] been reported" (resulting in 347 arrests) and "1,347 domestic dispute cases which resulted in 126 arrests" (personal communication, November 15, 1990). Thus, only 28% of the domestic violence calls resulted in arrest and 126 arrests were made when the dispatcher had already determined no violence had occurred. Notably, these calls total 2,621, more than the entire number of domestic assaults reported to the police during 1989.

The police chief has noted that the new policy has created some problems: a heavy and time consuming docket in J&DR Court; magistrate resistance to issuance of warrants and negative comments to police officers; and an extremely heavy caseload for the Commonwealth Attorneys Office.

In response to the second problem, Granfield spoke to the Chief Magistrate and received an assurance of cooperation. Nevertheless, Granfield advised police officers to "fully document" specific problems with any magistrate so that the information could be forwarded to the Chief Magistrate (personal communication, November 15, 1990, p. 2).

There are several other problems, however, that the police chief did not address that resulted from information uncovered by Slaght et al. in the Needs Assessment; namely:

- police response to domestic violence calls in the survey ranged in length from four minutes to 2 hours;
- seven calls for ambulances during the survey period were made by the police but none of those cases resulted in an arrest; and
- there seemed to be no police consistency in providing information on community resources.

Magistrates.

Magistrates in Fairfax County illustrate reasons that data about wife assault is incomplete as well as some of the complexities of the problem. Their attitudes both compound reporting problems and create enforcement difficulties. Slaght et al. (1990) quoted the magistrates' representative on the Coalition as stating that the magistrates frequently fail to issue arrest warrants because "they get tired of victims requesting warrants and then dropping the charges" (p. 6). This condition is also reflected in the police chief's report. The Magistrates' mandate, as noted earlier, is to issue a warrant based on probable cause that an assault has occurred, not on whether or not they think the victim is likely to prose-cute. And, although the Magistrates agreed to conduct a one month sur-vey of the number of direct requests from victims for arrest warrants, they failed to provide any data to the Coalition. Similarly, although the Magistrates' Office agreed to be on the Coalition, representation has only recently been resumed after a 2-year absence.

Attorneys.

The Coalition found no way to access members of the Fairfax Bar Association concerning the number of clients who turn directly to them for relief from spousal assault (Slaght et al., 1990). The Family Law Section of the Fairfax Bar Association has no Subcommittee on domestic violence. Consequently, there is no way to evaluate the response of attorneys in pri-vate practice to the problem of assaulted women.

Courts.

The Fairfax County Commonwealth Attorney recently stated the guiding principle of the Circuit Court is to serve the "best interests of the public"; whereas the juvenile court is to serve the "best interests of the juvenile" (R. Horan, personal communication, November 6, 1990). Assigning spousal assault to the J&DR Court suggests that the goal is to preserve the best interests of the family. This can be seen to imply that spousal assault is a family matter rather than a societal matter. Edwards (1989) claims this type of reasoning creates a "public/private divide" that "affect[s] the assessment of whether a domestic assault prosecution is in the public interest" (p. 223).

Nevertheless, assigning spousal assault to J&DR Court is proba-bly a good idea in Fairfax County because its case load is lighter, cases are heard more quickly, and the range of options are broader. The court is also better able to identify repeat offenders. The Chief Judge is specifically interested in stopping any type of assault and has assigned an intake offi-cer to counsel victims of spousal assaults. Unlike General District Court, a specific time is set for all preliminary hearings on spousal assaults, and the court room is closed to the public. Neither the J&DR Court nor the General District Court has procedures in place to count the number of men charged or convicted of assaults on their female intimates.

Changes in the Fairfax judicial system are due primarily to the personal efforts of the Chief Judges of the Circuit Court and J&DR Court. Buzawa and Buzawa (1990) point out that "the Judiciary retains the poten-tial of leading the criminal justice system by example or direction" because "they are the ultimate authority having the power to ratify or con-demn the actions of the police and prosecutors" (p. 65). Because structure exists independently of any individual, theoretically, the changes being made in Fairfax in time will solidify into structure. However, if any one of the individuals propelling the change leaves, nothing assures that the agencies involved will not revert back to ignoring the problem.

IMPLICATIONS FOR RESEARCH

The pro-arrest and pro-prosecution policies that have been implemented in Fairfax County have resulted in increased charges and convictions for spousal assaults. But, it remains to be proven if they will reduce male assaults on their female intimate partners. For this complex problem, solutions depend on much more information than is currently available. A number of questions should be examined, including:

- What do victims of male violence want from the legal system?
- Will the new pro-arrest and no-drop policies cause women to stop calling the police?
- Does arrest alone reduce the chance of repeated violence?
- What percentage of arrested abusers are actually tried in court? What percentage are dismissed? What effect does this have on recidivism?
- Does a police officer's view of male assaults on women in intimate relationships affect his or her rate of arrest? Is there an increased chance of further violence if the police are called and do not arrest?
- Is police response consistent? Do all officers provide resource information to all victims?
- What percentage of requests for preliminary protective orders are granted by magistrates? Is this in line with judicial response for such orders?
- What happens to women who turn to lawyers, physicians, clergy, and mental health-care providers rather than the police? Are they more or less successful in ending the violence directed at them?
- Will violence against women increase in a depressed economy?
- Do counseling, therapy, and/or men's violence programs reduce recidivism?
- What percentage of women return to their husbands after their arrests? Are they at a greater or lesser risk for abuse?
- What percentage of women return to their husbands after a shelter stay? Are they at a greater or lesser risk for abuse?

- What percentage of the victims of spousal homicides previously turned to the criminal justice system for assistance with spousal assaults?

Answering many of these questions depends on developing common definitions and finding ways to access and accurately compile data from all public and private service providers.

CONCLUSION

Male assaults on women in intimate relationships are of serious magnitude both in the United States and in Fairfax County, Virginia. Although we have been unable to identify a single cause of such behavior, we do know that men's greater size, strength, and financial resources, coupled with society's recognition of men as heads of the family and its reluctance to interfere in private matters, combine to create a situation in which men can use violence to prevent, contain, and/or end conflicts and thereby impose their will. Accordingly, as society raises the cost of physically abusing a female intimate, the incidents of such physical abuse should decrease. This hypothesis forms the basis of Virginia's attempts to criminalize wife abuse.

Fairfax County police are enforcing a pro-arrest policy, and the office of the Commonwealth Attorney is attempting vigorous prosecution. Communication between police and support agencies is enhanced by the Domestic Violence Coalition. An alternative-to-sentencing program is in place to help change the assaulter's behavior. Accessing private sources of services to assaulted women remains a problem, and budget cutbacks could undermine shelter availability as well as A Men's Program. Additional research is needed to evaluate the strengths and weaknesses of the new policies and programs.

But, if society fails to challenge the concept of male entitlement and to stress and teach productive conflict resolution skills, there is little hope that abusive men will alter their behavior. True resolution will require finding and funding programs that will help intimate partners reframe and resolve their conflicts without resorting to violence. The changes that have occurred, however, do provide a means to empower women to end the violence perpetrated against them and give a strong message to assaulters and to society that physical assault is criminal violence regardless of the relationship of the parties and, therefore, is against the law.

REFERENCES

Adams, D. (1988). Treatment models of men who batter. In K. Yilo & M. Bograd (Eds.), *Feminist perspectives* (pp. 176-199). Newbury Park, CA: Sage.

Bandura, A. (1973). *Aggression—A social learning analysis.* Englewood Cliffs, NJ: Prentice-Hall.

Black's Law Dictionary, 5th Ed. (1979). St. Paul: West Publishing Co.

Buzawa, E.S., & Buzawa, C.G. (1990). *Domestic violence, the criminal justice response.* Newbury Park, CA: Sage.

Code of Virginia 1950 Annotated. (1988-1991) Vols. 4 and 4A & Vol. 4A Supplement. Charlottesville: The Michie Co.

Dobash, R.E., & Dobash, R. (1979). *Violence against wives.* New York: The Free Press.

Dobash, R.E., & Dobash, R. (1988). Research as social action. In K. Yilo & M. Bograd (Eds.), *Feminist perspectives* (pp. 51-74). Newbury Park, CA: Sage.

Dutton, D.G. (1988). *The domestic assault of women.* Newton: Allyn & Bacon.

Edwards, S.M. (1989). *Policing domestic violence.* London: Sage.

Fairfax County Police Department. (1990, July 1). *Domestic violence policy and domestic violence police lesson outline.*

French, M. (1985). *Beyond power.* New York: Ballantine Books.

Ganley, A.L. (1981). *Court mandated counseling for men who batter: A three-day workshop for mental health professions.* Washington, DC: Center for Women's Policy Studies.

Gelles, R.J., & Cornell, C.P. (1990). *Intimate violence in families* (2nd ed.). Newbury Park, CA: Sage.

Kantor, G.K., & Straus, M.A. (1990). Response of victims and the police to assaults on wives. In M.A. Straus & R.J. Gelles (Eds.), *Political violence in American families* (pp. 473-487). New Brunswick, NJ: Transaction Publishers.

Kelly, L. (1988). How women define their experiences of violence. In K. Yilo & M. Bograd (Eds.), *Feminist perspectives* (pp. 114-132). Newbury Park, CA: Sage.

Langan, P.A., & Innes, C.A. (1986). *Preventing domestic violence against women.* (NCJ-102037). Washington, DC: U.S. Department of Justice.

Marcus, E. (1990, August 30). Justice Department rape statistics called unrealistically low. *The Washington Post,* p. A9.

Margolin, G., Sibner, L.G., & Gleberman, L. (1988). Wife battering. In V.B. Van Hasselt, R.L. Morrison, A.S. Bellack, & M. Hersen (Eds.), *Handbook of family violence* (pp. 89-117). New York: Plenum Press.

Martin, D. (1976). *Battered wives.* San Francisco: Glide Publications.

Metropolitan Washington Council of Governments. (1976). *The treatment of rape victims in the metropolitan Washington area.* Washington, DC: Author.

Pence, E., & Shepard, M. (1988). Integrating feminist theory and practice. In K. Yilo & M. Bograd (Eds.), *Feminist perspectives* (pp. 133-157). Newbury Park, CA: Sage.

Phelps, A.W. (1977). Domestic relations in Virginia (3rd ed.). Charlottesville: The Michie Co.

Ptacek, J. (1988). Why do men batter their wives? In K. Yilo & M. Bograd (Eds.), *Feminist perspectives* (pp. 133-157). Newbury Park, CA: Sage.

Russell, D.E.H. (1990). *Rape in marriage.* Bloomington: Indiana University Press.

Salveson, M.N. (1986). Sexism and the common law: Spousal rape in Virginia. *George Mason University Law Review, 8*(2), 369-384.

Sigler, R.T. (1989). *Domestic violence in context.* Lexington: Lexington Books.

Slaght, E.F., Zaucha, L., & Sheffield, J. (1990). *A needs assessment of domestic violence in Fairfax County, Virginia.* Final report presented to the Fairfax County Interagency Coalition on Domestic Violence, VA.

Stanko, E.A. (1988). Fear of crime and the myth of the safe home. In K. Yilo & M. Bograd (Eds.), *Feminist perspectives* (pp. 75-88). Newbury Park, CA: Sage.

Straus, M.A. (1978). Wife beating: causes, treatment, and research needs. In *Battered women: Issues of Public Policy.* Washington, DC: U.S. Commission on Civil Rights.

Straus, M.A., & Gelles, R.J. (1990). *Physical violence in American families.* New Brunswick, NJ: Transaction Publishers.

Straus, M.A., Gelles, R. J., & Steinmetz, D.K. (1980). *Behind closed doors.* Garden City, NY: Anchor Press/Doubleday.

Terry, M.S. (1991). Attorney General's Task Force addresses domestic violence. *The Law Digest, 5*(1), 1-3.

U.S. Department of Justice. (1990). *Criminal victimization in the United States, 1988* (NCJ. 122024). Washington, DC: Author.

U.S. Department of Justice. (1991) *Federal Bureau of Investigation Uniform Crime Report Annual Publication, Crime in the U.S.A.* Washington, DC: Author.

Virginia Law Women. (1979). *Your legal rights as a woman: A handbook for Virginians.* Charlottesville: University of Virginia Law School.

Walker, L.E. (1979). *The battered woman.* New York: Harper & Row.

Warshaw, R. (1988). *I never called it rape.* New York: Harper & Row.

3

Mediator Differences in Perception of Abuse: A Gender Problem?

Charity B. Gourley
George Mason University

Mediation is a process by which parties in conflict attempt to reach a mutually satisfactory agreement with the assistance of a third-party mediator. Mediation advocates consider an outcome negotiated by the parties themselves preferable to a decision imposed arbitrarily by judges with lawyers in an adversarial courtroom setting. When violence or threats of violence have been part of the pattern of the relationship of the mediating parties, it may be more difficult to maintain safety and fairness in the mediation process.

Violence may be a problem in any type of mediation situation, but I focus specifically on mediation as practiced in the United States in disputes involving domestic violence. *Domestic violence* is defined as "the threat or use of physical force to gain control over a current or former partner in an intimate relationship [which] results in fear and emotional and/or physical suffering" (Lerman, Kuehl, & Brygger, 1989, p. 3), and it may include the use of "verbally or emotionally abusive language that has a controlling or coercive effect on the other person" (MediatioNetwork of North Carolina, 1989).

I review the literature related to the controversy over whether or not mediation should be attempted in family disputes in which abuse may be present, I address concerns about the training received by mediators, and I discuss procedures for screening potential cases of abuse.

THE MEDIATION PROCESS

Mediation has been promoted as a helpful conflict resolution process for disputes ranging from neighbors with barking dogs (interpersonal) to decisions about the location of hazardous waste sites (community) to warfare across geopolitical borders (international). Divorcing couples also are using the services of mediators to work out details of the dissolution of their marriage, including arrangements for their children regarding custody, financial support, and visitation. Mediation in the United States generally consists of parties in conflict meeting with a so-called "neutral" third party (sometimes co-mediators or a team of mediators) for one or more sessions, averaging 1-3 hours each, and extending from 1 day to several years, depending on the type of conflict. An average divorce and child custody mediation might be three to five sessions.

The mediator role is to structure and guide the problem-solving process, establish groundrules for expected behavior (such as no interrupting), assist in generating options for solutions, and to write up the agreement after parties have mutually defined the conditions of what they have agreed to do. Many mediators are volunteers who have been trained in the process and who practice as co-mediators teamed with experienced mediators before mediating alone. Others are professionals who are paid for their services.

Persons in conflict are more likely to turn to the established judicial process than to the relatively new and unfamiliar process of mediation. But mediation has the advantages of allowing the parties to maintain responsibility for and control of their conflict and its resolution, generate more mutually beneficial options than previously considered, create more mutually satisfactory outcomes, and learn skills for addressing future conflicts in an ongoing relationship. Mediation usually costs less than litigation and is generally quicker.

Voluntary Versus Mandatory

Mediation was conceived as a voluntary and cooperative out-of-court process, but it is increasingly being used by the judicial system as a means of clearing overcrowded dockets by mandating litigants to participate in mediation. Lost is the belief that when people voluntarily submit to a process within which they control their own problem solving and discover solutions they believe to be of their own making, they are more likely to adhere to the resulting agreement. Mandatory mediation stuck onto an institutional philosophical base may settle people's disputes without truly resolving them.

Safe and Fair

Overloaded court dockets and the increasing need to seek less costly financial alternatives to litigation have created a great interest, according to attorney Bruch (1988), in the "appropriate role in family law for extra-judicial procedures," such as mediation. When parties go to mediation, the mediator is responsible for structuring a process of negotiation that is appropriate to the conflict and ensuring that the process is both safe and fair.

Bruch and many others (Kuehl, 1989; Lerman, 1984; Marks, 1988; Pagelow, 1990; Skaggs, 1988; Sun, 1988; Woods, 1987) are not happy with the results of mediation in family disputes, however. They describe women as being more cooperative than men and succumbing to mediator pressure to compromise by agreeing to unsatisfactory terms. Some critics say that the newly won power gained by women in divorce and child support cases through the court system is now being lost through mediation. Mediation is perceived as encouraging both parties to be generous in reaching an agreement to their dispute. Therefore, if the woman gives as much as the man, she loses because she had less to give in the first place.

Critics are particularly concerned with pressure to agree to joint custody, which increases contact between parents and is potentially risky in families with high interparental conflict. Few states require judges to consider spousal abuse in determining custody. Because of the large number of cases of ongoing violence even after separation and divorce, a resolution was passed by Congress in 1990 that credible evidence of physical spousal abuse should constrain granting child custody to the abusive spouse. Congresswoman Morella (1990), sponsor of the resolution, maintained that domestic violence is a "brutal criminal act, mostly but not always committed by men against women" that continues because "too many people look the other way, and our judicial system has often been guilty of indifference."

Divorce mediators Erickson and McKnight (1990) maintain that some history of spousal abuse is present in half of all divorce mediation cases, and Morella (1990) says that 53% of men who abuse their wives also abuse their children. If the mediator is not sensitive to abuse dynamics, the woman may feel intimidated in negotiations with her abuser and experience even further losses (Saunders, 1990; Sun & Woods, 1989). Mediators must be accountable for the fairness of what happens behind the closed doors of a mediation session. The harsh facts of domestic violence mean that mediators must also be aware of the potential for harm when their clients are outside the mediation session.

Neutrals Versus Advocates

The prevalence of abuse and of imbalance in power between conflicted parties poses serious challenges to the mediator as a *neutral*, a term officially adopted and promoted by some dispute resolution professionals. A power imbalance exists in mediation when one party has more power than the other, whether that power is physical, financial, or emotional. Laue (1982) maintains that all intervention alters the power configuration of the dispute, so all intervention is advocacy and, as a result, there are no neutrals.

Because of women's limited expectations of what they are entitled to, women have to struggle to perform equally in a bargaining situation. Leitch (1986/1987) therefore recommends affirmative action on behalf of women in order to achieve a balanced agreement.

Although a mediator is committed to impartiality, Moore (1988) believes the mediator has an ethical obligation to help the disputing parties to reach a fair agreement that will endure. He recommends that the party who is perceived to have less power should openly be helped to learn negotiation skills in order to have a productive exchange. Salem (1982) encourages dispute resolvers to not pretend to be neutrals, but to be advocates of a good process that alters the power imbalance and leads to meaningful movement toward the goal of justice. Folger and Bernard (1985) describe the interventionist approach in which the mediator has a particular value orientation, such as the wish to equalize power disparities in the parties or to move toward a desired outcome. Interventionists secure settlements that the mediators think are fair and consistent with their own ideological approach.

There is support, then, for mediators to maintain an ethical attitude of impartiality, but to not hold a strict interpretation of neutrality. The intention is to protect and educate the perceived weaker party in order that responsible mediation can take place, which sometimes means mediators become active interveners, not for a particular party, but for an effective process.

Sonkin, Martin, and Walker (1985) insist that mediators need to become aware of their own attitudes about violence and how those attitudes affect choice and effectiveness of intervention in cases of domestic violence. This includes understanding the beliefs and values they hold regarding men and women, sex roles, relationships, anger and conflict, as well as acknowledging their personal experience with violence, whether it be as a victim, a perpetrator, or an observer. To maintain mediation integrity, mediators who become advocates for affirmative action on behalf of the perceived weaker party must be clear with themselves and explicit with the disputants about their ideological orientation.

THE EFFECT OF CULTURAL PERCEPTIONS
AND VALUES ON MEDIATION

Mediation is a communication process that reflects the cultural context in which it occurs. That context may differ depending on the cultural and subcultural groups with which the disputants and the mediators identify. Women and men can be considered to form subcultural groups due to differences in their expectations and patterns of behavior. According to Tannen (1990), this results in communication often having different meanings for women and men. Tannen cites research demonstrating gender differences in children's patterns of communication within their own sex groups. She maintains that for women and girls, intimacy is the fabric of relationships, and talk is the thread from which it is woven. Female talk is inclined toward intimacy and inclusion. Men and boys form more hierarchical groups and talk more competitively, with members seeking to avoid subordinate positions. The intention of male talk is to maintain independence and a higher status.

Gilligan (1982; Gilligan, Ward, & Taylor, 1988), from a different theoretical perspective, makes a similar kind of distinction between the decision-making criteria of women and men. Gilligan discerned a tendency from early childhood for females to value relationships, cooperation, and an ethic of care more, whereas males value rules, rights, competition, and an ethic of justice. Gilligan's studies showed girls solving a moral dilemma from a perspective of being within a relationship (a "care perspective"), whereas boys dealt with the same moral dilemma from a stance of what is logical and right (a "justice perspective").

Such theories and their substantial empirical support suggest male and female mediators are likely to interpret conflicting parties' communication quite differently. In one mediation case, when I told my male co-mediator I thought I heard undertones of abuse emerging in the child custody case we were handling, his angry response told me I was touching a live wire that we had not been trained to handle. Our job, he responded, was to get an agreement signed, not "play therapist." My concern increased when I consulted the director of our mediation program, a retired military man, and he dismissed the reported violence with the comment that I was being "too sensitive" because "these things happen in all families." On my own initiative, I probed further in our mediation case and elicited a tale of numerous episodes of physical violence by the husband, some of which were witnessed by the child. When my co-mediator later commented that he might have behaved the same way—if his wife had done what our client's wife reportedly had done—I began to wonder about abuse and mediation as a gender issue.

Gendered perceptions of the mediator role are of interest to Weingarten and Douvan (1985). They discovered that female mediators envisioned the mediator role as collaborative and as a process of transformation and change affecting all of the parties, including the mediators. Male mediators were more likely to look at their personal performance and to envision their role as one of acting on the other parties. Men used the terms *neutral* and *objective* to define themselves and described the mediation process as a chess match or prisoners' dilemma game, whereas women saw themselves as a bridge between the parties. The male mediators thought mediator gender did not make any difference, but the women thought their "sex-linked socialization and roles" had a "relevant and valuable" effect on mediation (p. 353). Many women claimed their gender "led them to ask questions and look at aspects of process and role" that their male colleagues never described (p. 353). Some female mediators thought their male co-mediators tended to develop a concept of a solution and then push the parties toward it. This corresponds with group situation studies, according to Weingarten and Douvan, in which men focus on getting the task accomplished, whereas women tend to listen and focus more on interpersonal aspects, such as emotional tone and feelings.

Both female mediators and female clients may be disregarded. Belenky, Clinchy, Goldberger, and Tarule (1986) maintain that:

> girls and women have more difficulty than boys and men in asserting their authority or considering themselves as authorities, in expressing themselves in public so that others will listen, in gaining respect of others for their minds and their ideas, and in fully utilizing their capabilities and training in the work world. (p. 5)

Women often feel unheard and unheeded when they believe they have something important to say. The evidence is strong that in mixed groups men tend to talk more than women, and women are more likely to be interrupted than are men (Mader & Mader, 1990).

In child custody mediation, I have had women clients who asked permission, at the second or third mediation session, to read a written statement entailing the points they wished to make. In these cases, the wives were not as assertive as the husbands in expressing themselves during previous sessions, and the women were interrupted frequently by their husbands, and sometimes by my male co-mediator. I assume the women felt frustrated because they had not made themselves fully heard nor gained respect for their views, so they were attempting to balance the uneven verbal scales. I knew about the studies on interrupting women, so I was not surprised to observe the husbands and even my male co-mediator interrupt the wives. But I was chagrined to realize that I also occasionally interrupted the women.

Rifkin, Millen, and Cobb (1991) maintain that mediation can privilege certain persons over others by the way in which turn-taking is structured. They found that mediators construct a controlling frame within which participants' disputes are negotiated and that frame frequently develops from the telling of the story of the conflict by the first person to talk. People's ability to participate effectively is linked to how they are positioned in the process. Rifkin and associates perceive a need to pursue research that examines "the influences of gender and cultural issues in the mediation forum" (pp. 162-163). For women who already feel disempowered in negotiation situations, their position in turn-taking may help or further hinder their effective participation. Mediator awareness is important in constructing the negotiation frame. Still unknown is whether gender attributes influence mediator strategy.

If there really are no differences in the perception and behavior of mediators toward domestic violence, Taylor (personal communication, June 1991) maintains that no harm has been done by raising the question of gender differences. If, however, gender differences are a factor affecting the treatment of domestic violence, to ignore the differences could have dangerous consequences. Taylor believes that men and women perceive the world around them in different ways and that they also perceive each other differently, whether or not differences are actually there. If this can be shown to be true, it has great implications for mediation, as well as other helping fields. Knowing the way mediators and clients involved in a conflict perceive the issue at hand is as important as understanding the formal substance of the dispute.

RESEARCH ON GENDER DIFFERENCES

Although I do not assume universal gender traits for all men and women across all culture groups, I do assume tendencies for women and men to behave in certain fairly predictable patterns that are linked to the cultural conditioning each person has experienced during his or her formative years. For that reason, an exploration of research on gendered communication can show how this relates to mediation.

Research on Gender Differences

In research on communication styles in conflict management, Yelsma and Brown (1985) used the theoretical concept of sex-role traits to group results showing that persons with feminine traits tend to use more accommodative strategies, avoid conflict situations, take on the peace-keeper role, use more expressions of support and solidarity, and use more facilitative behaviors. Persons with masculine traits tend to use more verbal and physical aggression and are more dominant in conversations. These findings were measured on the Bem (1974) Sex-Role Inventory, a tool for grouping people into four categories of psychological traits: masculine, feminine, androgynous, and undifferentiated. Consensus has not been reached on how to apply findings based on sex-role trait research. Hall and Taylor (1985) claim that discussions of sex-role traits and psychological androgyny are flawed because the statistical methods used are faulty.

Meta-analysis, a procedure that combines statistics from many related studies and calculates the results, is valued by some researchers as a systematic probe of research findings. In a recent meta-analysis of studies of language use, Smythe and Schlueter (1989) found that reported gender differences are not convincingly significant, and differences within groups of women possibly are greater than between men and women. A meta-analysis of communication behaviors by Pruett (1989) revealed men as more dominant, contentious, and dramatic, and women as more attentive, open, animated, and friendly.

From meta-analysis, Hyde (1990) perceived small gender differences in cognitive abilities, with men measuring only slightly higher in mathematical ability and one type of spacial ability, and no significant difference in verbal ability. Again, within-gender group differences were larger than between-gender group differences.

More significant gender differences are apparent in a meta-analysis of social behavior studies. The largest differences occur in nonverbal behaviors in which Hyde (1990) found women significantly better than men in understanding the nonverbal cues of others, expressing emotions using nonverbal communication, recognizing faces, having more expressive faces, and emitting fewer speech errors. Women are approached more closely by others and are slightly higher in conforming behavior than are men. Women are more likely to offer help in long-term nurturant situations (e.g., tutoring), and men are more likely to help in short-term situations (e.g., automotive problems) and in perceived dangerous situations. Hyde found men moderately more aggressive than women. If aggressive behavior might produce harm to the victim, guilt, anxiety, or danger to oneself, women were much less likely than men to be aggressive. Hyde noted a slight two-decade decline in the magnitude of observed gender differences in the areas of aggression and cognitive abilities.

More gender-based information needs to be gathered in natural social settings. When women and men are interacting under natural rather than contrived conditions, research results should reveal gender differences and similarities more accurately.

Gender and Mediation

In spite of considerable study of gender differences in communication, more research is needed on what effect gendered perceptions and behavior can have on the process and outcome of mediation. Substantial theory and some research data make it reasonable to predict that female and male mediators will behave differently in mediation conditions.

A case study of mental health therapists (Broverman, Broverman, Clarkson, Rosenkrantz, & Vogel, 1970) is illustrative. Both male and female therapists revealed sex-role stereotypes (similar to those held by laypeople) that defined mentally healthy adults of unspecified sex by the same strongly positive qualities that were attributed to healthy men (e.g., highly competent and self-confident). In contrast, healthy women were considered to have very different qualities that were more likely to be viewed negatively (e.g., tactful, gentle, expressive of feelings). In a 1984 follow-up study, the therapists' attitudes about mentally healthy men and adults had changed—more value was placed on being aware of feelings—but ideas about mentally healthy women had not changed. If therapists are subject to their own cultural values in interpreting client behavior and deciding appropriate treatment, mediators also need to look at how their personal biases affect their mediation interactions and decisions.

Limited Nature of Gender-Based Theories and Research

Much theorizing and research related to both gender and mediation is developed by white academics and is based in the experiences of white middle-class Americans. Black feminist thought, says Collins (1991), emphasizes that it is important to understand the interconnections among race, gender, and class oppression and to not allow analysis of one group to become privileged over another. Addressing discrimination at one level (e.g., gender) may still leave a person locked into an oppressive situation at another level (e.g., race). In other words, balancing the gender scales in mediation may still leave a disputant disempowered at another unaddressed level in an oppressive social system. Coffman (1990) says that when gender is separated from race, age, class, and sexual orientation, it is distorted by being removed from the effects of its social context, and questionable research findings may result. Current research, limited as it is, still points to important questions about ways gender differences may complicate mediation.

VIOLENCE AND MEDIATION

Violence and threats of violence are potential underlying issues in all cases of conflict, but they are seldom systematically addressed in mediation. Of reported victims of domestic violence, 95% are women (Lerman et al., 1989). Half of all divorce cases contain some history of spousal abuse (Erickson & McKnight, 1990). And Morella (1990) claims that 53% of men who abuse their wives also abuse their children.

Denial of Violence

Gathering accurate information is difficult because abuse is commonly denied or discounted by both the victim and the abuser (Girdner, 1990; Robinson, this volume). The reasons for denial are many and varied: embarrassment, the victim's fear of retaliation by the abuser, the victim blaming herself for the abuse, guilt, shame, fear of consequences, and even the *Stockholm syndrome*—the phenomenon of fondness and protectiveness that sometimes develops between hostages and their captors, even when death threats are present. The psychological characteristics of hostages resemble those observed in battered women, say Graham, Rawlings, and Rimini (1988), and are the result of being in a life-threatening relationship. Concentrating on survival requires subordinates to avoid direct, honest reaction to destructive treatment by dominants, and any such pattern is likely to be carried into mediation.

Lerman (1984) maintains that society's tolerant attitude toward battering in male-female relations is implicated as a cause of the violence. She cites Dobash and Dobash's claims that violence against women by their spouses is one expression of the patriarchal structure of society—the exercise of power and control by the dominant over the subordinate. When public agencies, such as law enforcement, courts, doctors, and clergy (and mediators, I would add), fail to provide the protection and assistance needed by victims of abuse, these agencies perpetuate the violence and therefore become part of the problem. The inadequate response appears as denial by not taking the abuse seriously.

As these agencies of society model denial of the abuse, the abuser and the victim are socialized to deny it, too.

Because of pressures to minimize or deny abuse, Sonkin et al. (1985) assume that even when domestic violence is revealed to mediators, it is usually worse than either party admits. When violence is denied by the mediation community, perpetuation of abuse and harmful mediation outcomes may follow.

Mediation or Court?

Professionals responsible for family disputes disagree as to whether or not mediation should even be attempted in cases of domestic violence. Many mediators are not trained to recognize or deal with violence. Some insist without question that abuse cases need the protection of traditional court processes (Hart, 1990; Pagelow, 1990). Others maintain that mediation can be helpful when used with appropriate guidelines (Grebe, 1989; MediatioNetwork, 1989).

Some mediators who are sensitive to the issue of spousal abuse believe mediation can serve a constructive purpose. On a continuum, with "we can mediate anything" at one end and "no mediation of abuse under any circumstances" at the other, Chandler (1990, 1991) says the mediation field is in the process of sorting out which cases may be appropriate to mediate with a process specifically constructed for abuse situations. Smith (1991) emphasizes that abuse, assault, and stopping the violence are never negotiable issues because it is both unacceptable and illegal for one person to hit, batter, or otherwise abuse another person.

Screening for Mediation Appropriateness

Chandler's (1990, 1991) three-stage program in Hawaii—screen, referral to pre-mediation training and counseling, mediation—screens during intake with a series of questions constructed to surface the issue of abuse if it is present. If sensitive screening indicates that mediation may benefit this particular case, the disputants are then referred to a pre-mediation training and counseling program, with about 60% actually attending. Some might not get back into mediation, and others might go elsewhere for counseling. Pre-mediation programs were initiated and are run by battered women's shelters and church groups and are generally for women. Counselors help women learn to negotiate from an empowerment base. A support person may subsequently attend mediation with the woman. If a woman has taken out a court protection order, Chandler views that as promising evidence of initiative to take control of her own life, which makes it possible for her to negotiate from a position of strength rather than from fear or submissiveness.

Examples of questions asked by various mediation programs during intake screening and caucusing in private sessions include: Have you been physically abused during your relationship? If yes, when was the last incident? Do you have any reason to fear physical abuse from your spouse now? If yes, what is the basis of that fear? Do you have any type of protection order? Has there been emotional abuse, such as intimidation? Do you feel, as a result of the abuse, you are less able to communicate with your spouse on an equal basis? How have you made decisions in the past? How would you like decisions to be made in mediation? What would have to change in order for that to happen?

Girdner (1990) drew on her considerable mediation experience in developing her Conflict Assessment Protocol (CAP)—a triage tool to screen for abuse and for appropriateness of mediation. Her triage categories include those persons most likely to: (a) benefit if mediation proceeds as usually conducted; (b) benefit in mediation with specific ground rules, resources, and skills made available; and (c) experience harm from participation in mediation. Mediators must develop skills through training and experience to perceive elusive abuse situations. Even though some abuse may have occurred in cases falling into the second category, Girdner believes indications are favorable for positive progress through a specially designed mediation process that deals openly with the issue of abuse, encourages the abused spouse to pursue law enforcement remedies such as protection orders, requires anger management classes or therapy for the abuser, and recommends services for battered women or therapy to the abused spouse.

Based on extensive divorce mediation experience, Erickson and McKnight (1990) agree that the question is not whether to mediate cases of spousal abuse, but how to develop the experience, education, methods, and techniques for mediating these especially difficult cases. If the divorcing couple have children, they will still have future contact while parenting their children. Erickson and McKnight believe mediation in combination with therapeutic and legal processes can help parents develop new behaviors toward one another and aid future decision making regarding their children's needs. They see mediation and court processes as having the same goal: to establish guidelines to be followed while the couple settle marriage business matters and begin to act as separate parents.

Erickson and McKnight's (1990) screening method lists indicators of past or present abuse, which if observed during mediation, indicate the need for further enquiries. Some of these indicators may be present in nonabuse cases, but the mediator must be diligent about uncovering any history of abuse. Indicators for the husband are: (a) anger, blames wife as source of their problem; (b) wife initiated divorce, husband resists; (c) refuses to move ("if she wants the divorce, let her move out"); and (d) controlling behavior (e.g., managing all finances). Indicators for the wife are: (a) she initiated the divorce; (b) speaks in low tones, avoids open disagreement; (c) difficulty expressing needs; (d) masks comments about the past ("things have been difficult; we can't go on like this; it is hard on the children") without mentioning physical or emotional abuse; (e) has no lawyer because husband controls the money; (f) facial and body expressions of fear; and (g) no direct eye contact with her husband.

Erickson and McKnight (1990) say there is never a valid excuse or reason for abuse and violence. They make a strong but nonjudgmental statement about the violence while attempting to establish a safe environment to end the relationship through mediation. They educate the wife about legal protection orders, how to get police protection if threatened, names and phone numbers of shelters for battered women, and they detail boundaries for contact between husband and wife during child visitation exchanges. They further advise the wife to retain an attorney who is knowledgeable about both the mediation process and spousal abuse, ask spouses to have their attorneys present for consultation during mediation, and suggest that the abused spouse have an advocate present for emotional support during mediation. They refer the husband to local programs for abusers (although some communities may not have them) and make sure he clearly understands local laws regarding the legal repercussions if abuse continues.

If the issue of violence surfaces in mediation, Girdner (1990) and Erickson and McKnight (1990) maintain mediators need not establish its validity, but should acknowledge it as of concern to at least one party and then assess the risk of mediating. Girdner uses power-balancing techniques to ensure fair negotiations and an agreement reached without coercion. Advocates for victim's rights, however, see no reason why victims of abuse should have to continue to have a relationship with their abusers. The power configuration may arguably be altered if the safety of the mediating parties is assured outside of mediation and a safe and fair process is facilitated within mediation. But Lerman (1984), Adams (1988), and others insist that the abuser needs to be confronted with his abusive behavior and accept personal accountability for his conduct, in order for behavioral change to occur.

Not all cases belong in mediation, Girdner (1990) and Erickson and McKnight (1990) agree, especially when the abused wife is unable to identify her own needs as separate from the abuser's needs, or when the abuser continues to be controlling and accepts no responsibility for the abuse, or if other factors are present that indicate a strong likelihood of future violence, such as recent assaults or purchase of a weapon. When clients are excluded from mediation, however, mediators have a responsibility to provide safety information and appropriate referrals, although there is a serious lack of referral alternatives for clients caught in abuse.

MEDIATION ACCOUNTABILITY

Critics of mediation express considerable concern about inadequate training and accountability by mediators and judges in identifying domestic violence and naive attitudes about the control abusers have over victims. I have been a mediator since 1985, and none of the community programs in which I was trained for community, juvenile, and child custody mediation addressed abuse as an issue I might encounter. I remember with shame my first mediation case. My personal notes simply say, "woman beaten, trying to leave." A woman who had been living with a man for 2 years had taken their baby and moved out. The man charged her with theft of goods from their apartment, but his true intention apparently was to maintain control and get her to come back. She firmly insisted the relationship was ended. I thought I was doing reality testing when I pointed out their ongoing connection through their mutual responsibility for their child. Looking back, I believe I undermined the steps she had taken toward self-respect when I sounded like I supported the man's claims on her. Statistically, that case was considered a success because an agreement was reached about the household items. On reflection, however, I consider it a failure because of my unenlightened approach to the abuse issue.

Some critics (Lerman et al., 1989; Skaggs, 1988; Sun, 1988) believe the open court system provides more protection than the typically closed-door private mediation session that has little mediator accountability and no review of mediation agreements. Only the legal system has the power to enforce support orders, remove the batterer from the home, arrest when necessary, and enforce the terms of any decree if a new assault occurs. Without extensive training on the nature of abuse, Lerman (1984) believes mediators risk perpetuating the violence rather than removing it.

With appropriate guidelines, Corcoran and Melamed (1990) support mediation of spousal abuse cases as an opportunity for the divorcing couple to commit themselves to a new relationship without intimidation or violence. In their eyes, divorce mediation can be a route to empowerment and responsibility for both parties and a vehicle to avoid perpetuating the victimization of the abused spouse. I believe such happy outcomes are more likely with improved mediator training.

MEDIATOR TRAINING

The Society for Professionals in Dispute Resolution (SPIDR) and the Academy of Family Mediators (AFM) are professional organizations that have emerged in recent years to serve dispute resolvers. They are attempting to establish standards for mediator training and conduct for a field that is made up of both professionals and volunteers. AFM maintains an approved list of members who conduct high-quality mediator training programs. Mediator skills can be updated in workshops at annual SPIDR and AFM conferences. Mediation training is also conducted by community mediation programs, which were early pioneers in the field of dispute resolution.

The following framework could be used to select new mediators, to train both new and experienced mediators in domestic violence conditions, and to evaluate current mediator behavior. Honeyman (1990) considers role plays to be the best currently available method to test for mediation skills. Actors, who are familiar with mediation, play the role of parties in a simulated conflict. Well-regarded, experienced mediators evaluate candidates as they mediate two to three varied mock conflicts. During the information-gathering stage, evaluators note whether the candidates learned enough about the situation to make sound judgments about which paths to pursue or abandon, and then determine the reasons why candidates decided to investigate particular facts and exclude others. Mediators need to be able to investigate thoroughly enough to surface any issues like abuse that may be uncomfortable for either the mediator or the disputants. Honoroff, Matz, and O'Connor (1990) say the values orientation of mediators is reflected in mediation decisions, and evaluators should observe cues that mediator candidates may be avoiding particular issues.

Areas of mediator weakness could be remedied by having (a) trainees observe experienced mediators at work, (b) trainees be observed by experienced mediators, and (c) continuing education dealing explicitly with issues and strategies of which mediators may be unaware or uncomfortable. Sexism and other types of prejudice and bias should be specifically addressed. As with Chandler's (1990, 1991) program, 10-12 hours of education on spouse abuse should be required, to be conducted by persons with related experience, such as social service agency personnel, directors of shelters for battered women, and directors of mediation programs, like MediatioNetwork (Smith, 1991), where abuse guidelines are actively practiced. In addition, continuing education in nonverbal and cross-cultural communication is recommended to sensitize mediators to cues other than what the parties say and to become familiar with gender differences in communication.

CONCLUSION

Mediator training and the practice of mediation are not presently meeting the needs of persons in abusive situations. Abuse is an invisible issue—hidden from mediators by their clients, hidden from mediator trainees by their training programs, and hidden from social discourse by a patriarchal system that does not take it seriously. Until the field of mediation faces up to its contribution to this problem, abuse will remain one of what Murray (1989) calls hidden, underlying, and deep-rooted conflicts crouching within the visible disputes—not simply a barrier to true dispute resolution, but a lurking, potentially dangerous killer.

The research indicates differences in male and female behavior, notably in the way mediators tend to perceive and respond in mediation. Mediators must become more knowledgeable about how their mediation behavior may be influenced by their gender, race, age, class, and even sexual orientation. Denial of abuse by clients was discussed, but if it is the mediators who are denying signs of abuse in their clients' relationship, what is behind that denial? Because the abuser appears more likely to be the husband, is a male mediator more inclined to deny signs of abuse or make excuses for abusive incidents than a female mediator?

Mediators also need to become explicitly aware of the philosophical base from which they practice mediation, in order that their biases are made clear to themselves as well as to their clients. Do they hold a view of themselves as neutrals? If so, what are they ethically willing to overlook to remain truly neutral? Do they see themselves as advocates? If so, what are the ethical boundaries constraining their advocacy?

When I discuss with friends and mediation colleagues the issue of domestic abuse and violence, I discover an extreme lack of awareness that this is either a pressing issue or an issue that needs to concern mediators. Personal experience with this low level of awareness or concern, more than any other factor, discourages me from giving the resounding "Yes" I want to give to the question, "To mediate or not to mediate?" Mediation programs must honestly face the domestic violence issue and incorporate into every stage of their responsibility—training, intake procedures, and the mediation process—guidelines that will educate mediators and truly protect the abused from further abuse. Until then, mediation may not be the best process for reaching a fair and safe outcome in cases involving domestic violence.

Violence in our society is a social problem, and it must be addressed by the social system that tolerates or even encourages it. There is currently no satisfactory solution to the problem of a person who is trying to break off a relationship with another person who is abusive. Civil protection orders do not guarantee that a victim is out of danger from further abuse. It is merely a piece of paper that tells abusers to stay away from their victims. Chandler (1991) reminds us that these are real people in real situations who need real help. A functionally sound alternative or complement to court processes may be found in those mediation programs reported in this chapter that have implemented well-structured procedures both for eliciting hidden issues like abuse and for providing counseling, education, and support for parties in abuse cases. In combination with court processes that have the power to enforce orders, well-run mediation programs may do more good than abandoning people solely to the court system. When more enlightened guidelines become standard procedure in training and practice, mediation may become the humane and effective forum it was meant to be.

REFERENCES

Adams, D. (1988). Treatment models of men who batter: A profeminist analysis. In K. Yllo & M. Bograd (Eds.), *Feminist perspectives on wife abuse* (pp. 176-199). Beverly Hills, CA: Sage.

Belenky, M.F., Clinchy, B.M., Goldberger, N.R., and Tarule, J.M. (1986). *Women's ways of knowing: The development of self, voice, and mind.* New York: Basic Books/Harper Collins Publishers.

Bem, S.L. (1974). The measurement of psychological androgyny. *Journal of Consulting and Clinical Psychology, 42,* 155-162.

Broverman, I., Broverman, D., Clarkson, F., Rosenkrantz, P., & Vogel, S. (1970). Sex role stereotypes and clinical judgements of mental health. *Journal of Consulting and Clinical Psychology, 34,* 1-7.

Bruch, C.S. (1988). And how are the children? The effects of ideology and mediation on child custody law and children's well-being in the United States. *International Journal of Law and the Family, 2,* 106-126.

Chandler, D.B. (1990). Violence, fear and communication: The variable impact of domestic violence on mediation. *Mediation Quarterly, 7,* 331-346.

Chandler, D.B. (1991, June). Panel discussion on spouse abuse issues in mediation at the National Peacemaking and Conflict Resolution Conference in Charlotte, NC.

Chodorow, N. (1989). *Feminism and psychoanalytic theory.* New Haven, CT: Yale University Press.

Coffman, S.J. (1990). Developing a feminist model for clinical consultation: Combining diversity and commonality. *Women and Therapy, 9,* 225-273.

Collins, P.H. (1991). Learning from the outsider within: The sociological significance of black feminist thought. In M.M. Fonow & J.A. Cook (Eds.), *Beyond methodology: Feminist scholarship as lived research* (pp. 35-59). Bloomington, IN: Indiana University Press.

Corcoran, K.O., & Melamed, J.C. (1990). From coercion to empowerment: Spousal abuse and mediation. *Mediation Quarterly, 7,* 303-316.

Erickson, S.K., & McKnight, M.S. (1990). Mediating spousal abuse divorces. *Mediation Quarterly, 7,* 377-388.

Folger, J., & Bernard, S. (1985). Divorce mediation: When mediators challenge the divorcing parties. *Mediation Quarterly, 10,* 5-24.

Gilligan, C. (1982). *In a different voice: Psychological theory and women's development.* Cambridge, MA: Harvard University Press.

Gilligan, C., Ward, J.V., & Taylor, J.M. (Eds.). (1988). *Mapping the moral domain: A contribution of women's thinking to psychological theory and education.* Cambridge, MA: Center for the Study of Gender, Education and Human Development at Harvard University Graduate School of Education.

Girdner, L. (1990). Mediation triage: Screening for spouse abuse in divorce mediation. *Mediation Quarterly, 7,* 365-376.

Graham, D.L.R., Rawlings, E., & Rimini, N. (1988). Survivors of terror: Battered women, hostages, and the Stockholm Syndrome. In K. Yllo & M. Bograd (Eds.), *Feminist perspectives on wife abuse* (pp. 217-233). Newbury Park, CA: Sage.

Grebe, S.C. (1989). Ethical issues in conflict resolution: Divorce mediation. *Negotiation Journal, 5,* 179-190.

Hall, J.A., & Taylor, M.C. (1985). Psychological androgyny and the masculinity X femininity interaction. *Journal of Personality and Social Psychology, 49,* 429-435.

Hart, B.J. (1990). Gentle jeopardy: The further endangerment of battered women and children in custody mediation. *Mediation Quarterly, 7,* 317-330.

Honeyman, C. (1990). On evaluating mediators. *Negotiation Journal, 6,* 23-36.

Honoroff, B., Matz, D., & O'Connor, D. (1990). Putting mediation to the test. *Negotiation Journal, 6,* 37-46.

Hyde, J.S. (1990). Meta-analysis and the psychology of gender differences. *Signs: Journal of Women in Culture and Society, 16,* 55-73.

Kuehl, S.J. (1989). Against joint custody: A dissent to the General Bullmoose theory. Family and Conciliation *Courts Review, 27*(2), 37-45.

Laue, J.H. (1982). Ethical considerations in choosing intervention roles. *Peace and Change, 8*(2/3), 29-40.

Leitch, M.L. (1986/1987). The politics of compromise: A feminist perspective on mediation. *Mediation Quarterly, 14/15,* 163-175.

Lerman, L.G. (1984). Mediation of wife abuse cases: The adverse impact of informal dispute resolution on women. *Harvard Women's Law Journal, 7*(1), 57-113.

Lerman, L., Kuehl, S.J., & Brygger, M.P. (1989). *Domestic abuse and mediation: Guidelines for mediators and policymakers.* Washington, DC: National Woman Abuse and Prevention Project.

Mader, T.F., & Mader, D.C. (1990). *Understanding one another: Communicating interpersonally.* Dubuque, IA: Wm. C. Brown.

Marks, L.A. (1988, Winter). Domestic violence cases. *NCADV Voice* [National Coalition Against Domestic Violence].

MediatioNetwork of North Carolina. (1989). Domestic violence policy. (Revised April 7, 1989). Domestic violence guidelines for application of domestic violence policy. (Revised May 18, 1989).

Moore, C.W. (1988). Techniques to break impasse. In J. Folberg & A. Milne (Eds.), *Divorce mediation: Theory and practice* (pp. 251-176). New York: Guilford Press.

Morella, C.A. (1990, December 9). Keep wife-beaters away from the kids: Why do courts give them custody? *The Washington Post*, p. K5.

Murray, J.S. (1989). Designing a disputing system for Central City and its school. *Negotiation Journal, 5,* 365-372.

Pagelow, M.D. (1990). Effects of domestic violence on children and their consequences for custody and visitation agreements. *Mediation Quarterly, 7,* 347-363.

Pruett, B.M. (1989). Male and female communicator style differences: A meta-analysis. In C.M. Lont & S.A. Friedley (Eds.), *Beyond boundaries: Sex and gender diversity in communication* (pp. 107-120). Fairfax, VA: George Mason University Press.

Rifkin, J., Millen, J., & Cobb, S. (1991). Toward a new discourse for mediation: A critique of neutrality. *Negotiation Journal, 9,* 151-164,

Salem, R.A. (1982). Community dispute resolution through outside intervention. *Peace and Change, 7,* 91-103.

Saunders, D.G. (1990). *Child custody decisions in families experiencing woman abuse.* Manuscript submitted for publication.

Skaggs, K. (1988, Winter). Why mediation is bad for battered women. *NCADV Voice* [National Coalition Against Domestic Violence].

Smith, P. (1991, June). Panel discussion on spouse abuse issues in Mediation at the National Peacemaking and Conflict Resolution Conference in Charlotte, NC.

Smythe, M.J., & Schlueter, D.W. (1989). Can we talk?? A meta-analytic review of the sex differences in language literature. In C.M. Lont & S.A. Friedley (Eds.), *Beyond boundaries: Sex and gender diversity in communication* (pp. 31-48). Fairfax, VA: George Mason University Press.

Sonkin, D.J., Martin, D., & Walker, L.E.A. (1985). *The male batterer: A treatment approach.* New York: Springer.

Sun, M. (1988, Winter). Battered women and mediation: The national picture. *NCADV Voice* [National Coalition Against Domestic Violence].

Sun, M., & Woods, L. (1989). *A mediator's guide to domestic abuse.* New York: National Center on Women and Family Law.

Tannen, D. (1990). *You just don't understand: Women and men in conversation.* New York: William Morrow.

Weingarten, H.R., & Douvan, E. (1985). Male and female visions of mediation. *Negotiation Journal, 1,* 349-358.

Woods, L. (1987). Women's progress and the mediation backlash. *Grapevine, 18*(6).

Yelsma, P., & Brown, C.T. (1985). Gender roles, biological sex, and predisposition to conflict management. *Sex Roles, 12,* 731-747.

4

Secretarial Positioning: Gender Ambivalence and Harassment

Patricia J. Sotirin
David James Miller
Michigan Technological University

> [W]oman is at once Eve and the Virgin Mary. She is an idol, a servant, the source of life, a power of darkness; she is the elemental silence of truth, she is artifice, gossip, and falsehood; she is healing presence and sorceress; she is man's prey, his downfall, she is everything that he is not and that he longs for, his negation and his raison d'etre .
>
> —de Beauvoir (1948/1952)

GENDER AND AMBIVALENCE

Since the time de Beauvoir authored her celebrated treatise on women's domination, the recognition that ascriptions of "feminine gender" frequently are used in service of the subordination and oppression of women has become commonplace. One of the most striking features of such ascriptions, as de Beauvoir saw, is that the "nature" of the gender attributed to the second sex is contradictory. The contradictory "nature" of feminine gender abides in the social practices that constitute women as feminine, practices that are themselves contradictory.[1]

[1]Talk of the per se "nature" of such gender amounts to a reification of these practices.

The contradictions of feminine gender at once presume and reproduce a certain ambivalence toward women. This ambivalence is blatantly displayed, for example, in religious instruction and rite that regards women as both the source of life and the denizen of sin, mortality and death, as is the case in the tension between images of women as madonna or whore in Christianity (Nelson, 1979). It is manifest in the adoration of the virgin mother and the persecution of women as witches (Dworkin, 1974, 1976). This ambivalence is seen again in the tension regarding women's bodies, their sensuality and sexuality, as both the embodiment of good and the incarnation of evil (Rich, 1976).

Of course, these examples represent caricatures of a much subtler process. For the most part, the ambivalence toward women produced and reproduced by the contradictory practices that constitute feminine gender is nowhere so flagrant. Nevertheless, such examples point to a less perceptible process constituting the gender ascribed to women, a process whereby the trust of women is tempered with a suspicion that women—women as embodiments of feminine gender—cannot be trusted.

Our thesis here is that the ambivalence of trust and suspicion resulting from the contradictory practices constituting feminine gender can make such gender a site of conflict. We develop interrelated arguments to warrant this thesis. The first concerns gender ambivalence in organizational positions. We contend that gender as such is an aspect of organizational positions. Given that the contradictory practices constituting feminine gender produce the sort of gender ambivalence we just described, it follows that feminine-gendered organizational positions will manifest characteristics of this ambivalence. We demonstrate this point by discussing gendered positions and then show how gender ambivalence is inscribed in a particular position, the secretarial position.

Our second argument concerns gender ambivalence and conflict. Given that the ambivalence of feminine gender is constituted in contradictory practices, and that contradiction may be the site of conflict, then positions in the organization that manifest this ambivalence will be constituted as sites of conflict. We describe mediations among the contradictions that constitute the secretarial position and then consider a particular conflict situation, sexual harassment, at the site of those mediations.

THE GENDERING OF ORGANIZATIONAL POSITIONS

In organizational theory, the concept of partial inclusion focuses attention on the fact that organizations neither require nor desire the full range of human behavioral and relational capacities (Katz & Kahn,

1966).[2] In accord with the dictates of bureaucratic rationalization, only behaviors and relations that are functional to the organization have a proper place in the organization (cf. Weber, 1958). And what is functional to the organization is determined, at least in principle, in terms of the articulation of the division of labor and the coordination of roles.

The division of labor creates a rationalized hierarchy of specialized organizational tasks. The coordination of roles operates as a system of functionally derived interdependencies. Expectations, rewards, sanctions, and other control mechanisms enforce these interdependencies. Role in this sense circumscribes the relations and behaviors that are to be included or excluded from the organization.

The division of labor and the coordination of roles together delineate the *proper place* of any individual in the organization. This proper place is not merely a structural location described by organizationally sanctioned behaviors and relations. It designates an organizational ethos, a mode of occupying organizational space (Sotirin & Miller, 1990). The doctrine of partial inclusion warrants the abstraction of certain behaviors and relations from the total context of an individual's life.

The legitimacy of such a designation derives in part from the apparent sensibleness of the division of labor and the coordination of roles as abstract and neutral operational arrangements (Acker, 1990). Bureaucratic ideals of impartiality and interchangeability imply that the tasks and behaviors circumscribed are genderless. But the implication is neither borne out in practice nor tenable in principle.

In its conception, the division of labor draws on ascriptions of masculine gender. For example, the separation of planning from execution duplicates patriarchical presumptions of authority, privilege, and responsibility. Further, the ideals of impartiality and objectivity are premised on an ethic of justice that characterizes masculine moral codes (Gilligan, 1982). In practice, the division of labor creates a differentiation among workers ostensibly drawn on the assignment of tasks but implicitly involving gender, race, age, and other social distinctions (Hearn & Parkin, 1987). Such divisions are integral to the relations of authority

---

[2]The term *partial inclusion* has become a commonplace in management theory and as such, the tension that the phrase was meant to mark is often passed over. But in its original application, partial inclusion stood in contrast to *total inclusion* (Allport, 1933). Partial inclusion served to designate a situation in which the composition of a group consisted of an abstract aggregate of the common segments of the behavior of individuals, a necessary fiction if the group was to get things done (Allport, 1933, p. 96). The contrast to total inclusion served to bring the segmental character of partial inclusion into relief. For total inclusion "implies the inclusion of an endless variety of desires, emotions, habits, and thoughts integrated within each human . . . . In other words, an aggregate of unique individuals far too complex to be characterized adequately through any abstracted uniformity of action or desire" (Allport, 1933, p. 97).

and control accomplished through the coordination of roles.

The coordination of roles is premised as well on ascriptions of masculine gender. The concept of work role itself can be understood as underwritten by a gender subtext (cf. Smith, 1987). The notion that organizational roles can be isolated from a worker's life context requires "a particular gendered organization of domestic life and social production" (Acker, 1990, p. 149). That is, men can devote themselves to fulfilling work-role expectations because women are held primarily responsible for those demands that would intrude on such commitment.

The impersonal universality of work role is male-gendered and relies on the minimal responsibility socially assigned to men for domestic, emotional, and reproductive (procreation, childrearing, and children's socialization) labor. The embodiment of abstract roles requires men's bodies, responsibilities, and privileges. In contrast, "Women's bodies—female sexuality, their ability to procreate and their pregnancy, breast-feeding, and childcare, menstruation, and mythic 'emotionality'—are suspect, stigmatized, and used as grounds for control and exclusion" (Acker, 1990, p. 152).[3]

Positions in the organization, then, are gendered from the outset. Furthermore, masculine domination is inscribed in the very conception of rational organizational arrangements of task and role. In this context, the possibility for feminine gender oppression becomes part of the ethos of certain organizational positions.

THE SECRETARIAL POSITION AND AMBIVALENCE

The secretarial position provides the most visible example of gendered positioning. As a feature of the modern office, the secretarial position has been (and is) overwhelmingly occupied by females.[4] Furthermore, ascriptions of feminine gender characterize the ethos of this position and pervade task and role dimensions. Accordingly, anyone who fills it must contend with the gendered ethos of the secretarial position. Striking contradictions, however, constitute this position. These contradictions reproduce the suspicions that express an ambivalence toward feminine gender in all dimensions of the positioning of secretaries.

---

[3]For related discussions of the division of labor and the coordination of roles as historically gendered, see Kanter (1977); Burrell (1984); Ferguson (1984); Hearn, Sheppard, Tancred-Sheriff, & Burrell (1989); Acker (1990).

[4]Since the 1950s, labor statistics have shown that one of the leading occupations for women has consistently been secretarial work (Baxandall, Gordon, & Reverby, 1976; Women's Bureau, 1985). In line with this, the percentage of secretaries who are women has remained above 98% since the 1950s (in 1991, for example, women occupied 99% of all secretarial positions; Bureau of Labor Statistics, January 1992, Employment and Earnings Report).

The relevant dimensions in determining organizational positioning of any sort are task, role, and character. It is in character that the lived attributes of ethos or proper place are abstracted from the level of concrete action. In other words, character is the abstract formulation of proper place. In secretarial positioning, this formulation is characterized by gender ambivalence, making the proper place of a secretary a site of contradictions.

The Contradictions of Secretarial Labor

Secretarial tasks involving the routine management of information, although invaluable to the operation and integrity of organizational information systems, are devalued in practice. Specific tasks of information sorting, filing, and routing demonstrate this ambivalence. In sorting in-coming, out-going, and in-process information, secretaries perform the celebrated gatekeeper function. Charged with screening requests for managerial attention, secretaries are responsible for determining the boundaries between what deserves attention and what does not and for assembling and prioritizing the information that deserves attention.

However, Feldman and March (1981) contend that the "ordinary competence and minor initiative" involved in such pragmatic assessments amount to a display of and commitment to pre-established procedural rationalities. As Weick (1979, p. 249) has argued, the determination of what deserves attention and what does not is always made within a "climate of accountability" that denigrates or prohibits mutation and unjustified variation from these rationalities. Making distinctions between what deserves attention and what does not is for the most part the mere enactment—the recognition and manipulation—of organizational codes of protocol and authority (Lalonde, 1986).

In disseminating information, secretaries appear to be responsible for creating communicative forms and managing communicative flows. However, with respect to the former, secretaries are typically restricted to the use of institutionalized formats, both oral and written, that display an array of indices for bureaucratic rationality (e.g., standardization of format and content, etiquette of address, impersonal voice, neatness, and so on). Although such restrictions are often expressed as a concern for clarity, efficiency, and professionalism, they in fact impose a rational regimen that mitigates against variation.

With respect to the flow of communication, secretaries are restricted for the most part to the use of routine practices that control the information load on the rest of the system (cf. Huber & Daft, 1987, p. 146). These practices include secretaries as mediators but not as creators of messages. Indeed, when secretaries attempt to create information other than that routinely expected or requested, others in the organization tend to devalue or disregard the messages as unimportant or trivial unless they are substantiated by those in formal positions of authority or responsibility (Louis, 1980; Stohl, 1986). Secretaries perform a conduit function; they must be adept at recognizing and respecting extant relations of communication and authority.

Within the bureaucratic "climate of accountability," in which quantity is its own justification, paperwork relentlessly proliferates. In this climate, secretarial responsibility for disseminating information is often reduced to endless duplication. The secretary becomes an accoutrement (see later) to the computer, the photocopy machine, and other technologies for text and graphics reproduction.

As both bane and mainstay of secretarial work, filing is a characteristic task responsibility. However, filing information, like sorting it and passing it along, often involves little more than a manipulation of codes. Filing systems are self-organizing storage systems—incoming information gets filed into existing categories or into categories related to those that already exist (Weick, 1979).

The drudgery of filing is related not only to the lack of challenge but to the nonproductiveness of the task. Eighty-five percent of the records most organizations keep are never referred to and 95% of all references that are made are to records filed for less than 3 years (Pringle, 1989, p. 187). Organizations often collect information as much for symbolic as for instrumental value to create the appearance of decision rationality and accountability, and hence legitimacy. Much of what gets filed gains status as information from the place assigned it in the filing system. This accords with the emphasis on preserving written records in bureaucracies; value accrues from the keeping of records rather than from the usefulness of the records themselves.

In addition, storage, retrieval, and disposal of organizational records involve processes of selection and retention that defer firm distinctions between what can and cannot be discarded. In this system, the criteria for discard are ambivalent, contingent on time and space considerations, and sensitive to shifts in interpretive contexts. Expiration dates, storage capacities, and changes in context-dependent considerations alter the boundaries between what is worth saving and what is not until ultimately, the distinction itself appears to give way.

In summary, the contradictions of secretarial labor emerge out of the tensions between what is valued and devalued in the operation of organizational information and communication systems. Although ostensibly charged with important responsibilities for sorting, disseminating, and filing, in practice, these tasks often involve little more than the rote observation of protocol. Secretarial labor is devalued along with the tasks themselves; the trust placed in secretaries for critical information management services is undermined by a suspicion that secretarial work is best performed in routinized ways in accord with rigid standards that minimize opportunities for secretarial autonomy and creativity.

The Contradictions of Secretarial Role

Bureaucracy assimilates individuals to organizational roles. The hallmarks of bureaucratic roles include detailed job descriptions, impersonal relations, and personnel interchangeability. In the bureaucratic system, the particular individual who occupies a secretarial role at any given time is disposable. However, the secretarial role itself, for a variety of reasons, is considered indispensable. Three arguments for the indispensability of the secretarial role are the indispensability of the role in the interpersonal relation of boss-secretary; the indispensability of the role within the informal systems of managerial status and reward; and the indispensability of the role in the automated office. In each of its guises, indispensability gives way to dispensability.

Kanter (1977) has observed that given the interpersonal commitments characterizing the boss-secretary relation, the secretarial role resists bureaucratization and is often considered indispensable. The indispensability of this role emerges in a contextual shift from the impersonal and instrumental bureaucratic relationship to a personal and affective relationship. This personal and affective relationship has come to be characterized in terms of a conjugal metaphor (Beechey, 1987; Pringle, 1988; Tepperman, 1976). A discourse of the office wife emerged in debates at the turn of the century over the proper place for (middle-class) women (Davies, 1982; Pringle, 1988; Rothman, 1978). In this discourse, the ideal attributes of the traditional white, middle-class wife in relation to her husband were displaced onto the secretary: docility, deference, loyalty, subservience, and dependence. The secretarial role, as a caretaking relation, requires services beyond those detailed in formal job descriptions and is compensated in terms of emotional as well as monetary reward.

But this discourse fails to constitute the secretary as interpersonally indispensable. The secretarial role remains fundamentally inscribed by the bureaucratic codes of interchangeability and impersonal relations. In the current climate of economic uncertainty, the secretarial role is often a target of downsizing and re-entrenchment efforts, notwithstanding the personal boss-secretary relationship.

In addition, the discourse of the office wife has itself been modified in accord with the sociocultural reinterpretations of conjugal obligations since the 1960s (Friedan, 1963). The office wife, like the middle-class housewife, has reconsidered her conjugal obligations in the wake of the dispersion of the feminine mystique and no longer makes coffee unreflectively (Carroll, 1983). A modernist discourse of occupational professionalism—the career woman—has gained prominence and although it has not replaced the discourse of the office wife, it has introduced ambiguating connotations of teamwork, career independence, and assertive femininity (Pringle, 1988).

The secretary as a team player and a career woman may be indispensable to the office team in terms other than those associated with her role as office wife. The discourse of professionalism downplays the conjugal intimacy of the boss-secretary relationship. Moreover, both in-house and referral counseling services have become readily available. Although not tied to shifts in the discourses of the secretarial role, this increased availability indicates that the secretary is not indispensable for the emotional support or caretaking dimensions integral to the boss-secretary relationship.

A second argument for indispensability is that the secretarial role is a status symbol within informal systems of managerial reward, status, and social prestige (Braverman, 1974; Kanter, 1977). While almost anyone in the organization can request secretarial services, those who can claim possession ("she's my secretary") and exclusive use of secretarial services ("check with me before you give any work to my secretary") have greater status and usually a higher position in the hierarchy. The assignment of a personal secretary is taken as a sign of managerial reward and significance. In addition, the secretary assists in preserving and advancing managerial privilege and status both literally and metaphorically by protecting territorial claims and managerial privacy (Murphee, 1987).

Nonetheless, this dimension of secretarial indispensability remains inscribed by capitalist bureaucratic dynamics and is undermined by the system drive to maximize cost efficiencies, accumulate capital, and realize technological capacities. Braverman (1974) argues that in the inexorable drive to capital accumulation, the executive secretary as a status symbol is targeted for elimination as an inefficient diversion of capital and energy and an ostentatious display of executive privilege reminiscent of the traditional social office. He predicts that corporations will reorganize the boss-secretary relation around service pools and computer technologies, deskilling workers, centralizing authority, and restricting autonomy. Although debates over this "proletarianization" thesis remain unresolved (cf. Barker & Downing, 1980; West, 1982), the lack of resolution itself questions the claim that the secretarial role is indispensable as a status symbol.

Finally, there is the claim that the secretarial role is indispensable in terms of expanded domains of technical skill, expertise, and capacities for productivity. Those who celebrate the promise of technological innovations claim that new office technologies have enriched the secretarial role from office wife to executive extender by "eliminating some of the schlepp work" (Carroll, 1983, p. 131; Eckersley-Johnson, 1976). Technological innovation in the office involves changes in tasks and changes in relations of authority and responsibility. Of the first, Carroll (1983) is enthusiastic: "I believe that office automation will give secretaries an opportunity to upgrade their jobs while reducing or eliminating many of the time-consuming duties that they find least desirable" (p. 131). Less sanguine observers argue that the career opportunities for women represented by new positions and job classifications created by implementing new technologies are often transitional or temporary. For example, research by the Coalition of Labor Union Women at a Bell Telephone company indicated that "women and minority workers . . . are often moved into positions that may be transitional or may be vulnerable especially to further change or to elimination" (Gregory, 1986, p. 16).

Just as ambiguous is the significance for secretaries of technologically inspired changes in relations of authority and responsibility. Barley (1988) suggests that relations of authority may be renegotiated around shifts in technical skill and expertise. That is, when it is the secretary who can use sophisticated computer programs and not the boss, the secretary may negotiate greater latitudes of authority and autonomy in the area of her program expertise. In this sense, secretarial indispensability might well be redefined around technological opportunities.

The possibility for such redefinitions creates a new ambivalence toward the secretarial role, however. The secretarial role without technological opportunity is undesirable ("stuck with the typewriter" vs. becoming a specialist in desktop publishing). Developing those opportunities beyond the strictures of the secretarial position may be more desirable than preserving the role itself (promotion to a position in the computer department rather than staying a secretary with enhanced computer skills). One way or the other, the secretarial role is given up as disposable.

The claim that the secretarial role is indispensable in the automated office becomes even more ambiguous in situations that reduce secretaries to little more than machine accoutrements (Machung, 1988). This reduction historically has been justified by observations of a supposed coincidence among women's biological traits, social characteristics, and the demands of technological processes and equipment. For example, arguments about their "natural" propensity for office work, arising from the coincidence of natural feminine traits like patience, dexterity, and attention to detail, and social characteristics like docility and dependability, often justified hiring women as clerks and typists. This reduction to machine accouterments also justified such surveillance practices as productivity quotas and keystroke monitoring (Davies, 1982). The contemporary equivalent in the automated office is electronic surveillance (Nine to Five, 1987; Tepperman, 1976).

Although the secretarial role may be indispensable as the human element in the automated office, reducing the secretary herself to an element of the technological system often increases the possibilities for labor exploitation and oppressive working conditions. These may include increased productivity quotas, stress and other health risks (like carpal tunnel syndrome), as well as monitoring and other bureaucratic labor controls (like physical and task isolation). There are, then, unresolved tensions inherent in both the promises and the threats of the automated office for the secretarial role. In summary, ambiguity pervades all three claims for indispensability. As an office wife or team player, as a status symbol, or as an integral part of the electronic office of the future, the secretarial role ambivalently is promoted as indispensable and dismissed as disposable.

The Contradictions of Secretarial Character

In delineating the desirable traits of the secretary, one secretarial manual asserts that a "top-notch" secretary must be polite, pleasant, friendly, fair, thoughtful, cooperative, humble, tolerant and considerate, loyal, sensitive, courageous, honest, self-controlled, flexible and adaptable, diplomatic and observant of etiquette, well-groomed, endowed with a sense of humor, enthusiastic, and responsible (Eckersley-Johnson, 1976). These traits characterize a feminine gentility that overwrites all aspects of the secretarial role. Pringle (1988), for example, argues that the literacy, general knowledge, and competence of secretaries are "treated not so much as skills as characteristics which a lady has, along with a well-groomed appearance, a well-modulated voice, maturity, poise and grace and the ability to converse intelligently with managers" (p. 133). Secretaries are to be office ladies, an identity signifying a certain ideal of respectable womanhood that balances assertiveness, submissiveness, and attractiveness.

But the desirable traits of the secretary do not appear to guarantee that the secretarial role is treated with respect. A tension between expectations of respectability and suspicions of disrespectability marks secretarial character. We illustrate this tension as it appears in three character traits generally deemed important to the secretarial role: demeanor and appearance, availability, and flexibility/adaptability.

A respectable secretary should look like a lady—an "office lady"—and display the appropriate demeanor and appearance (Carroll, 1983). But the proper appearance can be taken as a sign of both respectable womanhood and sensual opportunity. The office lady is also the sexy secretary or everybody's mother. Whether sexy or maternal, the sensual component of the secretarial ethos invokes ambivalence toward the feminine that expresses itself as a tension between trust and suspicion. The suspicion of feminine sensuality in the secretarial ethos is organized in institutional lore and popular discourses around images of the sexy secretary and attendant associations of ill-repute.

Pringle (1988) argues that in the postwar consumer economy, sexuality as a commodity and a preoccupation in popular culture found expression in the figure of the secretary (literally and metaphorically). The boss-secretary relation came to be viewed in popular media as a "war of the sexes" waged in the office as "a kind of erotic war zone" (pp. 12-13). Hearn and Parkin (1984) name the boss-secretary relationship as the archetypal office sex fantasy (p. 121) and the secretary as the archetype of the organizational sexual stereotype (p. 145). Additionally, they point out that the office itself frequently has been the featured setting for pornographic images:

> [G]irls are shown studiously taking dictation in owlish glasses and severe hairstyles, quite unconscious that their neat white blouse is completely open down the front and the boss is absentmindedly playing with their breasts. Office girls cannot open a filing cabinet without revealing that they have nothing on under their respectable grey skirts. (Miles, 1983, p. 34, cited in Hearn & Parkin, 1984, p. 149)

These images involve what Hearn and Parkin (1984) refer to as a "pornographic code" constituting secretaries/girls as objects of male fantasy and heterosexual desire. Reframed by this code of male desire, the feminine gentility of the office lady is rendered suspect—the performance of respectability underscored by a certain disreputableness. A secretary's ascribed concern with fashion and maintaining her appearance takes on additional significance as a sign of sexual trumpery—a deceit, a tawdry finery, a "cheap" appearance designed to titillate. Demeanor and appearance, then, do not guarantee secretarial respectability but are also interpreted as indications of disrepute. These traits of the respectable secretary reproduce the ambivalence between trust and suspicion.

Similarly, ambivalence is evident in secretarial availability. To do a respectable job as a secretary requires a certain availability. By definition, a secretary's services are at the disposal of others in the organization, especially those in managerial positions, an availability often confounded by presumptions/perceptions of sexual availability.

Gutek and Morasch (1982) suggest that presumptions and perceptions of secretarial availability for sexual sport, adventure, and entertainment express "sex-role spillover," a presumed equivalence between work-role and sex-role identities that constitutes the secretarial role itself as sexualized. The presumption of work-role and sex-role equivalence expressed in secretarial availability draws on the historical entanglement of class and sexual relations in the social office. Benet (1972) observes that during the 1920s and 1930s respectable men of higher social status regarded working-class women in office typing pools—like the women who worked as domestic servants or shop assistants before them—as available for sexual entertainment. Pringle (1988) notes that during the 1950s and 1960s, more explicit discourses of sexuality in popular and office cultures added an emphasis on the female body and feminine sexual attractiveness.

Elements of this legacy persist under various guises. They persist in the age bias that disadvantages older secretarial women. In this sense, "old ladies" or "ugly ladies" signify sexual unavailability, and "girls"—even if they are "ugly girls"—signify sexual availability. Elements also persist in the continued emphasis on secretarial femininity and sexuality (in the language of liberal feminism, assertive femininity and self-confident sexuality). And elements also persist on the job as part of a working woman's assets and in the secretarial training programs and schools as "personal development" training (Pringle, 1988; Valli, 1986). These residual elements contribute to the suspicion that secretarial availability involves sexual availability.

Flexibility is also a dimension of secretarial work relations because the secretary frequently is called on to respond to demands and requests from people other than her boss. These may include people who work for or with her boss, visitors, and any person in the organization at a higher hierarchical level than her boss who requests secretarial support services. Flexibility as a design feature of secretarial work relations means that the services of "my girl" are not restricted by boundaries of managerial territoriality, status, and possession. Flexibility, then, imbues the role with a kind of promiscuity that resonates to the myth of the sexual secretary, particularly in its connotations of pliability and tractability.

AMBIVALENCE AS A SITE OF CONFLICT IN THE SECRETARIAL POSITION

The Mediation of Secretarial Contradictions

The contradictions of character permeate the ethos of the secretarial position; Pringle (1989) observes that what a secretary does is overshadowed by what she is taken to be. Suspicion of a disreputableness in the secretarial character warrants the disrespectful practices that express the devaluation of secretarial tasks and role. For example, secretaries are suspected of neglecting or failing to fulfill task and role responsibilities in part because of certain innate characteristics (frivolity, emotionality, domestic and interpersonal preoccupations) and task-disruptive social practices (gossiping, bitching, or participating in women-centered ceremonies and rituals at work).

Contrary to the doctrine of partial inclusion, the secretarial ethos is constituted as a locus of what is partially excluded: the emotional, private, intimate dimensions of human sociality that contradict organizational claims to a rational structure of social cooperation based on instrumental relations. In this regard, Kanter (1977) observes that the boss-secretary relationship is a "pocket of the personal inside the bureaucratic," whereas Machung (1988) calls secretarial work "the craft of love."

Little wonder then that secretarial role expectations extend well beyond rational-functional organizational responsibilities. In many organizations, secretaries still are expected to perform a variety of domestic services (making coffee, sewing on buttons) and personal services (making doctor appointments, buying birthday gifts). Boundaries on these services are interpersonally and situationally negotiated; what is required in order to do a respectable job as a secretary and what is permissible within the bounds of respectability remain renegotiable and ambiguous. Further, these negotiations over boundaries instantiate ambivalence toward the feminine. So, in living out her position as a repository of the personal, the secretary comes under suspicion—she might always exceed the bounds of moral, emotional, and sexual respectability.

Ambivalence, Contradiction, and Conflict

Gender ambivalence and the contradictory constitution of secretarial ethos frame an alternative account of the sexual harassment of secretaries. The sexual harassment of secretaries is a conflict situation circumscribed by the contradictory constitution of secretarial ethos or proper place. Such harassment involves a set of sociosexual practices that express those contradictions and the gender ambivalence.[5] In particular, the suspicions and contradictions of secretarial character expand the latitudes of proper organizational relations and conduct to include paternalism, subtle sexual discrimination, and comments and behaviors with sexual content catego-

---

[5]We adopt a broad conception of sexual harassment, concurring with the definition used for U.S. governmental guidelines: "Specifically sexual harassment is deliberate or repeated unsolicited verbal comments, gestures, or physical contact of a sexual nature that is unwelcome" (Gutek & Nakamura, 1982, p. 188). Equal Employment Opportunity Commission (EEOC) prosecution of harassment emphasizes the situational nature of such conflicts and proceeds on a case-by-case basis to take context into account (Wallace, 1982). Not only is sexual harassment configured by a broad range of behavioral and situational exigencies but by a variety of relational forms as well including paternalism, sexual aggression, or gender-based discrimination (Gottfried & Fasenfest, 1984).

rized as social pleasantries—compliments, invitations, jokes, intimate forms of informal address, casual social touching, gestures, suggestive facial movements, the giving of unwanted gifts, or letters.

The secretary's everyday negotiations over the latitudes of respectability often involve tolerating aspects of suspicion, devaluation, and disrespect. Gutek and her colleagues have documented this tolerance and report that secretaries tend to underreport incidents of sexual harassment, accepting a whole array of sociosexual behavior as appropriate (Gutek & Morasch, 1982). In their tolerance, secretaries reproduce the conditions facilitating their harassment; in effect they participate in constituting their own vulnerability. Meissner (1986) comments on one aspect of this complicity when he observes, "Men's and women's identification of some forms of harassment as flattering prevents men from recognizing their terrorism and makes women party to their own subordination" (p. 59).

Sexual harassment can be taken as a form of discipline or control over the threat posed by secretarial ethos. The emotional-connective character of secretarial ethos re-asserts that which is excluded from instrumental relationships and behaviors. In this sense, secretarial ethos poses the possibility of an alternative model of organizational sociality.

This perspective on the sexual harassment of secretaries complements and integrates in a critical manner several of the models of sexual harassment advanced in recent literature on sexual harassment in organizations. Despite their differences, the context of ambivalence, as well as contradiction and gendered organizational positioning appear relevant to each model.

The sex-role spillover model developed by Gutek and her colleagues takes sexual harassment in the organization to be a form of role conflict based on counterposed behavioral expectations (Gutek, 1988, 1989; Gutek & Cohen, 1987; Gutek & Dunwoody, 1987; Gutek & Morasch, 1982; Gutek & Nakamura, 1982). The model proposes that aspects of sex-role are imposed on the expectations and interpretations of work-role behaviors and possibilities. Gutek argues that in pink-collar positions, work-role and sex-role merge. Because of this, pink-collar workers often fail to recognize harassment as such and accept sexual overtures as part of the job (Gutek & Cohen, 1987; Gutek & Morasch, 1982). But that secretaries often accept harassment is not necessarily a failure to recognize harassment as a conflict situation. Rather, it is a consequence of the ambiguity experienced in such conflict situations given the contradictory ascriptions of their sexual character. What is problematic about the spillover model is the distinction drawn between sex role and work role because it implies the gender neutrality of work role.

The organizational model takes sexual harassment in the organization to be a form of conflict of interests emerging out of the distribution of opportunity structures inherent to organizational hierarchy (Tangri, Burt, & Johnson, 1982). The organizational model holds that harassment may be perpetrated by either males against females or females against males depending on their location in the hierarchy and such other contributing factors as work role set characteristics and sex ratios, organizational norms, job tasks and requirements, and the existence of grievance procedures. The model concedes that because women typically occupy the structurally disadvantaged locations in the organizational hierarchy, they are in general more vulnerable to the economic, emotional, and physical consequences of harassment. A communication-oriented variation of the organizational model suggests that organizational cultures may be either "harassment prone" or "harassment sensitive" (Fairhurst, 1986) and that the ambiguities and strategies involved in harassment situations vary accordingly.

But although vertical stratification and other structural characteristics affect the occurrence of sexual harassment, hierarchy itself expresses the more basic sociohistorical contradiction of gender discussed above. The organizational model misses the contradictions that frame the harassment situation. Consequently, it provides only a partial account of why secretarial vulnerability to such conflicts is continually reproduced even as individual secretaries or organizations attempt to alter particular conditions for its occurrence.

The sociocultural power model takes sexual harassment in the organization to be a form of male-female conflict derived from the relations of power characterizing patriarchal domination (Gottfried & Fasenfest, 1984). This model asserts that sexual harassment is a means of male control over women's labor—productive and reproductive. In the organization, harassment is a form of paternalism, "the conflict between men and women based on sexuality stemming from patriarchal relations in the family" (Gottfried & Fasenfest, 1984, p. 99). Harassment reproduces the structure of patriarchal domination by restricting the development of interpersonal relations at work to reifications of "femaleness," specifically mistress/object or mother/subject. But this model oversimplifies the experience of sexual harassment as it fails to recognize the mediated contradictions constituting gendered positions in the workplace. It is the complexity of the contradictions that renders the experience of harassment confusing and difficult for secretarial women and makes tolerance and complicity as likely as confrontation and resistance.

Summarily, sexual harassment situations are complex, involving interpersonal, organizational, and societal aspects. The contradictions of positioning as we have elaborated them above entangle these aspects in ways that become difficult to distinguish in everyday instantiations. In addition, sexual harassment situations are multidimensional, involving not only gender but also racial or ethnic, age, and socioeconomic aspects. Each of these brings its own configurations of contradictory practices. Finally, sexual harassment situations are communicatively difficult, involving behavioral, perceptual, and interpretive ambiguities and incongruities (Bingham, 1991; Booth-Butterfield, 1986; Fairhurst, 1986; Hickson, Grierson, & Linder, 1991). These inherent difficulties are exacerbated in situations such as those common to the secretarial position, in which gender ambiguities confound frames of interpretation and constrain the possibilities for communicative interaction.

COMPLICATIONS AND EXTENSIONS

Although this chapter has focused on the tensions inherent to the gender contradictions in bureaucratic life, our discussion of sexual harassment indicates that the overdetermination of organizational positioning includes even more complications. The secretarial position is complexly overdetermined by multiple articulations among the tensions and contradictions of race, class, age, gender, bureaucracy, and other crucial—or at least relevant—dimensions. Consider, for example, the "double articulation" of race, gender, and bureaucratic principles and practices (Hall, 1985). What happens to the respectable/lack of respectability contradiction when the ideal of white feminine gentility is displaced? And without this mainstay, do the ambiguities and negotiations of sexual harassment conflicts become re-anchored in alternative relations of subordination, or do they become more fluid and structurally critical? Furthermore, how are the contradictions within and among gender, bureaucracy, and race configured in such conflict situations—how is secretarial positioning and attendant vulnerabilities and possibilities altered for women of color whose lives are circumscribed by compounded ambivalences?

Furthermore, if we take account of class histories and ascriptions, our discussion begins to address the "multiple jeopardy" of gender, race, and class (King, 1988). How are class-based presumptions of servitude, sexuality, and subordination instantiated in secretarial positioning and how are their contradictory practices articulated to those of gender, bureaucracy, and race (cf. Valli, 1986)? We have already noted the class-inflected history of presumptions of sexual availability; clearly such suspicions inflect harassment situations but what are the particulars and significances of their instantiation and mediation? And what of age? These questions and others not yet set forth circumscribe the limits of the present work; it is our hope they will also sketch out the possibilities of work to come.

REFERENCES

Acker, J. (1990). Hierarchies, jobs, bodies: A theory of gendered organizations. *Gender and Society, 4,* 139-158.

Allport, F. (1933). *Institutional behavior: Essays toward a re-interpreting of contemporary social organization.* Chapel Hill: University of North Carolina Press.

Barker, J., & Downing, H. (1980). Word processing and the transformation of the patriarchal relations of control in the office. *Capital and Class, 10,* 64-97.

Barley, S. (1988). Technology as an occasion for structuring: Evidence from observations of CT scanners and the social order of radiology departments. *Administrative Science Quarterly, 31,* 78-108.

Baxandall, R., Gordon, L., & Reverby, S. (Eds.). (1976). *America's working women.* New York: Random House.

Beechey, V. (1987). *Unequal work.* London: Verso.

Benet, M.K. (1972). *Secretary: An enquiry into the female ghetto.* London: Sidgwick & Jackson.

Bingham, S.G. (1991). Communication strategies for managing sexual harassment in organizations: Understanding message options and their effects. *Journal of Applied Communication Research, 19,* 88-115.

Booth-Butterfield, M. (1986). Recognizing and communicating in harassment-prone organizational climates. *Women's Studies in Communication, 9,* 42-51.

Braverman, H. (1974). *Labour and monopoly capital.* New York: Monthly Review Press.

Burrell, G. (1984). Sex and organizational analysis. *Organizational Studies, 5*(2), 97-118.

Carroll, M.B. (1983). *Overworked and underpaid.* New York: Fawcett Columbine.

Davies, M. (1982). *Woman's place is at the typewriter.* Philadelphia, PA: Temple University Press.

de Beauvoir, S. (1952). *The second sex.* New York: Vintage Books. (Original work published 1948).

Dworkin, A. (1974). *Woman hating.* New York: E.P. Dutton.

Dworkin, A. (1976). Remembering the witches. In A. Dworkin (Ed.), *Our blood: Prophecies and discourses on sexual politics* (pp. 15-21). New York: Harper & Row.

Eckersley-Johnson, A.L. (Ed.). (1976). *Webster's secretarial handbook.* Springfield, MA: Merriam.

Fairhurst, G.T. (1986). Male-female communication on the job: Literature review and commentary. In M. McLaughlin (Ed.), *Communication Yearbook 9* (pp. 83-116). Beverly Hills, CA: Sage.

Feldman, M.S., & March, J.G. (1981). Information in organizations as signal and symbol. *Administrative Science Quarterly, 26,* 171-186.

Ferguson, K. (1984). *The feminist case against bureaucracy.* Philadelphia: Temple University Press.

Friedan, B. (1963). *The feminine mystique*. New York: Norton.

Gilligan, C. (1982). *In a different voice: Psychological theory and women's development*. Cambridge, MA: Harvard University Press.

Gottfried, H., & Fasenfest, D. (1984). Gender and class formation: Female clerical workers. *Review of Radical Political Economics, 16*, 89-103.

Gregory, J. (1986). *Pay equity and career opportunity. In Women, clerical work, and office automation: Issues for research* (pp. 15-16). Report of a conference sponsored by the Women's Bureau with The Panel on Technology and Women's Employment National Research Council. Washington, DC: U.S. Department of Labor Women's Bureau.

Gutek, B.A. (1988). Women in clerical work. In A. Stromberg & S. Harkers (Eds.), *Women worklives: Theories and facts in perspective* (pp. 225-240). Mountain View, CA: Mayfield.

Gutek, B.A. (1989). Sexuality in the workplace: Key issues in social research and organizational practice. In J. Hearn, D.L. Sheppard, P. Tancred-Sheriff, & G. Burrell (Eds.), *The sexuality of organization* (pp. 56-70). London: Sage.

Gutek, B.A., & Cohen, A.G. (1987). Sex ratios, sex role spillover, and sex at work: A comparison of men's and women's experiences. *Human Relations, 40*, 97-115.

Gutek, B.A., & Dunwoody, V. (1987). Understanding sex in the workplace. In A. Stromberg, L. Larwood, & B.A. Gutek (Eds.), *Women and work: An annual review* (Vol. 2, pp. 249-269). Newbury Park, CA: Sage.

Gutek, B.A., & Morasch, B. (1982). Sex-ratios, sex-role spillover, and sexual harassment of women at work. *Journal of Social Issues, 38*, 55-74.

Gutek, B.A., & Nakamura, C.Y. (1982). Gender roles and sexuality in the world of work. In E.R. Allgeier & N.B. McCormick (Eds.), *Changing boundaries: Gender roles and sexual behavior* (pp. 182-201). Mountain View, CA: Mayfield.

Hall, S. (1985). Signification, representation, ideology: Althusser and the post-structuralist debates. *Critical Studies in Mass Communication, 2*, 91-114.

Hearn, J., & Parkin, W. (1987). *Sex at "work": The power and paradox of organization sexuality*. New York: St. Martin's Press.

Hearn, J., Sheppard, D.L., Tancred-Sheriff, P., & Burrell, G. (1989). *The sexuality of organization*. London: Sage.

Hickson, M. III, Grierson, R.D., & Linder, B.C. (1991). A communication perspective on sexual harassment: Affiliative nonverbal behaviors in asynchronous relationships. *Communication Quarterly, 39*, 111-118.

Huber, G.P., & Daft, R.L. (1987). The information environments of organizations. In F.M. Jablin, L.L. Putnam, K.H. Roberts, & L.W. Porter (Eds.), *Handbook of organizational communication: An interdisciplinary perspective* (pp. 130-164). Newbury Park, CA: Sage.

Kanter, R.M. (1977). *Men and women of the corporation*. New York: Basic Books.

Katz, D., & Kahn, T.L. (1966). *The social psychology of organizations*. New York: Wiley.

King, D. (1988). Multiple jeopardy, multiple consciousness: The context of a black feminist ideology. *Signs, 14,* 42-72.

Lalonde, G. (1986). Getting past the receptionist on the phone or in person. In P.J. Frost, V.F. Mitchell, & W.R. Nord (Eds.), *Organizational reality: Reports from the firing line* (3rd ed. pp. 3-6). Glenview, IL: Scott, Foresman.

Louis, M.R. (1980). Surprise and sense-making: What newcomers experience in entering unfamiliar organizational settings. *Administrative Science Quarterly, 25,* 226-251.

Machung, A. (1988). 'Who needs a personality to talk to a machine?': Communication in the automated office. In C. Kramarae (Ed.), *Technology and women's voices: Keeping in touch* (pp. 62-81). New York: Routledge & Kegan Paul.

Meissner, M. (1986). The reproduction of women's domination in organizational communication. In L. Thayer (Ed.), *Organization—communication: Emerging perspectives* (pp. 51-66). Norwood, NJ: Ablex.

Murphee, M.C. (1987). New technology and office tradition: The not-so-changing world of the secretary. In H. Hartmann (Ed.), *Computer chips and paper clips: Technology and women's employment* (Vol. 2, pp. 98-135). Washington, DC: National Academy Press.

Nelson, M. (1979). Why witches were women. In J. Freeman (Ed.), *Women: A feminist perspective* (2nd ed., pp. 451-468). Palo Alto, CA: Mayfield.

Nine to Five. (1987). *Office workers survival guide.* Cleveland, OH: 9 to 5, the National Association of Working Women.

Pringle, R. (1988). *Secretaries talk: Sexuality, power and work.* London: Verso.

Pringle, R. (1989). Bureaucracy, rationality and sexuality: The case of secretaries. In J. Hearn, D.L. Sheppard, P. Tancred-Sheriff, & G. Burrell (Eds.), *The sexuality of organization* (pp. 158-177). London: Sage.

Rich, A. (1976). *Of woman born: Motherhood as experience and institution.* New York: Bantam Books.

Rothman, S.M. (1978). *Woman's proper place: A history of changing ideals and practices, 1870 to present.* New York: Basic Books.

Smith, D.E. (1987). *The everyday world as problematic: A feminist sociology.* Boston: Northeastern University Press.

Sotirin, P.J., & Miller, D.J. (1990, November). *The coercion of romance.* Paper presented at the Speech Communication Association Conference, Chicago, IL.

Stohl, C. (1986). The role of memorable messages in the process of organizational communication. *Communication Quarterly, 34,* 231-249.

Tangri, S.S., Burt, M.R., & Johnson, L.B. (1982). Sexual harassment at work: Three explanatory models. *Journal of Social Issues, 38,* 33-54.

Tepperman, J. (1976). *Not servants, not machines: Office workers speak out!* Boston: Beacon Press.

Valli, L. (1986). *Becoming clerical workers.* Boston: Routledge & Kegan Paul.

Wallace, P.A. (1982). Appendix: EEOC guidelines on discrimination because of sex. In *Women in the workplace* (pp. 219-235). Boston: Suburn House Publishing.

Weber, M. (1958). *The protestant ethic and the spirit of capitalism.* New York: Scribner.

Weick, K.E. (1979). *The social psychology of organizing* (2nd ed.). Reading, MA: Addison-Wesley.

West, J. (1982). New technology and women's office work. In J. West (Ed.), *Work, women and the labour market* (pp. 61-79). London: Routledge & Kegan Paul.

Women's Bureau, U.S. Department of Labor. (1985). *The United Nations decade for women, 1976-1985: Employment in the United States.* Report from the world conference on the United Nations dedicated for women 1976-1985. Washington, DC: U.S. Government Printing Office.

Introduction to Part II

Much conflict has less visible manifestations than physical and sexual abuse, but still can have debilitating consequences for men as well as women. In daily conflictual relations, women and men manage their disagreements in ways that make a difference, often a negative one, for their careers and home lives. Here gender role beliefs can legitimate differences in how men and women treat each other, and gender schemata can bias interpretations of behavior. Beliefs that men are aggressive and dominant can justify their having the upper hand or final word. Beliefs that women are sensitive and nurturant can generate consistent interpretations of ambiguous behavior as, for example, ideally suiting them for reproductive labor or as willing to make compromises or accommodations in conflict. Conflictual daily relations between men and women can help maintain the social order by strengthening beliefs about gender differences even when no such differences occur. Women and men need not behave differently for their behavior to be interpreted differently, and beliefs about gender differences can compel attention at the expense of other differences such as those due to race, class, or ethnicity.

All the chapters in Part II emphasize the importance of seeing contextual factors beyond sex differences in conflicts between men and women. They show why counts of women and men, by what they do in conflicts, are insufficient to understand the impact of gender. As we noted in Chapter 1, feminist theorists (Ferguson, 1989; hooks, 1984, 1989; Spelman, 1988; and many others) have made clear that the experience of maleness and femaleness is modified by race and class. Further modifications of gender result from other life experiences, so that what it means to "be" a woman is affected, for example, by whether she is Caucasian, physically handicapped, lesbian, poor, or urban, just as what it means to "be" a man is affected by similar experiences. Difference (among women and men and between women and men) is a topic of intensive debate today and doubtless will remain so as long as differences are associated with value judgments, hierarchy and, thereby, conflict. Because difference is also unlikely to disappear as a defining feature of life, treating it carefully and cautiously is important (Epstein, 1988; Harding, 1987; Jagger, 1990; Rhode, 1989, 1990).

Each of the five chapters in Part II examines ways in which men and women differ in managing conflict.[1] Euwema and van de Vliert, as reported in Chapter 5, "The Influence of Sex on Managers' Reactions in Conflict with their Subordinates," found that female nurses are treated more harshly by hospital managers for norm violation than are male nurses, and they compare the ability of two theories to account for this bias. According to discrimination theory, women are treated more harshly than men because they and their efforts are socially devalued. According to identification theory, sex discrimination is more apparent than real. People tend to be favorably biased toward those with whom they identify. Because it is easier to identify with same-sex than with opposite-sex others and because there are more male than female managers in most organizations, women appear to be the targets of sex discrimination when in fact biased treatment results from identification rather than sex per se. In comparisons of male and female managers' responses to violations by a male or female nurse, Euwema and van de Vliert find discrimination theory to make more accurate predictions than identification theory; female managers were particularly harsh in their attitudes toward female nurses.

In Chapter 6, "Conflict Management and Marital Adjustment Among African-American and White Middle Class Couples," Beinstein Miller discusses a different site of conflict, the marital relationship. She

---

[1]Unfortunately, most of the chapters give too little direct attention to differences among the men and women studied. In noting the influences of power, expertise, locations, and relationships, as well in questioning the size (and hence "real" significance) of differences found, these authors provide a foundation for raising many more questions about differences within the sex groups. But, only the chapter by Beinstein Miller explicitly identifies such cultural modifications of gender as a factor to be considered. More of this kind of focus is needed.

compares African-American and white couples' adjustment as a function of their marital beliefs and use of conflict management strategies. Her results indicate more similarities in marital beliefs, adjustment, and use of conflict strategies than differences between husbands and wives, but somewhat different associations between their marital adjustment and use of conflict strategies. Adjustment by wives, for example, appeared to be less influenced by use of conflict strategies than was adjustment by their husbands. Among white husbands, conflict avoidance was associated with good adjustment; among African-American husbands, conflict avoidance was associated with poor adjustment. These results highlight the importance of treating conflict behavior as an independent as well as dependent variable in understanding differences in women's and men's experience of conflict in close relationships. They also highlight the importance of taking race into consideration because approaches to conflict appeared to have opposite effects among African-American and white males.

Ruble and Schneer (chapter 7) raise the question of why gender stereotypes about men's and women's conflict behavior persist when the few consistent differences found in their conflict behavior are quite small. In "Gender Differences in Conflict-Handling Styles: Less Than Meets the Eye?", they report research in which senior business students and employees of organizations responded to questions about their use of five conflict management strategies: accommodation, avoidance, collaboration, competition, and compromise. Using four samples and two conflict instruments they found only two small gender differences in self-reported behavior. In the work setting, women reported somewhat greater use of compromise than men, whereas men reported somewhat greater use of competition than women. Among the employee sample, there were no differences away from work. These results suggest that gender may be a poor predictor of conflict management style and that stereotypes persist because of the influence of social situations as well as the influence of our beliefs on perceptions of behavior.

The final two chapters in this section also raise questions about previous research on gender differences in conflict. In Chapter 8, "Gender and Conflict: What Does Psychological Research Tell Us?" Keashly shows how inconsistent the results from empirical studies have been. She demonstrates that other variables besides gender (e.g., status, power, and expertise) account for differences in conflict behavior and these other variables, because they covary with gender, often explain gender differences. Results also depend on the type of measurement taken, for example, the more global the measurement and novel the situation, the greater is the opportunity for gender stereotypes to influence people's responses. When similar measures are used to compare conflict behavior in similar kinds of relationships, men and women indicate preferences for using similar strategies. Keashly shows, as do Ruble and Schneer, that differences are small, although often statistically significant. When found in close relationships, differences favor somewhat greater confrontation and emotional expression by women than by men and somewhat greater conflict avoidance by men than by women. When found at work, differences favor somewhat more compromise by women than by men, but even these differences, as those in close relationships, are not always found. Position and status, particularly at work, may make an important difference. Equally important seem to be gender stereotypes and their influence on the perception of conflict behavior. Differences between women and men are sometimes perceived when in fact they have behaved the same way.

In Chapter 9, "Gender Differences in Negotiating Behavior and Outcomes: Fact or Artifact," Watson compares the ability of theories based on sex-role socialization and theories based on power difference to explain gender differences in negotiating behavior. She examines studies in which the effects of gender and power were simultaneously tested and finds the most evidence for the power perspective. Equally important, she finds evidence for gender-power interactions that current theories do not predict. This evidence suggests that men and women might handle power and powerlessness differently. Men, for example, have been found to behave more confidently in powerless positions than have women and women have been found to behave more dominantly in powerful ones. This type of evidence, she argues, suggests we should be using more complex models of gender, power, and conflict.

The expectations of these authors to find gender differences in conflict behavior and intentions reflect the power of our socialization and gender role beliefs. In some cases, expectations are confirmed. For example, Euwema and van de Vliert show that hospital managers, regardless of their sex, blame female workers more than male workers for norm violation. Ruble and Schneer demonstrate expected although small differences in women's and men's use of competition and compromise in work settings, even as they question the practical significance of such findings. Beinstein Miller finds expected differences in conflict avoidance and engagement among married couples.

In other cases, expectations are not confirmed. For example, Ruble and Schneer find no differences between men and women in conflict management away from work, and Keashly reports that sometimes you see differences and sometimes you do not. These inconsistencies could be due to contextual differences that allow gender beliefs to influence perception to different degrees. Watson also reports inconsistent evidence for gender differences and, when expected differences are obtained, other factors such as power, status, and expertise with which they co-occur account for more variation in conflict behavior than does gender.

The contributions of all the authors in part II remind us how gender beliefs often compel our attention and distract us from other factors in conflicts that also make a difference. Their work underscores the importance of power as modified by gender in different contexts and the complex interrelationships among these factors.

Finally, these studies of gender difference lead to important questions about the possibilities for cooperative approaches, such as those expected of women, to work successfully in a context of competitive approaches, such as those expected of men. Watson, for example, points out that even though women in the bargaining literature have been portrayed positively, due to their cooperation, this behavior can make them unsuccessful as bargainers. Can cooperative approaches to conflict succeed in the context of competitive systems? How can we answer this question when competitiveness and power are gendered, correlated and deemed necessary within our social system? These difficult questions must be addressed for effective conflict resolution theory and practice.

REFERENCES

Epstein, C. F. (1988). *Deceptive distinctions: Sex, gender, and the social order.* New Haven, CT: Yale University Press.

Ferguson, A. (1989). *Blood at the root: Motherhood, sexuality & male dominance.* London: Pandora Press.

Harding, S. (1987b). The instability of the analytical categories of feminist theory. In S. Harding & J. F. O'Barr (Eds.), *Sex and scientific inquiry* (pp. 283-302). Chicago: University of Chicago Press.

hooks, b. (1984). *Feminist theory: From margin to center.* Boston: South End Press.

hooks, b. (1989). *Talking back: Thinking feminist, thinking black.* Boston: South End Press.

Jagger, A.M. (1990). Sexual difference and sexual equality. In D.L. Rhode (Ed.), *Theoretical perspectives on sexual difference* (pp. 239-254). New Haven, CT: Yale University Press.

Rhode, D.L. (1989). *Justice and gender.* Cambridge, MA: Harvard University Press.

Rhode, D.L. (Ed.). (1990). *Theoretical perspectives on sexual difference.* New Haven, CT: Yale University Press.

Spelman, E.V. (1988). *Inessential woman: Problems of exclusions in feminist thought.* Boston: Beacon Press.

5

The Influence of Sex on Managers' Reactions in Conflict with Their Subordinates*

Martin C. Euwema
Utrecht University
Evert van de Vliert
Groningen University

Research on sex differences in managerial conflict behavior is limited and inconclusive. There is only partial empirical support for the stereotypic idea that men deal in a more direct and harsh way with conflict than women (Ansari, 1989; Chusmir & Mills, 1989; White & Roufail, 1989). Also, studies on the often made distinction between "male" (task-oriented) and "female" (relation-oriented) leadership have not yielded much support for different leadership styles of men and women (Beijer, 1988; Ting-Toomey, 1986; White, 1981).

Inconclusive results of research on sex differences in conflict management might be due partially to two oversights. First, studies seldom focus on the sex of both manager and subordinate but instead focus on one or the other. Yet, studies of attribution and social influence have

*We thank Jeffrey Goldstein and Jacob Rabbie for their helpful suggestions.

demonstrated that a manager's behavior is jointly influenced by his or her sex and the sex of his or her subordinate (Ansari, 1989; Carli, 1989; Kaufman & Shikiar, 1985; Zammuto, London, & Rowland, 1979). Second, research pays little attention to the influence of sex on the determinants of conflict behavior, such as perceptions of conflict, attributions for conflict, and emotional experience in conflict, even though these might affect the conflict behavior of men and women differently (Deutsch, 1973; Filley, 1975; Thomas & Pondy, 1977). The central question in our study concerns the influence that sex of both manager and subordinate has on managerial conflict behavior and on determinants of this behavior.

THEORETICAL PERSPECTIVES AND HYPOTHESES

An important source of conflict is the role behavior of the subordinates. When a subordinate does not behave according to the norms and rules within the organization, the manager must correct this subordinate. This is an essential, but also difficult task for a manager. Criticizing subordinates can easily result in escalating conflicts, especially when the manager reacts angrily and aggressively and the subordinate becomes defensive, a quite common pattern (Baron, 1989; Bergmann & Volkema, 1989; Renwick, 1977).

A manager who is confronted with deviant behavior can react in several different ways. We differentiate among five styles of conflict behavior: forcing (using power to get things done), avoiding the conflict, accommodating to the opinion and behavior of the subordinate, compromising, and trying to reach an integrative solution of the conflict (Blake & Mouton, 1964; Rahim, 1986; Thomas,1976). What are the determinants of the conflict behavior of the manager?

Determinants of Conflict Behavior

For studying the determinants of conflict behavior we use Filley's (1975) process-model on conflict. Figure 5.1 shows the upper part of Filley's model.

Antecedent conditions are the characteristics of a situation which generally lead to conflict. Filley (1975) distinguishes nine antecedent conditions. One of these is behavioral regulation. An example of this is the violation of role prescriptions by a subordinate.

Perceived conflict is a logically and impersonally recognized set of conditions that are conflicting to the parties. In our case, this includes the perception of and attributions made by the manager. We can differ-

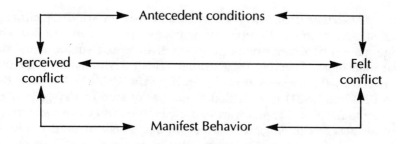

Figure 5.1. Conflict process

entiate between judgment of seriousness of the conflict issue and the attributions made about the causes of the deviant behavior.

Felt conflict is a personalized conflict relationship, expressed in feelings of threat, hostility, fear, or mistrust. The perceived conflict has a direct impact on the emotions of the manager. This emotional reaction can be described in terms of role stress. Role stress refers not only to anger and irritation, but also to doubts and thoughts on how to deal with the situation.

Perceptions, attributions, and feelings are closely interrelated. Anger and frustration are especially high when the manager attributes the cause of the deviancy to personal characteristics ("she is irresponsible," "he is dumb") or even negative (harmful) intentions by the subordinate ("he's trying to make a fool of me," "she is fighting my power," "he wants to sabotage the project"). High stress often results in simplifying, negative stereotypes (Walton, 1987).

Perceived and felt conflict result in *manifest conflict behavior*. Negative intentional attributions often result in harsh, aggressive reactions toward the deviant (Green & Mitchell,1979; Thomas & Pondy, 1977). High stress facilitates aggressive behavior and inhibits cooperative and problem-solving behavior (Baron, 1989; Johnson & Tjosvold, 1983).

Our central hypothesis is that the sex of both parties influences the behavior of the manager as well as the determinants of this behavior: the perceived conflict and the felt conflict. For each of these dependent variables we discuss the influence of the sex of the manager and the sex of the subordinate. We formulate eight hypotheses in total.

Influence of Sex on Perceived Conflict: Judgment of Seriousness and Attributions

What influence does the sex of the parties have on the perceived conflict? Two theories on sex discrimination offer partly conflicting predictions about the relation between sex and judgment and attribution processes. These theories are discrimination theory and identification theory.

Discrimination-theory assumes that women are discriminated against. According to this theory, managers (both men and women) judge male subordinates more positively than female subordinates and treat men more favorably than women. This discrimination is mainly explained by the higher status of men (Bernard, 1972). In line with this theory, White (1981) reports that a number of studies gave empirical support to the idea that males are expected to perform more successfully than females and in which the success of males was attributed to internal causes, for example, their skills, whereas the success of females was attributed to external causes, for example, chance. In case of failure the attributions would be the reverse: Male failure is attributed to bad luck, whereas female failure is attributed to a lack of skills.

Discrimination-theory leads to the expectation that deviant behavior by women will be evaluated more negatively and attributed less to the circumstances than comparative deviant behavior by men. According to discrimination theory the managers' sex would not influence these discriminating judgments and attributions.

Identification theory assumes that persons identify best with same-sex others (Ansari, 1989) and make the most positive judgments of those with whom they can identify. According to this theory, managers do not necessarily discriminate against women, but rather judge their own sex more positively than the opposite sex. Women are apparently discriminated against because managerial positions are occupied mainly by men, and male managers favor men. Female managers would similarly favor women. Attributions about success and failure in work are influenced by this identification process: Managers' perceptions and attributions basically favor members of their own sex (Dobbins, 1986; Kaufman & Shikiar, 1985).

Both theories have received empirical support. We therefore compare hypotheses from both theories. Hypotheses 1a and 2a are based on discrimination theory, which states that the behavior of men will be perceived more positively than the behavior of women. Hypotheses 1b and 2b are derived from identification theory, which leads to the expectation that male managers will perceive less conflict with a deviant man than with a deviant woman, whereas female managers will perceive less conflict with a deviant woman than with a man.

H 1a. Deviant behavior by male subordinates is judged as less serious than deviant behavior by female subordinates, by both male and female managers.

H 1b. Deviant behavior by subordinates is judged as less serious by same-sex than by opposite-sex managers.

H 2a. Deviant behavior by male subordinates is attributed less to the person and more to (mitigating) circumstances than deviant behavior by females, by both male and female managers.

H 2b. Deviant behavior by subordinates is attributed less to the person and more to (mitigating) circumstances by same-sex than by opposite-sex managers.

Influence of Sex on Felt Conflict: Experienced Stress

Felt conflict focuses our attention on the emotions of the manager. We were unable to find a single study on the influence of sex on experienced stress in conflict situations. The manager will probably feel frustration, anger, fear, threat, and perhaps confusion. From theories on "male" and "female" leadership it seems reasonable to assume that conflict leads in general to a stronger emotional response by women than by men. Lipman-Blumen (1980), for instance, suggests that a woman, by definition, needs to like the people with whom she has to work and that she also needs to feel liked. Hennig and Jardim (1977) express the same idea in the context of giving and receiving feedback. According to these authors, women are oriented to, and feel more comfortable with, giving positive feedback, whereas men deal more easily with negative feedback. If women are more concerned about good working relationships, it seems reasonable that women experience more stress when these relationships are threatened by conflict. A subordinate's deviant behavior, which impedes cooperation and requires negative feedback, would be expected to result in higher stress for female than male managers.

H 3. Male managers experience less stress if confronted with deviant behavior than female managers.

Influence of Sex on Conflict Behavior

Some studies have shown no sex differences in organizational conflict behavior (Chusmir & Mills, 1989; Renwick, 1977; Temkin, Cummings, & Wayland, 1986; Whinter & Green, 1987). Others have found women to be more compromising and accommodating and less forcing than men (Kilmann & Thomas, 1975; Rahim, 1983). Men appeared to be more directive, assertive, and forceful in organizational negotiations than women, whereas women appeared to be more oriented to communication and cooperation (Bernard, 1972; Logue, 1987; Rossi & Todd-

Mancillas, 1987; Turner & Henzel, 1987; Yelsma & Brown, 1985). At least in organizational conflict, there is some indication that men prefer forcing more than women do, whereas women have stronger preference for compromising.

> H 4. Male managers prefer more forcing and less compromising than female managers.

To test our fourth hypothesis we compared the conflict strategies of male and female managers. Results from prior research suggested that choice of strategy would also depend on the sex of their subordinate. Rossi and Todd-Mancillas (1987) and Todd-Mancillas and Rossi (1986) have explored the difference in conflict behavior of male and female managers in conflict with male and female subordinates. In these studies, Brazilian male managers preferred power strategies, such as threat and negative sanctions, over communicative strategies, when in conflict with female subordinates. In conflict with male subordinates, men preferred communicative strategies. Female Brazilian managers were not influenced by the sex of their subordinate. Dobbins (1986), too, examined the effect of sex of both parties on managerial conflict. He used U.S. students in the role of managers dealing with male or female subordinates. Dobbins found that female managers reacted in a more forcing way toward males than toward females, whereas the male managers were not influenced by the sex of their subordinates.

Although these studies have different results, both support the identification theory, according to which managers react more positively toward subordinates of their own sex than toward subordinates of the opposite sex. Discrimination theory, in contrast, leads to the expectation that managers, regardless of their sex, will use more cooperation and less force with men than with women.

> H 5a. Managers will choose less forcing and more accommodating and integrating strategies in conflict with male than with female subordinates.

> H 5b. Managers will choose less forcing and more accommodating and integrating strategies in conflict with same-sex than with opposite-sex subordinates.

METHOD

Respondents

All participants (100 men and 115 women) in this study were managers responsible for patient care in several hospitals in the Netherlands. Their average age was 32, and the average experience in a management position was 4 years.

Procedure

A videotaped conflict was shown to the participants. In this film (3 minutes) a nurse (male or female) violates hygienic prescriptions in binding a patient's wound. The responsible manager witnesses this behavior and confronts the nurse with his or her faults. The nurse behaves defensively, and the conflict starts to escalate. The unfinished argument ends when the nurse leaves the manager's office with a cynical remark.

Respondents were asked to identify with the patient-care manager in the film and were questioned for their reaction after the nurse had left the manager's room.

Independent Variable

The sex of the subordinate (nurse) was manipulated by making two versions of the videotape. The situation, spoken text, and behavior were identical. The only difference was the sex of the nurse, who was played either by a professional actor or actress.

The manager in the film was in both cases the same professional actress. She made her comments in a straightforward, rational, and problem-oriented manner. The video suggested that the escalation of the conflict was caused mainly by the nurse. The camera shots were focused on the nurse. The purpose of this camera position was to facilitate an optimal identification from the respondents with the manager on the video.

Control Questions

Five control questions were added to check the reality of the filmed conflict. The conflict issue was considered highly realistic. All the respondents had experienced a similar conflict in their managerial practice. The behavior of both parties during the confrontation was also judged as realistic. Male and female respondents did not differ on these items. Thus, the stimulus situation was highly realistic and recognizable to the respondents.

Measures of Dependent Variables

All responses were made on 7-point Likert-type scales ranging from "very unlikely" (1) to "very likely"(7).

Perceived conflict.

The judgment of seriousness of the situation was measured by agreement with four statements (Cronbach's α = .80): "The nurse is not allowed to behave like this"; "Most nurses think you should not do this"; "This is against professional prescriptions"; "This is a serious matter."

Causal attribution was measured by responses to three separate questions (with intercorrelations -.14; -.10; .14): "Was this unhygienic behavior caused by the patient?" "Was this behavior caused by the circumstances?" "Was this behavior caused by the nurse?"

Felt conflict.

The experienced stress was measured with a 5-item scale (α = .83) with questions like: "Would you be upset?" "Would you be irritated?" "Would you be wondering what to do?"

Conflict behavior.

To estimate the managers' conflict responses we developed a new instrument for measuring use of the five conflict resolution strategies: avoiding, accommodating, compromising, problem solving, and forcing. We chose to develop a new instrument because none of the existing lists is validated for The Netherlands and also because of the limitations of the existing instruments (Rahim, 1983; Van de Vliert & Kabanoff, 1988). The list offers 20 behavioral tactics, classified into five styles. Respondents answer how likely they would be to use every tactic in this specific conflict. Validation took place in a preliminary investigation. The Cronbach's alphas of the subscales were satisfactory, as were the low intercorrelations between the scales, both in the preliminary as well as in the main investigation. Examples of the items, of which four per style were given, are "I would agree with the other" (accommodating, Cronbach's α =.73); "I would try to reconcile our opinions" (problem solving, α =.63); "I would make it clear that I will not tolerate this" (forcing, α =.78); "I would insist that we both give and take on this matter" (compromising, α =.65); "I would avoid any further confrontation" (avoiding, α =.80).

RESULTS

Hypotheses were tested with a 2 x 2 (Sex of Manager x Sex of Nurse) analysis of variance. Results are shown in Table 5.1.

Perceived Conflict

Judgment of seriousness of the deviant behavior.

The behavior of a male nurse is judged less deviant and less serious than exactly the same behavior by a female nurse. The sex of the respondent (the manager) has no influence on this judgment, as can be seen in Figure 5.2a. This result confirms Hypothesis 1a and implies a rejection of Hypothesis 1b.

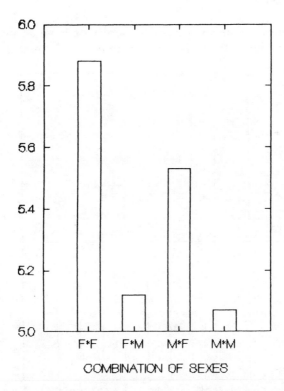

Figure 5.2a. Influence of sex on perceived conflict: Seriousness

Note: For figures 5.2a-5.4d: F*F: Female manager with female nurse; F*M: Female manager with male nurse; M*F: Male manager with female nurse; M*M: Male manager with male nurse.

Causal attributions.

Deviant behavior by the male nurse is attributed more to the patient and situation and less to the personal characteristics of the nurse than is deviant behavior by the female nurse. The sex of the responding managers has no influence on this attribution (see Figure 5.3b). This supports Hypothesis 2a, but not Hypothesis 2b.

Felt Conflict

The respondents' sex does have an impact on perceived stress, but not in the expected direction. As shown in Figure 5.3, male managers report more tension than females, especially in conflict with male nurses. We have to reject our third hypothesis.

Conflict Behavior

Sex of the manager and sex of the subordinate have an impact on the intended behavior of the manager. Generally, female managers rate forc-

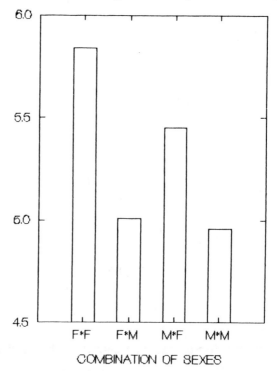

Figure 5.2b. Influence of sex on perceived conflict: Cause is nurse

Table 5.1. Means, Standard Deviations, and Test Values of the Perceived and Felt Conflict, and Conflict Behavior of Male and Female Managers in Conflict With Male and Female Subordinates

	Sex Manager				F (1,214)	
	male		female		a (sex manager)	
	M	sd	M	sd	b (sex nurse)	
					c (interaction)	
Perceived Conflict						
This is a serious situation						
Deviant is male	5.07	1.17	5.12	1.17	a	.62
Deviant is female	5.53	1.19	5.88	1.00	b	12.78**
					c	.93
Attribution: cause is the nurse						
Deviant is male	4.96	1.62	5.01	1.56	a	1.05
Deviant is female	5.45	1.36	5.84	1.54	b	9.35**
					c	.65
Attribution: cause is the patient						
Deviant is male	2.94	1.69	2.65	1.52	a	1.01
Deviant is female	2.38	1.51	2.26	1.51	b	4.34*
					c	.14
Attribution: cause is circumstantial						
Deviant is male	3.58	1.61	3.26	1.85	a	2.56
Deviant is female	3.10	1.62	2.64	1.83	b	4.72*
					c	.08
Felt Conflict						
Stress by manager						
Deviant is male	5.30	.88	4.64	1.11	a	12.78**
Deviant is female	5.35	.89	5.08	1.25	b	3.11
					c	1.81
Conflict Behavior						
Avoiding:						
Deviant is male	1.62	.64	1.90	1.13	a	.59
Deviant is female	1.77	.88	1.66	1.07	b	.26
					c	2.13
Integrating:						
Deviant is male	5.15	1.00	4.78	1.25	a	.01
Deviant is female	4.57	1.11	4.95	1.49	b	1.17
					c	4.92*
Accommodating:						
Deviant is male	1.68	.67	1.91	1.05	a	.01
Deviant is female	1.75	.86	1.48	.60	b	2.55
					c	4.44*

Table 5.1. Means, Standard Deviations, and Test Values of the Perceived and Felt Conflict, and Conflict Behavior of Male and Female Managers in Conflict With Male and Female Subordinates (cont.)

Compromising:						
Deviant is male	3.04	1.46	3.30	1.20	a	3.80*
Deviant is female	2.78	1.21	3.24	1.44	b	1.19
					c	.31
Forcing:						
Deviant is male	4.50	1.48	3.70	1.35	a	6.06*
Deviant is female	4.56	1.53	4.42	1.48	b	5.36*
					c	2.72

* $p < .05$.
** $p < .001$.

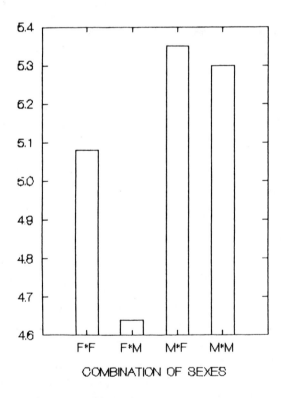

Figure 5.3. Influence of sex on felt conflict

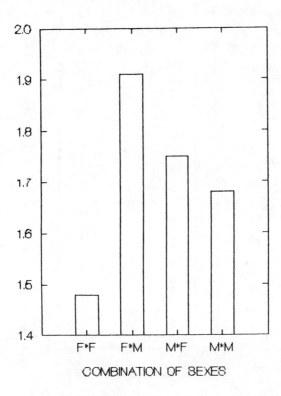

**Figure 5.4a. Influence of sex on conflict behavior:
Accomodating behavior**

ing lower and compromising higher than male managers, which supports our fourth hypothesis. However, the subordinate's sex also makes a difference in managers' choice of strategy, as indicated in Fig. 5.4a, b, and d.

Female managers rate forcing higher and accommodating lower when they are in conflict with a female rather than male subordinate, but the subordinate's sex does not influence ratings of forcing and accommodation by male managers. These outcomes support Hypothesis 5a.

Male managers rate integrative behavior higher when they are in conflict with a male rather than female subordinate, but the subordinate's sex does not influence ratings of integrative responses by female managers. These results also support Hypothesis 5a.

Although our hypotheses concerned sex differences in managers' perceptions, feelings, and behavior in conflict, we also tested Filley's (1975) model that manifest conflict behavior would be influenced by perceptions and feelings about conflict. Specifically, we tested the effects of

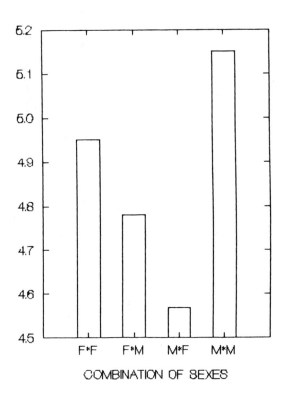

**Figure 5.4b. Influence of sex on conflict behavior:
Integrating behavior**

perceived seriousness of the violation, attributions for the violation, and confrontational stress on ratings of conflict responses and compared these effects among male and female managers in a series of multiple regression analyses. Ratings of seriousness, stress, and attributions were entered simultaneously in analyses of each conflict "style." These analyses were conducted separately for the total sample and for its four subgroups: male managers with male subordinates, male managers with female subordinates, female managers with male subordinates, and female managers with female subordinates. Ratings that explained statistically significant variance in conflict "styles" are shown in Table 5.2.

As indicated by the regression analyses, *perceived seriousness* of the violation is associated with higher ratings of forcing and lower ratings of avoidance, accommodation, and compromising. These results are due primarily to the responses of male managers, although female managers also rate avoidance low and forcing high if the subordinate is male

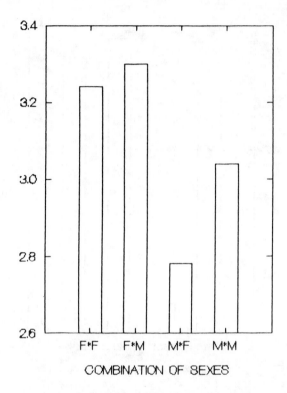

**Figure 5.4c. Influence of sex on conflict behavior:
Compromising behavior**

and the violation is perceived as serious.

Felt stress is associated with lower ratings of avoidance and
higher ratings of forcing, problem solving, and compromising responses. Both male and female managers rate compromising and problem
solving responses higher when their stress is high and the subordinate is
a female. Additionally, stress is associated with higher ratings of forcing
among male managers with female subordinates and with lower ratings
of accommodation among female managers with male subordinates.

The influence of *attributions* for the violation depends on the sex
of both manager and subordinate. Of particular relevance is the influence of blaming the violation on the subordinate. Among female managers with female subordinates, blaming the subordinate is associated
with lower ratings of avoidance and accommodation, but this association is not statistically significant among female managers with male
subordinates. Among male managers with male subordinates, blaming

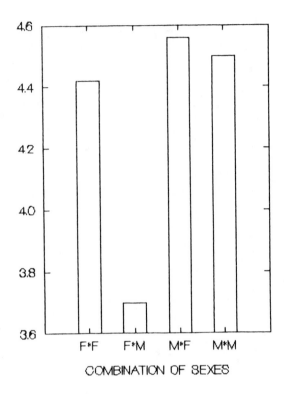

**Figure 5.4d. Influence of sex on conflict behavior:
Forcing behavior**

the subordinate is associated with higher ratings of forcing, but this association is not statistically significant among male managers with female subordinates.

Overall, these results suggest that perceptions of seriousness, feelings of stress, and blaming the subordinate reduce inclinations to avoid conflict, increase inclinations to use forceful responses, and increase inclinations to use problem solving and compromising responses if the subordinate is female.

DISCUSSION

In this chapter we focused on two points: the importance of paying attention in research to the sex of both parties in a dyadic conflict and the importance of paying attention to determinants of conflict as well as manifest

Table 5.2. Influence of Norm, Attribution and Stress on Managerial Conflict Behavior

Styles	Dyads[a]: General	Female-Female	Female-Male	Male-Female	Male-Male
Avoiding	$F_{(2,212)} = 13.2^{**}$ $r2 = .11$	$F_{(1,45)} = 18.3^{**}$ $r2 = .29$	$F_{(1,50)} = 7.2^{*}$ $r2 = .13$	$F_{(1,66)} = 6.4^{*}$ $r2 = .09$	n.s.
β	norm = -.24 stress = -.20	att.1 = -.54	norm = -.35	norm = -.30	
Accommodating	$F_{(2,212)} = 26.5^{**}$ $r2 = .20$	$F_{(1,45)} = 16.1^{**}$ $r2 = .26$	$F_{(2,49)} = 16.0^{**}$ $r2 = .29$	$F_{(1,66)} = 29.2^{***}$ $r2 = .31$	$F_{(1,46)} = 8.7^{*}$ $r2 = .16$
β	norm = -.40 att.1 = .13	att.1 = -.51	att.2 = -.49 stress = -.33	norm = -.55	norm = -.40
Forcing	$F_{(3,211)} = 20.9^{**}$ $r2 = .23$	$F_{(1,45)} = 7.9^{*}$ $r2 = .15$	$F_{(1,50)} = 6.7^{*}$ $r2 = .12$	$F_{(2,65)} = 7.7^{*}$ $r2 = .19$	$F_{(2,45)} = 14.0^{**}$ $r2 = .39$
β	norm = .24 stress = .26 att.1 = .18	att.2 = -.39	norm = .34 stress = .28	norm = .30 att.1 = .29	norm = .42
Problem Solving	$F_{(2,212)} = 11.0^{*}$ $r2 = .09$	$F_{(1,45)} = 6.0^{*}$ $r2 = .12$	n.s.	$F_{(2,65)} = 12.9^{**}$ $r2 = .28$	n.s.
β	stress = .26 att.3 = .15	stress = .34		stress = .43 att.3 = .25	
Compromising	$F_{(2,212)} = 11.3^{**}$ $r2 = .10$	$F_{(1,45)} = 16.7^{**}$ $r2 = .27$	$F_{(1,50)} = 11.1^{**}$ $r2 = .18$	$F_{(2,65)} = 7.0^{*}$ $r2 = .18$	n.s
β	norm = -.25 stress = .23	stress = .52	att.2 = .43 stress = .23	norm = -.38	

[a] the combination of sexes in the dyads. The first person refers to the manager, the second to the deviant subordinate.
Norm: this is a serious situation; att.1=cause is the nurse; att.2 cause is the patient; att.3 cause is circumstantial; $^{*}p < .05$. $^{**}p < .001$

conflict behavior. Results from this study indicate that understanding of sex discrimination in organizational conflict requires both considerations.

First, we found a main effect of the sex of the subordinate on judgments and attributions made by the manager. Second, the sex of the manager had main effects on his or her felt stress and behavioral intentions. Third, the behavioral intentions of the manager were influenced further by the sex of his or her subordinate. Finally, the specific sex composition of the dyad moderated the impact of perceived seriousness, felt stress, and attributions of blame on managerial conflict behavior.

Experienced Stress

One unexpected result was that male managers rated stress higher than did female managers. Although we cannot be certain of the reason for this difference, we can offer three possible explanations for it.

One explanation might be that male managers have greater need than female managers to control behavior by their subordinates. Violations by subordinates would therefore be more frustrating for them than for females and result in greater stress.

A second explanation for the higher stress among male managers might be its operationalization as irritation and worrying about what to do. Although women generally are seen as more emotionally expressive than men, there is an exception for anger and aggression. Anger is seen as a typical male reaction and is tolerated more from men than from women (Baker-Miller, 1976; Smith et al., 1989). Higher stress among male than female managers might therefore be partially explained by their stronger irritation and anger.

The third explanation might stem from the fact that managers were asked to take the role of the female in all conditions, which could have created more stress for males than females. Equally possible is that male managers were reporting stress that they thought a female manager would feel. Although instructions were to identify and report personal feelings, and although we did not find sex differences in judgments of the manager in the film, possible sex differences in identification are a serious limitation of our study. This suggests a replication study in which the sex of the manager in the film would be varied.

Discrimination or Identification?

In this study we compared the ability of hypotheses from discrimination and identification theories to explain discrimination against women in organizations. According to the results, discrimination theory does a better job than identification theory.

Male and female managers alike considered violation by a female subordinate to be more serious than violation by a male subordinate and were more inclined to blame the female than male subordinate for the violation. Female managers in particular reported intentions to use more forceful behaviors and less accommodative ones with female than male subordinates. Male managers reported intentions to use more integrative behaviors with male than female subordinates. These findings correspond with the conclusion of Ott (1985) that managers have a more positive attitude toward male than female subordinate nurses. We conclude that hypotheses from discrimination theory explain these results better than do hypotheses from identification theory. One exception might be the tendency for stress to increase intended use of integrative and compromising responses among both male and female managers when the subordinate is female.

The most remarkable result of this study is probably the way female managers treat subordinates of their own sex. Female managers seem to discriminate against women more than do male managers. This phenomenon is described by several authors (Chodorow, 1978), but a satisfying explanation is still lacking. We cannot be confident about a single explanation for this pattern of sex discrimination but will offer four possibilities.

First, the tendency for women to discriminate against their own sex might have been due to their stronger identification with the female manager. Stronger identification might incline them to be tougher with subordinates who behave defensively. Another possible explanation is offered by Ott (1985), who used the image of Cinderella for the female nurse and the prince for the male nurse. With these images a female manager would judge behavior of the prince more positively and correct him in a friendlier way than she would Cinderella, who has to know her place. Yet another possibility is that hygiene is associated more strongly with women's than with men's general roles and so violation of hygienic practice is more serious for women than for men. Other deviant behavior besides unhygienic wound care would need to be studied to test this possibility. A final explanation for discrimination of women by women can be derived from theories about sex-specific socialization. Chodorow (1978) argues that mothers are more critical of their daughters' than sons' behavior. This pattern might be reproduced in the hierarchical relations between female managers and their male and female subordinates and be particularly relevant for Dutch health care in which women in managerial positions traditionally do not have children, identify very strongly with their work, and value "caring" highly.

Further Investigations

The results of this study are in contradiction with the findings of Rossi and Todd-Mancillas (1987) that only male managers differentiate in their reactions toward men and women. Also, the results differ from Dobbins's (1986) conclusions that females react more mildly toward women than toward men. Further investigation is needed and justified, especially when we consider the limited design of all these studies. Special attention should be payed to the the direct and moderator effects of sex on the determinants of conflict behavior. Other important contingencies include the type of conflict, occupation, working relationship, and cultural values.

Practical Relevance

The results of our study are relevant for all managers, but especially for those in health care. The results underscore the importance of using systematic and explicit evaluation criteria, methods of correction, and strategies for handling conflicts with all subordinates. Education and later training should draw attention to the influence of sex-role expectations and their influence on discrimination behavior, including judgments and attributions for violations.

REFERENCES

Ansari, M.A. (1989). Effects of leader sex, subordinate sex, and subordinate performance on the use of influence strategies. *Sex Roles, 20,* 283 293.

Baker-Miller, J. (1976). *Toward a new psychology of women.* Boston: Beacon Press.

Baron, R.A. (1989). Negative effects of destructive criticism: Impact on conflict, self-efficacy, and task performance. In M.A. Rahim (Ed.), *Managing conflict: An interdisciplinary approach* (pp. 21-31). New York: Praeger.

Beijer, C. (1988). *Differences and similarities between male and female managers in terms of personality traits.* Discussion paper, Netherlands International Institute for Management, The Netherlands.

Bernard, J. (1972). *The sex game.* Englewood Cliffs, NJ: Prentice-Hall.

Bergmann, T.J., & Volkema, R.J. (1989). Understanding and managing interpersonal conflict at work: Its issues, interactive processes, and consequences. In M.A. Rahim (Ed.), *Managing conflict: An interdisciplinary approach* (pp. 8-19). New York: Praeger.

Blake, R.R., & Mouton, J.S. (1964). *The managerial grid.* Houston, TX: Gulf.

Carli, L.L. (1989). Gender differences in interaction style and influence. *Journal of Personality and Social Psychology, 56*(4), 565-576.

Chodorow, N. (1978). *The reproduction of mothering.* CA: Regents of University of California.

Chusmir, L.H., & Mills, J. (1989). Gender differences in conflict resolution styles of managers: At work and at home. *Sex Roles, 20,* 149-163.

Deutsch, M. (1973). *The resolution of conflict: Constructive and destructive processes.* New Haven: Yale University Press.

Dobbins, G.H. (1986). Equity vs. equality: Sex differences in leadership. *Sex Roles, 15,* 513-525.

Filley, A.C. (1975). *Interpersonal conflict resolution.* Glenview, IL: Scott Foresman.

Green, S.G., & Mitchell, T.R. (1979). Attributional processes of leaders in leader-member interactions. *Organizational Behavior and Human Performance, 23,* 429-458.

Hennig, M., & Jardim, A. (1977). *The managerial women.* London: Pan Books.

Johnson, D.W., & Tjosvold, D. (1983). Constructive controversy: The key to effective decision making. In D. Tjosvold & D.W. Johnson (Eds.), *Productive conflict management: Perspectives for organizations* (pp. 46-68). New York: Irvington.

Kaufman, C.G., & Shikiar, R. (1985). Sex of employee and sex of supervisor: Effect on attributions for the causality of success and failure. *Sex Roles, 12,* 257-269.

Kilmann, R.H., & Thomas, K.W. (1975). Interpersonal conflict handling behavior as reflections of jungian personality dimensions. *Psychological Reports, 37,* 971-980.

Lipman-Blumen, J. (1980). Female leadership in formal organizations: Must the female leader go formal? In H.J. Leavitt (Ed.), *Readings in managerial psychology* (pp. 341-362). Chicago: The University of Chicago Press.

Logue, B.J. (1987). *Argumentativeness in the organization: Employees assess its acceptability.* Paper presented at the annual meeting of the Eastern Communication Association, Syracuse, NY.

Ott, M. (1985). *Assepoesters en kroonprinsen* [Cinderellas and kings-to-be], Amsterdam: SUA.

Rahim, M.A. (1983). A measure of styles of handling interpersonal conflict. *Academy of Management Journal, 26,* 368-376.

Rahim, M.A. (1986). *Managing conflict in organizations.* New York: Praeger.

Renwick, P.A. (1977). The effects of sex differences on the perception and management of superior-subordinate conflict: An exploratory study. *Organizational Behavior and Human Performance, 19,* 403-415.

Rossi, A., & Todd-Mancillas, W.R. (1987). *Gender differences in the manage-*

ment of four different personnel disputes with male and female employees. Paper presented at the annual meeting of the Western Speech Communication Association, Seattle, WA.

Smith, K.C., Ulch, S.E., Cameron, J.E., Cumberland, J.A., Musgrave, M.A., & Tremblay, N. (1989). Gender-related effects in the perception of anger expression. *Sex Roles, 20*, 487-499.

Temkin, T., Cummings, H.W., & Wayland, A. (1986). The use of conflict management behaviors in voluntary organizations: An exploratory study.. *Journal of Voluntary Action Research, 15*, 1, 5-18.

Thomas, K.W. (1976). Conflict and conflict management. In M.D. Dunnette (Ed.), *Handbook of industrial and organizational psychology* (pp. 889-935). Chicago: Rand McNally.

Thomas, K.W., & Pondy, L.R. (1977). Toward an "intent" model of conflict management among principal parties. *Human Relations, 30*, 1089-1102.

Ting-Toomey, S. (1986). Conflict styles in black and white subjective cultures. In Y. Kim (Ed.), *Current research in interethnic communication* (pp. 75-89). Beverly Hills, CA: Sage.

Todd-Mancillas, W.R., & Rossi, A.M. (1986). *Additional findings on differences between Brazilian men and women managers in their managing of conflicts with employees.* Paper presented at the annual meeting of the International Communication Association, Chicago, IL.

Turner, L.H., & Henzel, S.A. (1987). Influence attempts in organizational conflict: The effects of biological sex, psychological gender, and power position. *Management Communication Quarterly, 1*(1), 32-57.

Van de Vliert, E., & Kabanoff, B. (1988, August). *Toward theory-based measures of conflict management.* Paper presented at the 48th annual meeting of the National Academy of Management, Anaheim, CA.

Walton, R.E. (1987). *Managing conflict: Interpersonal dialogue and third party consultation.* Reading, MA: Addison Wesley.

Whinter, D.A., & Green, S.B. (1987). Another look at gender-related differences in leadership behavior. *Sex Roles, 16*, 41-56.

White, J.W., & Roufail, M. (1989). Gender and influence strategies of first choice and last resort. *Psychology of Women Quarterly, 13*, 175-189.

White, M.C. (1981). Achievement, self-confidence, personality traits, and leadership ability: A review of literature on sex differences.. *Psychological Reports, 48*, 547-569.

Yelsma, P., & Brown, C.T. (1985). Gender roles, biological sex, and predisposition to conflict management. *Sex Roles, 12*, 731-747.

Zammuto, R.F., London, M., & Rowland, K.M. (1979). Effects of sex on commitment and conflict resolution. *Journal of Applied Psychology, 64*, 227-231.

6

Conflict Management and Marital Adjustment Among African-American and White Middle-Class Couples*

Judi Beinstein Miller
Oberlin College

Empirical research on gender and conflict typically examines conflict management as a function of gender. Whether at sociocultural, organizational, or interpersonal levels, variation in conflict and its management is taken to be the dependent variable and gender the independent variable. In some cases, variation is attributed to gender differences in values, power, or some combination of values and power. In other cases, it is attributed to social structural inequalities that produce power imbalances between men and women. This chapter also examines gender differences in conflict management behavior, but as a secondary rather than primary purpose. Instead of focusing on the contribution of gender to conflict and its management, this chapter asks whether men and women's conflict management behavior influences their adjustment in

---

*An earlier version of this chapter was presented at the International Network Conference on Personal Relationships, Normal, IL, May 1991.

close relationships and whether their cultural beliefs about conflict modify its influence. Research is reported in which the marital adjustment of African-American and white spouses is compared as a function of their conflict management strategies and beliefs about marriage. Its emphasis is on conflict management and adjustment by African-American husbands and wives because African-American marriage is particularly at risk for dissolution. Its purpose was to determine whether the experience of conflict has the same meaning for African-American and white husbands and wives, as evidenced by its apparent influence on their adjustment to marriage.

Increasingly lower rates of marriage and higher rates of marital dissolution among more African-Americans than whites have created concern over relations between African-American women and men (e.g., Gary, 1987; Staples, 1989). These trends are accompanied by lower marital satisfaction among more African-American than white couples, particularly among men, regardless of status (cf. Ball & Robbins, 1984; Glenn & Weaver, 1981). Explanations for such trends are often located in social structural disparities that create conflict between African-American women and men (cf. Aborampah, 1989; Tucker & Taylor, 1989, for reviews of these disparities). One disparity is the relatively low male-female ratio that results from more frequent accidents, homicides, war casualties, and imprisonment among African-American than white men. The relative scarcity of African-American men has led to increasing independence among African-American women, which can frustrate African-American males' expectations for heterosexual relationships and thereby lead to conflict (Franklin, 1984). At the same time, awareness of scarcity pressures African-American women into sharing men and accepting them on their own terms (Braithwaite, 1981), which can frustrate their expectations for heterosexual relationships and also lead to conflict.

A second disparity stems from socioeconomic constraints that prevent many African-American men from acquiring economic resources. Because African-American men often do not marry until they are able to act as providers, these constraints inevitably delay their decision. Moreover, because traditional gender roles are as important for African-Americans as for whites (if not more important, according to Hershey, 1978), the inability to continue providing resources can raise doubts about their masculinity and attractiveness as husbands. It is difficult for African-American men to acquire full masculine status, as defined traditionally, because they are blocked from achievements that are required by the male role. African-American women learn to take care of themselves for this reason also, which can raise doubts about their femininity and attractiveness as wives. Consequently, both women's and men's expectations for gender role complementarity can be frustrated, which can create potential for conflict between them (Franklin, 1984). Expectations for gender role complementarity may therefore be dysfunctional for many African-American heterosexual couples.

Other factors that might perpetuate conflict between African-American women and men would be those that impair conflict resolution. These factors might also originate in expectations that are dysfunctional for African-American couples. The purpose of this study is to examine one such set of expectations, those governing strategies for conflict management. Specifically, its hypothesis is that the internalization of traditional, white norms for conflict management would contribute to African-American marital dissatisafaction by impeding communication and limiting conflict resolution.

The possibility that African-American marital dissatisfaction might result in part from internalization of dysfunctional conflict management styles is based on the observation of communication differences between African-Americans and white Americans. Kochman (1981) suggested that African-American communication is more intense, assertive, and confrontational than white communication, at least among lower class African Americans, and limited research supports these differences (cited by Gudykunst & Lim, 1985). In contrast, it is common for many mainstream U.S. couples to avoid confrontation, especially if their marital values are traditional (Fitzpatrick, 1988). African-American couples who are committed to traditional marital beliefs may have therefore internalized conflict strategies that undermine their preferred patterns of communication and resolution of marital problems. To explore this possibility, African-American and white middle-class couples were asked to provide information about their marital beliefs, conflict strategies, and marital adjustment, so that the influence of their beliefs and strategies on marital adjustment could be compared. Of additional interest was whether African-American and white spouses would differ in marital adjustment and, if so, whether the difference could be explained by their marital beliefs or use of conflict strategies. Gender differences in conflict strategies were also expected because a variety of researchers have reported greater relationship care by women than men and more direct and affiliative responses in situations of conflict with intimates (e.g., Rusbult, 1987; White, 1989).

METHOD

Participants

Twenty-seven African-American couples and 23 white couples were recruited from the staff of a midwest college campus and from lists of church members provided by local ministers. Their average annual gross income was $40,000-50,000. Nearly half had obtained a bachelor's degree or more advanced degree and another 40% had at least some college education. They had been married an average of 20 years and had an average of two children. There were no statistically significant differences in these characteristics among African-American and white couples except for one; White couples were somewhat better educated (Wilcoxin rank sum, $z = 2.06$, $p = .039$). Couples were contacted by phone and, if willing to participate in the study, were sent questionnaires for each spouse, with instructions to fill them out separately and privately.

Measuring Instruments

Three previously validated instruments were included in the questionnaire; Fitzpatrick's (1988) Relational Dimensions Instrument, Spanier's (1976) Dyadic Adjustment Scale, and Rahim's (1983) Organizational Conflict Inventory. Fitzpatrick's Relational Dimensions Instrument was used to estimate the couples' marital beliefs. Responses to this instrument are typically used to cluster couples into three ideal types: traditionals, who value sharing and espouse conservative and ritualistic beliefs about their marriage; independents, who favor autonomy and change but place equal value on sharing affection and space; and separates, who also value autonomy but share their joys, sorrows, and ordinary times less often than other types of couples and engage in more controlling behaviors. Spouses who disagree about their beliefs are categorized as mixed. Estimates from previous studies are for approximately 20% to be traditional, 22% independent, and 17% separate (Fitzpatrick, 1988). Figures from the current study were 42%, 22%, and 2% respectively, indicating twice as many traditional couples as would be expected from previous research, a difference due probably to recruitment of the majority of couples from local churches. Because of the imbalance in couple type and small sample size, marital beliefs were not indicated by couple type. Instead, scores on the eight subscales of the instrument were factor analyzed and factor scores used to indicate spouses' marital beliefs. Internal reliabilities (Cronbach's alpha) for these subscales ranged from .44 to .84 and had an average alpha of .66, which is low but comparable to that reported by Fitzpatrick. Principal components analysis produced three factors that corresponded to beliefs associated with the three couple types. The first factor was characterized by beliefs in separate and controlling behaviors, the second by sharing of self and space, and the third by traditional values and conflict avoidance.

Spanier's Dyadic Adjustment Scale was used to measure spouses' consensus, affection, and marital satisfaction. Reliabilities for these subscales were .77, .68, and .81, respectively. Responses to items from all subscales were averaged to obtain an index of marital adjustment. Its reliability was .88.

Rahim's Organizational Inventory was used to estimate spouses' use of five conflict strategies. Based on Blake and Mouton's (1964) conflict management model, these strategies reflect the extent to which partners are concerned for self, other, or both self and other. Thus, there are subscales for integration strategies and for compromise strategies, which focus on both partners' concerns. There is also a subscale for domination strategies that focuses on one's own concerns and a subscale for accommodation strategies that focuses on the partner's. The final subscale includes conflict avoidance strategies. Although the instrument was originally designed in Likert format, a true-false format was used instead, which resulted in a reduction of the subscales' reliabilities. These ranged from .60 to .65, except for the avoidance subscale, which had a reliability of .83. Due to the social desirability of many scale items, the format also resulted in many ceiling effects. As an example, 84% endorsed all integration items and 98% all but one. Items were therefore discarded if more than 80% agreed they were true or false. This left 17 items out of an original 35. When factor analyzed, responses to these 17 produced six factors, the first four of which were interpretable as avoidance, accommodation, domination, and compromise strategies, respectively. Factor scores for these four strategies were then used to estimate spouses' use of conflict management strategies.

RESULTS

Gender and Race Comparisons of Beliefs, Strategies, and Adjustment

Scores for marital beliefs, conflict strategies, and marital adjustment were compared in a series of MANOVA's, using race as a between-couple factor and gender as a within-couple factor. These comparisons yielded two differences in marital beliefs. African-Americans endorsed traditional beliefs more than whites did [$F(1,48) = 5.21$, $p = .027$], and husbands endorsed beliefs about separate and controlling behavior more than their wives did [$F(1,48) = 7.56$, $p = .008$]. There were also marginally significant tendencies for whites to make stronger endorsements of sharing than did African Americans [$F(1,48) = 3.32$, $p = .075$] and for husbands to make stronger endorsements of traditional beliefs than did their wives [$F(1,48) = 3.51$, $p = .067$].

Avoidance was the only conflict strategy that differed by race and gender. African Americans reported avoiding conflict more often than did whites [$F(1,48) = 5.57$, $p = .022$] and husbands reported avoiding conflict more often than did their wives [$F(1,48) = 16.83, p < .001$].

Marital adjustment scores also differed by race and gender. White spouses scored higher than African-American spouses [$F(1,48) = 4.15$, $p = .047$], and wives scored higher than their husbands [$F(1,48) = 5.16$, $p = .028$]. The first difference was due primarily to higher satisfaction scores among more white than African-American spouses [$F(1,48) = 10.43$, $p = .002$] and the latter to marginally higher consensus scores [$F(1,48) = 3.88$, $p = .055$] and satisfaction scores [$F(1,48) = 2.91$, $p = .095$] among wives than their husbands.

Effects of Marital Beliefs on Use of Conflict Strategies

Hierarchical regression analyses were use to test the effects of race (dummy coded), gender (dummy coded), and marital beliefs on conflict strategy use. Main effects of race, gender, and belief scores were assessed first, their two-way interactions second, and three-way interactions third. These analyses produced statistically significant main effects primarily, indicating that marital beliefs had the same impact on African-American as on white spouses and on wives as on husbands. Equations with main effects of race, gender, and marital belief scores entered simultaneously accounted for statistically significant variance in avoidance, accommodation, and domination scores. The more traditional were spouses' beliefs, the higher were their avoidance and accommodation scores (standardized $\beta = .49$, $t = 5.69$, $p < .001$ and standardized $\beta = .28$, $t = 2.69$, $p = .009$, respectively). The stronger were their beliefs about sharing, the lower were their domination scores (standardized $\beta = -.20$, $t = -2.00$, $p = .048$). When marital beliefs were statistically controlled, race made no difference in use of these strategies. Gender, however, continued to make a difference in use of avoidance. As before, men scored higher than women (standardized $\beta = .22$, $t = 2.59$, $p = .011$). Only in the case of compromise strategies did marital beliefs appear to have a different influence among African-American than among white couples. In this case, the addition of race x belief interaction terms accounted for additional statistically significant variance in strategy scores [R^2change = .12, $F(3,91) = 4.48$, $p = .006$]. The final equation yielded three effects. Beliefs about sharing decreased use of compromise strategies among African-American spouses (standardized $\beta = -.35$, $t = -2.66$, $p = .009$) but increased it among white spouses (interaction term, standardized $\beta = .38$, $t = 2.94$, $p = .004$). Traditional beliefs also increased compromise marginally among white but not African-American spouses (interaction term, standardized $\beta = .26$, $t = 1.93$, $p = .056$).

Effects of Conflict Strategies on Marital Adjustment

The major question posed by this study is whether use of the same conflict strategies would have different effects on marital adjustment of African-American and white spouses, once their marital beliefs were statistically controlled. Two separate sets of analyses were used to address this question. In the first, marital adjustment scores were regressed hierarchically on the race, gender, marital belief, and conflict strategy scores of all spouses and on all gender x strategy and race x strategy interactions (see Table 6.1). Race, gender, and marital belief scores were entered first, conflict strategy scores second, race x strategy and gender x strategy interactions third, and race x gender x strategy interactions fourth. Because gender x strategy interactions made no significant difference in adjustment scores, these and their three-way interactions with race were eliminated from the analysis, leaving only main effects and race x strategy interactions. Among both African-American and white spouses,

Table 6.1. Effects of Beliefs and Strategies on Adjustment Standardized

	b	Standardized β	t
Step 1:			
Race (White)	.10	.14	1.57
Gender (Male)	-.04	-.06	-.67
Beliefs			
Separatist	-.11	-.28	-3.44**
Sharing	.14	.37	4.00***
Traditional	-.02	-.04	-.39
$[R^2 = .33, F(5,94) = 9.25***]$			
Step 2:			
Avoidance	-.12	-.31	-2.38*
Accommodation	.02	.05	.41
Domination	-.03	-.08	-.72
Compromise	.02	.04	.30
$[R^2\text{change} = .02, F(4,90) = .76]$			
Step 3:			
White x avoidance	.20	.37	3.21**
White x accommodation	-.08	-.14	-1.29
White x domination	-.01	-.02	-.20
White x compromise	.04	.08	.64
$[R^2\text{change} = .08, F(4,86) = 3.22*]$			

Note: Regression coefficients are from the final model; final model adjusted $R^2 = .35$, $F(12,87) = 5.11$, $p < .001$. ***$p < .001$. **$p < .01$. *$p < .05$.

beliefs about sharing increased adjustment, and beliefs about separate and controlling behavior decreased it. African-American spouses continued to score somewhat lower in adjustment than did white spouses, even after marital belief scores were statistically controlled, but the difference was not statistically reliable. Use of avoidance strategies increased adjustment among white spouses, but reduced it among African-American spouses. No other effects were statistically significant, including the effect of gender. Thus, conflict avoidance, which was associated with traditional marital beliefs, appeared to be dysfunctional for African-American couples as initially suspected. Comparisons with all two-way and three-way interaction terms used up many degrees of freedom (i.e., 21 out of 100), however, and made other, potential differences difficult to demonstrate. A second set of hierarchical regressions was therefore run in which marital adjustment scores of husbands and wives were analyzed separately.

In each regression, spouses' race and marital belief scores were entered first, conflict strategy scores second, and race x strategy interactions third. Then their partners' strategy scores were entered, followed by race x partner strategy interactions. Thus, it was possible, in the final model, to test the influence of each partner's conflict strategies, while controlling statistically for strategy use by the other partner. Scores for domination and compromise strategies were excluded from these regressions because their effects on adjustment were negligible when race and marital belief scores were statistically controlled. Moreover, it was desirable to enter fewer than the full set of predictors because each analysis was based on half the sample.

These separate analyses indicated that the effect of conflict strategies on marital adjustment was due primarily to the responses of husbands (see Table 6.2). Small although statistically significant variation in wives' adjustment scores was explained by their marital belief scores alone. Beliefs about sharing increased their adjustment and beliefs about separate and controlling behaviors decreased it. Once marital beliefs were statistically controlled, race, conflict avoidance, and accommodation made no statistically significant difference in their marital adjustment, although the direction of race and conflict avoidance effects was consistent with those for the entire sample.

In contrast, over half the variation in the husbands' adjustment scores was explained by race, conflict avoidance, and accommodation scores, together with their marital belief scores. Husbands' marital adjustment, like their wives', was increased by beliefs about sharing and decreased by beliefs about separate and controlling behaviors. Additionally, conflict avoidance decreased the adjustment of African-American husbands and increased the adjustment of white husbands.

Both African-American and white husbands' adjustment was decreased by their wives accommodation of them, whereas only white husbands' adjustment was decreased by being accommodating. There was a statistically nonsignificant tendency for accommodation by African-American husbands to increase their marital adjustment.

DISCUSSION

African-American couples in this study had lower marital adjustment scores than white couples and endorsed more traditional beliefs about their marriages. Because traditional beliefs were associated with conflict

Table 6.2. Effects of Beliefs and Strategies on Wives' and Husbands' Adjustment

	Wives' Adjustment Standardized			Husbands' Adjustment Standardized		
	b	β	t	b	β	t
Step 1						
Race (White)	.11	.14	.87	.14	.19	1.75#
Own beliefs						
Separatist	-.10	-.25	-1.70#	-.13	-.36	-3.67***
Sharing	.17	.43	2.79**	.13	.37	3.62***
Traditional	.05	.12	.64	-.02	-.06	-.46
	$[R^2 = .23,$ $F(4,45)] = 3.45^*]$			$[R^2 = .47,$ $F(4,45) = 9.84^{***}]$		
Step 2 (Own strategies):						
Avoidance	-.09	-.23	-1.07	-.15	-.41	-2.62*
Accommodation	-.04	-.10	-.52	.07	.19	1.51
	$[R^2$ change $= .01,$ $F(2,43) = .39]$			$[R^2$ change $= .01,$ $F(2,43) = .23]$		
Step 3 (Own strategies):						
White X avoidance	.16	.27	1.26	.20	.38	2.86**
White X accommodation	-.04	-.07	-.37	-.14	-.24	-1.86#
	$[R^2$ change $= .04,$ $F(2,41)] = 1.17]$			$[R^2$ change $= .11,$ $F(2,41) = 5.43^{**}]$		
Step 4 (Partner's strategies):						
Avoidance	.04	.10	.61	.05	.13	1.17
Accommodation	.02	.07	.44	-.09	-.24	-2.31*
	$[R^2$ change $= .01,$ $F(2,39) = .24]$			$[R^2$ change $= .07,$ $F(2,39) = 3.94^*]$		

Note: Regression coefficients are from the final model; final model adjusted R^2 for wives = .12, $F(10,39)$ = 1.65 and for husbands = .56, $F(10,39)$ = 7.34***. ***$p < .001$. **$p < .01$. * $< .05$. #$p < .10$.

avoidance, they reported greater conflict avoidance as well. Because males reported greater conflict avoidance than females, African-American males were the most likely to report avoiding conflict. Marital adjustment scores of African-American males were also the lowest of the four subgroups [planned comparison $t(96) = 3.31$, $p < .001$]. This result replicates findings from previous research that African Americans tend to hold traditional, even conservative attitudes toward marriage and the family and report less marital happiness than whites, due perhaps to greater difficulties in maintaining traditional marital roles.

One reason why marital adjustment scores were lower among African-American than white spouses in this study appears to be their avoidance of conflict. Indicators of marital adjustment were positively related to conflict avoidance among whites but negatively related among African Americans, especially among males. That African Americans nonetheless reported greater conflict avoidance than whites suggests they are valuing traditional, mainstream marital expectations that may conflict with other, perhaps cultural expectations for conflict engagement and active confrontation. This explanation is consistent with Kochman's (1981) claim that contentiousness and competitiveness in conflict are valued by African Americans and with other results from this study that beliefs about sharing increase compromise among whites but not among African Americans.

By the same reasoning, accommodation also should have been dysfunctional for African-American couples because giving in to one's partner can bypass an exchange of arguments. Yet, no such effect was found, other than for accommodation by African-American wives to reduce their husbands adjustment, and this effect was similar for white husbands. It was white, not African-American, husbands whose adjustment was reduced by accommodating their wives. The effect of being accommodating, although statistically unreliable, was opposite for African-American husbands. Exactly why this result was obtained is subject to speculation. It may be that frequent accommodation of one partner by the other signifies an inequitable distribution of care and power in a relationship and that it is this inequity that results in lowered marital adjustment. If so, then race differences in the exchange of rewards between husband and wife should be questioned. Specifically, why might white but not African-American husbands' marital satisfaction suffer when they overbenefit their wives? One possibility is that African-American husbands expect to accommodate their wives because accommodation is associated with traditional beliefs about marriage and African-American husbands espouse stronger traditonal beliefs than do white husbands. Or it could be that African-American husbands' accommodation is in exchange for other resources provided by their wives and does not amount to overbenefit. Because incomes are typically lower in African-American than white families, there has been greater necessity for African-American than white wives to work both outside and inside the home. Accommodation by their husbands might therefore reduce this inequity.

It is also unclear why the use of conflict strategies did not have the same apparent impact on wives' marital adjustment as on husbands'. One possibility stems from the tendency of wives to avoid conflict less than their husbands did (or at least to report doing so). Wives might therefore be less disturbed than their husbands by conflict. Certainly their central caretaking role in the family would suggest they had considerably more practice than their husbands in negotiating conflict. As an example, Vuchinich (1987) found that mothers rather than fathers were the ones who diffused family conflict at the dinner table. In the present study, a small but statistically significant negative correlation was obtained between wives' but not husbands' conflict avoidance scores and number of children ($r = -.24$, $p = .049$), which supports the possibility that women's experience in negotiating conflict may reduce their tendencies to avoid it. Conflict and its management may thus pose less of a threat to wives' than husbands' adjustment.

There were few main effects of gender in this study, but those that occurred are consistent with previous research and theory. Husbands endorsed beliefs about separate and controlling behavior more strongly than their wives did, including beliefs about having privacy, separate activities, and assertive encounters with their spouse. Husbands were also somewhat more likely than their wives to endorse traditional beliefs about marriage, for example, that a woman should take her husband's name, that infidelity is inexcusable, and that their children should be taught the traditions and customs of their heritage. Neither of these differences is surprising in view of men's long-standing dominance in marriage. The maintenance of traditional arrangements and separate activities is advantageous for the maintenance of asymmetries in power. Indeed, it is possible although speculative that conflict avoidance, which men reported using more often than women did (even after marital beliefs had been statistically controlled), also furthers power asymmetries by preserving the status quo. Conflict avoidance can clearly serve more than one function, and the possibility that men and women may use avoidance differently raises an important question for future research.

Yet, even though husbands' and wives' endorsements of beliefs differed somewhat, the impact of their beliefs on marital adjustment was the same. The more they endorsed beliefs about shared time and space, the higher were their marital adjustment scores. The more they endorsed beliefs about separate and controlling behavior, the lower were their marital adjustment scores. Wives scored higher in marital adjustment than did their husbands, but this gender difference disappeared when the effect of their marital beliefs was statistically controlled. It was their marital beliefs rather than gender that made a difference in marital adjustment. Husbands appeared to be less well-adjusted than their wives, but this was due to their somewhat stronger endorsement of beliefs about separate and controlling behavior.

These results should be interpreted cautiously, due to the relatively low reliability of scales and small sample size. Still, they suggest the possibility that traditional white tendencies to avoid conflict in marriage may be dysfunctional for African-American couples. African-American marriage is accompanied by a history of disadvantages. Communication patterns that interfere with marital problem solving and understanding may well increase its difficulties. It is important to note that race continued to make a marginally significant difference in the adjustment scores of husbands, independent of their marital beliefs and conflict strategy scores. This suggests that conflict management strategies and marital beliefs operate in conjunction with other, race-linked factors to limit marital adjustment among African-American men. Noteworthy too is that conflict management styles could be a consequence as well as cause of marital adjustment. Additional research is required to replicate these results, tease out cause-and-effect relationships, and ascertain their applicability to the larger African-American population. Additional research might also examine other mainstream expectations which affect the adjustment of African Americans and whites in opposing ways.

REFERENCES

Aborampah, O.M. (1989). Black male-female relationships: Some observations. *Journal of Black Studies, 19*, 320-342.

Ball, R.E., & Robbins, L. (1984). Marital status and life satisfaction of black men. *Journal of Social and Personal Relationships, 1*, 459-470.

Blake, R.R., & Mouton, J.S. (1964). *The management grid.* Houston, TX: Gulf.

Braithwaite, R.L. (1981). Interpersonal relations between black males and black females. In L.E. Gary (Ed.), *Black men* (pp. 83-96). Beverly Hills, CA: Sage.

Fitzpatrick, M.A. (1988). *Between husbands and wives: Communication in marriage.* Beverly Hills, CA: Sage.

Franklin, C.W. (1984). Black male-black female conflict: Individually caused and culturally nurtured. *Journal of Black Studies, 15*, 139-154.

Gary, L.E. (1987). Predicting interpersonal conflict between men and women: The case of black men. In M.S. Kimmel (Ed.), *Changing men: New directions in research on men and masculinity* (pp. 232-243). Beverly Hills, CA: Sage.

Glenn, N.D., & Weaver, C.N. (1981). The contribution of marital happiness to global happiness. *Journal of Marriage and the Family, 43,* 161-168.

Gudykunst, W.B., & Lim, T. (1985). Ethnicity, sex, and self-perceptions of communicator style. *Communication Research Reports, 2,* 68-75.

Hershey, M.R. (1978). Racial differences in sex-role identities and sex stereotyping: Evidence against a common assumption. *Social Science Quarterly, 58,* 583-596.

Kochman, T. (1981). *Black and white: Styles in conflict.* Chicago: University of Chicago Press.

Rahim, M.A. (1983). A measure of styles of handling interpersonal conflict. *Academy of Management Journal, 26,* 368-376.

Rusbult, C.E. (1987). Responses to dissatisfaction in close relationships: The exit-voice-loyalty-neglect model. In D. Perlman & S. Duck (Eds.), *Intimate relationships: Development, dynamics, and deterioration* (pp. 209-237). Beverly Hills, CA: Sage.

Spanier, G.B. (1976). Measuring dyadic adjustment: New scales for assessing the quality of marriage and similar dyads. *Journal of Marriage and the Family, 38,* 15-28.

Staples, R. (1989). Changes in black family structure: The conflict between family ideology and structural conditions. In B.J. Risman & P. Schwartz (Eds.), *Gender in intimate relationships: A microstructural approach* (pp. 235-244). Belmont, CA: Wadsworth.

Tucker, M.B., & Taylor, R.J. (1989). Demographic correlates of relationship status among black Americans. *Journal of Marriage and the Family, 51,* 655-668.

Vuchinich, S. (1987). Starting and stopping spontaneous family conflicts. *Journal of Marriage and the Family, 49,* 591-601.

White, B.B. (1989). Gender differences in marital communication. *Family Process, 28,* 89-106.

7

Gender Differences in Conflict-Handling Styles:
Less Than Meets the Eye?

Thomas L. Ruble
Joy A. Schneer
Rider College

Conventional wisdom suggests that men and women have different styles of handling interpersonal conflict. This wisdom was expressed recently in *Time* magazine in a special issue on women. As interpreted in *Time*, men are expected to emphasize an "all or nothing" approach whereas women are expected to be open, emphasizing a problem-solving approach (Rudolph, 1990).

To some extent, these gender differences may reflect socialization processes. Researchers suggest that girls and boys are raised differently, resulting in alternative ways of handling conflict (Rose & Larwood, 1988). Girls are socialized to value relationships and maintain harmony while boys are socialized to value status and seek victory. This is thought to translate into women taking a cooperative stance in conflict situations, whereas men are more competitive.

In this chapter, we examine whether expected gender differences are reported in conflict situations. If so, we estimate the extent of the differences to determine whether gender is a meaningful predictor of conflict behavior. The research focuses on self-reports of five different "styles" of handling interpersonal conflict.

Conflict-Handling Styles

In the 1960s, Blake and Mouton (1964) introduced a two-dimensional model for classifying managerial styles and conflict-handling orientations. This model has been reinterpreted on numerous occasions and different versions appear in the literature. Although the various interpretations use slightly different terms, a representative version of the model is that of Thomas and his colleagues (Ruble & Thomas, 1976; Thomas, 1976; Thomas & Kilmann, 1986). The model developed by Thomas identifies the two dimensions of conflict behavior as assertiveness (concern for self) and cooperativeness (concern for the other party). Within these two dimensions, five conflict- handling styles are classified: (a) avoiding (unassertive, uncooperative), (b) competing (assertive, uncooperative), (c) accommodating (unassertive, cooperative), (d) collaborating (assertive, cooperative), and (e) compromising (intermediate in both assertiveness and cooperativeness). The model is diagrammed in Fig. 7.1.

Avoiding involves sidestepping or withdrawing from conflict situations. Competing represents an attempt to win one's position at the expense of others. Accommodating involves the sacrifice of one's own

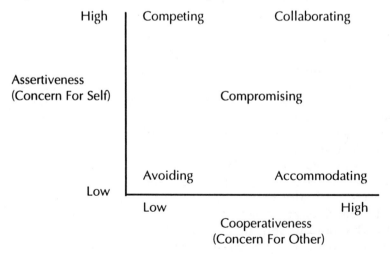

Figure 7.1. Conflict-handling styles

position to allow the satisfaction of others. *Collaboration* is associated with mutual gain or joint problem solving. This style involves exchanging information in order to achieve optimal or creative solutions to conflict. *Compromising* represents a give-and-take, middle ground approach to identifying solutions.

The two-dimensional model is based on the assumption that people develop somewhat stable preferences for certain styles. Although individuals may use all five styles to some extent, it is assumed that they tend to rely on certain styles. Thus, conflict-handling styles are viewed as relatively stable personal dispositions or individual differences.

Gender Differences in Conflict-Handling Styles

As we find in many fields, research on gender differences in conflict handling styles has yielded mixed results. Kilmann and Thomas (1977) found that male students were more likely than female students to report competing in disagreements with teachers, whereas females were more likely to report compromising than males. Chanin and Schneer (1984) found that female students were more likely than male students to report the use of compromising in a business simulation group setting, whereas males were more likely to report the use of collaborating than females. Rahim (1983a) reported gender differences on four of the five conflict-handling styles for a sample of U.S. managers. Compared to men, women were higher on compromising, collaborating, and avoiding and lower on accommodating. No differences were observed for competing. Chusmir and Mills (1989) surveyed managers representing three hierarchial levels in three occupational groups. No gender differences were found for conflict handling behavior at work or at home when the effects of hierarchial level were controlled.

Related research on organizational influence styles also has yielded mixed results. Kipnis, Schmidt, and Wilkinson (1980) found no gender differences in the use of several influence tactics similar to the five conflict-handling styles. On the other hand, Mainiero (1986) found that women were more accommodating than men in coping with organizational powerlessness.

Despite conventional wisdom, this small set of studies on conflict-handling styles does not provide strong evidence of expected gender differences. The research indicated some tendency for women to score higher on compromising, whereas gender differences on the other four styles were inconsistent.

Although some statistically significant differences were found for gender, the practical significance of these results may be minimal. Statistical significance levels alone do not indicate the magnitude of the

158 Ruble & Schneer

differences observed (Friedman, 1968; Hays, 1963; Kerlinger, 1986; Rosnow & Rosenthal, 1989). In behavioral research, minor differences may reach levels of statistical significance if the sample is particularly large.

Previous research on conflict-handling styles did not assess the magnitude of gender differences. Thus, conflict-handling differences may exist between men and women, but they may be too small to help predict what any individual person would do in a conflict situation. In the present research, the analysis of conflict-handling styles includes a determination of the magnitude of gender differences. This analysis provides some basis for judging the practical significance of the findings.

General Issues in Research on Gender Differences

Before addressing specific questions pertaining to conflict-handling styles, it is useful to recognize that research on gender differences involves a set of difficult issues (cf. Frieze, Parsons, Johnson, Ruble, & Zellman, 1978). According to Deaux (1984), gender may be viewed as a "subject variable" or as a "social category." Research on gender as a subject variable focuses on how men and women differ in fixed personal characteristics such as behavior, traits, or capabilities. Research on gender as a social category focuses on how people perceive gender differences and, subsequently, respond to the perceived distinctions between women and men. These views may lead to divergent interpretations of research if perceived gender differences are incongruent with actual gender differences.

Conventional wisdom and expectations for gender differences tend to reflect the subject variable approach. According to this view, gender differences in conflict-handling styles should be relatively consistent across samples, measures, and settings. Deaux (1984) suggests that fixed gender differences are relatively weak determinants of behavior. Even when statistically significant differences are found, gender accounts for a relatively small proportion of variance in behavior.

Research Questions

The present research examines the issue of gender differences in conflict situations by evaluating self-report measures of conflict-handling styles from four different samples. Three major questions are addressed:

1. Do men and women differ in their self-reports of conflict-handling styles?
2. If differences are reported, are those differences consistent

across different samples and different measures?
3. If consistent differences are reported, what is their practical significance in predicting how people will respond to conflict?

METHOD

Instruments

Although early conflict instruments tended to have measurement problems, (cf. Thomas & Kilmann, 1978), two recent instruments seem to have improved psychometric properties: (a) the Thomas-Kilmann Conflict Mode Instrument (MODE; Kilmann & Thomas, 1977; Thomas & Kilmann, 1986) and (b) the Rahim Organizational Conflict Inventory (ROCI-II; Rahim, 1983b). Although both instruments measure the five conflict-handling styles, the MODE instrument uses a forced-choice format with 30 pairs of items, whereas the ROCI-II uses a rating format with 28 Likert-type items. This research uses both instruments to insure that the results are not instrument specific.

A comparison of the psychometric properties of the two instruments suggests that the ROCI-II probably is more reliable than the MODE instrument (Kilmann & Thomas, 1977; Rahim, 1983b; Womack, 1988). For the present samples, estimates of coefficient alpha for the five scales ranged from .27 to .79 for the MODE instrument and from .63 to .85 for the ROCI-II. The alpha coefficients for the ROCI-II tend to fall in a range considered acceptable for research purposes (cf. Nunnally, 1978). Due to the forced-choice format of the MODE instrument, which pairs a given style with all other styles, it is not clear that coefficient alpha provides the best estimate of internal consistency reliability. Nevertheless, findings based on the MODE instrument should be interpreted with caution.

Respondents

The more than 600 hundred respondents include four different samples: (a) 62 employees of business, government, and nonprofit organizations who completed the MODE instrument, (b) 211 senior business students who completed the MODE instrument, (c) 174 senior business students who completed the ROCI-II instrument, and (d) 198 senior business students who completed the ROCI-II instrument.

The employee sample completed the MODE instrument twice, first for conflicts at work and a second time for conflicts away from work. This sample was drawn primarily from middle-level managers and professional employees with college degrees. Data were not available regarding specific occupations and levels within the middle management range.

The student samples completed the conflict-handling instruments in the context of a computerized business simulation. As an integral part of a business policy course, students were divided into four-person teams who functioned in the roles of top corporate executives. The teams made quarterly decisions for their companies simulating 3 years of business operation (3 months real time). The students completed the instruments near the end of the simulation period according to how they handled conflict within their teams.

Data Analysis

Inferential statistics (t tests) were used to estimate the probability that gender differences could appear by chance. If there was a low probability of obtaining differences by chance (i.e., $p < .05$), the results were termed statistically significant. If an observed difference was statistically significant, we concluded that at least some difference in conflict-handling styles existed between women and men. However, because significance levels alone do not indicate the extent of the differences, follow-up procedures are recommended to assess the magnitude of effects (cf. Friedman, 1968; Hays, 1963; Kerlinger, 1986; Rosnow & Rosenthal, 1989).

A variety of measures can be used to assess magnitude of effects. Omega-squared (ω^2) provides a conservative estimate of the proportion of variance in a dependent variable that may be attributed to the effect of an independent variable (Hays, 1963; Kerlinger, 1986). This study used estimates of omega-squared to assess the magnitude of gender differences.

RESULTS

Employee Sample

Comparisons between men and women were made separately for conflicts at work and away from work. Mean ratings of conflict-handling styles are presented in Table 7.1. The means were compared by independent-samples t tests. For work situations, women reported a tendency to compete less than men ($p < .05$) and compromise more ($p < .01$). For situations away from work, no differences were found between men and women. Thus, for 8 of the 10 comparisons between women and men, no

TABLE 7.1. Mean Ratings of Conflict-Handling Styles for Females versus Males in Work and Nonwork Situations

| | Conflict Style: MODE Instrument | | | | |
	Avoid	Compete	Accomm	Collab	Compro
Nonwork					
Female (27)	6.52	3.04	7.52	6.33	6.33
Male (35)	6.68	3.77	8.06	5.86	5.83
t	0.27	0.98	0.94	0.76	1.06
Work					
Female (27)	5.93	5.00	4.67	6.52	7.93
Male (35)	5.54	6.60	4.91	6.43	6.60
t	0.64	2.03*	0.41	0.15	2.83**

Note: Sample size in parentheses.
* $p < .05$. ** $p < .01$.

significant differences were obtained.

Estimates of ω^2 were .05 and .10 for competing and compromising at work, respectively. Thus, gender differences accounted for approximately 5% and 10% of the variance in competing and compromising in conflicts at work. However, because the results were not transsituational, these effects cannot be considered as fixed personal characteristics of men and women.

Student Samples

Mean ratings of conflict-handling styles for the three student samples are presented in Table 7.2. The first sample completed the Thomas-Kilmann instrument (MODE). Two statistically significant differences were found. Female students reported a tendency to compete less than males ($p < .01$) and compromise more ($p < .05$). These differences are the same as those obtained with the MODE instrument for work settings. However, the magnitudes of the effects were lower in the student sample. Estimates of ω^2 were .03 and .02 for competing and compromising, respectively.

The second student sample completed the Rahim instrument (ROCI-II). Again, gender differences were found for competing and compromising. Women reported a tendency to compete less ($p < .001$) and compromise more ($p < .01$) than men. Estimates of ω^2 were .09 and .05 for competing and compromising, respectively. The third student sample also completed the ROCI-II instrument, but gender differences did not reach customary levels of statistical significance. However, differences for competing and compromising reached levels often reported

Table 7.2. Mean Ratings of Conflict-Handling Styles for Female versus Male Students in a Business Simulation

	Avoid	Compete	Accomm	Collab	Compro
		Conflict Style			
		MODE Instrument			
Sample 1					
Female (103)	4.72	5.57	3.87	7.52	8.27
Male (108)	4.78	6.84	3.37	7.47	7.54
t	0.19	2.80**	1.57	0.19	2.38*
		ROCI Instrument			
Sample 2					
Female (105)	2.55	3.08	3.38	4.34	3.89
Male (69)	2.54	3.47	3.37	4.30	3.64
t	0.13	4.17**	0.22	0.66	3.17**
Sample 3					
Female (127)	2.46	3.12	3.56	4.33	3.94
Male (71)	2.37	3.30	3.60	4.22	3.82
t	0.92	1.92	0.62	1.60	1.73

Note: Sample size in parentheses. Due to differences in format and scoring for the MODE and ROCI instruments, the mean ratings are not comparable between instruments.
* $p < .05$. ** $p < .01$.

as marginally significant ($p < .10$). The direction of the differences was consistent with results from the previous samples with women reporting a tendency to compete less and compromise more than men. Estimates of ω^2 were .01 for both competing and compromising.

Summary of Results

A summary of the magnitudes of effect is presented in Table 7.3. The estimates of ω^2 due to gender differences are presented for the four samples. For the employees, the results cover only the work setting.

An average for estimates of ω^2 indicate that approximately 4.5% of the variance in both competing and compromising can be attributed to gender differences. These averages are close to the 5% estimate of Deaux (1984) for the upper bound of gender effects in a variety of social psychological studies.

TABLE 7.3. Estimates of Omega-Squared for Gender Differences in Competing and Compromising

Conflict Style	Competing	Compromising
Sample		
Employees-work	.05	.10
Students 1	.03	.02
Students 2	.09	.05
Students 3	.01	.01
Average	.045	.045

DISCUSSION

This research was directed toward three specific questions. First, do males and females differ in self-reports of conflict-handling styles? The answer appears to be "somewhat." Five different conflict-handling styles were examined. For each of the five styles, five comparisons between men and women were tested for statistical significance. Of the 25 tests, 6 comparisons yielded statistically significant differences. No significant differences were found for conflicts away from work. This result is consistent with the research of Chusmir and Mills (1989). In addition, no significant differences were obtained for accommodating, avoiding, or collaborating styles in work- or task-oriented settings. However, statistically significant gender differences were found for competing and compromising in work- or task-oriented settings.

Second, if differences are reported, are those differences consistent across different samples and measures? The answer appears to be "for some styles in work- or task-oriented settings." For competing and compromising, the pattern of gender differences was relatively consistent for employees at work as well as for the students participating in a business simulation. In general, women reported greater tendencies to compromise and lesser tendencies to compete compared to men. In three sets of comparisons, the differences for competing and compromising reached customary levels of statistical significance, whereas in the fourth set of comparisons the differences approached statistical significance. This pattern of results was consistent across the different instruments as well.

Third, if consistent differences are reported, what is their practical significance in predicting how people will respond to conflict? The answer appears to be "very limited." Consistent with prior research, relatively consistent gender differences were found for competing and compromising. However, the effects of gender were small, accounting for approximately 5% of the variance in these two conflict-handling styles.

Based on this evidence, one should not feel confident in predicting a person's conflict-handling style based solely on knowledge of their gender.

Limitations

In evaluating these results, the limitations of this research must be acknowledged. The data for all four samples were obtained from self-reports of conflict-handling styles. Clearly, this represents a limited measure of actual conflict-handling behavior. Given the limitations of self-report measures (Podsakoff & Organ, 1986), caution is urged in generalizing to behavioral differences.

Another limitation was that the settings were dominated by a business orientation. Most, although not all, of the employee sample worked for profit-directed firms. The three student samples completed the conflict instruments in the context of a business simulation. Moreover, prior research suggests that women who choose to go into business may model the behaviors expected of men in business (Rose & Larwood, 1988). Thus, gender differences in the population at large may be underestimated in this study due to the nature of the respondents.

Finally, coefficient alpha estimates for the MODE instrument raise questions about its reliability. However, results based on the MODE were reasonably consistent with results based on the ROCI-II. Still, results based on the MODE instrument should be interpreted with caution.

Conclusions

The results of this research reflect different types of respondents, instruments, and settings. The heterogeneity in this study sets it apart from previous research on conflict-handling styles. We found some consistent gender differences in work/task settings for two of the five conflict-handling styles—women reported competing less and compromising more than men. However, estimates of the magnitude of effects suggest that the practical significance of these gender differences is questionable as gender accounted for an average of only 5% of the variance in competing and compromising.

Why, then, does conventional wisdom about gender differences persist? Despite these findings, it is hard to discount beliefs about gender differences in conflict-handling behavior. In daily experiences we often see a pattern of gender differences. Perhaps this is because gender acts as a social category that affects our perceptions and interpretations of a person's behavior (Deaux, 1984).

Gender stereotypes and role expectations may have a strong

influence on behavior or the interpretation of behavior (cf. Ruble & Ruble, 1982). Perhaps by our own behavior, we may elicit gender-stereotyped behavior from others we engage. Research on the "Pygmalion Effect" and "expectancy confirmation processes" suggests that individuals act in a way expected of them (cf. Bass, 1990; Darley & Fazio, 1980). Or, we may perceive and/or attribute an individual's behavior to the effects of gender even though the behavior was based on other factors. Deaux (1984) has suggested that causal attributions for male and female performance are related to gender-based expectations.

The processes noted here could lead to the persistence of stereotypes despite the finding that gender has limited value in predicting a person's conflict-handling behavior. Thus, actual gender differences in conflict behavior may be "less than meets the eye."

REFERENCES

Bass, B.M. (1990). *Handbook of leadership.* New York: The Free Press.

Blake, R.R., & Mouton, J.S. (1964). *The managerial grid.* Houston, TX: Gulf.

Chanin, M.N., & Schneer, J.A. (1984). A study of the relationship between Jungian personality dimensions and conflict-handling behavior. *Human Relations, 37,* 863-879.

Chusmir, L.H., & Mills, J. (1989). Gender differences in conflict resolution styles of managers: At work and at home. *Sex Roles, 20,* 149-163.

Darley, J.M., & Fazio, R.H. (1980). Expectancy confirmation processes arising in the social interaction sequence. *American Psychologist, 35,* 867-881.

Deaux, K. (1984). From individual differences to social categories: Analysis of a decade's research on gender. *American Psychologist, 39,* 105-116.

Friedman, H. (1968). Magnitude of experimental effect and a table for its rapid estimation. *Psychological Bulletin, 70,* 245-251.

Frieze, I., Parsons, J., Johnson, P., Ruble, D., & Zellman, G. (1978). *Women and sex roles: A social psychological perspective.* New York: Norton.

Hays, W.L. (1963). *Statistics for psychologists.* New York: Holt, Rinehart & Winston.

Kerlinger, F.N. (1986). *Foundations of behavioral research* (3rd ed.). New York: Holt, Rinehart & Winston.

Kilmann, R.H., & Thomas, K.W. (1977). Developing a forced-choice measure of conflict-handling behavior: The "MODE" instrument. *Educational and Psychological Measurement, 37,* 309-325.

Kipnis, D., Schmidt, S., & Wilkinson, I. (1980). Intraorganizational influence tactics: Explorations in getting one's way. *Journal of Applied Psychology, 65,* 440-452.

Mainiero, L.A. (1986). Coping with powerlessness: The relationship of gender and job dependency to empowerment-strategy usage. *Administrative Science Quarterly, 31,* 633-653.

Nunnally, J. (1978). *Psychometric theory.* New York: McGraw-Hill.

Podsakoff, P.M., & Organ, D.W. (1986). Self-reports in organizational research: Problems and prospects. *Journal of Management, 12,* 531-544.

Rahim, M.A. (1983a). A measure of styles of handling interpersonal conflict. *Academy of Management Journal, 26,* 368-376.

Rahim, M.A. (1983b). *Rahim organizational conflict inventories.* Palo Alto, CA: Consulting Psychologists Press.

Rose, S., & Larwood, L. (1988). Charting women's careers: Current issues and research. In S. Rose & L. Larwood (Eds.), *Women's careers: Pathways and pitfalls* (pp. 3-21). New York: Praeger.

Rosnow, R.L., & Rosenthal, R. (1989). Statistical procedures and the justification of knowledge in psychological science. *American Psychologist, 44,* 1276-1284.

Rudolph, B. (1990). Why can't a woman manage more like. . . a woman? *Time,* p. 53.

Ruble, D., & Ruble, T. (1982). Sex stereotypes. In A. Miller (Ed.), *In the eye of the beholder: Contemporary issues in stereotyping* (pp. 188-252). New York: Praeger.

Ruble, T.L., & Thomas, K.W. (1976). Support for a two-dimensional model of conflict behavior. *Organizational Behavior and Human Performance, 16,* 143-155.

Thomas, K.W. (1976), Conflict and conflict management. In M. Dunnette (Ed.), *Handbook of industrial and organizational psychology* (pp. 889-935). Chicago: Rand McNally.

Thomas, K.W., & Kilmann, R.H. (1978), Comparison of four instruments measuring conflict behavior. *Psychological Reports, 42,* 1139-1145.

Thomas, K.W., & Kilmann, R.H. (1986). *Thomas-Kilmann conflict mode instrument.* Tuxedo, NY: Xicom.

Womack, D.F. (1988). A review of conflict instruments in organizational settings. *Management Communication Quarterly, 1,* 437-445.

8

Gender and Conflict: What Does Psychological Research Tell Us?

Loraleigh Keashly
University of Guelph

In this chapter, I discuss the ways in which social psychologists conceptualize and study gender and conflict with an eye toward directions for future research. To accomplish this task, I begin with an exploration of the meaning of the terms *gender* and *conflict*. With respect to sex and gender, I focus on the reciprocal nature of biological distinctiveness and the sociocultural definitions of women and men and highlight the value of examining gender-related behavior in a social context. I also discuss the multiple meanings of conflict as reflections of differential emphasis on objective and subjective criteria, drawing attention again to the importance of conflict behaviors as social phenomena.

Based on a review of selected studies, I demonstrate that a number of variables (some of which co-vary with gender) influence conflict behavior and often explain more variation in conflict behavior than does gender. I argue that processes and outcomes of conflict depend on the nature of relations between conflicting parties (including intimacy and relative status), the specific situational context in which they conflict, and the beliefs they hold about conflict. The way in which conflict behavior is operationalized (measured) is shown to affect the results of these studies.

A major theme from this review is that although the evidence indicates more similarities than differences in the conflict behavior of women and men, people continue to believe that there are sizable differences. I suggest we pay more careful attention in our future research to the interplay among gender-linked beliefs, perceptions, and behavior in conflict.

What is Gender?

Social psychologists have emphasized the importance of distinguishing between the concepts of *sex* and *gender* (Rhode, 1990). Briefly, sex refers to the biologically based distinctions between woman and man (chromosomal and hormonal). Gender refers to the cultural, social, and power implications of this biological differentiation (i.e., the beliefs about, expectations, interpretations, and experiences of women and men in our society; Rhode, 1990; Unger, 1989). The distinction between these concepts reflects different perspectives or assumptions about causality. The use of the term *sex* conveys the assumption that the characteristics studied are an essential part of the person's personality—stable and coherent. Thus, "sex differences" in social behavior may be viewed as inherent in the nature of men and women, whereas "gender differences" originate in the social system rather than within the person (Unger, 1989). Use of the concept of *gender differences* implies that traits and behaviors attributed to men and women are a reflection of societal beliefs, expectations, and prescriptions for people based on biological distinctiveness. In effect, sex forms the basis of a social categorization system that is gender (Deaux, 1984). Knowing someone is a man or a woman cues in a whole set of expectations and beliefs that have implications for our behavior and ways of dealing with these individuals and ultimately for their behavior toward us (Deaux & Major, 1990).

I prefer to use the term *gender* because it captures and acknowledges the complex and reciprocal nature of biological and social elements of women and men's experience and behavior. It directs my interests as a social psychologist to the study of behavior within the social context as cognitively and interactively expressed. In particular, use of the term *gender* rather than *sex* highlights the importance of moving beyond a description of gender-linked behavior to an examination of the social mechanisms by which these "differences" are created (Unger, 1990).

Hare-Mustin and Marecek (1988) argue that any discussion of gender requires an exploration of the meaning of difference. Currently, there are three distinct views of gender differences (Rhode, 1990). The first could be labeled *denial* (or beta bias; Hare-Mustin & Marecek, 1988) because it disputes the extent or essential nature of differences between women and men. From this perspective, researchers point to influences within methodologies that have exaggerated gender differences. Although some differences are accepted, the essentiality of their nature is not. Thus, research and thinking that focus on delineating social, cultural, and situational influences on gender-linked behavior can challenge the biological and individual-differences perspectives (e.g., Deaux & Major, 1990; MacKinnon, 1990). Caution needs to be taken in adopting this viewpoint because an emphasis on lack of difference may inadvertently perpetuate using men and their norms as the standard of comparison, leaving the system essentially unchallenged (Rhode, 1990). This viewpoint also fails to acknowledge the importance of social positions typically occupied by women (Hare-Mustin & Marecek, 1988).

The second view of gender differences accepts and addresses the value placed on these differences (alpha bias; Hare-Mustin and Marecek, 1988). Attention is focused on describing and celebrating women's experience, a perspective exemplified by the work of Gilligan (1982) on the "different voice" of women. This perspective is essentialist in nature as it maintains traditional dichotomies while acknowledging the similarities between women and men and the social origins of their roles. Like denial, it reinforces social expectations and beliefs and may continue to restrict opportunities for both sexes (Rhode, 1990). Additionally, it tends to ignore differences among women with respect to race, ethnicity, class, and age (Hare-Mustin & Marecek, 1988).

These two perspectives reflect the current status of gender research. Tests of gender differences in social behavior (e.g., influence, helping, conflict) are characterized by a "now-you-see-it, now-you-don't" quality (Unger, 1981). Sometimes women and men do the same things and sometimes they do not. Such inconsistency requires attention to more than whether women and men may or may not differ, but to the conditions under which these differences arise. Perhaps the greater issue is not so much the debate over differences but "the consequences of stressing such differences in particular contexts" (Rhode, 1990, p. 5).

The third view challenges traditional conceptualizations of difference as dualism and focuses instead on patterns and dimensions of difference. This approach seeks to remove differences as the exclusive focus of gender-linked questions (Rhode, 1990). For example, although research on female-male differences occurs as less than perfect correlations or statistical frequencies, we tend to interpret the numbers in dualistic terms. These "tendencies" in our interpretation of data do not permit an exploration of gender as a social process and instead highlight gender as a static quality, legitimizing male-female as fundamental social categories (Hare-Mustin & Marecek, 1988). Such dichotomization ignores the variability among women and men associated with social class, race, age, marital status, and cultural background (Sherif, 1982). Several authors (Deaux & Major, 1990; Jaggar, 1990; MacKinnon, 1990) have argued that the dichotomization is based on viewing inequality as an effect of gender differences as opposed to the cause of them. The perspective that inequality can generate differences challenges the oppositional categories. Instead of focusing on dualisms it focuses on differing dimensions of difference and the situations under which they arise (Rhode, 1990).

As a social psychologist, I am concerned with social origins and meanings of gender. When I refer to gender difference, it is with expectations of variations in difference by situation. When I interpret gender difference, it is with sensitivity to the correlates and underlying dimensions of social behaviors.

What is Conflict?

In much of social psychological research, the researcher provides the description or simulation of conflict and examines how people respond to and within it (Felstiner, Abel, & Sarat, 1980/1981). This practice allows great variation in definitions of conflict (Peterson, 1983) that may not be consistent with the "disputants'" interpretation of the situation (see Pinkley & Northcraft, 1990). Scholars' descriptions of conflict have varied along dimensions of outcome (constructive or destructive; differential gain or misperception), degree of competitiveness, actual conflict behavior versus intention to behave (not openly expressed), structure of the interaction (e.g., fight, debate, game), objective versus subjective criteria, and so on (Peterson, 1983). This is not surprising given the complexity of conflict and the values and interests of researchers. However, failure to make these distinctions explicit may lead to apparently inconsistent results as these may represent very different events and processes. Moreover, the practice of imposing definitions for conflict may ignore the conflicting parties' perspectives and the reasons for their behavior.

Evidence suggests that different individuals describe or experience the "same" conflict or situation differently. The work of Pinkley (1990; Pinkley & Northcraft, 1990) and Sheppard (1984; Sheppard, Blumefeld-Jones, Minton, & Hyder, 1990) suggests that conflict parties interpret or frame a conflict along a number of dimensions and that this framing affects their choice of goals and strategies for dealing with the conflict. Conflict interpretations have been found to vary with gender (Kelley et al., 1978; Pinkley & Northcraft, 1990), role (e.g., mediator-disputant; Pinkley, 1990; victim-perpetrator; Baumeister, Stillwell, & Wotman, 1990), and status of the conflict parties (Hare-Mustin &

Marecek, 1988), which suggests the importance of studying social contexts of conflict as well as conflict parties' interpretations. When scholars ignore these aspects of conflict, they may be describing and explaining different phenomena than the ones that have actually created conflict. A parallel theme can be seen in studies of gender-linked behavior when the assumption is made that one group's experience (men's) tells us a great deal about another group's (women's) experience or when variables correlated with group membership (e.g., status, power, education, experience) are not used as statistical controls.

As a social psychologist I am concerned about careful conceptualization of the situation, the persons involved and their relationships to each other, and about the operationalization by appropriate methodological procedures such as manipulation checks, use of self-referent situations, the monitoring of relevant co-variables, and descriptions from the participants' perspectives.

Thus, to answer the question "what is conflict?" requires acknowledgment of these features, even though most of the studies examined in this chapter fail to do so sufficiently (Northrup, 1989). Studies addressing the issue of gender and conflict need to be assessed in terms of these features and their influence on reported results and interpretations. In the following review, I attempt to identify those circumstances in which women and men experience conflict, noting gender differences when present. I begin by summarizing early experimental research, then go on to discuss more recent work according to interpersonal contexts and other features of conflict.

Lessons From Early Research on Conflict and Gender

In their 1975 book, *The Social Psychology of Bargaining and Negotiation*, Rubin and Brown reviewed approximately 100 studies that focused on the relationship between sex and various aspects of bargaining behavior. They noted that results fell into three categories: (a) no difference in bargaining performance for males and females, (b) males behaving more cooperatively than females, and (c) females behaving more cooperatively than males. To explain such "inconsistent" findings, they focused their explanations on the structure of the situation and the differential perception of situational cues. They argued that women and men did not differ in their abilities and skills at bargaining but that they were sensitive to different cues in the bargaining situation. Women were more attuned to interpersonal aspects of the relationship, whereas men attended more to the task of maximizing their gains. Thus, men would compete or cooperate depending on whether it would allow them to maximize their gains, whereas women would compete or cooperate

depending on the behavior of the other person, which is an interpretation consistent with sex-role expectations.

Renwick (1977) has argued that the results from this type of gaming research are limited in their generalizability because the relationships
studied were not ongoing and had limited opportunities for communication between the members of the dyad. Under such circumstances, subjects may tend to "fall back" on sex-role expectations for behavior. Thus,
it becomes important to investigate women's and men's behavior in conflict situations other than bargaining or gaming situations.

The interpersonal relationship is an important context within
which to explore gender-linked conflict behavior for two reasons. First,
much of the work on the strengths of women and men focuses on the
dimensions of connection and separation, respectively (Markus &
Oyserman, 1989), which should make the interpersonal relationship a
fertile ground for gender-linked behavior. Second, research results from
the related area of social influence differ depending on the nature of the
relationship between the influencer and the target, for example, supervi-
sor-subordinate, parent-child, or friend-friend (e.g., Atkinson, 1987;
Eagly, 1983; Howard, Blumstein, & Schwartz, 1986; Kipnis, 1984). These
results suggest that characteristics of partners' relationships such as their
sex composition, relative status and power, and degree of emotional
connection might make a difference in conflict as well.

Inconsistencies in results from early research have also been
related to the methodological differences in studies. Unger (1981)
argued that sex of subject effects were more likely to be obtained in field
than in laboratory studies because: (a) subjects in laboratory settings
would be more conscious of social desirability and objectivity than
would subjects in field settings; and (b) norms governing sex roles
would be overridden by norms of social objectivity in the lab. In contrast, Fagenson (1990) argued that gender-linked differences in leadership and management behavior would be typically found in laboratory
studies rather than in the field because lab experiments are short term,
artificial, and make social roles and their associated stereotypical behavior salient. In field settings, participants have self-selected into jobs and
organizations that yield "relatively homogeneous settings with relatively similar people in them" (p. 269). Such contradictory perceptions of
methodological differences warrant attention to the research setting as
an origin of gender-linked conflict behavior (Eagly & Johnson, 1990).

Other methodological differences could also influence research
results. These include participants' awareness of being studied (the issue
of unobtrusive-reactive measurement), specificity of the conflict situation and novelty of the conflict issues. For example, it is reasonable to
hypothesize that the more general and novel the conflict situation, the

more likely it will be for people to "fall back" on general expectations for behaviors, which include sex-role expectations. Gender-linked behavior, therefore, would be more likely in novel and/or global situations than in familiar or specific ones.

Along with differences in the research setting, the measurement of study variables has come under scrutiny. With respect to the independent variable, is gender being used as a subject variable or as a stimulus variable (Deaux, 1984)? That is, do men and women behave differently or are they perceived to behave differently, regardless of their actual behavior? Unger (1989) has commented that finding gender-linked social behavior is more likely in settings in which the data involve the evaluations of and responses to a man or woman by others. Of particular interest is whether perceived gender differences are based on actual differences in behavior. Evidence from research on other social behaviors suggests that perceptions of behavior often reflect the sex-role bias of the observer, not actual differences between women and men actors (e.g., Korabik, Baril, & Watson, 1990).

With respect to the dependent variable, how is conflict behavior operationalized and measured? Conflict behavior can be assessed by global measures of conflict style such as the Thomas-Kilmann (T-K) MODE instrument, Hall's Conflict Management Survey, Rahim's Organizational Conflict Instrument, and the Conflict Tactics Scale (e.g., Chusmir & Mills, 1989; Korabik et al., 1990; Shockley-Zalabak, 1981); by self-report in specific situations (e.g., Canary, Cunningham, & Cody, 1988); by narrative (Pinkley & Northcraft, 1990; Gwartney-Gibbs & Lach, 1991); by behavioral observation (e.g., Burrell, Donohue, & Allen, 1988; Korabik et al., 1990); and by perceptions of other's behavior (e.g., Renwick, 1977). Such different approaches can also lead to different conclusions about gender-linked behavior. Evidence suggests that finding gender-related behavior is more likely under measurement conditions that: (a) limit individuality of responses in favor of predetermined alternatives, and/or (b) appear to strip behavior from its historical and cultural context (Gruber & White, 1986; Unger, 1990). These conditions are typical of the majority of the research reviewed in this chapter.

In the discussion that follows, I have grouped studies of gender and conflict that have been published since 1975 according to the relationship being studied (e.g., intimate, work, and stranger) rather than by type and setting of measurement. Consequently, it is important to keep in mind differences that could be due to these latter factors. The studies are representative but not exhaustive of current psychological research. My conclusions are intended to illuminate those features of conflict situations and their study that are consistently associated with findings of gender-linked conflict and influence behavior.

THE STUDIES

Intimate Relationships (Partners and Friends)

Studies of conflict in close relationships indicate more similarities than differences between women's and men's conflict management behavior. Sometimes women emphasize expression of feelings and criticism more than men do, and sometimes men emphasize denial and avoidance more than women do, but otherwise their reports of conflict management are similar.

Canary et al. (1988), for example, asked undergraduate students to describe a "typical" conflict in a close relationship and then to endorse the degree to which they used each of 47 tactics in dealing with the situation. Women were more likely to report using personal criticism and showing anger, whereas men were more likely to report denying the existence or extent of the conflict. Gruber and White (1986) had undergraduates rate the extent to which they used a number of personal power strategies in order to get their way with others. Women and men reported equal rates of feminine-typed strategies, but men reported using more masculine strategies. White and Roufail (1989) provided undergraduates with a list of 43 influence strategies and asked them (a) to indicate the frequency with which each would be used in "getting their own way" in interpersonal relationships, and (b) to identify the strategies of first choice and of last resort. Women and men did not differ in the hierarchy of strategies that they chose, but women and men did differ in the reported frequency of use of particular strategies. Women reported using negative emotion (such as crying, pouting, getting angry) more frequently than did men, whereas men reported using more coercive strategies than did women. Interestingly, these results parallel the patterns of influence noted between less and more powerful people (Hare-Mustin & Marecek, 1988; Kipnis, 1984). Ruble and Stander (1990), using the Thomas-Kilmann MODE instrument, compared women's and men's preferred conflict management styles "at work" and "in a social setting." Women and men did not differ in their preferred styles in social settings. Both preferred, in descending order, to accommodate, avoid, compromise, collaborate, and, least of all, to compete.

In studies in which participants use predetermined tactics or styles to indicate their conflict behavior in heterosexual partnerships, specifically, results are similar. Buunk, Schaap, and Prevoo (1990) had Dutch undergraduates indicate their own and their partners' style of conflict management. Men perceived themselves and were perceived by their partners as both avoiding emotional discussion and smoothing over differences. Women perceived themselves and were perceived by their partners as dealing more directly with the conflict in terms of pushing and problem solving. Chusmir and Mills (1989) found no differences, however, in conflict management styles that women and men preferred to use at home with their partners. Both preferred to use the following conflict strategies in descending order: accommodation, collaboration, compromise, avoidance, and competition—a finding somewhat similar to that of Ruble and Stander (1990), except that collaboration was ranked higher and avoidance lower by Chusmir and Mills' participants than by Ruble and Stander's.

According to Kelley et al.'s (1978) research, women's and men's reports of behavior in specific conflict situations may differ from their generalizations about typical conflicts. These researchers provided specific scenarios to couples who then selected from a predetermined list of comments what they would say or do in each of the situations. Women portrayed themselves, as did their partners, as more emotional and critical of the male's insensitivity. In turn, men portrayed themselves, as did their partners, as logical, unemotional, showing open anger, and providing reasons for a delay. These results, which are consistent with sex-role stereotypes, are also consistent with the findings of Buunk et al. (1990) and Canary et al. (1988). Thus, within the context of specific conflict situations, men are described as "conflict avoidant" and women as "conflict confrontive." But it is important to add that Kelley et al. also found non-sex-typed comments used more frequently than sex-typed comments by both women and men and concluded that women's and men's conflict behavior is largely interchangeable.

Emotional commitment, gender composition of the dyad, and relative status of the partners have also been found to play a role in women's and men's conflict behavior. Three studies examined the relationship between liking or commitment and use of conflict tactics among heterosexual couples. Billingham and Sack (1987), working with undergraduates, found that the more emotionally committed a couple was, the more they reported using reasoning and verbal aggression strategies. Still, irrespective of emotional involvement, the women reported using more reasoning and more verbal aggression than did the men in the sample. Interestingly, men perceived their female partners as engaging in more physical violence than vice versa. Again, women were characterized as more direct in managing conflict with their male partners.

In some contrast are Fitzpatrick and Winke's (1979) findings, which are based on undergraduates' use of conflict tactics with same-sex and opposite-sex others. Women and men endorsed similar strategies in dealing with opposite-sex others. The greater their emotional involvement, the more likely they were to report using strategies of emotional appeal (e.g., promise to be more loving) and personal rejection (e.g., withhold affection, ignore). The less involved they were, the more likely they were to use strategies of manipulation (acting nice, being pleasant) and nonnegotiation (refuse to discuss, repeating point of view). Women and men differed in how they dealt with same-sex friends, however. Women reported using more personal rejection, emotional appeal, and empathic understanding (e.g., focus on mutual needs) strategies, whereas men relied more on nonnegotiation strategies. Interestingly, the differences between women's and men's responses for same-sex relationships parallel differences for opposite-sex relationships that are high versus low in emotional involvement and may be related to theoretical distinctions between female connection and male autonomy that are often found in the literature.

Baxter and Shepherd (1978) found that attachment to the partner rather than gender made a difference in women's and men's approval of different management styles. The more emotional involvement their participants reported, the more likely they were to report using direct strategies, which emphasize emotional connection between partners. Thus, it may be that the relationships for which women and men are reporting conflict behavior differ in attachment and that gender differences in conflict behavior are due to these differences.

Two common features of the research reviewed thus far are reliance on undergraduate student samples and use of context-limited self-report instruments. Atkinson (1987), reviewing gender roles in marriage and family research, points out that the relationships of undergraduates are often relatively new and may not reflect the character of long-term relationships held by older couples. Self-reports may not accurately reflect actual behavior and its perception in a conflict situation. Hence, it is important to study long-term relationships using other than a self-report format.

Two recent studies of marital communication and interaction fit these requirements. Both found no difference in strategy use between wives and husbands. Bell, Chafetz, and Horn (1982) interviewed 30 married couples to identify decisions over which there was disagreement and strategies that had been used to resolve the conflict. Women and men mentioned similar strategies in the following descending order: influence, authority, control, and manipulation. Still, husbands tended to win the conflicts regardless of the strategies employed by them or their wives. These "wins" occurred regardless of their situation-specific resources or beliefs in the legitimacy of the various strategies. Bell, Chafetz, and Horn found that other resources such as educational level of the husband, labor force status of the wife, and family traditionalism were related to outcome. These three are social indicators of status and power, a point to which I return later.

In the only study of actual conflict behavior, Burggraf and Sillars (1987) analyzed audiotaped discussions of 77 heterosexual couples on issues of disagreement. They coded the tapes for instances of avoidance, competition, and cooperation and found little evidence of gender-linked verbal conflict styles, noting rather a tendency for communication acts to be reciprocated within a couple. Because they did find differences according to the couples' marital beliefs, they concluded that the norms of the couple influenced their verbal conflict behavior more than their gender did. Burggraf and Sillars (1987) note that their findings differ from those of self-report studies and may result from the interactive and reciprocal nature of conflict behavior. They argue that "self-reports are removed from the immediate influence of the partner's eliciting actions. Further, self-reports access images of self which may be swayed by stereotypes of appropriate sex-role behavior" (p. 291).

Whether the gender of one's partner influences conflict behavior has also been addressed. Women and men in Fitzpatrick and Winke's (1979) study reported using similar strategies with opposite-sex others but somewhat different strategies with same-sex others. But same- and opposite-sex relationships were not comparable because same-sex others were friends and opposite-sex others were romantic partners. Thus, women's and men's responses could not be clearly attributed to having either a male or female "partner" but may have been related to nuances in relationship definition.

Research on heterosexual and homosexual couples affords opportunities to compare the influence of partner's sex in love relationships. Falbo and Peplau (1980), for example, asked homosexual and heterosexual women and men to indicate how they got their way with their romantic partner. Gender-linked behavior was found only among heterosexuals, with men more likely to report using strategies labeled as *bilateral* and *direct* (e.g., bargaining and reasoning) and women more likely to report strategies labeled as *unilateral* and *indirect* (e.g., withdrawal and expression of negative feelings). These results parallel the findings on balance of power, such that those who preferred and saw themselves as having more power than their partner reported using more bilateral and direct strategies (see also Kipnis, 1984), and provide some support for the argument that (at least, self-reported) gender-linked influence and conflict behavior may reflect gender-linked differences in power (Eagly, 1987).

To identify the relative contributions of gender, sex-role orientation, and structural bases of power, Howard et al. (1986) compared influence strategies perceived to be used by both partners of naturally occurring heterosexual, homosexual, and lesbian couples.[1] Although sex

---

[1]Couples independently indicated the extent to which their partner would do each of 24 influence tactics in order to get their way. Six categories of influence were identified: manipulation (hints, flattery, reminding of past favors), supplication (pleading, crying, acting helpless), bullying (threats, insults, violence), autocracy (insisting, claiming greater knowledge, asserting authority), disen-

of the actor was not related to use of tactics, sex of the partner was related. Partners of men (heterosexual women and homosexual men) were perceived to use manipulation and supplication more than were partners of women (heterosexual men and lesbian women). Thus, "positions of weakness increase the likelihood of using weak tactics" (p. 107). However, even after controlling for structural bases of power, sex and sex-role orientation continued to account for significant variance in perceived use of weak tactics. This result suggests that sex and sex-role orientation had independent effects on perception of the partner's conflict behavior, beyond that accounted for by power differences.

In summary of the studies of intimate relationships, the following points can be made. Both women and men are perceived (by self and other) to engage in accommodative, avoidant, compromising, collaborative, and competitive behavior in conflict situations. As Kelley et al. (1978) note, male and female conflict styles are largely interchangeable. That some differences exist should be no more intriguing than the high degree of similarity. Use of conflict management behaviors seems to depend on the degree of emotional connection, relative access to power, and gender of one's partner. The extent to which the former two aspects co-vary with gender is not clear except that it is not a perfect correlation.

Perhaps more importantly, the way "conflict behavior" is measured influences the findings. Self-reports on global conflict management style as well as perceptions of partner's style tend to result in more findings of gender-linked effects than self-reports or observations of behavior in specific conflict situations. This suggests that global assessments may tap into cultural stereotypes, whereas more situation-specific assessments identify behavior with multiple causes, of which gender is only one. Observations by Kelley et al. (1978) and Gruber and White (1986) that women and men perceived themselves to use less sex-typed strategies than they perceived women in general and men in general would use support such an interpretation. The "standards" or norms we apply to our own behavior may also differ from those we apply to others so that we see others as more sex typed than we see ourselves (Deaux & Major, 1987; Unger, 1989). Thus, conclusions that people's perceptions of themselves or others reflects their own and others' behavior in actual situations may be inappropriate.

---

gagement (sulking, use of guilt, leaving), and bargaining (reasoning, offer to compromise, offer trade-off). Structural bases of power were differences between the partners' income, education, and age. In addition, a measure of relative perceived attractiveness was also constructed. Interpersonal bases of power included relative commitment to the relationship (Who is more committed?) and general dependence in the relationship (Who would be more disrupted by a breakup of your relationship?).

Work-Based Relationships

Studies of conflict management in work relationships also reveal few gender-linked behaviors, even when global measures are used. Duane (1989) had union and management officials indicate, using the T-K Conflict MODE instrument, how they generally handle grievance-related issues. He found no gender-linked preferences for compromise and collaboration, but women reported preferring competition more and avoidance and accommodation less than did men. Women reported competition as their most preferred strategy, whereas men reported collaboration. This is a sharply different picture than would be expected based on sex-role expectations. Indeed, it is exactly opposite to what would be predicted.

Ruble and Stander (1990) used the T-K Conflict MODE to study conflict management "at work" and "in social settings" by employees of business and nonprofessional organizations. They found that women and men differed only in preferred strategies at work. In contrast to results from Duane (1989), men endorsed competition and compromise as their most preferred styles and accommodation as their least preferred, whereas women endorsed compromise as their most preferred and competition and accommodation as their least preferred. Using another standardized measure of conflict management styles (Hall's Conflict Survey), Shockley-Zalabak (1981) found no difference in either the order of strategies preferred or the strength of those preferences for women and men managers. The descending order of preference was for collaboration, compromise, avoidance, accommodation, and competition.

The samples in these three studies differ. Duane (1989) surveyed a very select group of union/management officials, Shockley-Zalabak (1981) a group of management personnel, and Ruble and Stander (1990) a much more heterogeneous group of workers. Thus, the dramatic difference in women's and men's preferences among these studies may reflect the nature and/or status of the jobs the participants hold.

Two studies provide some insight into the influence of organizational position or rank on preferred conflict management style. Using the T-K MODE instrument, Chusmir and Mills (1989) had managers of banking, industry, and nonprofit organizations indicate their preferred styles of conflict management at home and at work. At work there was a relationship between position level and conflict management style, although the nature of this relationship was not reported. When position levels were held constant, however, women and men did not differ in preferred conflict management styles. Overall, collaboration and compromise were most preferred, whereas accommodating and competing were least preferred, an ordering similar to that found by Ruble and

Stander (1990) and Schockley-Zalabak (1981). Revilla (1984) had top, middle, and first-line college administrators respond to the same instrument and found that work experience and the nature of the organization, rather than gender of the respondent, were related to variability in conflict management style. These administrators reported that they competed and collaborated less but compromised and avoided more than a comparable group from business and government. In addition, more experienced administrators reported more competition, less compromise, and more assertiveness in general than those with less experience.

These studies, using global estimates of conflict behavior at work parallel the findings from studies of "intimate relationships" that use similar measures. Although there is some evidence for sex-role congruent behavior, there is more evidence for sex-role incongruent behavior, and most often no difference in preferences between women and men. The results of Revilla (1984) and Chusmir and Mills (1989) suggest that rank and experience may be stronger influences than gender. Because, as Eagly (1987) and others argue, women tend to have lower rank and less experience than men in organizations, it is important to examine research in which these characteristics are related to women's and men's conflict behavior.

Korabik, Baril, and Watson (1990) hypothesized that gender differences would be found only among "naive" managers. They assessed conflict behavior using self-reports, perceptions of others, and observations of behavior. MBA students completed the Rahim Organizational Conflict Instrument-II to assess their preferred conflict management styles and then role played a supervisor with three subordinates while being videotaped. As predicted, gender-linked preferences for conflict management style were found only among naive or inexperienced supervisors, in that women reported preferring collaboration, accommodation, and compromise more than men. There were no gender-linked differences in role-play performances, however, nor in outcomes attained by women and men. Still, women and men who used similar styles were evaluated differently by subordinates. Supervisor effectiveness was more negatively associated with competition and more positively associated with accommodation for women than for men. This result parallels that of Wiley and Eskilson (1982), who found that experienced managers (82% men) evaluated women and men differently depending on the power strategy they used. Women were viewed as more effective when they used reward power, whereas men were viewed as more effective when they used expert power.

Another two studies examined supervisor gender and confidence in the supervisory role as they relate to actual use of various influence strategies. In the first (Instone, Major, & Bunker, 1983), undergraduates who acted as supervisors in a simulated organizational setting were authorized to maintain standards among subordinates by using various influence strategies, including pay increases and decreases, transfer, firing, training, and positive, negative, or general talks. Most of the gender-linked differences found were weak and of marginal significance. Women used fewer attempts overall and a more limited range of strategies than men. They tended to use more coercive strategies and fewer rewarding strategies. However, women also had lower confidence in their supervisory abilities than men, and this explained the differences in number of influence attempts and choice of strategies. Among women and men in equal power positions, with equal access to resources, Instone et al. (1983) found little gender difference in supervisory behavior.

Koberg (1985) used the same simulation and found that women and men undergraduates did not differ in use of reward, coercive, or expert strategies when dealing with worker compliance. Unlike results from Instone et al., self-confidence in this study was not gender-linked. Similarly, Burrell, Donohue, and Allen (1988) found that gender differences in actual mediator behavior occurred only among untrained as distinguished from formally trained mediators. Thus, the evidence is that experience and training may be more powerful than gender in influencing actual conflict behavior.

As in close relationships in which the partner's gender and status make a difference in conflict management, so in work relationships the subordinate's and supervisor's gender require consideration. Renwick (1977) had women and men managers indicate how likely they were to use each of the five conflict management styles to handle differences with immediate supervisors. Using the same scales, managers also estimated how their supervisors responded. Women and men did not differ in self-reported styles of conflict management, citing compromise, collaboration, accommodation, competition, and avoidance in descending order. But women viewed their supervisors (all male) as less assertive (i.e., avoiding, accommodating, and compromising) than did men. Although there were no female supervisors in this study with whom to compare results for male supervisors, gender-linked differences were not apparent in subordinate behavior, at least toward male supervisors.

Offerman and Schrier (1985) examined the impact of gender and role (supervisor vs. subordinate) on undergraduates' self-reported use of social influence strategies in a hypothetical organizational dispute. Women were more likely than men to report using personal/dependent strategies (e.g., smile, tell them need support) and negotiation strategies (e.g., compromise), whereas men were more likely to report using indirect strategies (e.g., hints, manipulate) and reward/coercion. Women stressed strategies that focus on connection with the other and deny status difference, whereas men stressed strategies that acknowledge status differences (e.g., acting powerless or powerful). When responding as supervisors, both women and men were less likely to use withdrawal and negotiation and more likely to use unilateral strategies than when responding as subordinates. These responses parallel the strategies of the powerful and powerless. Role and gender did not interact. Unlike Renwick's (1977) participants, women and men believed they would respond somewhat differently, regardless of their role. The differences may result from differences in measurement, as Offerman and Schrier (1985) used a broad range of specific behaviors, whereas Renwick represented each style by a single statement.

Kipnis, Schmidt, and Wilkinson (1980) compared compliance-gaining strategies used by women and men with superiors, colleagues, and subordinates. Exchange strategies (remind of past favors, offer help), ingratiation strategies (act humbly, praise), and upward appeal strategies (support of higher ups) were reported equally for use with subordinates and co-workers and less for use with superiors, who evoked rational strategies (reasons, logic) most often. Job status was closely associated with the use of particular tactics. The higher respondents' positions in the organization, the more often they used direct tactics and the less often they were dependent on superiors. At similar levels of status and in similar status relationships, women and men chose similar tactics when attempting to get their way.

Only Instone et al. (1983), among these studies of position and experience, examined the impact of subordinate's gender on women's and men's conflict behavior. They found little impact of worker sex on actual supervisory behavior. The only effect was that female workers received more positive and encouraging talks from their supervisors (regardless of gender) than did their male counterparts. Their results were replicated by Offerman and Kearney (1988), who additionally found that participants responded differently to female and male supervisors. When considering interaction with a female supervisor, people were less likely to choose reasoning and negotiation strategies and more likely to choose withdrawal from the conflict than when considering interaction with a male supervisor.

Although women and men did not believe they would respond differently as supervisors in Offerman and Schrier's (1985) research, subordinates believed they would respond differently to female and male supervisors in the 1988 study. This is akin to Korabik et al.'s (1990) finding that although female and male supervisors did not see themselves or behave differently, subordinates made a distinction. In a somewhat related study, Burrell et al. (1988) found that even though women and men mediators did not differ in their behavior during a mediation session, women mediators were perceived by disputants as being less controlling than the men.

Looking specifically at the gender composition of the subordinate and supervisor dyad, Zammuto, London, and Rowland (1979) examined the supervisor's perception of the subordinate's conflict management behavior using resident assistants and their supervisors. In addition, commitment of the resident assistants to their job and to their supervisor was also measured. Briefly, male supervisors perceived male advisees to withdraw more and confront less than female supervisors perceived either their male or female advisees to do. Males reporting to females were perceived to use more accommodating, compromising, and collaborative behaviors when committed to the position. However, females reporting to females were perceived to avoid these strategies when committed to the position. In addition, as commitment to supervisor increased, females reporting to females and males reporting to males were reported to collaborate more and compete less.

Studies of conflict management such as these suggest that some findings reflect sex-role bias on the part of the observer rather than actors' actual behaviors. This is not a benign conclusion. It suggests that perceptions of men's and women's conflict management behavior may depend more on others' reactions than on their abilities or behavior (Korabik et al., 1990).

The summary of research on work relationships includes conclusions similar to those based on the research about personal relationships. Women and men are perceived and believed to engage in an equally extensive range of conflict behaviors. However, these behaviors (and, perhaps more so, the perception of these behaviors) are also influenced by the gender of the perceived, the gender of the target, and features of the dyadic relationship such as commitment, status, and role. Clearer in research focused on the work relationship is that actual gender differences in behavior are few and often accounted for by gender-linked differences in status, rank, experience, and self-confidence. Indeed, Ruble and Schneer (1991) found that only 5% of the variance in competing and compromising styles (which showed the most consistent gender-linked differences across four samples in their study) was due to gender of the respondent. Such estimates of effect size corroborate other results as to the stronger influence of variables other than gender.

Gender-linked conflict behavior is also more likely to be found in studies in which measurements do not identify a specific relationship and, more particularly, a specific conflict situation. The inconsistency of gender-linked behaviors when found, that is, they are sometimes sex-role congruent and sometimes sex-role incongruent, supports the value of studying situations in which sex-role expectations or norms are salient and influential (see Deaux & Major, 1987, 1990).

Stranger Relationships

It could be argued that many studies of workplace relationships also fall into the category of stranger relationships, as most involve role playing between strangers. However, a few have used tasks that are uncharacteristic of workplace relationships and, hence, are of interest here. Using a buyer-seller negotiation simulation with same-sex dyads, Pruitt, Carnevale, Forcey, & Van Slyck (1986) found no differences in actual negotiation behavior or outcome for women and men. However, there were differences in women's and men's perceptions of their behavior as negotiators. Consistent with sex-role stereotypes, men saw themselves as more competitive, whereas women saw themselves as more cooperative, more trusting of the other negotiator, and more powerless despite the lack of discernable differences in actual behavior.

Similarly, using a social dilemma paradigm, Stockard, Van de Kragt, & Dodge (1988) found no difference in the cooperative behavior of women and men, although women described themselves as acting more for altruistic reasons and men described themselves as acting more for selfish or principled motives. Thus, expressed motives coincided with sex role expectations, whereas overt behavior was not discriminably different. Worth noting is that both the negotiation and social dilemma simulations demanded very specific negotiation behavior, leaving little room for the operation of other norms. That women and men behaved similarly in these studies points to the importance of situational factors as compared to "inherent" differences.

The "gap" between perceptual and behavioral measures appeared in another study of women's and men's conflict behavior that used a different paradigm than those considered previously. Molm (1985) investigated the impact of structural power imbalances in same-sex and opposite-sex dyads on behavioral and cognitive dimensions of power use. Participants were randomly assigned to be the more or less powerful person and interacted with one another via computer-operated test consoles in different rooms. They were given two response choices: a social exchange response that would produce a reward for the other and an individual behavior that would produce a reward for themselves. Total earnings would depend on both participants' responses. Participants were instructed to maximize their own gains. Women and men in powerful positions did not differ in actual use of power and were evaluated similarly, but power use was differentially related to evaluation of the more powerful person, depending on the less powerful person's sex. Power use by a powerful partner influenced women's perceptions of the partner's competence but was unrelated to men's perception of the partner. Sex composition of the dyad also influenced perceptions of the powerful other. In opposite-sex dyads, evaluations of the powerful person were influenced less by power use than in same-sex dyads. It appears as though gender became a differentiating characteristic in opposite-sex dyads and affected the links between actual behavior and attributions of power without differentially affecting actual behavior or overall attributions.

Together, these studies suggest that even when there is no discernable gender-linked difference in overt behavior and perceptions of behavior, the processes underlying perceptions of behavior may be gender-linked. Thus, in understanding the relationship of gender with influence generally and with conflict in particular, not only the goals, motives, intentions, and perceptions of the members of the dyad should be considered but also the processes by which these relate to behavior (Deaux & Major, 1987).

Some Conclusions About Gender and Conflict

Overall, it is clear that women and men are equally capable of the conflict behaviors described in these studies. Thus, the research provides little evidence of gender differences in abilities and skills related to conflict management. Rather it supports Deaux's (1984) argument that women and men have similar potentials. Second, there is evidence among these studies that sex-role expectations appear to influence behavior and perceptions of behavior in particular circumstances. Gender-linked conflict behavior appears to occur most often when the relationship context or situation is vaguely defined, when perceptions of the other's behavior are assessed, when short-term relationships in opposite-sex dyads are the focus, and when global self-report assessments are used.

Third, these studies provide evidence of influences and norms other than sex-role expectations that may affect and influence conflict and behavior. In the realm of intimate, ongoing, personal relationships, "the intimacy and temporal permanence of family relationships allow spouses to abandon culturally determined standards for behavior and replace them with personally negotiated norms" (Burggraf & Sillars, 1987, p. 278). Similarly, within the organizational context, structural bases of power, experience, and job status are stronger influences on behavior than is gender per se. To discover these more specific norms requires research methods and measurement strategies that are sensitive to conflict at different levels of analysis (e.g., intrapersonal, interpersonal, group, and intergroup) and that capture its dynamic nature in specific situations. Little research to date has used such methods or measures.

Fourth, evidence suggests that the experience and meaning of conflict may differ for women and men. Several studies not discussed earlier highlight gender-linked differences in experiences of conflict. In focused interviews with women and men clerical and maintenance workers, Gwartney-Gibbs and Lach (1991) found that the origin, processes, and outcomes of workplace disputes differed somewhat for women and men. Although both spoke of conflicts about family and day care, benefits, and grievance, women more often reported interpersonally oriented conflicts that were not being managed by institutionalized dispute resolution methods. Some women chose to make lateral moves to get out of the situations that affected their movement hierarchically in the organization.

Weingarten and Douvan (1985) spoke with equally well-known and well-respected female and male mediators about how they viewed and carried out their roles as mediators. Women viewed their goal to be an understanding of parties and their differences, whereas men saw their goal to be the development of an agreement. Men believed they should be neutral, whereas women believed they should facilitate balance between conflicting parties. Miller's (1991) work on women's and men's interpersonal conflict scripts found little difference in the components of the script but differences in how the components went together. Men perceived the offended to be the one who decides when the conflict is over, whereas women perceived that both the offended and the offender needed to agree. Each of these studies indicate the importance of looking not only at "outcomes," whether in behavioral or perceptual terms, but also at processes of "achieving" outcomes and the interpretation of these outcomes by those involved.

Finally, worth attention is the persistence of beliefs in gender-linked behavior even when these behaviors are not found in research. Similarly noteworthy are differences in how women and men are treated and perceive themselves to be treated when their behavior differs little. The existence of perceived differences in behavior in the absence of observed differences promotes consideration of the impact of others' expectations on interactions in conflict. Do we deal with women and men differently as a result of these expectations? Do we assume "differences" are natural and inevitable and use them as a basis for discrimination? How do we deal with men and women who behave in sex-role incongruent ways, that is, those who behave "out of character"? Such questions need to be addressed more than researchers have done to date.

It is within a dynamic interplay of expectations, perceptions, and behavior that the role of gender in conflict lies. To speak of "gender differences" is a misnomer. To speak of "gendering" and "conflicting" may be more accurate. By far the majority of our research in gender and conflict is static and contextless. Our measurements and our research methods need to reflect this more dynamic nature in order to transform our description and understanding of conflict and of gender.

REFERENCES

Atkinson, J. (1987). Gender roles in marriage and the family: A critique and some proposals. *Journal of Family Issues, 8*(1), 5-41.

Baumeister, R.F., Stillwell, A., & Wotman, S.R. (1990). Victim and perpetrator interpersonal conflict: Autobiographical narratives about anger. *Journal of Personality and Social Psychology, 59*(5), 994-1005.

Baxter, L.A., & Shepherd, T.L. (1978). Sex-role identity, sex of other, and affective relationship as determinants of interpersonal conflict-management style. *Sex Roles, 4*(6), 813-825.

Bell, D.C., Chafetz, J.S., & Horn, L.H. (1982). Marital conflict resolution: A study of strategies and outcomes. *Journal of Family Issues, 3*(1),111-132.

Billingham, R.E., & Sack, A.R. (1987). Conflict tactics and the level of emotional commitment among unmarrieds. *Human Relations, 40*(1), 59-74.

Burrell, N.A., Donohue, W.A., & Allen, A. (1988). Gender-based perceptual biases in mediation. *Communication Research, 15*(4), 447-469.

Burggraf, C.S., & Sillars, A.L. (1987). A critical examination of sex differences in marital communication. *Communication Monographs, 54,* 276-294.

Buunk, B.P., Schaap, C., & Prevoo, N. (1990). Conflict resolution styles attributions to self and partner in premarital relationships. *The Journal of Social Psychology, 130*(6), 821-823.

Canary, D.J., Cunningham, E.M., & Cody, M.J. (1988). Goal types, gender, and locus of control in managing interpersonal conflict. *Communication Research, 15*(4), 426-446.

Chusmir, L.H., & Mills, J. (1989). Gender differences in conflict resolution styles of managers: At work and at home. *Sex Roles, 20*(3/4), 149-163.

Deaux, K. (1984). From individual differences to social categories: Analysis of a decade's research on gender. *American Psychologist, 39*(2), 105-116.

Deaux, K., & Major, B. (1987). Putting gender into context: An interactive model of gender-related behavior. *Journal of Personality and Social Psychology, 94*(3), 369-389.

Deaux, K., & Major, B. (1990). A social-psychological model of gender. In D.L. Rhode (Ed.), *Theoretical perspectives on sexual difference* (pp. 89-99). New Haven, CT: Yale University Press.

Duane, M.J. (1989). Sex differences in styles of conflict management. *Psychological Reports, 65,* 1033-1034.

Eagly, A.H. (1983). Gender and social influence: A social psychological analysis. *American Psychologists, 38,* 971-981.

Eagly, A.H. (1987). *Sex differences in social behavior: A social role interpretation.* Hillsdale, NJ: Lawrence Erlbaum Associates.

Eagly, A.H., & Johnson, B.T. (1990). Gender and leadership style: A meta-analysis. *Psychological Bulletin, 108*(2), 233-256.

Fagenson, E.A. (1990). At the heart of women in management research: Theoretical and methodological approaches and their biases. *Journal of Business Ethics, 9,* 267-274.

Falbo, T., & Peplau, L.A. (1980). Power strategies in intimate relationships. *Journal of Personality and Social Psychology, 38*(4), 618-628.

Felstiner, W.F., Abel, R.L., & Sarat A. (1980/1981). The emergence and transformation of disputes: Naming, blaming, claiming. . . . *Law and Society Review, 15*(3/4), 631-654.

Fitzpatrick, M.A., & Winke, J. (1979). You always hurt the one you love: Strategies and tactics in interpersonal conflict. *Communication Quarterly, 7,* 3-11.

Gilligan, C. (1982). *In a different voice: Psychological theory and women's development.* Cambridge, MA: Harvard University Press.

Gruber, K.J. & White, J.W. (1986). Gender differences in perceptions of self's and others' use of power strategies. *Sex Roles, 15*(1/2), 109-118.

Gwartney-Gibbs, P.A., & Lach, D.H. (1991). Workplace dispute resolution and gender inequality. *Negotiation Journal, 7*(2), 187-200.

Hare-Mustin, R.T., & Marecek, J. (1988). The meaning of difference: Gender theory, postmodernism, and psychology. *American Psychologist, 43*(6), 455-464.

Howard, J.A., Blumstein, P., & Schwartz, P. (1986). Sex, power, and influence tactics in intimate relationships. *Journal of Personality and Social Psychology, 51*(1), 102-109.

Instone, D., Major, B., & Bunker, B.B. (1983). Gender, self-confidence, and social influence strategies: An organizational simulation. *Journal of Personality and Social Psychology, 44*(2), 322-333.

Jaggar, A.M. (1990). Sexual difference and sexual equality. In D.L. Rhode (Ed.), *Theoretical perspectives on sexual difference* (pp. 239-254). New Haven, CT: Yale University Press.

Kelley, H.H., Cunningham, J.D., Grisham, J.A. Lefebvre, L.M., Sink, C.R., & Yablon, G. (1978). Sex differences in comments made during conflict within close heterosexual pairs. *Sex Roles, 4*(4), 473-492.

Kipnis, D. (1984). The use of power in organizations and in interpersonal settings. In S. Oskamp (Ed.), *Applied social psychology annual* (Vol. 5, pp. 179-210). Beverly Hills, CA: Sage.

Kipnis, D., Schmidt, S.M., & Wilkinson, I. (1980). Intraorganizational influence tactics: Explorations in getting one's way. *Journal of Applied Psychology, 65*(4), 440-452.

Koberg, C.S. (1985). Sex and situational influences on the use of power: A follow-up study. *Sex Roles, 13*(11/12), 625-639.

Korabik, K., Baril, G.L., & Watson, C. (1990). *Managers' conflict management and leadership effectiveness: The moderating effects of sex.* Unpublished manuscript, University of Guelph, Guelph, Ontario, Canada.

MacKinnon, C.A. (1990). Legal perspectives on sexual difference. In D.L. Rhode (Ed.), *Theoretical perspectives on sexual difference* (pp. 213-225). New Haven, CT: Yale University Press.

Markus, H., & Oyserman, D. (1989). Gender and thought: The role of self-concept. In M. Crawford & M. Gentry (Eds.), *Gender and thought* (pp. 100-127). New York: Springer-Verlag.

Miller, J.B. (1991). Women's and men's scripts for interpersonal conflict. *Psychology of Women Quarterly, 15,* 15-29.

Molm, L.D. (1985). Gender and power use: An experimental analysis of behavior and perceptions. *Social Psychology Quarterly, 48*(4), 285-300.

Northrup, T.A. (1989). The dynamic of identity in personal and social conflict. In L. Kriesberg, T.A. Northrup, & S.J. Thorson (Eds.), *Intractable conflicts and their transformation* (pp. 55-82). Syracuse, NY: Syracuse University Press.

Offerman, L.R., & Kearney, C.T. (1988). Supervisor sex and subordinate influence strategies. *Personality and Social Psychology Bulletin, 14*(2), 360-367.

Offerman, L.R., & Schrier, P.E. (1985). Social influence strategies: The impact of sex, role, and attitudes toward power. *Personality and Social Psychology Bulletin, 11*(3), 286-300.

Peterson, D.R. (1983). Conflict. In H.H. Kelley, E. Berscheid, A. Christensen, J.H. Harvey, T.L. Huston, G. Levinger, E. McClintock, L.A. Peplau, & D.R. Peterson (Eds.), *Close relationships* (pp. 360-396). New York: Freeman.

Pinkley, R. (1990). Dimensions of conflict frame: Disputant interpretations of conflict. *Journal of Applied Psychology, 75*(2), 117-126.

Pinkley, R.L., & Northcraft, G.B. (1990). *Cognitive interpretations of conflict: Implications for dispute processes and outcomes.* Unpublished manuscript.

Pruitt, D.G., Carnevale, P.J.D., Forcey, B., & Van Slyck, M. (1986). Gender effects in negotiation: Constituent surveillance and contentious behavior. *Journal of Experimental Social Psychology, 22,* 264-275.

Renwick, P.A. (1977). The effects of sex differences on the perception and management of superior-subordinate conflict: An exploratory study. *Organizational Behavior and Human Performance, 19,* 403-415.

Revilla, V.M. (1984). *Conflict management styles of men and women administrators in higher education.* Unpublished doctoral dissertation, University of Pittsburgh, PA.

Rhode, D. (1990). Theoretical perspectives on sexual differences. In D.L.

Rhode (Ed.), *Theoretical perspectives on sexual difference* (pp. 1-9). New Haven, CT: Yale University Press.

Rubin, J.Z., & Brown, B.R. (1975). *The social psychology of bargaining and negotiation.* New York: Academic Press.

Ruble, T.L., & Schneer J.A. (1991, January). *Gender differences in conflict handling styles.* Paper presented at the Conference on Gender and Conflict, George Mason University, Fairfax, VA.

Ruble, T.L., & Stander, N.E. (1990). *Effects of roles and gender on conflict-handling styles.* Unpublished manuscript, Rider College, Lawrenceville, NJ.

Schockley-Zalabak, P. (1981). The effects of sex differences on the preference for utilization of conflict styles of managers in a work setting: An exploratory study. *Public Personnel Management Journal, 10,* 289-295.

Sheppard, B.H. (1984). Third party conflict intervention: A procedural framework. *Research in Organizational Behavior, 6,* 141-190.

Sheppard, B.H., Blumenfeld-Jones, K., Minton, J.W., & Hyder, E. (1990). *Informal conflict intervention: Advice and dissent.* Unpublished manuscript, Duke University, Durham, NC.

Sherif, C.W. (1982). Needed concepts in the study of gender. *Psychology of Women Quarterly, 6,* 375-398.

Stockard, J., Van de Kragt, A.J.C., & Dodge, P.J. (1988). Gender roles and behavior in social dilemmas: Are there sex differences in cooperation and its justification? *Social Psychology Quarterly, 51*(2), 154-163.

Unger, R.K. (1981). Sex as a social reality: Field and laboratory research. *Psychology of Women Quarterly, 5*(4), 645-653.

Unger, R.K. (1989). Sex, gender, and epistemology. In M. Crawford & M. Gentry (Eds.), *Gender and thought: Psychological Perspectives* (pp. 17-35). New York: Springer-Verlag.

Unger, R.K. (1990). Imperfect reflections of reality: Psychology constructs gender. In D.L. Rhode (Ed.), *Theoretical perspectives on sexual difference* (pp. 102-149). New Haven, CT: Yale University Press.

Weingarten, H.R., & Douvan, E. (1985). Male and female visions of mediation. *Negotiation Journal, 1*(4), 349-358.

White, J.W. (1988). Influence tactics as a function of gender, insult, and goal. *Sex Roles, 18*(7/8), 433-448.

White, J.W., & Roufail, M. (1989). Gender and influence strategies of first choice and last resort. *Psychology of Women Quarterly, 13,* 175-189.

Wiley, M.G., & Eskilson, A. (1982). The interaction of sex and power base on perceptions of managerial effectiveness. *Academy of Management Journal, 25*(3), 671-677.

Zammuto, R.F., London, M., & Rowland, K.M. (1979). Effects of sex on commitment and conflict resolution. *Journal of Applied Psychology, 64*(2), 227-231.

9

Gender Differences in Negotiating Behavior and Outcomes: Fact or Artifact?

Carol Watson
Rider College

Many long-standing assumptions about gender differences have been challenged and debunked by researchers since the late 1970s. In the organizational arena, this process of challenging and discrediting old assumptions has been particularly evident in the leadership field (e.g., see Powell, 1990). However, relatively little such activity has occurred with respect to conflict management in general and negotiation in particular.

The lack of attention to whether assumed gender differences in negotiating behavior really do exist may reflect the fact that researchers considered gender differences in this area fairly extensively during the 1950s, 1960s, and early 1970s, and generally agreed on a favorable view of women (see Rubin & Brown, 1975, for the most recent review). The image of women that has emerged from research on negotiation and bargaining has been one of cooperative fair-mindedness as against men's image of competitive selfishness (e.g., Vinacke, 1959). This positive overarching image of women is somewhat misleading, however, because women's cooperativeness has generally been equated with weakness and ineffectiveness. Despite the early recognition that cooperation is important for mutually satisfactory outcomes from conflict (Blake & Mouton, 1964; Deutsch, 1949), researchers interested in negotiation and bargaining have generally adopted the view that winning is the desired outcome regardless of how the other party fares. Thus, although women have frequently been portrayed as nicer negotiators than men, because niceness does not help one to win, men have been credited with being more effective negotiators than women.

Given the lack of recent attention to gender differences in negotiating and the mounting evidence from the leadership field that gender differences do not hold when women achieve positions of power, it is important to revisit the question of whether there are gender differences in negotiating behavior and/or outcomes, or whether previously observed differences may be an artifact of status and power differences between men and women in the United States. The purpose of this chapter, therefore, is to review the more recent research pertinent to this question (since Rubin & Brown's review was published in 1975). Four theoretical perspectives have been identified that provide competing predictions about the source of observed and/or assumed gender differences in negotiation and conflict management:

1. The sex-role socialization perspective.
2. The situational power perspective.
3. The gender/power additive perspective.
4. The expectation states theory perspective.

Research relevant to these four perspectives is reviewed in an effort to clarify whether gender differences in negotiating behaviors and outcomes do exist or whether they are an artifact of status and power differences.

THEORETICAL BACKGROUND

The Sex-Role Socialization Perspective

The sex-role socialization perspective predicts that men and women will negotiate differently because of the different behavioral expectations associated with their respective gender roles. Women in U.S. culture are taught to be nurturant and supportive. Therefore, women are expected to avoid direct confrontation and to be softer, more accomodative negotiators than men. Men are taught to be tough and task-oriented. Thus, they are expected to be harder, more competitive negotiators than women.

As pointed out earlier, this has been the predominant view in the negotiation and bargaining literature although the empirical data do not provide consistent support for it (see Rubin & Brown, 1975). Nevertheless, women are generally believed to be softer negotiators, to prefer an accomodative style, to be generous, and to be more concerned that all parties are treated fairly than about gaining positive substantive outcomes for themselves (Terhune, 1970; Vinacke, 1959). Men, on the other hand, are believed to be tough negotiators, to make many demands and few concessions, and to be more concerned about winning positive substantive outcomes for themselves than about how the other party fares (Bartos, 1970; Terhune, 1970). Men are also believed to be more flexible negotiators than women, using a tit-for-tat strategy more often and being better at finding rational strategies that allow them to maximize gains (Terhune, 1970).

Although the previous paragraph details the prevailing version of the sex-role socialization perspective, some researchers have found support for a more negative depiction of women bargainers. For instance, women have sometimes been found to lock into an unrelenting competitive stance when their partners refuse to cooperate, and this behavior has been construed by some as vindictive (Rapoport & Chammah, 1965; Tedeschi, Shlenker, & Bonoma, 1973). Still others have questioned women's negotiating competence, claiming that women's behavior in negotiations is similar to that of men who do not understand the rules of the game (Caplow, 1968; Kelley, 1965), an explanation more consistent with the socialization perspective.

The bottom line here is that gender differences have frequently been found in studies of negotiation, bargaining, and conflict. The effects are often weak and inconsistent, yet they are prevalent. Although some have attributed these differences to women's greater concern for relationships and fairness, and others have attributed them to women's incompetence, disinterest, or vindictiveness, virtually no one has concluded that women are effective negotiators or bargainers.

The Situational Power Perspective

The situational power perspective questions the existence of gender differences. According to this view, observed gender differences are an artifact of men's and women's differential access to power in U.S. society (Epstein, 1970; Kanter, 1977; Meeker, & Weitzell-O'Neill, 1977; Terborg, 1977). This approach was popularized by Kanter (1977) who has argued that women behave the way any person in a low power position would behave. According to this perspective, observed gender differences should disappear once women obtain positions with power.

In support of the situational power perspective, status has been shown to determine the amount of power a person has in interactions with others (Berger, Fisek, Norman, & Zelditch, 1977), and gender has been shown to be a status characteristic that confers higher status on men and lower status on women (Lockheed & Hall, 1975). Based on Berger et al.'s theory it has been proposed that women are not really any more motivated to help others or to prefer harmony and equality of outcomes than men in conflict situations, but that they are forced to behave this way because of their lower status (Meeker & Weitzel-O'Neill, 1977). The literature on disputing shows differences in the behavior of high- and low-power negotiators that exactly mirror the assumed gender differences in negotiator behavior and outcomes (Bartos, 1970). Because women generally have lower status and hence less power than men, and because women are more likely to be found in low status, low power occupations and positions than men, we may have been misled into assuming that observed differences between men and women are due to gender when in fact they result from status and power differences.

Gender/Power Additive Hypothesis

It is also possible that giving a person situational power does not eliminate the effects of his or her gender status. Some have argued that gender and power statuses combine additively to determine negotiation behavior and outcomes (Fagenson, 1990; Powell, Posner, & Schmidt, 1984; Terborg, 1977). From this perspective, both the sex-role socialization and the situational power hypotheses are correct. As a result, being male is expected to enhance one's situational power, whereas being female is expected to detract from it. Similarly, being male is expected to mitigate situational powerlessness, whereas being female is expected to exacerbate it. Thus, men in high power positions should be the most powerful, and hence the most competitive and successful negotiators, whereas women in low power positions should be the least powerful, and hence the least competitive and least successful negotiators. Because men are most often in high power positions and women in low power positions, attributing the observed differences in their negotiating behavior to gender alone might be erroneous. If this hypothesis regarding the additive effects of gender and power is correct, men in low power positions and women in high power positions should be equivalent and intermediate in their power and hence in their competitiveness and success.

Expectation States Theory Perspective

A more complex and theoretically developed model, derived from expectation states theory (Berger et al., 1977) as applied specifically to power relationships (Molm, 1986), predicts that the influence of gender and power will depend on whether negotiators are in same or mixed-sex pairs. According to this perspective, gender is activated as a status characteristic only in mixed-sex pairs because it is only in these pairs that gender differentiates the parties.

Expectation states theory proposes that status characteristics establish performance expectations in small group settings such that high status individuals (i.e., men) are expected to be more competent than low status individuals (i.e., women). Because of these expectations, high status individuals do in fact initiate more, they receive more positive reactions from others, and they have more influence. Thus, when a man and a woman negotiate, gender is expected to determine who is more powerful in the sense of controlling the negotiation, and hence who is more successful. When their situational power differs, gender is expected to interact with power in such a way that it diminishes a woman's power in the presence of a male and enhances a man's power in the face of a female. In other words, it will be only slightly easier for high power than lower power women to control negotiations with low power men, but it will be much easier for high power than low power men to control negotiations with low power women. To date, no studies have tested the full hypothesis, however, so the discussion here is restricted to pairs in which a power imbalance exists.

To summarize the various predictions these theoretical perspectives make about the negotiating behavior of men and women, let us consider what each perspective predicts with respect to competitive, self-oriented behavior. The prevailing version of the sex-role socialization theory hypothesizes that men, regardless of their situational power, will behave more competitively than women. The situational power theory predicts that high power individuals, regardless of their gender, will behave more competitively than low power individuals, regardless of their gender. The gender/power additive hypothesis predicts that gender status will combine with situational power in such a way that high power men will behave more competitively than anyone else, low power men and high power women will be equivalent and intermediate in competitive behavior, and low power women will behave least competitively. Finally, expectation states theory predicts that the additive effects of gender and power will be found in mixed-sex pairs but not in same-sex pairs. The impact of the opponent's gender is expected to exaggerate men's situational power advantage and minimize women's in mixed-sex pairs such that high power men should be significantly more competitive than their low power female opponents, but high power women should not be more competitive than their low power male opponents. In same-sex pairs only situational power should operate so that high power females with female opponents should be no less competitive than high power males with male opponents.

LITERATURE REVIEW

Sample of Studies

Altogether, 34 studies were found that have addressed the topic of gender differences in negotiation, conflict, power, or influence since 1975. Only 8 of these tested both gender and power, however, so it is these 8 studies that provided the data for this review (see Table 9.1 for a listing and brief description of the relevant studies).

Sixteen studies were excluded because they tested only gender, or gender combined with other independent variables not directly related to power. As an aside, the story these 16 studies tell about gender differences is just as confusing as that told by the 100 studies reviewed by Rubin and Brown (1975). In some cases, support for the positive, cooperative image of women bargainers was found (e.g., Kimmel, Pruitt, Magenau, Konar-Goldband, & Carnevale, 1980; Wall, 1976); in others, support for women as "illogical," inept, or disinterested, bargainers was found (e.g., Hottes & Kahn, 1974; Kimmel et al., 1980; Wall, 1976; Watson & Kasten, 1987); and in still others, no differences at all were found (e.g., Koberg, 1985; Pruitt, Carnevale, Forcey, & Van Slyck, 1986, Wall, 1977). In many cases, support for more than one of these perspectives could be found in the same study.

One new variable that has emerged in recent years as a potential mediator of gender differences is partner's gender. Several studies provided convincing evidence that gender differences are greater in same-sex pairs than in mixed-sex pairs (Carli, 1989; Mulac, Weimann, Widenmann, & Gibson, 1988). This possibility is considered in some detail later in the chapter because, as the reader may have noted, it conflicts with the predictions of the expectation states theoretical perspective. It is consistent with the socialization perspective, however, in that it rests on the assumption that individuals match their behavior to that expected from a partner. Thus, men should behave more gently with a female partner, whereas women should behave more forcefully with a male partner. These astereotypical behavior patterns should minimize gender differences in mixed-sex pairings compared to same-sex pairings in which the parties should exhibit high rates of gender-stereotypical behavior.

Nine studies were excluded because they were based on paper-and-pencil self-report measures rather than actual behavior or outcomes. The author's own past research has cast doubt on the predic-

Table 9.1. List and Description of the Studies Reviewed

	Subject Population[1]	Group Composition[2]	Task	Source of Power	Dependent Variable	Hypothesis Supported[3]
1. Dovidio et. al., 1988	U	MS	Reach agreement on 3 discussion questions	Expert and reward power	Visual Dominance	P
2. Kravitz & Iwaniszek, 1984	U	SS	Coalition formation	Number of votes and alternatives	Payoff differences	G x P
3. Molm, 1986	U	SS/MS	Prisoner's dilemma choice task	Control over own outcomes	Power usage	G x P
4. Putnam & Jones, 1982	G/U	SS/MS	Labor-management role play	Role	Bargainer tactics	P
5. Scudder, 1988	U	SS	Buyer-seller game	Role	Tactics and profit	G x P
6. Siderits et al., 1985	U	MS	Meliam Dialogues	Role	Expressions of hostility	P
7. Stake & Stake, 1979	U	MS	Reach agreement on discussion task	Performance-related self-esteem	Change in opinion	G x P
8. Watson, 1991	M	SS/MS	Negotiation role-play	Role	Feelings, behavior, and outcomes	P, G G x P

[1]U = undergraduates G = graduate students M = Managers; [2]SS = same-sex MS = mixed-sex; [3]P = situational power G = gender G x P = gender x power interaction.

tive validity of paper-and-pencil measures of conflict management styles (Baril, Watson, & Korabik, 1990). The low correlation between subjects' scores on conflict management inventories and their actual conflict behavior is another manifestation of the problem personality theorists have grappled with for several decades in trying to predict behavior from personality measures (Bem & Allen, 1974; Epstein, 1979; Mischel, 1968; Mischel & Peake, 1982). Some techniques have been recommended for improving the predictive validity of paper-and-pencil measures (e.g., Bem & Allen, 1974; Epstein, 1979), but they have not been adopted by researchers in the conflict area. Consequently, data based on self-reports are potentially misleading.

Finally, one study was excluded (Kollock, Blumstein, & Schwartz, 1985) because it was based on comparisons of hetero- and homosexual couples. The comparability of gay and lesbian couples to same-sex pairs of unacquainted strangers was thought to be sufficiently questionable to warrant exclusion of this study. (The results from this study supported the situational power perspective.)

Gender Versus Power as Predictors of Behavior and Outcomes

Four of the eight studies that examined power and gender found strong support for power and little or no support for gender as a predictor of behavior and/or outcomes (Dovidio, Ellyson, Keating, & Heltman, 1988; Putnam & Jones, 1982; Siderits, Johannsen, & Fadden, 1985; Watson, 1991) and are discussed later. The other four studies found interactions between power and gender (Kravitz & Iwaniszek, 1984; Scudder, 1988; Stake & Stake, 1979) and are discussed in the next section.

Dovidio et al. were interested in visual dominance in mixed-sex pairs of students (defined as the ratio of looking while speaking to looking while listening). They found that power, in the form of expertise (greater knowledge and/or familiarity with the subject being discussed), or, to a lesser extent, reward power (being asked by the experimenter to critique the other's arguments and award points or not), determined visual dominance. These researchers included a control condition in which neither party had reward power or greater expertise. In this condition, as predicted, men exhibited more visual dominance than women.

Putnam and Jones (1982) found that the bargaining behavior of industrial relations students who took part in a simulated labor/management dispute was determined by assignment to either a labor (low status) or management (high status) role. Subjects in the labor role used more offensive strategies (i.e., threats, rejections, demands, attacking arguments, etc.), whereas those in the management role used more defensive behaviors (i.e., retractions, accommodations, promises, commitments, rational arguments). Out of the many analyses these authors conducted on their data, the only gender difference that emerged was a trend ($p < .07$) for men to use more rejection statements than women.

Siderits et al. (1985) used a simulation (the Melian Dialogues) that is based on the actual historical confrontation between the elders of the tiny island of Melos (long-time allies of Sparta) and the admirals of Athens. This simulation pitted four-person groups of men against four-person groups of women who alternated in the high power Athenian roles and low power Melian roles during the simulation (order of role assignment was counterbalanced). The researchers were interested in what the impact of assignment to power roles would be on expressions of hostility and anxiety by members of the same-sex teams. The results showed a highly significant effect for role ($p < .0001$) and no effect for gender. The high power role elicited significantly more overtly hostile content, whereas the low power role elicited more covert hostility and anxiety regardless of the gender of the subjects or the order of participation. A gender main effect was found for amount of talking with men talking more than women ($p < .02$), but subsequent analyses that controlled for loquaciousness yielded the same findings with respect to expressions of hostility and anxiety.

Watson (1991) examined the impact of gender and power on the perceptions, behavior, and outcomes achieved by practicing managers who took part in a simulated negotiation. Participants were randomly assigned to either same-sex or mixed-sex pairs and within each pair, one person was assigned to a high power role, whereas the other was assigned to a low power role. Male and female managers differed significantly in the number of years they had worked and in their degree of acquaintance with their assigned partners so these variables were controlled for in the analyses. Watson found main effects for power and gender, but the number, as well as the strength, of the power effects was greater than that of the gender effects. The results showed that, regardless of gender, participants in the high power role felt more competitive, more powerful, more in control, expected more cooperation from their opponents, were more likely to use a problem-solving approach, were less likely to use promises, felt more satisfied with the outcome, and believed they had been more successful, but were actually less successful than participants in low power roles. The main effects for gender showed that women reported lower self-confidence before negotiating, less satisfaction with their own negotiating behavior, and believed they had been less successful than men.

These four studies indicate that power is a better predictor of bargaining behavior and outcomes than gender. The kinds of gender effects that remain once power differences are accounted for appear to be related to how women feel about the situation or themselves and to some aspects of their behavior, but not to their ability to influence or bargain.

Gender/Power Additive Hypothesis

The reader will recall that this hypothesis predicts that the effects of gender and power accumulate in such a way that men in positions of power will be more powerful, and hence competitive and successful, than women in low power positions. Low power men and high power women are viewed as intermediate and equivalent in power and therefore equal in competitiveness and success.

Five of the eight studies reviewed provide some insight into the validity of this hypothesis (Kravitz & Iwaniszek, 1984; Molm, 1986; Scudder, 1988; Stake & Stake, 1979; Watson, 1991). Little support was found for the additive prediction. Only Watson's results provided any support for this hypothesis, and even she found support for it on only 1 of 17 dependent variables. In line with the hypothesis, both men and women believed they had been more likely to obtain joint, win-win solutions when they had power than when they did not, and men in both power positions believed they had been more successful than women. Because neither behavioral data nor the experimenter's asssessment of outcomes supported this belief, it provides little support for the additive hypothesis.

Although a two-way interaction between gender and power was not predicted due to the absence of any theory along these lines, all five of these studies found some evidence of such an interaction. Both Molm and Watson found that men react to powerlessness differently than women do. Men in low power positions seem to engage in persuading behavior more frequently than women. In Watson's study, this entailed the behaviors of stating a position and then offering rational arguments to support it. Persuading is considered by negotiation theorists to be a competing tactic, but it is presumably the least aggressive of the possible competing tactics that a negotiator might employ (Pruitt, 1983). Watson also found a trend ($p < .10$) for low power women to win more points for themselves than high power men, the exact reverse of the additive interaction hypothesis.

In Molm's study, low power men "gave" more than low power women. Although this suggests a greater cooperativeness on the part of low power men, the nature of the "giving" leads to a somewhat different interpretation. Subjects in Molm's study took part in a Prisoner's Dilemma type of task. They could choose between pressing an "individual" button to give themselves points or an "exchange" button to give their partner points. They made these choices over a series of 300 rounds, never knowing how their partner would choose in advance, but always learning their partner's choice immediately after they had made their own choice. Each participant received six points from the other's exchange response. A power imbalance was created by varying the value of the individual choice: The high power party received six points for this choice while the low power party received only one point. Thus, the low power party would do better if he or she could induce the high power party to press the "exchange" button. Because communication was not allowed, the only way to induce exchange responses was to make them oneself and hope to persuade the other to do likewise through imitation or guilt. Thus, the "giving" behavior of low power men in Molm's study could be interpreted as more an effort to persuade than a truly cooperative or altruistic behavior.

The remaining three studies that permitted an evaluation of power versus gender found no main effects for either power or gender, but an interaction between them. In two of these studies (Kravitz & Iwaniszek, 1985; Scudder, 1988), having power caused men to behave in more competitive ways, as predicted, but it. . . . had less impact on women's behavior. In the third study (Stake & Stake, 1979), the opposite effect was found: Power (in the sense of performance related self-esteem) increased women's dominant behavior (i.e., number of opinions given and disagreements stated), but not men's.

In the Kravitz and Iwaniszek study, students took part in a coalition formation experiment. Power was manipulated by varying the resources (in the form of number of votes controlled) and number of coalition alternatives of the players. The study found that power differences led to larger payoff differences in all-male groups (taken as a sign of more competitive behavior among group members) than in all-female groups. However, the authors note "this difference was one of degree, not kind. The same type of effects were found in both genders, the only difference was in magnitude" (p. 546). Furthermore, many different analyses were performed on the data, and the authors conclude that the rate of statistically significant effects that included gender was quite low.

In Scudder's study, students took part in a buyer-seller negotiation. The seller always had more power than the buyer, but the magnitude of the power difference was varied (specifics on how this was done were not provided). The results showed that, contrary to predictions, women in positions of higher power failed to use more bottom-line statements (i.e., "This is my final offer") than women in positions of lower power, whereas men, as predicted, did vary in this behavior by power condition. However, there were no gender differences in profits obtained. Thus, although women in higher power positions may have used less aggressive tactics than men, this did not adversely affect their ability to bargain successfully.

In the Stake and Stake (1979) study, the results are questionable because of the peculiarities of the sample population. To match men and women on performance-self-esteem, the authors were forced to eliminate from the subject population the women with the lowest scores and the men with the highest scores. As a result, the authors acknowledge that they included in the study a group of women with unusually high self-esteem scores and a group of men with extremely low self-esteem scores. Consequently, the results may be of limited generalizability.

Overall, then, very limited support was found for the possibility that gender and power accumulate to the advantage of men and the disadvantage of women. There were more instances of interactions between gender and power suggesting the possibility that gender and power interact to determine behavioral responses to power and powerlessness.

Gender x Power x Other's Gender Interactions

Only two of the eight studies addressed the hypothesis derived from expectation states theory and both dealt only with pairs in which a power imbalance existed (Molm, 1986; Watson, 1991). Neither provided support for the hypothesis.

Molm found no gender differences in power use in mixed-sex or in same-sex pairs. She had also varied whether situational power was legitimated or not in her study, however, and she did find an effect for legitimation. Participants in the legitimated condition were publicly assigned to the high power role on the basis of their prior performance on a task that presumably was related to how well they would do in the experiment. Molm expected differences in mixed-sex pairs only when power was not legitimated because legitimation based on task competence should eliminate the impact of gender as a status characteristic according to expectation states theory. In fact, however, she found differences when power was legitimated rather than when it was not. Legitimation affected high power females in such a way that many of them became even tougher and more competitive than the high power men. These results certainly do not support an expectation states explanation.

Furthermore, Molm also found a significant difference between high power men and women in same sex pairs. Female-female pairs of bargainers were less likely to engage in a tit-for-tat strategy than male-male pairs. This is noteworthy because the tit-for-tat strategy has been found to be the best way to ensure positive, joint, long-term outcomes in mixed-motive situations (Axelrod, 1984). This difference suggests that women are least likely to settle on a cooperative pattern when they bargain with another woman, whereas men are most likely to do so when they bargain with another man.

The results from Watson's study are somewhat more equivocal but on balance also do not support the expectation states hypothesis. She found three significant and one marginally significant ($p < .07$) three-way interactions among gender, power, and opponent's gender. These interactions showed that low power women who had male opponents differed from other low power parties in unexpected ways. To begin with, these women engaged in significantly higher rates of threatening behavior than low power men who had female opponents. They also differed from low power women who had female opponents in that they felt they had been more powerful during the negotiation, they were more satisfied with the decision reached, and they felt marginally more successful at achieving cooperative solutions.

The nature of these findings is contradictory to the predictions of expectation states theory. The supposedly weakest participants (low power women facing a male opponent) were not expected to use the toughest tactics. Yet, they did. Threatening is considered the most aggressive of the competing tactics (Pruitt, 1983). Nor were these women expected to differ from low power women with a female opponent. The fact that low power women felt more cooperatively successful with male opponents than with female opponents contradicts the hypothesis that women should have more trouble with male opponents.

These two studies provide no support for the extension of expectation states theory to negotiating contexts. Nevertheless, they do provide some intriguing evidence that gender, power, and the gender of one's opponent do interact. Molm's study suggests that women in general may overreact to having power. Watson's study, on the other hand, suggests they may overreact to not having power when they face a male opponent.

CONCLUSIONS

The studies reviewed here do not provide overwhelming support for any one of the four theoretical perspectives examined. On balance, however, they provide stronger support for the view that gender differences in negotiation behavior are an artifact of power and status differences between men and women in U.S. culture than for the sex-role socialization perspective.

This conclusion rests on the fact that the situational power perspective received the strongest and most consistent support. One of the more convincing demonstrations of this is the study conducted by Dovidio et al. (1988) that contained a control condition in which gender was varied but power was not. Stereotypical gender differences were found when power was not manipulated, but these differences were eliminated by the inclusion of a power variable. Equally convincing is the study by Siderits et al. (1985) in which participants served as their own controls, taking both low power and high power roles in turn. In the high power role, participants of both genders displayed more hostility than when they were in the low power role.

By way of contrast, most of the studies reviewed found either no main effects for gender, main effects that disappeared when power was controlled, or effects that had no impact on the outcome of the interaction. The gender effects that remained over and above the effects of situational power were related to women's confidence about negotiating and to their feelings about their own negotiating performance. Although these feelings did not affect the outcomes women achieved, they did affect women's perceptions of their outcomes. Because such feelings may predispose women to avoid negotiating situations, they represent a potentially important difference between men and women.

Equally important, the studies reviewed also indicate that gender, power, legitimation of power, and opponent's gender interact in ways not predicted by current theory. Interactions between gender and power were not predicted, for instance, yet five of the eight studies yielded such interactions. In one study (Scudder, 1988), men were found to issue more "take-it-or-leave-it" statements when they had power than when they did not, but women's usage of such statements was unaffected by power. Thus, power affected men and women differently in this instance. Power per se did not cause women to adopt more aggressive behavior. What did lead to more aggressive behavior in powerful women was either external legitimation of their power status (Molm, 1986), or a strong sense of performance-related confidence (Stake & Stake, 1979). These two studies suggest that when women feel legitimately powerful, they become even more dominant than men. The sense of legitimacy seems to have this effect whether it is internally or externally induced.

Several studies found that men and women react differently to powerlessness as well (Molm, 1986; Watson, 1991). In both of these studies men responded to low power roles by adopting persuading tactics more so than women. This strategy is congruent with prescriptions from current theory (Savage, Blair, & Sorenson, 1989) in that "soft competition" is recommended to low power parties facing powerful opponents. Because persuading is viewed as the softest of the competing tactics (Pruitt, 1983), usage of this tactic would seem to follow theoretical recommendations.

Women's reaction to powerlessness depended on the gender of their opponent. When the opponent was a man, women adopted the highly aggressive threatening approach. This yielded marginally better outcomes for them than other low power parties achieved and left them feeling more powerful, more satisfied, and paradoxically, more convinced they had achieved cooperative outcomes. Although this highly aggressive approach worked for the low power women in Watson's study, it is not one that was expected nor predicted by any of the theoretical approaches considered. Nor is such an aggressive approach generally recommended for low power parties in a situation like the one Watson used (Gifford, 1989; Savage et al., 1989). The general consensus is that the low power party should not risk highly aggressive tactics because the high power party has the ability to retaliate with devastating consequences. It is therefore quite surprising that the aggressive tactics of low power women worked against high power men. Perhaps the men were caught off guard by the aggressiveness of their low power female opponents and/or kept themselves in check because their opponents were women.

Another unexpected finding was that women had particular difficulty negotiating with another woman in one of the studies. Molm found evidence of less cooperative behavior in female-female pairs compared to male-male pairs. It appeared to be the high power women who prevented cooperation. Neither expectation states theory, nor recent work on the impact of the other's gender predict such an effect. Expectation states theory assumes that gender is not an issue in same-sex pairs, whereas others who predict greater gender differences in same-sex pairs (Carli, 1989; Hall, 1984; Mulac et al., 1988) would have expected greater cooperativeness in female-female pairs. This latter prediction is based on the rationale that men and women have developed clear expectancies about how they ought to behave in same-sex groupings, and they act in ways that are consistent with their stereotypes. Thus, women are likely to be polite, friendly, and agreeable with each other, and men are likely to compete with each other.

The negotiating context introduces a dilemma for women, however. It dictates that they compete with each other, which is not the way women are expected to interact. Furthermore, in Molm's study one party had more power than the other. Powerful parties of both genders tended to exploit their power advantage. As a result, high power women may have behaved much more competitively than their low power female opponents expected. Rubin and Brown (1975) suggested that women are likely to retaliate against such violations by locking into a punitively competitive cycle. This suggests that powerful women may initiate a destructive competitive cycle with less powerful women when they behave in accordance with the demands of the negotiation context and their high power position. Perhaps greater cooperativeness in female same-sex pairs is to be expected primarily when women have equal status and power. There is some support for this possibility in the literature (i.e., Watson & Kasten, 1987).

Implications

Because so few studies could be found that have addressed the issues raised in this chapter, the implications drawn here necessarily remain speculative. It is hoped that, despite their tentativeness, they will stimulate researchers to look more deeply into the interplay between gender and power uncovered by this review.

One major finding of this review is that women are probably not inherently more cooperative than men in negotiating or bargaining situations. If this is correct, it implies on the one hand, that women are not worse negotiators than men as has generally been assumed. That is, given a reasonable degree of situational power, women are likely to be as oriented toward beating their opponents as men and as succesful at doing so. It also implies, however, that women are not nicer negotiators than men in terms of being more fairminded or compassionate as some feminist writers would have us believe (Gilligan, 1982; Rosener, 1990). Thus, we cannot count on women to provide a humanizing influence as they move into more powerful positions in society. Rather, women are likely to accept the rules of interaction as men have written them. This conclusion parallels very closely that drawn by researchers interested in leadership. As noted in the introduction, research on leadership has shown that when women achieve or are given leader roles, their behavior matches that of men in leader roles. Because the leader role confers situational power on its incumbent, it probably functions largely as situational power did in the studies reviewed here. Thus, the conclusion drawn here about the impact of situational power versus gender on negotiating behavior is consistent with the voluminous research on leadership.

The fact that women were found to be even more competitive and ruthless than men when they felt legitimated and/or confident in their power raises the disturbing possibility that women may not only fail to be more fairminded and compassionate when resolving conflicts, but may actually be even less so than men. Because this effect was found in only two studies, such an implication is on particularly weak footings. However, other researchers have noted similar results in some research settings (Rapoport & Chammah, 1965) and have drawn the conclusion that women are more vindictive negotiators than men. As disturbing as this implication is, the fact that women have at times been found to lock into an unrelenting competitive stance argues for further exploration of this phenomenon. Some have suggested that it occurs because women become personally offended by competitive or selfish responses to their cooperative overtures (Rubin & Brown, 1975). Others have attributed such presumably anomalous behavior to women's unfamiliarity with generally accepted rules of the bargaining "game" (Kelley, 1965). These findings have been in the literature for many years, but little attention has been paid to them. This would seem to be an important area for further research.

Women's image as cooperative negotiators was also damaged by the findings from one study (Molm, 1986) that women were less likely to establish cooperative relations with other women than men were with other men. This finding suggests that conflicts between women with unequal situational power may be more strained and difficult than those between differentially powerful men. If true, the questions here seem to revolve around whether this might occur because negotiating requires women to behave in astereotypical ways that are perceived as particularly offensive when they are enacted by other women, or whether women do not understand how to play the negotiating game with each other so as to establish a cooperative give-and-take interaction. Because more and more women are moving into powerful positions in a variety of organizations, their relations with one another in such settings provides another largely untouched research area.

Finally, there is the case of the disempowered women who faced a male opponent in Watson's simulation. Rather than behaving in a highly submissive way as predicted, these women were feisty and somewhat more successful than other participants in the study as well as generally pleased with the outcomes they achieved. The fact that their high power male opponents did not retaliate and crush them suggests that this might be the right approach for women in similar situations. Watson's participants were practicing managers, however, dealing with an intraorganizational conflict. Perhaps managerial women, because of characteristics that led them into managerial positions, are more able and/or willing to enact such an approach than average women would be. Such tactics may also be more acceptable in the business world than they would be in intimate, personal conflicts. Nevertheless, the possibility suggested by this finding deserves further exploration.

As noted earlier, these implications are speculative. Nevertheless, they provide some interesting avenues for future research. What seems clear from this review is that gender and power combine and interact in ways that current theory fails to address. The challenge facing us now is to move to more complex theories that include both gender and power rather than to continue treating gender as such an important variable in its own right.

REFERENCES

Axelrod, R. (1984). *The evolution of cooperation*. New York: Basic Books.

Baril, G.L., Watson, C., & Korabik, K. (1990). *Managers' conflict resolution behaviors as predictors of leadership effectiveness*. Paper delivered at the third annual convention of the International Association of Conflict Management, Vancouver, B.C., Canada.

Bartos, O.J. (1970). Determinants and consequences of toughness. In P. Swingle (Ed.), *The structure of conflict* (pp. 45-68). New York: Academic Press.

Bem, D.J., & Allen, A. (1974). On predicting some of the people some of the time: The search for cross-situational consistencies in behavior. *Psychological Review, 81*, 506-520.

Berger, J., Fisek, M.H., Norman, R.Z., & Zelditch, Jr., M. (1977). *Status characteristics and social interaction: An expectation states approach*. New York: Elsevier.

Blake, R.R., & Mouton, J.S. (1964). *Managing intergroup conflict in industry*. Houston, TX: Gulf.

Caplow, T. (1968). *Two against one: Coalition in triads*. Englewood Cliffs, NJ: Prentice-Hall.

Carli, L. L. (1989). Gender differences in interaction style and influence. *Journal of Personality and Social Psychology, 56*(4), 565-576.

Deutsch, M. (1949). An experimental study of the effects of cooperation and trust in group process. *Human Relations, 2*, 199-231.

Dovidio, J.F., Ellyson, S.L., Keating, C.F., & Heltman, K. (1988). The relationship of social power to visual displays of dominance between men and women. *Journal of Personality and Social Psychology, 54*(2), 233-242.

Epstein, C. (1970). *Women's place: Options and limitations in professional careers*. Berkeley, CA: University of California Press.

Epstein, S. (1979). The stability of behavior: On predicting most of the people much of the time. *Journal of Personality and Social Psychology, 37*(7), 1097-1126.

Fagenson, E.A. (1990). Perceived masculine and feminine attributes examined as function of individuals' sex and level in the organizational power hierarchy: A test of four theoretical perspectives. *Journal of Applied Psychology, 75*(2), 204-211.

Gifford, D.G. (1989). *Legal negotiation: theory and practice*. St. Paul, MN: West Publishing.

Gilligan, C. (1982). *In a different voice*. Cambridge, MA: Harvard University Press.

Hall, J.A. (1984). *Nonverbal sex differences: Communication accuracy and expressive style*. Baltimore, MD: Johns Hopkins Press.

Hottes, J.H., & Kahn, A. (1974). Sex differences in a mixed-motive conflict situation. *Journal of Personality, 42*(2), 260-275.

Kanter, R. (1977). *Men and women of the corporation.* New York: Basic Books.

Kelley, H.H. (1965). Experimental studies of threats in interpersonal negotiations. *Journal of Conflict Resolution, 9,* 79-105.

Kimmel, M.J., Pruitt, D.G., Magenau, J.M., Konar-Goldband, E., & Carnevale, P.J.D. (1980). Effects of trust, aspiration, and gender on negotiation tactics. *Journal of Personality and Social Psychology, 38*(1), 9-22.

Koberg, C. S. (1985). Sex and situational influences on the use of power: A follow-up study. *Sex Roles, 13*(11-12), 625-639.

Kollock, P., Blumstein, P., & Schwartz, P. (1985). Sex and power in interaction: Conversational privileges and duties. *American Sociological Review, 50,* 34-46.

Kravitz, D., & Iwaniszek, J. (1984). Number of coalitions and resources as sources of power in coalition bargaining. *Journal of Personality and Social Psychology, 47*(3), 534-48.

Lockheed, M.E., & Hall, K.P. (1975). Conceptualizing sex as a status characteristic: Applications to leadership training strategies. *Journal of Social Issues, 32,* 111-124.

Meeker, B.F., & Weitzell-O'Neill, P.A. (1977). Sex roles and interpersonal behavior in task-oriented groups. *American Sociological Review, 42,* 91-105.

Mischel, W. (1968). *Personality and assessment.* New York: Wiley.

Mischel, W., & Peake, P.K. (1982). Beyond deja vu in the search for cross-situational consistency. *Psychological Review, 89,* 730-755.

Molm, L.D. (1986). Gender, power, and legitimation: A test of three theories. *American Journal of Sociology, 91*(6), 1356-1386.

Mulac, A., Wiemann, J.M., Widenmann, S.J., & Gibson, T.W. (1988). Male/female language differences and effects in same-sex and mixed-sex dyads: The gender-linked language effect. *Communication Monographs, 55,* 315-335.

Powell, G.N. (1990). One more time: Do female and male managers differ? *Academy of Management Executive, IV*(3), 68-76.

Powell, G.N., Posner, B.Z., & Schmidt, W.H. (1984). Sex effects in managerial value systems. *Human Relations, 37,* 909-921.

Pruitt, D.G. (1983). Strategic choice in negotiation. *American Behavioral Scientist, 27*(2), 167-194.

Pruitt, D.G., Carnevale, P.J., Forcey, B., & Van Slyck, M. (1986). Gender effects in negotiation: Constituent surveillance and contentious behavior. *Journal of Experimental Social Psychology, 22*(3), 264-275.

Putnam, L.L., & Jones, T.S. (1982). Reciprocity in negotiations: An analysis of bargaining interaction. *Communication Monographs, 49*(3), 171-191.

Rapoport, A., & Chammah, A.M. (1965). *Prisoner's dilemma.* Ann Arbor: The Univeristy of Michigan Press.

Rosener, J.B. (1990, November-December). Ways women lead. *Harvard Business Review,* pp. 119-125.

Rubin, J.Z., & Brown, B.R. (1975). *The social psychology of bargaining and negotiation.* New York: Academic Press.

Savage, G.T., Blair, J.D., & Sorenson, R.L. (1989). Consider both relationships and substance when negotiating strategically. *Academy of Management Executive, III*(1), 37-48.

Scudder, J.N. (1988). The influence of power upon powerful speech: A social-exchange perspective. *Communication Research Reports, 5*(2), 140-145.

Siderits, M.A., Johannsen, W.J., & Fadden, T.F. (1985). Gender, role, and power: A content analysis of speech. *Psychology of Women Quarterly, 9*(4), 439-450.

Stake, J.E., & Stake, M.N. (1979). Performance-self-esteem and dominance behavior in mixed-sex dyads. *Journal of Personality, 47,* 71-84.

Tedeschi, J.T., Schlenker, B.R., & Bonoma, T.V. (1973). *Conflict, power, and games: The experimental study of interpersonal relations.* Chicago: Aldine.

Terborg, J. (1977). Women in management: A research review. *Journal of Applied Psychology, 62,* 647-664.

Terhune, K.W. (1970). Personality in cooperation and conflict. In P. Swingle (Ed.), *The structure of conflict* (pp. 193-234). New York: Academic Press.

Vinacke, W. (1959). Sex roles in a three-person game. *Sociometry, 22,* 343-359.

Wall, J.A. (1976). Effects of sex and opposing representative's bargaining orientation on intergroup bargaining. *Journal of Personality and Social Psychology, 33*(4), 371-381.

Wall, J.A. (1977). The intergroup bargaining of mixed-sex groups. *Journal of Applied Psychology, 62*(2), 208-213.

Watson, C. (1991). An examination of the impact of gender and power on managers' negotiation behavior: Implications for ADR Practitioners. *Proceedings of the Society for Professionals in Dispute Resolution* (pp. 154-162). Washington, DC: SPIDR.

Watson, C., & Kasten, B. (1987). *Separate strengths? How men and women negotiate* (Working Paper No. 1). Newark, NJ: Center for Negotiation and Conflict Resolution, Rutgers University.

Introduction to
Part III

The five chapters in part III present consequences of seeing gender in conflict. In so doing, they illustrate why conflict requires attention to power as it is modified by gender. These authors raise important basic questions: What is conflict? What are its objects and objectives? How is it gendered? What part do values and their gendering play in its management and resolution?

In Chapter 10, "'Gender Conflict': Connecting Feminist Theory and Conflict Resolution Theory and Practice," John Stephens portrays gender conflicts as conflicts of values and roles between people and discusses whether such conflicts can be resolved by mediation or other forms of what has come to be called *alternative dispute resolution*. Such procedures respond to cases rather than deeper-rooted problems such as power asymmetries in hierarchies. He emphasizes that specification of the issues in gender conflict is itself a contentious matter and that processes such as mediation, even though it may be sensitive to feminine values, may not provide solutions to gender conflicts, even in the short run. He suggests that problem-solving workshops may offer a better avenue to solutions, but he believes that the litmus test of their effectiveness should be women's experience with them. One unresolved issue in conflict and conflict resolution theories, Stephens finds, is that neither conflict resolution nor feminist studies has adequately conceptualized the parties, issues, and locations in gender conflict.

Angela Febbraro and Roland Chrisjohn critique the basis of much conflict research in Chapter 11, "A Wittgensteinian Approach to the Meaning of Conflict." They criticize empirical, data-driven approaches (e.g., classical test theory) to defining conflict on the grounds that meaning lies in people rather than patterns of correlation, and they argue instead, as did Wittgenstein, that conceptual clarification of concepts such as conflict should precede their empirical study. They demonstrate ways in which the meaning of conflict can be elaborated through usage, and they go on to show how current use of the term is based primarily on men's usage, which is adversarial and reflective of a power over approach, rather than being growth-promoting, which is reflective of a power with approach. Febbraro and Chrisjohn suggest that knowledge from prior conflict research should be reassessed and conflict reconceptualized along the lines described by Wittgenstein, including its usage in feminist discourse. Their insistence on conceptual clarification, similar to Stephens' focus on issue specification, makes gender an explicit part of the process.

Cynthia Chataway and Deborah Kolb identify one element that might be part of such a reconceptualization in Chapter 12, "Working Behind the Scene: Gender and Power in Informal Conflict Management." They provide case studies illustrating informal processes through which conflict is managed in organizations, processes that rely in part on empowering disputants. They discuss reasons why people without mediation credentials (frequently women) become involved in informal conflict management. Chataway and Kolb use a model in which conflict is first addressed intrapersonally by a variety of coping strategies, then interpersonally by informal conversations, and finally, although infrequently, by formal organizational procedures. They apply the model to the experience of three women who emerged as informal conflict mediators in their organizations. All three provided support to potential disputants by listening to their stories, offering alternative explanations and solutions, communicating their perspectives, and attempting to stage problem-solving discussions. Each had personal access to higher status decision makers; each disliked conflict; each wanted genuinely to help. In each instance conflict had developed between persons who were unequal in organizational status, and it was the lower status individual who turned to these women for help. These can be construed as empowering experiences in which mutual gain is born out of interdependence and care, a conclusion that fits appropriately into feminist theoretical positions.

Marcia Dewhurst and Victor Wall also examine women's talk in conflict situations, but from a slightly different perspective. In Chapter 13, "Gender and the Mediation of Conflict: Communication Differences," they examine mediators' use of formulations to clarify, reframe, and control mediation processes and the outcomes achieved by using different kinds of formulations. In general they find that more formulations are used in resolved than unresolved disputes, regardless of mediators' sex. However, they also find that female and male mediators differ somewhat in their use of formulations. Consistent with gender role expectations, female mediators use formulations to integrate disputants' points of view more often than male mediators, whereas male mediators use formulations to control the mediation process more often than female mediators. When disputes are resolved, disputants report as much satisfaction with male as with female mediators, but when disputes are unresolved they express greater satisfaction with sessions mediated by females. Nevertheless, they evaluate the male mediator's competence higher than the female's in these circumstances. These results raise important questions about the gendering and evaluation of behavior, in this case, talk. Are controlling behaviors perceived to be competent because they preserve order or because they are used by men? Why are integrating behaviors, which are associated with satisfaction, not also associated with competence? Is this a consequence of their being used more often by women, or is it because they equalize control and are irrelevant to order?

In the final chapter, "Overlapping Radicalisms: Convergence and Divergence Between Feminist and Human Needs Theories in Conflict Resolution," Ingrid Sandole-Staroste compares radical feminist theory and human needs-based conflict resolution theory, both of which advocate fundamental restructuring of society, but with different foci. Her comparison shows how John Burton, the primary human needs conflict theorist, reflects our concern for context by locating the roots of conflict in institutions and social structural arrangements that limit satisfaction of basic human needs. But his conception of context is incomplete. Feminists locate roots of conflict in institutions but also in individuals' acceptance of ideologies that value competition for power and other resources. Sandole-Staroste argues that a human needs perspective that ignores individual differences based on gender, race, and class is not neutral and may in fact obscure the needs of powerless persons. She advocates including gender as an analytic category in the study of conflict resolution because gender typically organizes thought, social activity, cultural beliefs, and institutions and is associated with power imbalances. Without a consideration of gender in all its complexity, solutions and prescriptions may be based on masculinist rather than human needs.

Taken together, these chapters focus the question of whether it is possible to resolve conflicts in a patriarchy, a point made directly by Stephens and Sandole-Staroste and one made indirectly by Chataway and Kolb. In discussing informal peacemaking within organizations, Chataway and Kolb present cases of women sought out, in part, because as women they were not seen as threatening. These cases remind us that in modern bureaucratic organizations (all hierarchal), conflicts do not get resolved, they get managed. Their chapter illustrates the distinctions made by Stephens between alternative dispute resolution (ADR) and conflict resolution as avenues to dealing with conflicts. Chataway and Kolb provide a major contribution to thinking about ADR because informal peacekeeping is rarely considered within that framework. Informal peacekeeping has not been so located, we suggest, because of its gender subtext. The analysis by Chataway and Kolb reminds us also that the role of power in hierarchies is to manage rather than resolve conflicts.

Ultimately, all three chapters—Stephens, Chataway and Kolb, and Sandole-Staroste—highlight the radical implications of the feminist critique: As long as there is hierarchy with its inherent inequalities between groups and classes of individuals, conflicts can be managed but not resolved. Regardless of which scheme for needs classification one uses, whether it is to accept the interpersonal needs described by Schutz (1966), the description of Burton (1990), or the contribution of Clark (1990a, 1991), one cannot find a way to fully satisfy those needs in a hierarchy. One can do so even less in a hierarchy arranged by gender, whether it be the current patriarchal arrangement that privileges male and what is male identified or some fictional matriarchy that privileges female.

Conflict resolution on a small scale has occurred in numerous small communities around the world (Clark, 1990b, 1991), Conflict resolution on a larger scale will not occur until the world is radically rearranged. According to the scholarship in this volume, only when cultural institutions, social organizations, and technological systems satisfy all human needs, those of women as well as men, will we be positioned to resolve rather than manage conflict. At the same time, because most cultures arrange gender and other individual differences hierarchically, the chapters in this part, combined with those from the first two parts, show how important it will be to continue improving all means of conflict management and to achieving sensitivity to the impact of gender and related differences.

REFERENCES

Burton, J. (ed.). (1990). *Conflict: Human needs theory*. New York: St. Martin's Press.

Clark, M.E. (1990a). Meaningful social bonding as a universal human need. In J.W. Burton (Ed.), *Conflict: Human needs theory* (pp. 34-59). New York: St. Martin's Press.

Clark, M.E. (1990b, November). *Rethinking the 'rational' society: A plea for some broad-based philosophizing*. Paper presented at 10th annual Lilly Conference on College Teaching, Miami University, Oxford, OH.

Clark, M.E. (1991, August). *On "science" and "nature"—"Human nature"*. Paper presented at annual conference of Council on Peace Research and Education, Fairfax, VA.

Schutz, W.C. (1996). *The interpersonal underworld*. Palo Alto, CA: Science & Behaviors Books.

10

"Gender Conflict": Connecting Feminist Theory and Conflict Resolution Theory and Practice*

John B. Stephens
The Ohio Commission on Dispute Resolution and Conflict Management

Feminist theory and conflict resolution theory[1] each approach social systems seeking analysis of unpeaceful situations and promoting change for greater individual development and social justice. However, the differences in their central concepts and assumptions are significant.

In this chapter I explore the connections of feminist and conflict resolution theories in two ways. First, I describe how feminist analysis challenges many of the conceptual bases of conflict studies and alterna-

---

*The views expressed are those of Mr. Stephens as a Ph.D. candidate at the Institute for Conflict Analysis and Resolution at George Mason University. They do not necessarily reflect the views or policies of the Commission on Dispute Resolution.

[1] I specify conflict *resolution* theory to exclude ethology and other contributions to conflict theory. The focus on resolution assumes human agency can modify conflictual situations through thoughtful—but not purely rational—techniques.

tive dispute resolution (ADR). Second, I analyze how two practices of peaceful conflict intervention—mediation and problem-solving workshops—relate to feminist analysis.

CONCEPTUAL ANALYSIS

Feminist theory and conflict theory are each heterogenous subjects. In fact, their internal debates parallel each other. Briefly, one focus of intrafeminist debate is the division between the legal assurance of sexual equality versus the reconstitution of the role (if any) of gender in society. Thus, proper remedies range from reformist measures (an Equal Rights Amendment to the U.S. Constitution or comparable worth legislation) to more transformative or revolutionary change (socialist economic reorganization or an androgynous social system). Although this is an oversimplified summary of a rich discussion, the differences center on divergent diagnoses of the sources of women's oppression: ranging from a "reformist" liberal-democratic color of feminism to a "radical," sometimes Marxist end of the feminism spectrum.

The parallel in conflict studies is the distinction between ADR and conflict resolution. Alternative dispute resolution, like liberal feminism, seeks reform of institutions and leans more toward system maintenance. Conflict resolution, like radical feminism, argues for broader and deeper social change. The latter claims a greater willingness to delineate and address the "fundamental causes" of large-scale conflict/oppression of women (see Figure 10.1).

As highlighted in Figure 10.1, the focus of this chapter is on conflict resolution and the practices of mediation and problem solving.[2] Before distinguishing these concepts from the others arrayed on the continuum, an example illustrating Figure 10.1 follows.

The scenario is a conflict between a landlord and tenant concerning an overdue rent payment and needed repairs to the property. An ADR approach would focus on the landlord and tenant as the two parties in dispute and would seek a settlement. A conflict resolution perspective would more likely see this conflict as a manifestation of a deeper, more fundamental conflict in the legal-property rights of landlords and tenants. Finally, peace activists might wish to focus on the "deeper" policy questions of affordable and safe housing and community-based ownership of property.

---

[2]The parallelism of Figure 10.1 is only intended to be a starting point for examining the connections between feminist and peace/conflict studies. I hope to move beyond this linear spectrum conception to a richer "landscape" of conflict-feminist ideas. For an interesting effort to move beyond the left-right liberal-conservative diagrams of U.S. political thought, see Selben & Steiner, 1991.

CONFLICT/PEACE *FIELDS OF STUDY*:

¦-----Peace Studies -----¦   ¦-----Alternative Dispute -----¦
                                                    Resolution
            ¦-----Conflict Resolution -----¦
CONFLICT/PEACE *PRACTICES*:

    Nonviolent Action----------Mediation ------------Arbitration
    Civil Disobedience   Mini-trials
    ¦------Problem-solving ------¦
◄---SOCIAL -------------------------------------- SYSTEM -----►
    CHANGE   MAINTENANCE
FEMINIST THOUGHT
Androgyny ---- Marxist ----Radical--------------------Liberal-
                                                    Democratic

Figure 10.1. Diagram relating the range of thought, practice, and advocacy in peace studies, feminist theory, conflict resolution, and ADR to a continuum of social change and system maintenance. The relations proposed are to provide a context for the discussion of the conceptual and practical concerns of connecting feminist thought and conflict resolution. It excludes other mechanisms that are even more system dependent and power based (e.g., legal trials, war).

If we now say the tenant is a woman and the landlord a man, we can raise different perspectives in feminist thought. If the landlord has made similar repairs faster or better for his male tenants, sex discrimination might be the focus of a liberal-democratic feminist critique. Similarly, one can develop other details of previous interactions between man-landlord and woman-tenant to raise issues of communication, role expectations, and oppression that would be of primary interest to other feminist theorists.

One concern is that a male landlord would only "hear" the concrete complaints about material problems and be deaf to (or ignore) the emotional content of the situation presented by the female renter. A "true" resolution might depend on addressing the affective issues (e.g., privacy, security, orderliness) as much or more than the contractual obligations. This perspective would resonate with the feminist critique of the legal system as being dominated by values favorable to men: adversarial, formalistic, individualistic, and so on.

This illustration is intended to provide a concrete reference for the abstract analysis that follows (see Figure 10.2). Yet, how one attempts to describe "a conflict" implies a framework or attitude toward what change is possible (with this scenario of a landlord/tenant dispute fitting within an ADR perspective).

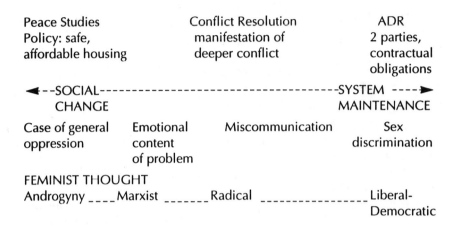

Figure 10.2. Illustrative scenario: "A landlord-tenant conflict"

Alternative dispute resolution focuses on intervention practices that are reformist and have less impact on system values. Arbitration, mini-trials, and mediation of family, consumer-merchant, landlord-tenant, or neighbor-neighbor conflicts are examples of ADR. The "alternativeness" of ADR rests in its separation from litigation or traditional positional negotiations to resolve disputes. A prime value of ADR practice is efficiency. ADR also includes some recognition of the inappropriateness of court proceedings for some kinds of social problems.

The ADR focus is on the particular case. Thus, ADR is synonymous with *conflict management* as a case-processing system. Only in rare instances do ADR mechanisms challenge the value of the superordinate adversarial, legal mechanism (or a partisan legislative forum) as a final resort if the "alternatives" fail.

Conflict resolution theory, as delineated by the Institute for Conflict Analysis and Resolution at George Mason University, argues the irrelevance of traditional settlement mechanisms to deep-rooted, protracted conflicts. Conflict resolution presumes that sources of the most serious and important conflicts lie at a deeper level than ADR mechanisms can reach, that they are battles over values or needs.

Returning to the illustration, ADR deals with a dispute of tenant versus landlord. Conflict resolution would analyze the similarities of disputes between tenants and landlords to understand the common causes and dynamics of these disputes. These deeper patterns would be "the conflict" in a conflict resolution approach. From a conflict resolution perspective, the ADR analysis looks only at manifestations of the more fundamental factors that define the conflict.

Some conflict resolution analysts promote separation from ADR by distinguishing between "resolution" and "settlement." *Resolution* is transformational; a resolution transforms all parties' views of the conflict. Instead of each side stating its positions and reaching a compromise, resolution seeks a deeper learning and the creation of a joint understanding of the conflict without one side giving in. Through a greater shared understanding of the factors in conflict, self-sustaining solutions to the conflict are attainable. Until this deeper level is addressed, argues the conflict resolution paradigm, there will be only temporary settlements of surface disputes that are bound to break down because the root cause of the conflict is left intact.

I focus on the broadest level of *gender conflicts*—the idea that a structured pattern of inequality and oppression of women causes conflicts in a variety of social settings. The inherent disempowerment of women—by valuing femininity as less important for exercising power and authority in the public realm—is a central theme of the feminist critique.

ADR and conflict management tend to look at manifestations of deeper gender oppression: sexual harassment, unequal pay, and family violence. Most conflict analysts may recognize the structural bases for conflicts involving gender, yet focus on particular disputes. I argue that ADR (to a greater degree) and conflict resolution (to a lesser degree) have a *conceptual* difficulty in considering "the gender problem," a difficulty that stems from three central concepts of both types of conflict analysis: *parties, issues,* and *location* of a conflict.

Parties

If one takes a structural approach to gender conflict, there appear to be two parties: men and women. Men oppress and women are oppressed. This simple division quickly blurs, however. We see many women apparently satisfied with traditional patriarchy—Phyllis Schlafly and the Eagle Forum supporters as one example—and some men striving to be feminist in their values and behavior. In most large-scale social conflicts (e.g., ethnic or racial clashes), one expects a certain amount of dissent within ranks, or "traitors" actually helping the "enemy." But gender conflicts seem different. The definition of the parties is not by sex, nor necessarily by gender. Men who support feminism (be they "feminists" or "co-feminists") do not lose the status of "men" by being pro-feminist. Similarly, women who oppose feminist reforms are still "women."

One should question whether there are only two ideas involved in constituting gender: femininity and masculinity. Is androgyny a balance between the two concepts, or is it a flexible amalgam of these traits? Or does androgyny stand outside the labeling of behaviors and attitudes as either feminine or masculine?

How do gay men, lesbians, and bisexuals fit into a gender scheme? We could say that they are advantaged or disadvantaged to the degree they have masculine or feminine traits. However, the differences in sexual orientation combined with the physiological sex difference certainly challenge the sexual bases for what is masculine and feminine, powerful or weak. How does feminism consider sexual harassment between homosexuals? Does patriarchy apply?

At this broadest level of categorizing groups and generalizing about their relation to privilege and power, the gender dichotomy is not necessarily decisive. Race, class, and sexual orientation are powerful divisions that complicate who is seen as powerful in a conflict. Within the operations of patriarchy, many feminist voices point to interlinking oppressions of sexism, racism, and classism (e.g., hooks, 1984). From this view, the gender conflict cannot stop at gender, but gender can only be understood within the characteristics of race, class, and so on.

Conflict studies depend on an ability to define parties in conflict by a distinguishing boundary characteristic. In gender conflicts, gender is not the border. Indeed, the parties cannot be dichotomously categorized. It is possible to have a masculine person as a feminist; or a woman opposed to the values of feminism. Thus, the label *gender conflicts* (implying most/all men against most/all women) is a misnomer.

A better beginning is to conceive of many conflicts between men and women (and women-women, men-men) as *value* conflicts. The values focus on the meaning and importance of gender and its application to traits, attitudes, and roles in society. Gender conflicts draw on moral questions of equality and privilege, and difference and commonality, as well as on practical everyday judgments of how men and women interact (e.g., washing dishes, fixing the car, handling heavier loads, traits of a good leader, etc.).

Kreisburg (1982) is one of the few widely recognized conflict resolution theorists who gives direct attention to gender and conflict. Kreisburg begins by stating that there are usually unambiguous differences between males and females physiologically, but that the *social* division of man/woman is not unambiguous. He then outlines some manifestations of women's disadvantage: in the family, education, occupation and earnings, political power, and so forth. He also offers an insight into gender status difference by citing a study in which girls were 10 times more likely than boys to say they wished they were boys than vice versa.

Kreisburg believes that a basic peculiarity of men and women as conflict groups is that "they live more intimately with each other than among themselves" (p. 49). This certainly is a good observation, given the mainstream values of sexual and emotional intimacy with the opposite sex. This observation is less accurate as one considers homosexual relations and different views on family and intimacy (e.g., *Diary of a Mad Housewife*). Nonetheless, Kreisburg points to a high level of interdependence—biological and social—that distinguishes men and women as conflict groups from other disputing groups.

If we see gender conflicts as conflicts of values and roles—centering on gender, but not defining the parties by gender—then the implication is that conflict resolution is a more appropriate analysis and approach for intervention than ADR. Conflict resolution focuses more on values (and needs) and a broader understanding of conflicts. Alternative dispute resolution more often seeks an interest-based settlement of differences, with less emphasis on the deeper educative role of conflict analysis and resolution.

Issues

Another central concept of conflict analysis is that of issues. A conflict has to be "about something"—and that something is labeled an issue (or issues). Issues are points of contention that define some question or value in which the parties perceive a difference between themselves. It is these differences that are seen as the guts of the conflict—what keeps it going.

What are the issues in gender conflict? Starting at the liberal, mainstream end of feminism the issues include child care, abortion rights, equal employment opportunity, equal pay for equal work and equal pay for work of comparable worth, and so on. These issues focus on positive steps to erase sexual discrimination in the public realm and to protect individual, private choice. Moving further along the system change/maintenance spectrum, other gender distinctions can point to structural bases for conflict issues. Maintenance of distinctions by dress, occupational aspirations, religious teachings, and role models are examples of these kinds of "issues."

Continuing toward the system change pole, one can define gender conflict as oppression due to hierarchy in general. The more radical feminist critiques point to the centrality of hierarchy in denying the development of women, poor people, and racial and ethnic minorities. In this view, the issue is hierarchy itself. This critique goes beyond seeking to eliminate hierarchy based on gender. It leaves no hierarchy unchallenged.

There are significant divisions in the views of what the issues are in gender conflict. It is a long reach from the issue of ensuring equal opportunity for women and men in a (presumably) meritocratic system, to challenging the idea of hierarchy or difference, or contesting the legitimacy of social roles. In a liberal feminist view, the aim is the increased *sharing* of valued social roles (e.g., men doing child care, women as engineers, doctors, lawyers, etc.). The more radical view seeks to completely transform social roles by envisioning nonhierarchical roles of diversity and equality.

Kreisburg (1982) applies the concepts of consensual and dissensual issues to gender conflict. *Consensual issues* are when parties agree on the value of some resource or status, but disagree on what is a fair division among themselves. *Dissensual issues* are differences in agreement on the basic goals of individual and societal pursuit (e.g., religion). Dissensus can be a basis for cooperation. Kreisburg notes that if different gender roles are accepted, there can be a basis for exchange, cooperation, and harmony. Kreisburg offers this view of issues of dissensus and consensus in gender conflicts:

> If men and women agree that power is good and if women demand that men have less power over them, then it follows that if women's demands are met, men must lose something that is desirable. But, women might argue that if men who value autonomy and freedom cease having so much power over women, men themselves would also be freer. (pp. 50-51)

If gender issues are dissensual, there should be some way to choose social roles and resources to satisfy different, but *compatible*, views by men and women of what is of value.

Yet Kreisburg's argument points beyond finding a new "fit" or balance between women and men to more fundamental changes. His approach is resonant with feminist argument for a transformation of the social order from power being perceived as "power over" (a controlling or dominator model) to power as "power with" (a co-equal, cooperative *combinatory* sense of power).

However, other feminists argue that gender inherently defines power relations (e.g., Daly, 1978; Kramarae, 1981; Spender, 1985). Following these views, "power" is not something "men" can give up, as Kreisburg implies, because "men" and "power" are confounded concepts. Perhaps only when gender has no more relation to power than eye color or ear size might the reconfiguration of power between women and men make sense. Otherwise, unless social roles of men and women are equally valued, some form of domination by those holding more highly valued roles is inevitable.

Like the conflicting analyses that arise from different feminist perspectives, what is at issue in conflicts concerning gender is itself a contentious matter. This makes defining "the conflict" more difficult. This difficulty, however, reflects one common and maddening feature of gender conflict(s)—continuing contention over what *should* gender *mean*?

There is a great need for a far-ranging dialogue about what the issues concerning gender are, how they are related, and what can be done about them. This must occur in order to gain a sufficient definition of what an issue is and what exactly are the *differences* on that issue. I do not mean to obscure important issues already commonly understood (e.g., equal political and labor rights, violence against women). I think it is fair to say that part of solving gender conflict lies in the pursuit of defining issues and their ramifications.

Location of Gender Conflict

ADR and conflict resolution also operate from the idea that conflicts are located somewhere. Wars, environmental protection, and labor strikes are defined in terms of some context—often a particular physical location. A consumer complaint focuses on a material product or service. The "where" (and "what" in similar physical terms) is part of delineating a conflict's location.

The "location" of gender conflict is problematic. The family, workplace, and political forums are places where conflict between women and men occur. But if those conflicts have a gender component, it usually transcends its location. If one traces the cause to gender role expectations, this source of conflict can most certainly be traced back to the socialization of children. Here, too, however, location is not singular. From children's clothing, to how boys and girls should play, to media images and societal norms, all of these factors help form the meaning and division of gender.

Conflict resolution has focused on deep-rooted conflicts: Ethnic and racial identity and security are common themes. In this sense, not only is the gender conflict deep rooted, it may be *comprehensive*. Only the similar social meanings of race, class, ethnicity, and sexual orientation approach gender's construction of individual and social identity, security, and expectations. Yet, it is clear that conflict resolution theory and research has never attended to gender with the same level of analysis or attention as it has given to race or class.

Hence, the levels of gender conflict are not only multiple, they are interlinked. The conflict within a "family" often stems from the need for a two wage-earner household. Questions of child care and housework affect consideration of work outside the home by one or more partners and the support of some third person to fulfill child care and housework needs. Similarly, the expectations of school—who takes home economics and who takes metal shop—help support certain kinds of expectations about college and work.

Summary

Conflict studies conceptualize conflicts as something parties do at some location over issues. From a general feminist conception of gender conflict, each of the three concepts—parties, issues, location—is problematic. However, one must draw boundaries for situations that call for valuable, near-term intervention: a husband abusing his wife, sexual harassment at work, or women seeking entry to all-male institutions. In these cases, ADR may provide essential localized settlement or management of a particular conflict. However, the root causes of conflicts involving gender must be addressed or resolution will not occur. Persistent recurrence of such conflicts demonstrates that ADR has not provided resolutions.

Conflict resolution has not yet addressed at the conceptual level the parties, issues, or interests in gender conflict(s). Nor have feminist studies to a much greater extent. Considerable progress in both areas is essential if either area of analysis is to address satisfactorily deep-rooted conflicts. I hope this initial clarification of concepts and perspectives can contribute to that process. In the meantime, however, disputes involving gender continually occur and are dealt with in political arenas, courts, and ADR venues. Conflict studies and especially ADR are not well equipped to address diffuse or structural conflict. Their aim is primarily the management of particular manifestations of contentious problems in society.

The continuing debate over parties, issues, and location goes beyond most of the interests of conflict studies. Feminist concerns are being addressed through peace studies far more than through conflict studies. From Galtung's (1969) conception of structural violence, to the growing links between feminism and peace activism (e.g., Brock-Utne, 1989), the advocacy aims of feminist analysis find a home in peace studies.

For example, peace studies often look at phenomena such as militarism in multidimensional or "holistic" ways. Also, Galtung argues that peace is not just "negatively" defined as the absence of overt violence. "Positive peace" includes just, nonoppressive relations that require the removal of structural forms of violence such as a hierarchy based on gender. Brock-Utne goes further and contends that peace education calls for androgynous relations.

MEDIATION AND PROBLEM SOLVING: APPLYING FEMINIST PERSPECTIVES

In this section, I examine two forms of conflict resolution and ADR practice, mediation and problem-solving workshops, in the light of feminist theory. These two processes highlight parts of the dialogues within both feminist and conflict studies and may illuminate the usefulness of the continuum previously discussed. First, I present and extend Bailey's (1989) analysis of different feminists' critiques of mediation as "female" and more or less capable of being "feminist" especially in view of field survey data of women and men who have been disputants in mediated divorces. These concrete data help balance the theoretical arguments Bailey explores with the practical question: Do many women think mediation *as they experience* it is empowering? Finally, I look at a more transformation-oriented conflict resolution practice—the problem-solving workshop—that would seem to be quite compatible with the feminist focus on the need for structural change. Oddly, this practice has been developed by men and one of its founders has only a cursory idea about how women's views might be important. Burton's understanding of the problem-solving workshop and "feminist views" are presented and critiqued.

Mediation

It has been intimated that some approaches in conflict resolution help redefine power and draw on values amicable to "female concerns." Bailey (1989) explores this idea in regard to mediation, placing the idea of mediation as a "female" process within a larger debate of feminist legal theory. She characterizes the contrasting views as the "different voice" approach associated with Carol Gilligan versus the "dominance" approach championed by Catherine MacKinnon.

MacKinnon (1987) characterizes gender issues as issues of power and hierarchy and suggests that only derivatively is it a difference. MacKinnon criticizes the different voices approach by saying that "difference" allows for the male view to be defined as "standard" and women's views to be defined as different. This only reinforces the traditional place of women's views as separate and secondary to male-dominated, oppressive power relations. In such a perspective, mediation would be "female" in that it is subordinated to traditional modes of power oppressive to women.

Gilligan (1982) draws her view from observed differences of how males and females approach moral problems. She argues that boys commonly operate from an "ethic of rights" (or "ethic of justice") in approaching moral problems. They focus on individual rights and universally applicable legal rules based on the assumption that individual autonomy is the decisive value. Girls, in Gilligan's study, exhibit an "ethic of care" with the preservation of relationships as the guiding value. Girls tend to approach problems in a more contextual manner and seek an outcome sensitive to the particular circumstances.

Bailey identifies legal theorists who build on Gilligan and relate the ethic of care with mediation and the ethic of rights with the legal system. Riskin (1984) believes the "perspective of caring and interconnection finds mediation much more hospitable" (p. 332) and Menkel-Meadow (1985) speculates that women lawyers might focus more on context, relationships, and care. Menkel-Meadow suggests that the "male" legal system—hierarchical, rule-based, and competitive—may be transformed by increasing numbers of women lawyers using a more cooperative form of legal practice (Bailey, 1989).

Bailey cites Rifkin's (1984) experience in which teaching law led Rifkin to see mediation as more consistent with a feminist pedagogy. Traditional legal pedagogy is hierarchical and "trains students to reject an analysis of social reality as it is subjectively experienced, and instead requires them to internalize a series of abstract rules" (Rifkin, 1984, p. 23). Rifkin views mediation as challenging these precepts by supporting a dialogue of subjective, emotional experience. The emphasis is on "the female concerns of responsibility and justice" instead of individual rights, thus mediation requires a feminist pedagogy.

Through Rifkin, however, we come full circle in the initial division of "different voice" versus "dominance" that Bailey identified. Rifkin cites MacKinnon and the potential for feminist theory to challenge patriarchy, in part, through the values embodied in mediation. The direction of Gilligan, Riskin, and Menkel-Meadow is to try to bring the two ethics together for a richer sense of morality and justice. Their vision is to seek a fruitful combination of the two ethics. Rifkin, however, views mediation and feminist values as the bases for challenging the "male" legal system.

Bailey (1989) reviews other dangers in the "different voices" model. Such an analysis can be interpreted to be supportive of stereotypes about an "inherent nature" of females. This could justify a division of labor oppressive to women without the kind of systemic structural changes sought by the radical and cultural feminists. Second, support of an essential difference between male and female natures can inhibit social change. Gilligan, however, carefully points out that her evidence provides no support for a conclusion of "inherency" (p. 2). Finally, the "voice of care" can be seen as the "voice of victim"—an expression of femaleness within patriarchy. MacKinnon fears that women may identify with this positively valued female stereotype, but ignore Gilligan's warning that human connection allows for both care and oppression (Bailey, 1989).

An important question is whether an ethic of care and an ethic of rights can be integrated. Bailey conceives Gilligan's work as arguing for such an integration to create a new model of adult moral development. Many criticize this idea arguing that in our current genderized realm, the two ethics cannot be truly integrated, and attempts to do so run the risk of co-optation. The co-optation danger is illustrated by Rifkin (1984). A mediated divorce settlement provided for child custody for the husband, no support for the wife (although she had no job), and a lump sum for the wife's share of the property. The wife's lawyer advised her against this settlement, and the wife chose to represent herself at the hearing. Her lawyer was so upset that he attended the hearing to address the judge on his objection to the agreement. The judge did accept the agreement after speaking with the wife at length.

Bailey (1989) views this case study as demonstrating the problem of women who define their power and interests in terms of an ethic of care who then face men who do not reciprocate. The husband "used her concern with preserving the relationship with her children against her by making possible damage to that relationship the price [for settlement]" (p. 6). The case shows the weakness of mediation's focus on care and concern for others without a concomitant alteration in the structure of male dominance of property and power. Mediation can be seen as a possible inroad against dominance in a different realm. Riskin (1984) only sees a woman client working against lawyer-client dominance, eventually representing herself in the postmediation court proceedings. Unfortunately, without a clearer idea of the conduct of the mediation, and how the conversation between the woman and judge satisfied the judge's concerns, this case leaves one troubled, but without sufficient information to judge this case as a "success," "failure," or something else.

Bailey's review sharpens the questions over the *meanings* of characterizing mediation as more friendly to women's concerns. Can valuing of the different voice lead to system change through women (and men) conducting their legal processes and disputes through mediation? Or, is the legal system dependent on hierarchy and able to accommodate mediation only as long as the dominant, hierarchical values have the final say, as they do now? Feminist values support mediation in some ways, but not in all ways (Gourley, this volume). If mediation fails, women are disempowered in adversarial, final legal proceedings. Finally, mediation may only seem to accommodate female values. If men do not go along with the ethic of care, mediation does not protect women from unequal and unjust results even when mediation "succeeds."

Bailey's (1989) conclusion is that the critique of oppressive relations must continue to be the consistent focus of feminism. Instead of focusing on mediation as "feminine," we should examine whether the practice of mediation reduces or perpetuates gender inequality. One such focus is provided by Kelly and Gigy (1989) in a report on one divorce mediation program. This mediation program was separate from the court system, but all settlements were referred to the spouses' lawyers for ratification. The respondents participated voluntarily in Kelly's study, so no claims can be made that the results extend to all mediated disputes.

Some critics suggest that spouses who choose mediation tend to be less angry than those pursuing court action. Thus, divorce mediation cases could be seen as easier to handle, and more positive outcomes may not be due to the mediation process. Kelly reports, however, that divorcing couples in this mediation program were not less angry and did not have better communication than couples pursing a court settlement. The main differences between the two groups were that spouses using mediation tended to be younger, more educated, and more likely to have children under 18 years old than those going to court.[3]

When spouses were asked if the divorce process (court/adversarial or mediation) helped them stand up for themselves, women in mediation had the highest positive response (Kelly, 1990). Interestingly, men who participated in mediation had the lowest positive response on the "standing up" question, with adversarial men and women in the middle. Women using mediation had higher satisfaction with their outcomes than women in adversarial settings. This included satisfaction with property division, alimony, custody, and child support, and their emotional comfort with the divorce settlement. Mediation helped both women and men better understand their children's needs and develop useful strategies to meet those needs.

Kelly noted that the opposition to mediation expressed by legal and political advocates for women is based on the belief that women are less powerful and are likely to be disadvantaged in all types of divorce mediation. Kelly and Gigy conclude that their findings do not support these concerns. Women who choose to end mediation do not seem to be disadvantaged: "Women appear to terminate mediation for essentially the 'right' reasons—feeling unempowered or overwhelmed by the data or the process, or perceiving their spouse as obstructive in negotiating fair agreements" (p. 279). Finally, even for those who terminated mediation, women, more than men, still would recommend mediation to a friend.

From Bailey (1989) we hear that mediation is not necessarily liberating for women. From Kelly and Gigy (1989) we learn that at least one setting of divorce mediation does empower women and offers greater satisfaction than traditional adversarial decisions. Using the framework I

---

[3]The data come from an ongoing longitudinal study (Kelly & Gigy, 1989). The sample of "adversarial" spouses is drawn from those filing divorce petitions in one California county and totals 225 individuals. The "mediation" spouses sought a divorce agreement through a voluntary process at a northern California mediation center. Questionnaires measured the attitudes previously reported. Given the differences between adversarial and mediation groups on education, age, and young children, observed gender differences may be these factors.

provided earlier, one might say that Kelly and Gigy's findings fit within an ADR perspective, whereas the debate Bailey presents focuses on deeper changes in the legal system. Alternatively, the litmus test of the legitimacy or power in mediation may be women's experience instead of theoretical analysis. My framework for analysis does not settle or resolve the discussion of the differences, but does highlight questions and assumptions that must be examined to assess the usefulness of mediation, and by extension ADR, for addressing conflicts involving gender.

Problem Solving

The development of the conflict resolution problem-solving workshop[4] to address large-scale conflicts was pioneered by Burton, Kelman, and others in the 1960s. Although the features of problem-solving workshops offer clear connections to feminist concerns, it is notable that its founders, and the predominant number of practitioners, are men.

The problem-solving workshop was conceived as a departure from diplomatic negotiations. A panel of facilitators is assembled to listen to representatives of parties in large-scale conflict and to seek an understanding of the causes of the protracted nature of the conflict (e.g., Turkish vs. Greek Cypriots, Protestant vs. Catholic in Northern Ireland). The panelists ask questions to try to expose the underlying values and needs that the adversaries express indirectly. The setting is a "workshop" because it is not designed to negotiate a short-term settlement, but is analytic and exploratory. The aim is for a deeper, more comprehensive and jointly developed analysis of the conflict as a basis for creating a new understanding of the situation that will be communicated to the political leaders of the conflict groups.

Kelman (1985), a social psychologist, focuses more on the psychological barriers and group dynamics that have lead to seemingly endless conflict. Burton (1987) stresses the need to help the adversaries "cost out" their current approach and different options in order to gain a more realistic view of the choices for continued conflict or steps toward settlement/resolution. In general tone, neither Kelman or Burton seem influenced by feminist analysis.

Burton (1987) says that, as part of assuring a balance of perspectives on the panel of facilitators, members should include both genders.[5] Could this be an unexpected feminist interest in co-facilitation from a

---

[4]*Problem solving*, widely used in individual and group settings, is distinct from the structured workshop described here. A problem-solving workshop is particular to efforts to resolve protracted intercommunal conflict and, within the last 4 years of Burton's thinking, attempts to address "basic human needs."

[5]Burton states that ethnic or class balance of the facilitative panel only may be relevant (pp. 43-44).

man who otherwise has not focused on this issue in his work? Unfortunately, Burton's guidance on gender is weak for two reasons.

First, his conception of gender is based on sex. Does this mean that any "woman" will do, or should there be one liberal and one radical feminist facilitator in order to have "balanced perspectives"? Moreover, if one seeks a feminist facilitator, sex (or gender) is not the decisive factor. Why couldn't a pro-feminist man meet the guidance for "balancing perspectives" on gender? Presumably, a woman feminist would have a greater degree of verisimilitude than a feminist man, but as I note shortly, this might be counterbalanced by other considerations.

Second, Burton (1987) offers gender balance as a general rule, but does not offer an illustration of how it might be important. I can envision a conflict between two patriarchal groups and wonder how a woman facilitator would be viewed. At least two choices are possible. One would be for the facilitative panel, if pro-feminist, to not allow the protagonists' values to dictate what gender people must be to act as legitimate facilitators. A different response, if one believes that the conflict is not "about gender," is to attend to the issues as defined by the parties and not be "provocative" with feminist observations. Rather than "insert" gender into the conflict, an all-male facilitative panel might be chosen.

Burton (1988) envisions a different political world where problem-solving processes replace hierarchical means of social control. Resonant with some feminist approaches (e.g., eco-feminism), he views the breakdown, even self-destruction, of traditional elite control of society through power politics. Further, he sees analytical problem-solving conflict resolution becoming institutionalized in some ADR processes.

Burton (1988) believes problem-solving workshops have the potential to take the place of the legal hierarchy and power-based negotiation and to "push societies toward a means of non-authoritative social control" (p. 23). This position certainly is harmonious with the radical feminist critique of hierarchy. Burton adds that, "While legal processes are coercive and prohibitive, [problem-solving] conflict resolution processes are positive means of social control which seek to establish nonconflictual relationships" (p. 23).

Burton's vision of problem solving is more social change oriented than mediation. Unfortunately, we do not have sufficient empirical evidence to provide a final evaluation of this vision. The practical illustrations Burton cites are heterogenous and not clearly transformative. He only offers general analytic work on mediation, adoption of ADR procedures by some federal agencies, and informal approaches to solving community problems[6]. Although these may promote deep social

---

[6]Burton compiled a broader statement of his views in four volumes published in 1990 (see Burton, 1990a, 1990b, and Burton & Dukes, 1990a, 1990b), but the earli-

change, the jury is still out on their large-scale effects and not all the examples Burton cites are related to problem-solving workshops.

What Burton's analysis does offer is an important point of contact with radical feminist perspectives. But as implemented to date, this theory has been largely silent on issues of gender conflict or on gender of the parties in conflict. Careful attention to the further development, application, and testing of Burton's needs theory (1990b) will be required to assess whether the silence on gender is yet another example of woman being subsumed within man, with the assumption that what meets the needs of men will meet the needs of women. It appears that feminist aspirations might benefit from adapting the problem-solving workshop as a practical tool and that the conflict resolution problem-solving workshop can benefit from sustained application of feminist analysis.

Feminist analysis can enhance the ideas of needs and values as a basis for protracted conflict between social groups (see Sandole-Staroste, this volume). Similarly, gathering groups of women and men together (e.g., co-workers) in a workshop setting to explore the meaning of gendered behavior—sexual harassment, job performance standards, policies on job skills, or pay structure that are gender biased—might be a way to inform, build cooperative understandings, and pursue a fundamental transformation of values, attitudes, and behavior.

Summary

I have analyzed gender conflict through the basic concepts of conflict resolution and by reviewing gender-related concerns in two particular conflict resolution practices: mediation and problem-solving workshops. The conceptual analysis has critiqued standard understandings of parties, issues, and location of conflict when applied to disputes involving gender differences. I argued that gender conflict is best conceived as a conflict of values among people rather than as a conflict between two genders— women and men. The issues in conflict are multiple, interlinked, and tied to one's basic assumptions about how gender is valued and what changes are necessary for a more just society. Consequently, the location of gender conflicts is similarly multiple and complex. I noted that peace studies have shown progress in incorporating feminist critiques into their concepts and analysis. The conceptual analysis has attempted to lay the groundwork for an improved connection between feminist and conflict analysis in order to better address deep-rooted conflicts.

---

er versions are cited due to their simplicity of statement, without being superceded by the 1990 publications.

As cases of application, I explored two concepts about whether ADR or conflict resolution is better suited to realizing feminist values. One argument is that mediation does not necessarily change the basic roots of male domination: property and power. Yet, there is at least some empirical evidence that voluntary divorce mediation may be more empowering of women than traditional court proceedings. Both points of view raise intriguing questions for the further analysis of conflict resolution through problem-solving workshops. The workshops as conceived are open to some of the transformative aims of radical feminism, but Burton's own consideration of gender relating to facilitators' perspectives is inadequately developed.

I believe this initial "map" of conflict resolution, feminist thought, and social change raises the following areas for further research:

1. The kinds of values involved in conflicts between parties of different genders;
2. Longer term effects, especially related to the deeper transformation of social relations, that alternative dispute resolution or conflict resolution activities enhance, or inhibit;
3. Problem-solving workshops as a concrete practice of raising awareness of feminist concerns in places where groups of women and men interact.

REFERENCES

Bailey, M.J. (1989, March). *Mediation as a "female" process.* Paper presented at the North American Conference on Peace and Conflict Resolution, Montreal, Quebec.

Brock-Utne, B. (1989). *Feminist perspectives on peace and peace education.* New York: Pergamon Press.

Burton, J.W. (1987). *Resolving deep-rooted conflict: A handbook.* Lanham, MD: University Press of America.

Burton, J.W. (1988). *Conflict resolution as a political system* (Working Paper #1). Fairfax, VA: Center for Conflict Analysis and Resolution.

Burton, J.W. (Ed). (1990a). *Conflict: Human needs theory.* New York: St. Martin's Press.

Burton, J.W. (1990b). *Conflict: Resolution and provention.* New York: St. Martin's Press.

Burton, J.W., & Dukes, F. (1990a). *Conflict: Practices in management, settlement and resolution.* New York: St. Martin's Press.

Burton, J.W., & Dukes, F. (Eds.). (1990b). *Conflict: Readings in management and resolution.* New York: St. Martin's Press.

Daly, M. (1978). *Gyn/ecology: The metaethics of radical feminism.* Boston: Beacon Press.

Galtung, J. (1969). Violence, peace and peace research. *Journal of Peace Research, 6*(3), 167-191.

Gilligan, C. (1982). *In a different voice.* Cambridge, MA: Harvard University Press.

hooks, B. (1984). *Feminist theory: From margin to center.* Boston: South End Press.

Kelly, J.B. (1990). Mediated and adversarial divorce: Respondents' perception of their processes and outcomes. *Mediation Quarterly, 24,* 71-88.

Kelly, J.B., & Gigy, L.L. (1989). Divorce mediation: Characteristics of clients and outcomes. In K. Kressel & D. Pruitt (Eds.), *Mediation research: The process and effectiveness of third-party intervention* (pp. 263-283). San Francisco: Jossey-Bass.

Kelman, H.C. (1985). Interactive problem solving: A social-psychological approach to conflict resolution. In W. Klassen (Ed.), *Dialogue toward inter-faith understanding* (pp. 293-314). Tantur/Jerusalem: Ecumenical Institute for Theological Research.

Kramarae, C. (1981). *Women and men speaking.* Rowley, MA: Newbury House Publishers.

Kreisburg, L. (1982). *Social conflicts* (2nd ed.) Englewood Cliffs, NJ: Prentice- Hall.

MacKinnon, C. (1985). Feminist discourse, moral value and the law—a conversation. *Buffalo Law Review, 34,* 11-87.

Menkel-Meadow, C. (1985). Portia in a different voice: Speculations on a women's lawyering process. *Berkeley Women's Law Journal, 1,* 39-63.

Rifkin, J. (1984). Mediation from a feminist perspective: Promise and problems. *Law and Inequality, 2*(1), 21-31.

Riskin, L.L. (1984). Toward new standards for the neutral lawyer in mediation. *Arizona Law Review, 26,* 329-62.

Selben, E., & Steiner, R. (1991). The American political landscape. *Utne Reader, 48,* 97-99.

Spender, D. (1985). *Man made language* (2nd ed.). London: Routledge & Kegan Paul.

11

A Wittgensteinian Approach to the Meaning of Conflict

Angela R. Febbraro
University of Guelph
Roland D. Chrisjohn
University of British Columbia

In this chapter, we examine some of the assumptions that have guided most psychological investigations of conflict and gender.[1] Attention to psychological assumptions is important because many are shared by all who study conflict; similarly, many of the results of psychologists' efforts are widely cited and used, not only by other academics and researchers, but by practitioners of conflict management and resolution as well. We also present an alternative approach to the meaning or conceptualization of conflict (or any psychological concept) based on the philosophical writings of Wittgenstein. Finally, we draw on the work of Penelope (1990) to demonstrate how the use of language within the con-

---

[1]As psychologists who have been trained within the discipline, we think we are in a good position to identify some of these assumptions, although we recognize that the degree to which they are held by individual psychologists will vary. We acknowledge that our discussion of these assumptions will reflect our own assumptions and concerns regarding conventional psychological theory, research, and practice. These become clearer in the course of this chapter.

text of a patriarchal society reflects the unequal power relationships between women and men; that, accordingly, conflict is often talked about in adversarial, "power-over" terms; that there exist alternative ways of conceptualizing conflict (and power); and that approaches to meaning that do not take into account the politics of gender relations and of language are poor candidates to offer much enlightenment regarding gender and conflict.

A WITTGENSTEINIAN APPROACH TO CONFLICT

Our critique of conflict research makes use of the work of Wittgenstein and his followers.[2] Introducing Wittgenstein's approach is not easy because his work ranged across many interrelated topics, and by his own admission he was not particularly successful in providing an intelligible road map. Moreover, we are involved in our own struggle to better understand Wittgenstein's ideas, so that what we present here is necessarily simplistic and highlights only those aspects of his work we have found useful. (For more comprehensive analyses of his work, see ter Hark, 1990; Baker & Hacker, 1982, 1983, 1985).

Some Major Points

Wittgenstein's (1953) later philosophy was concerned with language and how it is used to depict our world. His starting point was an objection to the assumption that words acquire their meaning via correlations with objects in the world. As harmless as this might sound, Wittgenstein traced the consequences of this assumption to a vast sea of troubles. In showing us the shoreline of this sea, he developed an original, alternative way of talking about our world.

Wittgenstein's investigations interest us in a variety of specifics. Foremost is his argument that empirical findings do not bear on conceptual matters. Until the conceptual problems have been worked out, what

[2]We have also explored several other approaches to meaning (e.g., linguistic approaches such as discourse analysis, hermeneutics, semiotics), but find these problematic for many of the same reasons we find traditional psychological or psychometric approaches wanting. For example, semioticians use elaborate analytical taxonomies and formal algorithms to interpret texts (Scholes, 1982); hermeneuticists and discourse analysts often try to uncover underlying, abstract dimensions of meaning (see Grimshaw, 1990, on the "proto-taxonomy" of conflict talk; Polkinghorne, 1988); traditional linguists espouse the notions of a universal grammar and context-independent syntactic rules; and sociolinguists, while trying to include social context in their analyses, often still try to develop discourse rules that are general and context-free (Mishler, 1979).

is or is not a useful empirical question is unknown. To give a simple example, suppose we find that hat size correlates significantly with individual differences in conflict resolution style. Have we made a useful empirical finding, or elaborated our conception of conflict resolution? The correlation does not diagnose itself; we can only resolve the issue by reference, for example, to how the concepts conflict and style are used in everyday language. Yet, have not presumptive interpretations of the meaning of such correlations been drawn by many who find correlations among gender and various conflict styles?

The measurement of psychological constructs is based on a positivist (or logical empiricist)[3] epistemology (Ellett, 1985; Febbraro, 1990; Norris, 1983). According to construct validity theory (Cronbach & Meehl, 1955), in order to ascertain that a particular psychological instrument (e.g., an intelligence test) in fact measures a particular theoretical construct (e.g., intelligence), objective, empirical data "must" be gathered. Typically, the psychometric properties of the instrument are assessed (e.g., its dimensionality, internal consistency) and its "validity" obtained (e.g., by assessing its correlation with other supposed measures of the construct). Without such data, psychologists cannot be sure they have measured a concept adequately. Further, because psychologists do not always agree about the meaning of a concept and are not certain about its ramifications, construct validation also provides a method for discovering correlates that (it is hoped) can enrich the understanding of a concept.

Wittgenstein pointed out that conceptualization must precede the data gathering, a point with which most psychologists would agree. Yet, as Taylor and Beinstein argue (this volume), research about gender may be based on a largely inadequately conceptualized construct. And, as we argue here, much research about conflict is equally poorly conceptualized (indeed, the whole notion of conceptualization, to the extent it reflects empiricist, objectivist philosophy, leads us astray). Beyond this basic point, users of data-driven research are inclined to make a number of missteps in their approach to conceptual clarification, especially reification or objectification; confusion of primitive metaphysical theories[4] with grammar (grammar in Wittgensteinian terms, is a set of rules for

---

[3]Although no uniform or "classical" definition of logical positivism (or logical empiricism) exists, there are a few generally agreed upon tenets that hold particular relevance for the present discussion. These include: (a) a belief in scientific realism (i.e., the idea that science seeks knowledge about one real world and that scientific truths are independent of observers); (b) the notion that science is the accumulation of value-free, objective facts; and (c) the idea that scientific concepts are precise, have fixed meanings, and can be described in terms of set-theoretical models or axiomatic, deductivist principles (Hacking, 1981).

[4]Primitive metaphysical theories, according to Baker and Hacker (1982), are unverified empirical assertions about the world that are confused with grammar

the use of a concept); confounding of metaphor with "reality"; and pursuit of classical category definitions for concepts that have no such limitations. Perhaps most insidiously, once such an approach becomes the unexamined ideology of a discipline, it becomes difficult to see these missteps as problems.

THE PRACTICE OF AN UNTENABLE EPISTEMOLOGY: AN EXAMPLE

The Thomas-Kilmann MODE Instrument

Because of its popularity in conflict research, and because we believe that it adequately represents the psychometric approach to conceptualization and measurement within psychology, we have chosen the Thomas-Kilmann (T-K) Management-of-Differences Exercise (MODE) Instrument (Thomas & Kilmann, 1974a) as our example of shortcomings in psychological research.[5] We do not wish to suggest that the T-K MODE Instrument is exceptional in any way, we could have selected other measures popular in conflict research, such as the Rahim Organizational Conflict Inventory (ROCI; Rahim, 1983), and our discussion would not have required radical alteration. However, before we offer our critique of the MODE, we describe what it is and how it works.

The T-K MODE Instrument was designed to assess the repertoire of conflict-handling skills that an individual uses in conflict situations (i.e., situations in which a person's wishes differ from those of another). Proposed are five conflict-handling styles or modes: competing, collaborating, compromising, avoiding, and accommodating.[6] These

---

(i.e., grammar in the Wittgensteinian sense, or roughly, "how a language operates"). People may *believe* that intelligence is innate, for example, but there is no predisposition in English (or in any other language) that this belief (or primitive metaphysical theory) must be so.

[5]We should clarify that the T-K MODE Instrument is not regarded as a measure of "conflict," per se; rather, it was designed by Thomas and Kilmann to provide profiles of individual behavior in situations of conflict. Still, we believe that to make the distinction between the meaning of a concept (e.g., conflict) and how it is "played out" in individual behavior is, in some ways, illusory. First, we question the meaningfulness of speaking of conflict as something abstracted from its context of individual behavior in conflict situations; and second (related to our first concern), we believe that this distinction contributes to the reification/objectification of both meaning and behavior. Moreover, even if we maintain the distinction, the same philosophical arguments that we will make would still apply, regardless of whether we were speaking of conflict per se, or of individual behavior in conflict situations.

[6]This five-category classification scheme was first introduced by Blake, Shepard and Mouton in 1964.

styles, according to Thomas and Kilmann's approach, are defined by two underlying dimensions: assertiveness/nonassertiveness and cooperativeness/noncooperativeness. An individual's style of dealing with conflict is determined by the relative combinations of the two dimensions: The competing style is considered to be high in assertiveness and low in cooperativeness; the collaborating style reflects high assertiveness and high cooperativeness; the avoiding style combines low assertiveness and low cooperativeness; the accommodating style results from high cooperativeness and low assertiveness; and, the compromising style reflects moderate amounts of both cooperativeness and assertiveness. Thus, conflict styles are defined conceptually by Thomas and Kilmann as a person's tendencies to behave cooperatively/noncooperatively and assertively/nonassertively in conflict. In practical terms, this amounts to relative preferences for competing, collaborating, compromising, avoiding, and accommodating behavior.

A person's preferences are measured by her or his responses to the 30-item forced-choice MODE Instrument, which presents pairs of desirability-matched statements written to reflect the conflict styles.[7] Respondents are asked to consider situations in which they find their wishes differing from those of another person and to respond by circling the statement in each pair that is most characteristic of their own behavior. Respondents receive five MODE subscale scores on the basis of their choices which, presumably, reflect their preferred style.

An Empiricist, Deterministic and Objectivist Foundation

As with all psychometric instruments based on classical test theory, the T-K MODE Instrument is founded on the idea that each one of a person's scores is a function of some portion of "true score" plus some portion of "error." Similarly, correlations between test scores on different test-taking occasions, which are often used to assess reliability, and correlations between test scores and other indicators of the behavior, which are used to assess its validity, are also based on this assumption. Indeed, most construct validation efforts involve the use of correlation coefficients, and the T-K MODE Instrument is no exception. Empirical research into the psychometric (and, potentially, "conceptual") properties of the MODE has been, not atypically, almost entirely correlational (Kilmann & Thomas, 1977; Thomas & Kilmann, 1978).

This research assumes the idea that meaning is inherent within a structure such as a network of correlation coefficients. As feminist and other philosophers have argued, however, one's perceptions (and con-

---

[7]In the instrument's original development, lists of items were generated to "operationalize" the five conflict-handling modes (Thomas & Kilmann, 1974b).

ceptions) of the world do not result solely from the "things" being perceived. Perceptions, even precisely recorded ones, are not objective and disembodied. They are influenced by the perceiver's experiences, expectations, and the contexts in which they are perceived (Bleier, 1984; Feyerabend, 1975; Haraway, 1987; Harding, 1986, 1991; Gergen, 1982; Keller, 1985; Kuhn, 1970). Others who have studied language and concept formation (e.g., Lakoff, 1987; Rosch & Mervis, 1975; Wittgenstein, 1953) have concluded it is fallacious to presume that empirical "effects" can completely inform us about meaning; empirical effects underdetermine putative psychological process.

People make sense of empirical effects on the basis of their prior understanding or experience. Therefore, to presume that empirical effects such as correlation coefficients inform us about the meaning of a concept is to commit the same logical error. Construct validity theory claims that correlations between scores on tests indicate connections between the concepts that they represent and, therefore, the ramifications of their respective meanings. It is important, however, that meanings not be confused with their correlates (Guttman, 1977; Wittgenstein, 1953). This principle is basic to any understanding of the appropriate inferences that can be drawn from correlation coefficients: Simply because two "things" are correlated with one another does not mean they are the same or conceptually related. Many possible explanations could account for empirical associations between variables. Empirically trained psychologists know this, but too often ignore the cautions of which they are aware.

In another vein, according to Thomas and Kilmann (1974a), conflict styles result from both personal predispositions and the requirements of situations. Similarly, an individual's preference for any particular conflict mode may be due to "temperament *or* [italics added] practice" (p. 11). We have difficulty, however, with a number of assumptions that underlie these suppositions.

First, as many feminist thinkers (e.g., Bleier, 1984; Haraway, 1987; Harding, 1986; Rosser, 1990;) and others (e.g., Levins & Lewontin, 1985) have explained, theories that suggest that behavior is due to biology or culture, or their interactions, rely on the false dichotomy between biology and culture (or between person and situation). Such a dichotomy, they argue, is based on the erroneous notion that an individual (or her or his "biology") can be meaningfully separated from her or his social and political context. Second, although Thomas and Kilmann do claim to consider situational or contextual factors in their theory of conflict, the notion of "conflict style" inevitably shifts the attention back onto the individual. As Hocker and Wilmot (1985) pointed out, individual style approaches to conflict (including psychometric instruments such as the MODE) treat such styles as if they were a trait belonging to a person. In addition, without repeated measures (which introduce their own problems), such instruments cannot reflect change over time, nor the variability that most of us enact in our lives. Indeed, to assign a person one label that supposedly captures their conflict style is a "gross oversimplification" (Hocker & Wilmot, 1985, p. 50), abstracted from context or culture. Conflict-measuring instruments that examine predispositions assume situational consistency and do not reflect variability associated with context, relationships, time, and so on (Hocker & Wilmot, 1985). Ultimately, individuals are seen as "functions" of the personality traits they "have," and their behavior, however changeable, is functionally or probabilistically determined. Too easily then comes the inference that something inherent operates to produce conflict-handling style, and given the appropriate circumstances (personal or situational), standard reactions will be elicited.[8]

Up to this point, our critique of the T-K MODE Instrument has been largely "philosophical." However, the MODE (and its use) can be criticized on other grounds as well. It is questionable, for example, whether the MODE can be "validly" used to study samples other than those that served as the original norm group in 1974 (339 managers at middle and upper levels of business and government organizations). Such a question seems especially relevant since in 1974 the norming group were doubtless almost exclusively male and white. Even if the instrument is valid for its original group, can it be assumed to measure accurately the same construct in women, and women of any class and race at that? Or working-class men or men of color? Measurement tools developed using such a sample may not generalize beyond white, middle- or upper-class managers or government officials.

Certain theoretical claims of the MODE have also been chal-

---

[8]We should mention, too, that we have concerns regarding Thomas and Kilmann's suggestion that temperament may determine, in whole or in part, an individual's conflict style. The word "temperament" (along with "predisposition") is often used in the psychological literature to refer to biological causes (e.g., Kagan & Snidman, 1991; Thomas, Chess, & Birch, 1968). Without clear evidence to support biological determinants of conflict style, however, we believe that the use of such words is potentially misleading and dangerous. Again, attention is deflected from the social, political, and historical conditions that may help us to understand situations of conflict, to inherent mechanisms such as "aggression" or aggressive instinct. For similar reasons, we are weary of empirical investigations into the "Jungian" (psychoanalytic) bases of the Thomas-Kilmann conflict styles (Kilmann & Thomas, 1975; Mills, Robey, & Smith, 1985). Such investigations emphasize and presuppose the existence of "underlying" or "hidden" traits/motives that determine (again, in mechanistic fashion) individuals' behavior in conflict situations. Further, such investigations share in common with objectivist theories and methodologies (classical test theory, construct validation) the search for an underlying, latent "object."

lenged. For example, using a nonmetric distance scaling program, van de Vliert and Kabanoff (1990) found that responses to the MODE clustered according to its proposed underlying two-dimensional structure, but that there was poor discrimination between competing and collaborating and between avoiding and accommodating. Additionally, a study by Carlin (1991) has even questioned the adequacy of a two-dimensional representation for the MODE. Her analysis favored a three-dimensional solution that was distinct in important ways from what Thomas and Kilmann have led us to expect (i.e., the compromising mode was not located "in the middle" of the multidimensional space).[9]

It is also unclear that the modes represent combined manifestations of two dimensions because each mode has been interpreted in a variety of ways. For example, according to Thomas and Kilmann (1974a), competing could include standing up for your rights, defending a position that you believe is correct, or simply trying to win, each of which can be evaluated differently with regard to a cooperativeness dimension. Similar distinctions in meaning are made with respect to the other three modes. And what does it mean to say that compromising is "intermediate" in both assertiveness and cooperativeness? For example, does it make sense to represent it as located somewhere "in the middle" of two-dimensional space? We are not convinced that it does make sense, on either conceptual grounds, or as Carlin's (1991) study has shown, empirical grounds.

To get around these problems, Wittgenstein provided an alternative to empirical approaches to conceptual clarification and illustrated it at various places in his work (e.g., Wittgenstein, 1953, 1958). He suggested that conceptual clarification be carried out by examining how a word is employed, through elaborating the circumstances of its use (Baker & Hacker, 1982). Wittgenstein considered that the meaning of a word is not obscure ("nothing is hidden"; Malcolm, 1986), but that ordinarily we get little practice in clarification. Hence, even though we can use a word perfectly well in everyday discourse, it takes effort to provide a clear overview of the meaning of a concept. We are not suggesting that obtaining this surview is a simple endeavor; we are suggesting it has not been done, for either the term *conflict* or *conflict style*.

---

[9]On a technical level, the MODE suffers from more than a few difficulties (van de Vliert & Kabanoff, 1990). Reliabilities of the subscales, often characterized as "moderate" by the developers, are in fact rather low (in the .60s), certainly too low to place confidence in any judgment made about a specific individual's "style" (Kaplan & Saccuzzo, 1982). Validities are based largely on correlations with other instruments as previously discussed. The forced-choice format creates linear dependencies in subscale scores, which makes multivariate analyses difficult (Clemens, 1965), influences univariate statistics in complex ways, and precludes evaluation of Thomas and Kilmann's assertion that we are capable of using all five modes.

Carrying out a conceptual clarification is likely to involve a host of activities, and although we can use our mastery of a language for conceptual clarification (i.e., we can explain our usage of words), we cannot give a "read out" of the meaning of a concept, for such a read out (or list of features) does not exist. However, anything that illustrates the manner in which a word is employed assists in its clarification. Wittgenstein was adamant that these activities did not constitute a "method" or a "technique"; belief in a technique demonstrates "contempt for the individual case," or the treatment of different concepts as if they had common properties or generalizable explications. Concepts, he insisted, had all kinds of uses, some similar to uses of other concepts, some unique. How other concepts are clarified may give us ideas or hints about where to start, but clarification cannot be reduced to a system. The only way to proceed is one concept at a time.

This brings us to another important point. Classical test theory, construct validity, and traditional scientific epistemology all assume a particular (objectivist) view regarding the appropriate way to categorize. According to this view, the world (and concepts) can be structured along set-theoretic, classical models in which concepts are defined by establishing their necessary and sufficient properties, differentiating them from other concepts, and placing them into mutually exclusive categories. Concepts (or constructs) and the methods used to define them reflect the assumption of an objective, disembodied reality. The viewpoint relies on assuming the knower is separate from the known. Lakoff (1987) and others (Harding, 1986; Keller, 1985) demonstrated how such a world view is untenable and provides no reliable foundation for an approach to meaning. Lakoff offered an alternative world view, which he called "experientialism,"[10] in which concepts are not defined in terms of sufficient and necessary properties. Instead, Lakoff argued, we can learn about linguistic categories by examining the metaphors in which they occur. For example, his discussions of the concepts of *anger* and *lust*—and of the similarity between the metaphors in which these two

---

[10]For a discussion of experientialism and its empirical support, see Lakoff (1987). Most of the support for this world view is drawn from linguistic and anthropological studies (e.g., Rosch's, 1973, work on color in the Dani language; Kay & McDaniel's, 1978, work on color categories; Lounsbury's, 1964, work on kinship categories). Wittgenstein also played an important role in exposing the problems in the classical theory of categories. He is associated with the ideas of family resemblance (i.e., members of a category may be related to one another without members having common properties); centrality (i.e., some members of a category may be better examples of the category than others); extendable boundaries (i.e., a characteristic of open-ended categories, such as "game"); and, membership gradience (i.e., at least some categories have degrees of membership and no clear boundaries).

concepts are used—help us to understand the way we conceptualize anger and lust. The conceptualization reflects the close association between sex and violence in Indo-European culture (without, however, suggesting that there is any necessary connection between the two). Lakoff's approach to learning about meaning is consistent with Wittgenstein's emphasis on everyday language, for it provides a way of elaborating the manifold uses of a term.

In Wittgenstein's own clarification tool kit were a number of useful devices, including elaborations of commonplace metaphorical expressions, descriptions of ordinary language games (vignettes showing how a word is used), and descriptions of discordant language games (scenarios showing how a word cannot be used). Baker and Hacker (1982) provide a description of 13 tools for conceptual clarification. Although we cannot restate here their excellent presentation, we consider it useful to apply their ground plan to the concept of *conflict*.

The Concept of Conflict

In ordinary English, conflict is a verb and a noun used to depict instances in which people do not get along, or disagree, or act on this disagreement. We recognize degrees of disagreement, from minor differences of opinion to organized (*sic*) warfare on a worldwide scale. We speak of disharmony between political opinions or personal tastes. Interestingly, as pointed out by Szasz (1987), "intrapsychic" conflict is a metaphorical extension of the socially formalized phenomenon.[11]

Hocker and Wilmot (1985) list some common metaphorical expressions more or less related to the concept of conflict. Other metaphors for conflict involve sensory distortion (e.g., "We don't see eye to eye"; "You don't hear what I'm saying"), physical problems of various sorts (e.g., "A square peg in a round hole"; "He grates on me"; "We're not on the same wavelength"), combine sensory and physical opposition (e.g., "We're at an impasse"), or compare conflicts of differing scale to one another (e.g., "He and I are at war"; "The USA and the USSR were eyeball to eyeball in the Cuban missile crisis"). Notice that there is no

---

[11]Herein lies another instance of reification or decontextualization within psychology: To personalize conflict (i.e., to locate it within an individual) serves to deflect attention away from the broader, historical, social, and political context of any particular conflict. Furthermore, such a deflection can contribute to a process of victim-blaming; for example, if a woman were involved in a conflict with her employer (i.e., she is being sexually harassed by her boss) and a personal view of conflict is presumed, it would be possible for observers to locate the conflict within the woman, rather than to understand it in terms of unequal power structures, systemic discrimination, or patriarchy (Caplan & Nelson, 1974).

thought that these expressions depict a real state of affairs (eyeball to eye-ball would be uncomfortable, regardless of how long it could be maintained); these are just examples of how we talk about conflict.

Conflict has a beginning and can have an ending, so it could have genuine duration. It does not have a location (i.e., it may occur between two people, but exists in neither one of them), although aggressive actions or disputes indicative of conflict occur in specifiable places (e.g., on a battlefield; inside a place of residence). As previously mentioned, we recognize differing levels of intensity or magnitude of conflict, on at least an ordinal scale. Conflict is not summonable as an act of will, but one can "look for trouble" or try to avoid disputes.

Conflict is not an objective feature of the world and is not defined by information about the external or the internal world; the context provides what is meant by conflict. There are no necessary or sufficient conditions the satisfaction of which entails an instantiation of conflict. Conflict has direction: We are usually in conflict about something or with someone.

The main use of the word "conflict" is as a description of a state of affairs between people and not as a personal disposition. Similar constructions are used intelligibly (e.g., "John has a contentious personality"), but again, conflict itself is but clumsily used in such circumstances. "Being in conflict" can only appropriately be a state of affairs for those who have language or will (i.e., humans). Humanity and Nature, or two dogs fighting, are only metaphorically in conflict. Finally, the criterial and/or symptomatic basis for the instantiation of conflict (see Baker, 1974, for a discussion of Wittgenstein's use of these terms) seems to develop from our earliest experiences with one another and so seems to be largely a problem for developmental psychology (Baker & Hacker, 1982).

This discussion merely begins the process of clarifying the concept of *conflict*. This process, although not simple, is not mysterious or hidden either, and does not require objective, scientific analysis. The process could continue indefinitely (i.e., the conceptual "category" of conflict has extendable "boundaries"). Still, we believe the process has been mystified, in a sense, by various disciplines that have grown up around the concept of conflict and rendered its study complex in ways that it is not (i.e., through objectification, reification, and decontextualization). For example, much of the work cited earlier has been concerned with supposed consistent styles of conflict management possessed by individuals. Some work examines the putative effectiveness of conflict resolution strategies, either as they "inhere" in individuals or as they are developed by special training programs. Still other work investigates short- or long-term mental health consequences of exposure to conflict situations. As we have seen, the typical psychological (or psychometric) approach to conflict research is built on shaky philosophical ground; the same arguments, we hold, would apply to these other (dubious) elaborations. On the other hand, analyses similar to the one laid out for conflict could be made for the variety of responses people have to conflict. What do people mean when they report avoiding conflict, or compromising, or collaborating, and so forth? We think it important that such efforts be made. Until they are, it may not be very meaningful how people are scored on a conflict style scale.

THE STUDY OF GENDER AND CONFLICT

To argue that researchers need to attend to what people mean by conflict is only part of what we have set out to accomplish, however. Our other purpose concerns the study of gender and conflict. In general, the literature on gender and conflict style abounds with inconsistent findings.[12] Burrell, Donohue, and Allen (1988) stated that this lack of a clear picture is reflected in Conrad's (1985) review of more than 100 studies on gender differences as predictors of conflict style. However, even if the literature were more consistent (or more directly concerned with the meaning of conflict per se), given what we consider the problematic nature of traditional empiricist methodologies, we believe it is impossible to rely on what has been "discovered" about gender and conflict on the basis of such studies.[13] In the following section, we briefly explore an alternative approach to the understanding of conflict that, in our view, has the potential to be more sensitive to gender issues than are traditional approaches.

Gender, Power, and Language: The Patriarchal Universe of Discourse

As insightful as Wittgenstein's ideas may be with regard to the meaning of psychological concepts, his work does little to enlighten the discourse on gender and conflict. In particular, Wittgenstein did not address the

---

[12]Some research (e.g., Kilmann & Thomas, 1977; Rahim, 1983) has found males to be more dominating and less compromising than females, whereas females use more regressive, prosocial, compromising, avoiding, and passive styles of conflict management (Shockley-Zalabek & Morley, 1984; cited in Burrell et al., 1988). Other studies report no differences in how females and males handle conflict situations (Bell, Chafetz, & Horn, 1982; Rubin & Brown, 1977; each cited in Burrell et al., 1988). Chusmir and Mills (1989), for example, found that, at home and at work, managers of similar level, regardless of gender, resolved conflict in similar ways.

[13]Psychology has also been criticized for making sexist assumptions about women and for its unfounded generalizations about females and ethnic/cultural minorities on the basis of white male samples; see Sherif (1987). These criticisms apply equally well to research on gender and conflict, as we have alluded to pre-

differential power relations among members of linguistic communities. In this regard, we have found Penelope's (1990) work especially enlightening, for in our view, any meaningful understanding of gender and conflict must take into account the unequal power relations between women and men, within and without situations of conflict.

How did Penelope (1990) accomplish this? She did this by detailing how certain words and sentence structures within the English language have been used as instruments of oppression. For example, she describes several of the linguistic ways in which men perpetrate their dominance over women:

1. using abstractions that are not explicit about events in the world;
2. attributing agency to abstract or inanimate objects;
3. suppressing human agency and responsibility for events and actions;
4. using inaccurate or distorted descriptions (e.g., euphemisms and dysphemisms) to make supposedly true statements about the world; and
5. using metaphor to emphasize selected aspects of events, objects, and people, and to hide other, equally significant features of experience.

Consistent with a Wittgensteinian approach to meaning, Penelope's work also urges us to examine closely the ways in which we use a concept in everyday language, that is, to understand the way people use words and grammatical structures to serve specific purposes. The following examples provide a brief illustration of some of these points.

"Domestic incidents" and "surgical strikes". When we use the phrase *domestic incident* in our everyday lives, we understand that we do not mean that someone accidentally broke a glass or spilled some milk.

---

viously. Moreover, many feminist philosophers and scientists (e.g., Harding, Keller) have argued that traditional positivist/empiricist science reflects a masculine epistemology, and is, therefore, problematic as a source of knowledge about women and men (or about any other area of study). This epistemology, as described earlier, is characterized by objectivity, detachment, and the tendency to split apart or abstract phenomena from their contexts. In psychology, for example, gender "effects" are isolated from context effects in ANOVA tables. Similarly, psychology's focus on the individual often leads researchers to ignore the broader social and political context in which people live. Indeed, Weisstein (1971) explains many psychologists' failure to understand women by their insistence on looking for inner traits that agree with gender stereotypes (and that are often buttressed by notions of biological determinism) and by their tendency to discount the importance of the broader social context.

Rather, we know that a conflict has taken place, that it has occurred in a place of residence, and that it has involved at least two people who are not strangers (and who may, in fact, be living together, married to one another, or related in some way). We may reasonably guess that a person, probably a man, has just battered, murdered, or raped another person, probably a woman. As Penelope explains, a phrase such as *domestic incident* is a euphemism for the violence that is directed by men, typically, against women; the phrase does not explicitly identify what was done, by whom (i.e., agency), or to whom. The use of such a euphemism serves to keep hidden this context of violence. Similarly, the phrase *abused woman* or *abused child* leaves unanswered who is responsible for the abuse; instead, the adjective "abused" draws attention to the woman or child and is used as if to describe something inherent about them (Penelope, 1990). Furthermore, the word "abused" implies that there exist appropriate *uses* for women and children and thus serves to define women and children as objects. These are some of the ways in which language can be used to serve the interests of particular groups of people (e.g., those who are in power, in this case, men) and to maintain, as it were, the status quo.

Similarly, the ways in which we, as members of a "western" linguistic community, talk about international conflicts (e.g., wars) reveals much about how we conceptualize such conflicts and about the context in which such conflicts are perpetrated. Human agency (e.g., the act of killing) is denied or cloaked through abstraction, metaphor, and euphemism, in order to present a certain picture of reality, and again, to serve the interests of particular groups. Thus, we hear phrases such as *surgical strikes, carpet bombing, collateral damage,* and *softening up a position,* instead of *people (specific names?) were killed (murdered? raped?) by military forces.* Presumably, to state explicitly that innocent people were killed for some unknown or questionable "cause" might render "the war effort" less popular. Furthermore, it can be seen that many of these metaphors possess gender-relevant, and often sexual, connotations (e.g., "softening up a position," "enemy thrust").[14] Cohn's (1987) account of the role that this specialized language (what she refers to as "technostrategic") plays in nuclear strategic thinking speaks eloquently to this very theme.

Cohn's account is a telling explication of how language can promote certain systems of thought while disallowing and excluding others. Like Penelope, Cohn argues that we must pay careful attention to the language we use, that is, "whom it allows us to communicate with and what it allows us to think as well as say" (p. 690). Through her analysis, we recognize the abstraction and euphemism of the metaphors used in

---

[14]See also Burke and McKeen (1989) and Gutek (1989) for discussions on how the language used in traditional, male-dominated industries often incorporates sports, sex, and war metaphors.

talk about nuclear war (e.g., "clean bombs," "penetration aids"). Cohn demonstrates how the imagery of the language reflects male sexuality, male power, and the association of weapons with domestic bliss, male birth, and male creation. Such language serves to minimize the seriousness of militarist activities and to deny their deadly consequences. And, once again, the link between sexuality and violence, as described in Lakoff's (1987) metaphorical analysis, rears its ugly head.

Cohn (1987) aptly warns that although the imagery of the metaphors used in technostrategic might be transparent (the general theme is that to disarm is to emasculate), individual motivations must not be read from such imagery. The imagery itself does not originate in particular individuals, but rather in broader social, political, economic, and cultural contexts. Still, as Cohn argues, the technostrategic conceptual system is an abstraction far removed from the concrete realities of what one is talking about and creating through discourse (killing, rape). The phrases *limited nuclear war* or *managing the nuclear arms race*, for example, seem to make sense only within this abstract conceptual system. Speaking of the realities of human suffering and mass murder would be alien to this discourse. However, although the discourse may be abstract and seems to make sense only within a "world of its own," it serves real, concrete, political purposes. Indeed, almost paradoxically, such an "abstract" conceptual system can only have meaning within a particular social and political context.

And although it is tempting to attribute such problems as militarism to language itself and, therefore, to conclude that we need only change the words in order to eliminate militarism, these and other problems do not reside within language, nor within individual language users. Without radical alterations in behavior, systems of thought, and existing power relations (i.e., contexts), changing words will make little difference (Cameron, 1985; Penelope, 1990; Spender, 1980). Language can be used for oppressive and violent purposes; but language itself cannot oppress—nor can it "break our bones" (cf. Penelope, 1990).[15]

Alternative Conceptualizations of Conflict and Power

As we have seen in our discussion of the everyday usage of *conflict*, the term is often used in situations in which people oppose one another or in which there is competition for mutually exclusive (or mutually desired) goals. Accordingly, conflict is conceptualized as a zero-sum

---

[15]Although Penelope does an excellent job of describing how language is used for oppressive purposes (i.e., to serve patriarchy), she "slips up" from time to time (as we all do), by attributing agency to language, rather than to those who use language (i.e., people).

game (Baron & Byrne, 1991). However, this adversarial notion of conflict reflects a particular approach to power, one requiring winners and losers (Waltz, 1954). Such a competitive notion of power, in which individuals possess power "over" others, is a masculine notion of power, reflective of a masculine world view (Gilligan, 1982; Miller, 1976; Schaef, 1985).[16] Thus, our everyday usage of *conflict*—which seems related to a particular notion of power—may well reflect a masculine world view and the patriarchal culture in which it makes sense. As we argued throughout this chapter, language must be understood within its social and political context. And, from our discussion of the metaphors of conflict, at least some of the "sexual politics" of conflict talk should already be apparent. In order to understand "gender and conflict," then, it is necessary to understand the politics of gender within patriarchy, the politics of language, and the politics of power; for the notion of power that informs our present dominant use of the terms *gender* and *conflict* is of a particular variety. Implicit in this understanding is the possibility of alternative conceptualizations of power and conflict.

An alternative notion of power, that is, a feminine or woman's notion, has already been described by some feminist writers (see especially, Gilligan, 1982; Miller, 1976). This alternative conceptualizes power in terms of promoting the development of each individual, rather than in terms of aggressing against, controlling, limiting, or destroying others. Gilligan refers to it as a power of care (similar, in essence, to an "ethic" of care). Accordingly, the nurturance, growth, and empowerment of others within the context of interpersonal relationships, and the maintenance of harmony with nature, are all considered vital (Belenky, Clinchy, Goldberger, & Tarule, 1986; Gilligan, 1982; Grant, 1988; Lunneborg, 1990). Ruddick (1989) discusses maternal power, expressed in keeping children healthy, creating schools, jobs, day cares, hospitals, and work schedules that serve the interests of both mothers and their children. Helgeson (1990) and Marshall (1984) describe women's ways of leadership in terms of care, compassion, empathy, nurturance, and inspiration—all connective values in which the importance of maintaining relationships is paramount. And, in contrast to seeing power as a zero-sum game, as is the case within the White Male System described by Schaef (1985), the Female System defines power as limitless, and as

---

[16]Our use of the terms *masculine* or *feminine* at various points in our discussion does not indicate an essentialist view of such terms. We do not believe for example, that a masculine world view is biologically determined, essential, or natural to the male sex; similarly for a feminine world view. Indeed, we have difficulties with the use of such terms in the first place; rather than being discrete, objective categories, our view is that femininity and masculinity are socially constructed dichotomies whose primary purpose is to serve patriarchal interests. See Stoltenberg (1989) for further discussion on these points.

increasing when given away or shared. Within the Female System, power is described as a capacity for the entire community as social, rather than individual, hierarchical, or as necessitating the domination of some by others.

If it is possible to conceptualize power in a radically different way (e.g., as nurturance and growth), then it is also possible to reconceptualize conflict. Indeed, Miller (1976) also discussed conflict from a woman's perspective. As she explains, conflict has been a taboo area for women, as women are supposed to be the quintessential accommodaters, mediators, adapters, and soothers. Yet, conflict is necessary if women are to build a different future and to empower themselves. In Miller's words,

> All of us, but women especially, are taught to see conflict as something frightening and evil. These connotations have been assigned by the dominant group and have obscured the necessity for conflict. Even more crucially, they obscure the fundamental nature of reality—the fact that, in its most basic sense, conflict is inevitable, the source of all *growth* [italics added], and an absolute necessity if one is to be alive. (p. 125)

Miller's call is for women to challenge the negative connotations, in patriarchal society, of the notion of conflict, to engage in conflict, and thus, to challenge the status quo and women's position in patriarchal society.

Unfortunately, within the present system of dominance relations in which we live, it seems difficult for to us to come up with metaphors of conflict in which "growth" is the primary image, rather than aggression (but see, perhaps, Popper, 1966). Still, we are reminded that, for the world to be different, more than words must change; so too must the political context in which words and concepts derive meaning.

CONCLUSIONS

It may seem anticlimactic that we conclude with nothing "more" than descriptions—no theories, no data. However, Wittgenstein stated that the end product of unravelling the knotty reasoning underlying philosophical confusion was not a theory, just "no knots!" Our intention was to draw attention to a number of, in our view, questionable assumptions underlying the traditional psychometric approach to meaning and to provide the outline for what we consider a more fruitful approach. Wittgenstein has shown us the philosophical problems with traditional assumptions and methodologies, whereas Penelope has raised our awareness of the social and political implications of these assumptions and of our discourses. Together, their work demonstrates the inadequacy of how gender, conflict, and power have been conceptualized by many psychologists thus far. We believe that the considerations raised herein render the status of a great deal of preexisting work on conflict up in the air. Certainly, a reexamination of results in light of these and related issues would seem to be a useful next step. As far as the study of conflict is concerned, the philosophical, social, and political implications of a fundamental reconceptualization could be revolutionary. We seek to develop a psychology of conflict that is more sensitive to issues of gender and power, more reflective, and of greater compass. We invite the reader to explore, on her or his own, the foregoing ideas, and to continue this process.

REFERENCES

Baker, G.P. (1974). Criteria: A new foundation for semantics. *Ratio, XVI*, 156-181.

Baker, G.P., & Hacker, P.M.S. (1982). The grammar of psychology: Wittgenstein's bemerkungen uber die philosophie der psychologie. *Language and Communication, 2(3)*, 227-244.

Baker, G.P., & Hacker, P.M.S. (1983). *Wittgenstein: Meaning and understanding*. Oxford: Basil Blackwell.

Baker, G.P., & Hacker, P.M.S. (1985). *Wittgenstein: Rules, grammar and necessity*. Oxford: Basil Blackwell.

Baron, R.A., & Byrne, D. (1991). *Social psychology: Understanding human interaction*. Boston: Allyn & Bacon.

Belenky, M.F., Clinchy, B.M., Goldberger, N.R., & Tarule, J.M. (1986). *Women's ways of knowing: Development of self, voice, and mind*. New York: Basic Books.

Blake, R.R., Shepard, H.A., & Mouton, J.S. (1964). *Managing intergroup conflict in industry*. Houston, TX: Gulf.

Bleier, R. (1984). *Science and gender: A critique of biology and its theories on women*. New York: Pergamon Press.

Burke, R.J., & McKeen, C.A. (1989). *Why can't women be more like men? Some thoughts on management development for women*. Unpublished manuscript.

Burrell, N.A., Donohue, W.A., & Allen, M. (1988). Gender-based perceptual biases in mediation. *Communication Research, 15(4)*, 447-469.

Cameron, D. (1985). *Feminism and linguistic theory*. London: MacMillan.

Caplan, N., & Nelson, S.D. (1974). On being useful: The nature and consequences of psychological research on social problems. *American Psychologist, 28*, 199-211.

Carlin, G.M. (1991). *A conceptual analysis of conflict management style mea-*

sures. Unpublished master's thesis, University of Guelph, Ontario, Canada.

Clemens, W.V. (1965). An analytical and empirical examination of some properties of ipsative measures. *Psychometric Monographs (Psychometric Society)*, 14.

Chusmir, L.H., & Mills, J. (1989). Gender differences in conflict resolution styles as managers: At work and at home. *Sex Roles, 20*, 149-163.

Cohn, C. (1987). Sex and death in the rational world of defense intellectuals. *Signs: Journal of Women in Culture and Society, 12*(4), 687-718.

Conrad, C. (1985). *Gender, interactional sensitivity and communication in conflict: Assumptions and interpretation*. Paper presented at the Speech Communication Association Convention, Denver, CO.

Cronbach, L.J., & Meehl, P.E. (1955). Construct validity in psychological tests. *Psychological Bulletin, 52*, 281-302.

Ellett, F.S. (1985). Psychological terms, logical positivism, and realism: Issues related to construct validation. *Educational Theory, 35*(3), 273-284.

Febbraro, A.R. (1990). *Construct validity, leadership, and meaning: Shaking the foundations*. Unpublished master's thesis, University of Guelph, Ontario, Canada.

Feyerabend, P. (1975). *Against method*. London: Verso.

Gergen, K.J. (1982). *Toward transformation in social knowledge*. New York: Springer-Verlag.

Gilligan, C. (1982). *In a different voice: Psychological theories and women's development*. Cambridge: Harvard University Press.

Grant, J. (1988). Women as managers: What they can offer to organizations. *Organizational Dynamics, 16*(3), 56-63.

Grimshaw, A.D. (Ed.). (1990). *Conflict talk: Sociolinguistic investigations of arguments in conversations*. Cambridge: Cambridge University Press.

Gutek, B.A. (1989). Sexuality in the workplace: Key issues in social research and organizational practice. In J. Hearn, D.L. Sheppard, P. Tancred-Sheriff, & G. Burrell (Eds.), *The sexuality of organizations* (pp. 56-70). Newbury Park, CA: Sage.

Guttman, L. (1977). What is not what in statistics. *The Statistician, 26*(2), 81-107.

Hacking, I. (Ed.). (1981). *Scientific revolutions*. Oxford: Oxford University Press.

Haraway, D. (1987). Animal sociology and a natural economy of the body politic, part I: A political physiology of dominance. In S. Harding (Ed.), *Sex and scientific inquiry* (pp. 217-232). Chicago: The University of Chicago Press.

Harding, S. (1986). *The science question in feminism*. Ithaca, NY: Cornell University Press.

Harding, S. (1991). *Whose science? Whose knowledge? Thinking from women's lives*. Ithaca, NY: Cornell University Press.

Helgeson, H. (1990). *The female advantage: Women's ways of leadership*. New York: Doubleday/Currency.

Hocker, J.L., & Wilmot, W.W. (1985). *Interpersonal conflict*. Dubuque, IA: Wm.C. Brown.

Kagan, J., & Snidman, N. (1991). Temperamental factors in human development. *American Psychologist, 46*(8), 856-862.

Kaplan, R.M., & Saccuzzo, D.P. (1982). *Psychological testing: Principles, applications, and issues*. Monterey, CA: Brooks/Cole.

Kay, P., & McDaniel, C. (1978). The linguistic significance of the meanings of basic color terms. *Language, 54*, 610-646.

Keller, E.F. (1985). *Reflections on gender and science*. New Haven: Yale University Press.

Kilmann, R.H., & Thomas, K.W. (1975). Interpersonal conflict-handling behaviour as reflections of Jungian personality dispositions. *Psychological Reports, 37*, 971-980.

Kilmann, R.H., & Thomas, K.W. (1977). Developing a forced-choice measure of conflict-handling behaviour: The "MODE" Instrument. *Educational and Psychological Measurement, 37*, 309-325.

Kuhn, T.S. (1970). *The structure of scientific revolutions*. Chicago: The University of Chicago Press.

Lakoff, G. (1987). *Women, fire, and dangerous things*. Chicago: The University of Chicago Press.

Levins, R., & Lewontin, R. (1985). *The dialectical biologist*. Cambridge: Harvard University Press.

Lounsbury, F. (1964). A formal account of the Crow- and Omaha-type kinship terminologies. In W.H. Goodenough (Ed.), *Explorations in cultural anthropology* (pp. 351-394). New York: McGraw-Hill.

Lunneborg, P. (1990). *Women changing work*. New York: Bergin & Garvey.

Malcolm, N. (1986). *Wittgenstein: Nothing is hidden*. Oxford: Basil Blackwell.

Marshall, J. (1984). *Women managers: Travellers in a male world*. New York: Wiley.

Miller, J.B. (1976). *Toward a new psychology of women*. Boston: Beacon Press.

Mills, J., Robey, D., & Smith, L. (1985). Conflict-handling and personality dimensions of project-management personnel. *Psychological Reports, 57*, 1135-1143.

Mishler, E.G. (1979). Meaning in context: Is there any other kind? *Harvard Educational Review, 49*(1), 1-19.

Norris, S.P. (1983). The inconsistencies at the foundation of construct validation theory. In E.R. House (Ed.), *Philosophy of evaluation: New directions for program evaluation* (pp. 54-74). San Francisco: Jossey-Bass.

Penelope, J. (1990). *Speaking freely: Unlearning the lies of the fathers' tongues.* Elmsford, NY: Pergamon Press.

Polkinghorne, D.E. (1988). *Narrative knowing and the human sciences.* New York: State University of New York Press.

Popper, K. (1966). *The open society and its enemies* (5th ed.). London: Routledge & Kegan Paul.

Rahim, M.A. (1983). A measure of styles of handling interpersonal conflict. *Academy of Management Journal, 26*(2), 368-376.

Rosch, E. (1973). Natural categories. *Cognitive Psychology, 4,* 328-350.

Rosch, E., & Mervis, C. (1975). Family resemblances: Studies in the internal structure of categories. *Cognitive Psychology, 7,* 573-605.

Rosser, S.V. (1990). *Female-friendly science: Applying women's studies methods and theories to attract students.* Elmsford, NY: Pergamon Press.

Ruddick, S. (1989). *Maternal thinking: Toward a politics of peace.* New York: Ballantine Books.

Schaef, A.W. (1985). *Women's reality: An emerging female system in a white male society.* San Francisco: Harper & Row.

Scholes, R. (1982). *Semiotics and interpretation.* New Haven: Yale University Press.

Sherif, C.W. (1987). Bias in psychology. In S. Harding (Ed.), *Feminism and methodology* (pp. 37-56). Bloomington: Indiana University Press.

Spender, D. (1980). *Man made language.* New York: Routledge & Kegan Paul.

Stoltenberg, J. (1989) *Refusing to be a man: Essays on sex and justice.* Portland, OR: Breitenbush Books.

Szasz, T. (1987). *Insanity: The idea and its consequences.* New York: Wiley.

ter Hark, M. (1990). *Beyond the inner and the outer: Wittgenstein's philosophy of psychology.* Boston: Kluwer Academic Publishers.

Thomas, A., Chess, S., & Birch, H. (1968). *Temperament and behaviour disorders in children.* New York: New York University Press.

Thomas, K.W., & Kilmann, R.H. (1974a). *The Thomas-Kilmann Conflict MODE Instrument.* Tuxedo, NY: XICOM Inc.

Thomas, K.W., & Kilmann, R.H. (1974b). Comparison of four instruments measuring conflict behaviour. *Psychological Reports, 42,* 1139-1145.

Thomas, K.W., & Kilmann, R.H. (1978). Comparisons of four instruments measuring conflict behaviour. *Psychological Reports, 42,* 1139-1145.

van de Vliert, E., & Kabanoff, B. (1990). Toward theory-based measures of conflict management. *Academy of Management Journal, 33*(1), 199-209.

Waltz, K.N. (1954). *Man, the state, and war: A theoretical analysis.* New

York: Columbia University Press.

Weisstein, N. (1971). Psychology constructs the female. In V. Gornick & B.K. Moran (Eds.), *Women in sexist society: Studies in power and powerlessness* (pp.207-224). New York: Basic Books.

Wittgenstein, L. (1953). *Philosophical investigations.* Oxford: Basil Blackwell.

Wittgenstein, L. (1958). *The blue and brown books.* Oxford: Basil Blackwell.

12

Informal Contributions to the Conflict Management Process

Cynthia J. Chataway
Harvard University
Deborah M. Kolb
Simmons College

At a recent conference, one of the authors presented three case studies of informal conflict management in organizations (Chataway, 1993). The cases described the informal conflict management activities of three women who have no formal mandate or special training to mediate in their organizations. The audience of dispute resolution professionals and others was divided about the effectiveness of this kind of informal work.

Some people, particularly those who do have a formal mandate to intervene—ombudspeople, mediators, and personnel officers—were concerned about what they heard. They rejected the suggestion that behind-the-scenes conflict resolvers make positive contributions to organizational functioning. Indeed, several in this group claimed that their own systematic efforts to resolve conflicts, in a way that made longterm organizational change possible, were actually undermined by the informal conflict managers in their organization.

Other members of the audience, particularly those who had personal experiences either in the role of informal conflict resolver or as organizational disputants themselves, were gratified by the presentation. They felt the presentation legitimated a difficult but necessary role in their organization. Some also stated their opinion that the formal efforts put forth by the first group were ineffective.

Emotions on both sides ran strong. A member of the audience suggested that the informal "natural helpers" should be supported and connected with each other so they would feel less isolated and could learn from each other. We also spent some time in this conference session discussing the possibilities for collaboration between the informal "helpers" and formal dispute resolvers.

This audience clearly recognized how pervasive is behind-the-scenes conflict[1] management. Our experience supports this. Not only do we find ourselves increasingly involved in this kind of activity, but learn that many colleagues, friends, and students, particularly women, similarly find themselves in this position. Therefore it is important for us to understand this role, see its relationship to other forms of organizational conflict management, and evaluate it in organizations and other settings.

Although the audience of practitioners at this conference acknowledged the prevalence of informal conflict management, the role has been almost invisible in research. Historically, empirical inquiry has focused on the sources or reasons for conflict and on the various structural and procedural mechanisms by which organizations are designed to manage it. These include structures for containing conflict (e.g., integrative roles, teams, and task forces), procedures for resolving differences (e.g., negotiation and problem solving), and dispute resolution procedures (e.g., grievance arbitration and mediation), among others (Miles, 1980; Pondy, 1967; Westin & Feliu, 1988). What people actually do in conflict situations, how they feel about it, how the different forms of conflict processing coexist, and how these affect the organizational order, have not historically been evaluated (Collins, 1975).[2]

In this chapter we explore the informal role in a number of ways. First, we examine how informal conflict management fits within the various processes for dealing with conflicts in organizations. Using data from case studies, we discuss the activities of three women involved in informal activities and how their efforts intersect with other conflict management mechanisms. In our analysis, we consider the ways in which the role can be gendered and the implications of this for people who perform the role in an organization.

---

[1]The terms *conflict* and *dispute* are used interchangeably in this chapter.

[2]When conflict has been studied, it has most often been examined in its most overt and extreme form of open confrontation. This may explain why conflict has often been conceived of as inherently damaging.

THE CONFLICT MANAGEMENT PROCESS

How a conflict is defined and dealt with involves a complex interaction of issues, players, contexts, and management processes. Our observations suggest that people rely first on their own resources in dealing with a dispute. They do this through a variety of coping strategies, and then sometimes through interactions with others on an informal basis. Only occasionally do people take their conflicts into a formal forum. This is an interactive, not necessarily linear process. In other words, disputants experiment with various forms of expression. By focusing on informal conflict management we shift the locus of inquiry from management structures and formal rules to the processes of conflict as they are expressed and acted on over the course of a dispute. This interactive process between perceived conflict and action is one of the essential ways that issues are made meaningful and are possibly resolved (Nader, 1965; Sarat, 1987).

The Contextual Interpretation of Conflict

Research has tended to situate the causes of organizational conflict in situations of diversity and interdependence. Such factors as personality differences, task interdependency, status inconsistency, jurisdictional ambiguity, communication obstacles and distortions, common resource dependency, performance/reward discrepancy, goal/structure clashes, disputes over authority and responsibility, competition, miscommunications, and diversity of the labor force (Lawrence & Lorsch, 1967; Pondy, 1989; Walton & McKersie, 1965) are all cited as potential catalysts of conflict. How these differences will be expressed and understood is a function of the forum in which they are being considered (Felstiner, Abel, & Sarat, 1981). As different strategies and resources are utilized in dealing with a perceived dispute, the dispute itself often becomes transformed. Elements initially considered salient can disappear, and other concerns that were initially unexpressed can emerge, depending on the people spoken to and the requirements of the particular dispute resolution forum accessed (e.g., the courts, union steward, or the media). For example, a dispute initially conceived of as a collective problem can become individualized when brought to a public dispute resolution forum such as a court (Felstiner et al., 1981). Conversely, a disagreement with a supervisor over how to carry out a certain task can become an institutional issue that has legal ramifications once it becomes part of a formal complaint system.

In order to understand how a given conflict will be expressed, one needs to attend to the dispute management resources available and to the collective, albeit implicit, judgments regarding their use. In other words, the culture in an organization with regard to the expression of conflict is very important. Conflict can be considered as a path to truth and creativity, as disloyalty to the organization, or as individual weakness. Even in an organization in which institutional norms and resources for grievance expression and resolution exist, the unofficial norm against acting on these principles or accessing these resources can be very strong. For example, in one high technology firm, "truth through conflict" was a central principle of decision making. However, the degree to which task conflicts were expressed depended on who was involved and people's judgments about whether members could "take it" (Kunda, 1991).

Generally, organizational cultures do not value the open expression of conflict. Indeed, written and unwritten norms and values regarding the suppression of conflict are pervasive in organizations (Argyris, 1986). Conflicts over a variety of issues and interests tend to be masked as rational discourse, misunderstandings, or personality problems, or they are controlled through rituals (Kolb, 1986; Kolb & Sheppard, 1985; Pettigrew, 1973). Organizational cultures most often foster a tendency to avoid and deny conflict, with the implication that conflict is undesirable and best suppressed in the interests of harmony and integration (Greenhouse, 1986). Members learn not to express their differences openly, to withhold relevant information, and even to delay dealing with the conflict on the informal level. Individuals sometimes cope with conflict for years, evidenced only by occasional grumbling and an unmeasured influence on work satisfaction, creativity, mental and physical health, and productivity.

In an organization that encourages conflict to be discussed openly, where conflict is addressed nonjudgmentally, and/or where structural change rather than individual deficits are considered first in the analysis and resolution of conflict, employees would be expected to publicly express their differences more often. Presumably they would become more skilled at confrontation and might not require the help of informal third parties as frequently. This does not suggest that they would cease to utilize informal resources, but rather that the informal processes would proceed in a somewhat different way.

Individual differences in personality, organizational status, reputation, and behavioral style also influence the way disputants perceive and respond to conflict. One's place in the organizational hierarchy is important. Position seems to influence the types of disputes experienced, the resources available, and the resources accessed. For instance, those lower in the hierarchy experience conflict regularly and make use of a wide range of strategies and resources in dealing with their disputes. Those higher in the organizational hierarchy, with more autonomy and control over their work, may experience conflict less often, but when it is experienced, they are more constrained in their modes of grievance against colleagues or superiors (Westin & Feliu, 1988). Organizational norms against the expression of conflict are stronger for middle and upper management, and formal mechanisms for expressing conflict are almost nonexistent. The most common experience across the organizational hierarchy seems to be that people must either "lump it" or find some indirect, informal, surreptitious way to address a grievance.

In addition to formal status in the organization, organizational reputation can have a profound influence on the avenues open to individuals to express a grievance. Men who have established their competence and commitment to organizational goals tend to find that their public protests are considered credible. The credibility of women, however, does not seem to be enhanced by proven competence and organizational loyalty to the same extent as for men (Bray, Johnson, & Chilstrom, 1982). This suggests that gendered norms and expectations constrain and influence the forms of grievance expression open to men and women in an organization. Research by Bray et al. suggests that despite a woman's history of successful contribution to an organization, she will find that her public expression of disagreement goes unaddressed, or worse, is discounted. Based on this experience, women may cease to utilize formal or public grievance processes and will utilize less visible processes to bring about change, not necessarily because they are more comfortable with this approach, but because this approach meets their needs more effectively or is the only avenue open to them.

Gender is an individual difference for which there is evidence of small to moderate, but important, behavioral differences. Research indicates little if any differences between men and women in skills and abilities (Deaux, 1984). However, men and women bring to organizations different experiences and perceptions of conflict, in part as a result of conditions that vary with sex, such as occupation, behavioral expectations, vulnerability to physical attack, and the sex-typing of social roles (Eagly, 1987). Women are reported (by themselves and by men) to be more concerned with others, more selfless, and in possession of a greater desire to be "at one" with others (i.e., communal). In contrast, men are thought to be (and consider themselves to be) more self-assertive, self-expansive, and in possession of a greater urge for mastery (i.e., agentic; Bakan, 1966).

These expectations exert a considerable influence on the behavior of men and women, particularly in situations in which gender roles and obligations are especially salient (Eisenberg & Lennon, 1983). Others tend to react positively to behaviors that are congruent with gender expectations, and they discourage or ignore incongruent behaviors (Bellinger & Gleason, 1982; Fagot, 1978; Hall, 1984; Rosenthal, 1988;

Skrypnek & Snyder, 1982). This accounts for the finding that the largest gender differences tend to be found mainly in self-reported rather than actual behaviors (Keashly, this volume).

Internal Coping

The initial response of an individual to a perceived conflict may not be readily apparent to others. Given the finding that people generally avoid or "lump" their differences (Bumiller, 1987; Felstiner et al., 1981; Greenhouse, 1986), it seems important to know more clearly what it is they are doing when they do not appear to be dealing with a dispute. Coping has not been a subject of research in organizations, but work in other fields provides some promising indications. Lazarus and Folkman (1984), for example, propose a taxonomy of eight coping strategies that differentiate the many ways that individuals cope with their difficulties. They suggest that by understanding the individual's internalized cultural and social norms we can begin to understand and predict what that individual will perceive as stressful and how that individual will react to or cope with a stressor, such as conflict on the job. Briefly, the eight coping strategies delineated by Lazarus and Folkman (1984) are (loosely ranked from most to least internal): wishful thinking, detachment, withdrawal, self-blame, tension reduction, positive thinking, problem solving, and seeking social support. Wishful thinking, detachment, withdrawal, and tension reduction all involve some form of avoidance of the problem, either temporary in order to gain some perspective, or more chronic. The strategies of self-blame and positive thinking are two sides of attempting to frame the problem internally. These six coping strategies help us untangle what is happening when individuals do not appear to be responding to an experienced conflict. The last two coping strategies, problem solving and seeking social support, involve a more overt "reaching out" for assistance to others who are not directly involved in the conflict. When and why disputants turn to others for advice, diversion, to spread rumors, and so on, is not well understood.

Informal Third Party

When a disputant moves beyond self-help or internal coping processes, another person from outside the conflict often becomes involved. Particularly in an organizational context in which conflict tends to be personalized and can have negative consequences for those involved, caution is usually exercised. It is difficult to envision an individual in any organization who would proceed into formal grievance procedures without the initial step of looking for support or advice, in order to let off steam, or for assistance in understanding the dispute more deeply. If only for confirmation that their grievance is warranted, disputants will talk to friends and colleagues whom they trust and whose opinions they respect before utilizing formal grievance procedures or making their complaint public.

Conflict is said to be informally managed when those without formal dispute resolution roles or responsibilities become involved in a dispute. Informal conflict managers can be sought out by disputants, or take the initiative themselves. Akin to what we know about more formal conflict management systems (Kolb, 1986), informal third parties also engage in different forms of intervention depending on their own personal resources and position with respect to the organization and the disputants. For instance, in conflicts between subordinates, managers tend to act as adjudicators, particularly when they are held accountable for related decisions and are concerned about precedent (Lewicki & Sheppard, 1985). Ombudspeople, on the other hand, who have rich networks in organizations, tend to mobilize those relationships to help complainants change their job situation (Kolb, 1987). Because research on informal conflict management is still very new, the implication of gender in this process is even less well understood. Our observations only begin to shed light on the gendered nature of this work and raise questions for future research.

Black and Baumgartner (1983) present one of the rare examples of a comprehensive theory of the third party that encompasses formal and informal responses to conflict. Their typology of third-party responses and roles acknowledges that all formal roles have their informal equivalents and that the informal processes are used more frequently than the formal. Even if a disputant decides to take a grievance to formal conflict management, informal processes generally continue concurrently and influence the formal processes as they unfold (Bartunek, Kolb, & Lewicki, 1992). Informal interaction and influence can also stabilize the formal process by providing a continuing forum for grievance management after the official settlement has been reached and by communicating perceptions and needs without requiring disputants to state them to each other or commit to them publicly.

Formal Third Party

Formal conflict managers are by definition institutionalized, public, and remunerated for the performance of their function. Because their organizational role is to mediate, or to represent those with grievances, they often work apart from the daily functioning of the organization. Thus, people occupying these roles can only respond to those conflicts that become public[3] and in which disputants are prepared to communicate the important factors in the dispute. Their knowledge of the organizational networks, norms, and history is often much more limited than that of the informal manager. Although the informal manager is often approached in order to make use of his or her personal connections and insider knowledge, the formal conflict manager's assistance is solicited when publicity or an outsider's objectivity are desired. Relatively few organizational complaints find their way into the institutionalized forums, and negative consequences (e.g., low performance evaluations, demotions) tend to follow (Kolb, 1987; Lewin, 1987).

Conflict left unaddressed will generally not disappear, but will appear in other forms of destructive behavior, such as passive resistance (Bartunek & Reid, 1992), foot dragging, dissimulation, false compliance, pilfering, (Scott, 1985) or re-emergence of the conflict (Burton, 1987). Even when dealt with formally, conflicts are rarely resolved. Instead they are processed in ways that rephrase, repress, or redefine them, so they continue to surface again and again in different ways (Merry & Silbey, 1984; Smith, 1989). In other words, the outcomes of most conflicts are other conflicts, with only temporary respites in between (Abel, 1982).

The existence of private, nonconfrontational approaches to conflict management helps to account for the relative infrequency of publicly articulated grievances (Miller & Sarat, 1981). Organizational ideals of harmony and integration are often upheld (in the public handling of disputes) because of private, behind-the-scenes, conflict management activities (Goffman, 1959). Grievances will be conceptually reframed when expressed to formal conflict managers to correspond to the norms of appropriate or strategic behavior. For example, an emotional, personalized, and/or irrational reaction will be "cleaned up" and explained publicly through a logical recounting of events. The informal and formal processes are interdependent and can occur concurrently in the service of projecting acceptable motivations, meeting needs and interests, and bringing about necessary changes in organizational functioning.

Men and women engaged in formal dispute resolution work seem to conceive of their work differently. Even when matched for success and reputation as mediators, women tend to conceive of their role as facilitating a balance of power between disputants, whereas men more frequently believe that their role is to function as a neutral. Female mediators more often report that the goal of mediation was to facilitate an understanding between the parties and an appreciation of differ-

---

[3]This notion of public includes those situations where a complainant seeks the services of an ombudsman who promises confidentiality (Rowe, 1987) because once a complaint enters the formal system, public claiming becomes more likely.

ences, whereas men tend to report the goal as the development of an agreement (Weingarten & Douvan, 1985).

We are not suggesting here that either informal or formal conflict management is inherently more valuable. The effect of informal interventions remains very much an open question. We are interested in the interconnections between the formal and informal contributions, their relative use in different situations, and the implication of gender in this process.

THE CONFLICT MANAGEMENT PROCESS: INFORMAL CONTRIBUTIONS

Any member of an organization can potentially find him- or herself in an informal conflict management role. Our research focuses on three caucasian American women in middle and upper level management.[4] Their experiences and reflections on their work form the basis for our analysis of the intersection of gender and informal conflict management. First, we present an introduction to the three women and their work and then use their insights and experience to describe the nature of informal conflict management and the intersection of conflict management, power, and gender in organizations.

Olivia Lane was a manager of executive training and development at a high-tech company, married to one of the firm's senior executives. She became a "go-between" among the senior vice presidents and different levels of the organization in a series of strategic and interpersonal conflicts. In one strategic planning task force, Lane used her position to arrange a series of meetings with a senior VP, the task force, and potential consultants. When it appeared that the task force would not speak up to support their own plan, Lane brought the conflict into the open. On other occasions, she helped individual managers deal with conflicts over work and career.

Patricia Loomis was in sales and training in a small but growing technology consulting firm. The president sought her out regularly for advice on "how to deal with people" because of her background in social work. Much of her informal conflict management work was between the president (Jack) and the senior vice president of operations (Liz). Loomis worked with Liz and Jack to help them communicate more constructively with each other and to reframe issues relevant to the com-

---

[4]These are the cases mentioned in the introduction that were presented at the conference. Each case is described in greater depth in Kolb (1992). The newness of the study of informal conflict management suggest the appropriateness of case study analysis (Merriam, 1990).

pany's success. Individually she coached them and helped them appreciate the impact that they had on each other.

Betty Armstrong was a senior professor who frequently assisted graduate students and junior faculty on a variety of professional and personal matters. For example, she helped a junior faculty member, Connie, strategize and confront a male colleague over a cancelled teaching assignment. In another situation, Armstrong orchestrated a tenure review that she felt was being compromised by negative comments made in one-on-one meetings. She arranged a committee meeting, talked with all parties in advance, and made sure each person on the committee participated equally so that minority opinions could not dominate.

All three women experienced the informal work they performed as gendered in some way. Each described herself as nonthreatening, easy to talk to, and sensitive to "people" issues. They related this characteristic to gender: "This is a typical thing a woman is good at. I'm not threatening; I'm sympathetic and I'm comfortable to speak to. They know that I will let them come in and talk and that I will listen." "I think they think that I will help them solve their problems." "From the start, people were aware of my psychology background, joked a little nervously about it, and slowly began to use it, coming to me for advice on how to deal with this person or that issue." However the three women resented the fact that they were continually being drawn in to work on "women's problems."

Hochschild (1983) observes that frequently women are expected to take on these kinds of functions within their organizations because the functions are seen as congruent with other gendered societal roles. "[W]omen in general are asked to look out for psychological needs more than men are. The world turns to women for mothering, and this fact silently attaches itself to many a job description" (Hochschild, 1983, p. 172). By looking at the context of their involvement as they described it, we next consider the gendered dimensions of disputing in organizations.

The Contextual Interpretation of Conflict

What types of disputes were these women drawn into, and how might their involvement have affected the way the conflicts were expressed and subsequently interpreted? Most of the stories they told were of conflict that had developed across levels of the organizational hierarchy, rather than between peers. Disputes were between senior and junior VPs, administrators and VPs, president and VP, and junior and senior faculty. Most requests came from the lower status party.

All three women expressed a sense of the value of the lower power disputants to the functioning, productivity, reputation, and values of the organization. They perceived that if their concerns were not dealt with to their mutual satisfaction, it would be a potential loss to the organization, as well as to the individuals concerned. The disputants were often described as constrained by their organizational positions. They felt either trapped, stretched, or unable to move forward constructively. They saw their choices as either to adjust, put up, or get out. Thus, the women were seen as a source of potential relief to the disputants.

In Lane's case, the VPs were unhappy about the historical lack of support for strategic planning. Feeling themselves blocked in the development of their ideas by an inability to influence organizational decision makers, they used Lane to transmit critical information about their frustrations to senior management. Lane responded to their expressed need for an ally and collaborator.

Loomis tried to help relieve a stalemate. Jack and Liz had great difficulty working together and this was affecting the firm's performance, not to mention the morale of its members. Although their interventions were at the interpersonal level, Lane and Loomis became involved in issues that had organizational implications. They did not intervene when issues of friendship or romance were involved, but rather when problems of communication, conflict, and personality seemed to be inhibiting the achievement of organizational goals.

Like Lane and Loomis, Armstrong tried to help people who were relatively powerless. Connie would have lost the teaching assignment without Armstrong's assistance. Armstrong decided on her own to pick up the tenure case because she thought the process was unfair— "these things get said and there's nobody to challenge them." She was also responsible for publicly labeling the tenure case as a conflict or problem to be solved. Without her involvement she felt the denial of tenure would have passed, unchallenged by a debate over values or interests. Although these situations had organizational implications, especially the tenure case, Armstrong became involved at least in part because she cared about the fate of the two lower status disputants.

In the meetings these three women orchestrated, issues that had been described privately as problems of power and relationship were framed mostly in impersonal, organizational terms: the need for a strategic plan, conflicts over authority or responsibility, and evaluation criteria. For example, people told Loomis privately about their fears that concessions would be used against them and that a particular manager was too controlling. However, in public the same conflict was framed as a need to develop adequate compensation for outstanding contributions to the company.

The informal efforts of these three women come more into focus when one considers what alternatives existed for the disputants. In Lane and Loomis's firms, no formal complaint procedure existed; in Armstrong's organization, the grievance process was deemed too public. One of the reasons these women became involved was because of the need to deal with conflict and at the same time for disputants to remain low profile as complainants. The VPs were more than happy to remain anonymous while Lane relayed their information and dissatisfactions. Lane knew the senior VP would be sensitive about any dissatisfaction within the task force, so instead of confronting him directly, she asked for his advice and orchestrated a discussion of his strategic plan as a forum for the expression of other plans. Loomis mediated among upper management, the president, senior vice president, and an administrator regarding their complaints about each other. In Armstrong's tenure case, one would not generally be able to appeal until after a negative decision. However, because Armstrong was able to assemble a mixed group of supporters and nonsupporters, she pressed people to take public positions for which they would be held accountable.

Internal Coping

What do we know from these cases regarding the efforts of the disputants to deal with the conflict themselves before requesting help from the informal conflict manager? In all cases the individuals were becoming more detached, either because of anger or apathy. The possibility that some of these disputants would leave the organization was very real. An employee came to Lane to inform her that she planned to resign. Lane's response was to inquire about openings in other departments and to quietly communicate the possibility of a transfer. In the task force case Lane intervened when she felt that the VPs had given up hope. Loomis seemed to take on much of Jack's responsibility for employee satisfaction and tried to deal with morale problems among certain administrators. In Armstrong's case a junior professor had written a potentially destructive and accusatory letter, and Armstrong helped her to develop a different strategy. The conclusion we draw from the cases is that, in most of the situations, disputants were unable to cope with the issue on their own so they asked for help.

Informal Third Party

Informal dispute resolution was not part of Lane's, Loomis's, or Armstrong's formal job descriptions, so why did they become involved? Their positioning in the organization, both personally and professionally, seemed to be important. In their self-descriptions these women stressed their desire to support both the organization and the individuals within it. In addition, their personal characteristics and skills were noticed by other members of the organizations.

Lane, Loomis, and Armstrong were in positions in which they were able to learn about emerging problems and conflicts and to use their access to important people to address the problems if necessary. Lane's involvement with the various task forces put her in touch with a network of vice presidents, hence she was privy to issues that concerned them. Those involved were also well aware that she was the wife of a senior executive. "If it hadn't been me pushing for this, it would have died. It's because I am Ed's wife. I can't imagine anybody else doing what I do. One of the VPs said that he listened to me 99% because I am Ed's wife." Loomis's experience in social work, first informally, and then via the human resource function, meant that people came to her with problems and difficulties they were having with others. Her friendship with the president, to whom she was a confidante, was also important. "It became clear to others in the company that I had a good relationship with Jack." Armstrong was involved with various women's groups which made her visible to the community of academic women who called on her for help. Her position as one of the very few senior women at the university singled her out and influenced the actions she took on behalf of other women (Kanter, 1977).

These three women described their informal work in very similar ways. They provided support by allowing people to tell their stories. They reframed people's understandings of their situation by providing alternative explanations and choices. They communicated the perspectives of the other people involved in the dispute, either directly by transferring a message, or indirectly during discussion. Less frequently, they looked for opportunities to orchestrate a constructive discussion between disputants regarding their conflicts.

In terms of their role, these women were all perceived, not as professional dispute resolvers, but as helpers and experts in human relations and organizational politics. Despite these perceptions, Lane and Loomis, in particular, minimized their expertise and accomplishment. Lane described her intervention at the meeting as happening "before I knew what I was doing," and Loomis asked the president why he "seems to listen to me." Although they gained satisfaction from their involvement, there was little suggestion that they felt they were ideally suited for the work. Rather, there was a sense that they were simply responding to a need or request. They utilized "everyday" skills of relaying information, facilitating discussion, and providing emotional support, alternative perspectives, and reframing, and thus they did not perceive their work as special. Sometimes they altered information to speak more constructively to the sensitivities of the recipient. At other times they created conditions for a more constructive dialogue between the disputants. As messengers they helped people to understand each other, acted as advocates, and used inside information as a basis for suggesting possible solutions to problems.

Lane and Loomis were surprised by their own influence and may have felt uncomfortable with it, as though power was somehow antithetical to their sense of self (Rodriguez, 1988). They worried about the legitimacy of their positions, problems with confidentiality and honesty, and the politics of their relationships. Loomis openly questioned the value of the work. "I worry sometimes that I am keeping a bad system alive. I am preventing them from hitting bottom. On the good side, I get them to see things from a broader perspective; I am teaching them about psychology."

What is so interesting is the willingness of these women to take on this burden. Although informal conflict management was not part of their jobs, they were willing to involve themselves in time- and energy-consuming work for which they would be recognized very little, if at all. Armstrong explained that she preferred to work behind the scenes, where her contributions remained invisible. "I wanted to orchestrate it. I was pretty invisible. I don't think, except for two people, that anyone realizes the hand I had in it."

Their personal motivations seemed to emerge out of a desire to help, in particular to help women whom they perceived as capable of contributing to the organization but who were impeded somehow in their work. Thus the progress of the disputants and that of the organization were perceived to be interconnected. When the informal conflict managers did get involved, they had specific visions for a better workplace in mind. Loomis described her agenda in the following manner: "Increasingly I began to take on causes, things I wanted changed. A lot of their treatment of people, especially the women, was very poor. I felt that [the top people] genuinely wanted to have a company that was better than others as far as human resources was concerned and yet they kept screwing up." Lane and Loomis, to some extent, placed the good of the organization above that of the individuals concerned. They seemed to become identified and involved only with cases they perceived to be important for the progress of the organization. However, their conception of what was best for the organization included facilitating the satisfaction of employees. Therefore, settling of conflicts involved assisting people on both sides. A dual motivation to help both sides was a central characteristic of each dispute described.

They were trusted, as evidenced by the extent to which people shared vulnerabilities about their work and their lives, although Loomis particularly had to work for this trust from Liz. Liz told her that as soon as she saw Loomis disagree with Jack and take a stand, that she knew she could be trusted. Trust is generated when one believes that the trusted person will act in one's best interest, rather than solely for personal gain. These women were in the extraordinary situation of frequently being trusted by both sides.

The three women also seemed to be genuinely motivated by the helping role, despite the time, energy, and risk involved. They expressed no desire to be remunerated for this work, and little expectation of thanks. They enjoyed taking responsibility for others, even though this sometimes involved risk to their own positions, especially when they orchestrated public meetings. Armstrong's advocacy in the tenure case exemplified this willingness to take risks on behalf of others. The meeting that she organized amounted to an open confrontation with the area chair. Similarly, Lane challenged the members of the task force to go public with their disagreements.

Finally, their attitudes about conflict also drove their participation. Loomis's comment was representative: "Sometimes I think this is a woman's thing. For myself, I am terrible at dealing with conflict. I want to make people get along. I don't like it when they disagree. I keep hoping that they'll see the good side of each other." Because they disliked conflict, they wanted to avoid its potentially disruptive tendencies. Ironically, their dislike of conflict seemed to engage them in it.

Formal Third Party

In none of these cases did the disputants consult a professional such as an ombudsperson or personnel officer. Over time, however, the involvement of the three women did become more formal. Lane was appointed liaison for the formal planning process, Loomis was asked to set up a human resource function, and Armstrong served on a growing number of women's issues committees. Thus, their informal roles were captured in some way and became, or were acknowledged as, important to the institutionalized activities. Further research should examine the potential influence that formal recognition of the informal mediator role has on the evolution of this role because its power may lie in its nonbinding, anonymous nature.

POWER AND GENDER

The diversity of the emotions expressed by these three women (pleasure, satisfaction, resentment, guilt, nervousness, and isolation) reflects both the power of the work described, its precariousness, and the possibility that gendered expectations may have in part imposed this work on these women. From the explanations given, it appears that their work was gendered on at least three levels.

On a personal level, they were willing to help others and expressed many values that are closely associated with women: reciprocity, connection, and caring, as opposed to hierarchy, separation, and power (Kimball, forthcoming). They described their strength as emanating from interdependence and their energy constructively directed for the mutual gain of the interconnected parts of the organization. Rather than manipulating, they facilitated the conditions for a convergence of opinions. Rather than engaging in an exclusive process, these women widened involvement in the discussion, including people who would otherwise have been left out. Sometimes they brought discussion into the open where more awareness and dialogue could be generated.

On a normative level, all expressed a sense that they had little choice, that their involvement was expected of them. They felt they were performing a female role: providing invisible support, doing social work, or even babysitting. Armstrong felt particularly burdened by the time required and the potential damage to her own position and legitimacy as a result of her involvement in informal conflict management.

On a situational level, in addition to their professional positions within the organization, these women did work which was complementary to the formal roles of the men in their organizations. The complementary nature of their work and relationships meant that their gender was particularly salient. The salience of gender, in turn, is expected to increase gender differences in behavior (Eisenberg & Lennon, 1983). Thus, the possibility of using their relationships for personal advantage was never mentioned. Instead they talked about the perceived needs of the individuals and the organization and the responsibility that came with their unique positions and relationships.

Although they said they felt they had little choice but to help the disputants, clearly many choices were made. Not least of their choices was the decision to describe their extensive informal work as justified because it was in the interests of the organization as well as the parties. Because the women gave no examples of people they had chosen not to help, the rationale that their informal contributions were always in the interests of the organization is called into question. One is left to wonder what the primary motivations were for helping in the cases described. Did they feel torn between organizational loyalty and alleviating the suffering of those who asked for help? What skills and professional interests were subverted or enhanced as they took on responsibility for dispute resolution within the organization?

Extensive previous research suggests that men in similar positions would be involved in similar activities, but that their work would be perceived differently by others and by themselves (Keashly, this volume). If women are perceived to be working for the interests of others, and men are perceived to be working for their own interests, this may affect other attributions made about them, such as their ambition, their exploitability, their judgment, or their time management skills. Perhaps if their efforts were perceived to be constructed at least in part for their own self interest, women mediators would not be perceived as less competent than men. The perception of lesser competence seems to persist even in situations in which male mediators did not help the parties to reach a successful agreement and female mediators did (Wall & Dewhurst, 1991).[5]

The three women were ambivalent about their informal contributions. None questioned that they had helped to alleviate the constraints on frustrated disputants, particularly lower status women. However, they were keenly aware that none of their interventions had challenged the existing organizational structures and cultures and that they had put themselves at risk. Why did they choose not to press for the structural changes they each knew were needed? Did they assume that they lacked the power to bring about such change? Perhaps their past experiences had taught them that public expressions of dissatisfaction would not be listened to, or accorded legitimacy, so they limited their efforts to behind-the-scenes work (Bray et al., 1982). Whatever the reason, the status quo ante remained: In Lane's case the relationship between the task force and upper management remained the same, the president continued to rely on Loomis for human relations work, and barriers to gender equity among faculty continued in Armstrong's department.

Their informal efforts did reduce the more virulent forms of conflict in organizations: angry outbursts, sabotage, exit, and dismissal, as well as apathy and disengagement. With their help, disputants appeared rational rather than angry, were transferred rather than quit, and took proactive action instead of feeling helpless. However the capacity of the respective organizations to deal with future conflicts was not enhanced. People would continue to rely on third parties as go-betweens who would try to reframe conflicts into a form congruent with the existing culture. Therefore, informal conflict management is likely to be most prevalent in organizations in which conflict is hidden and suppressed because these organizations derive considerable benefit from people who perform these invisible roles.

Research suggests that if differences are not recognized or publicly

---

[5]Women also perceive themselves as less competent than men, even when their productivity is objectively equivalent.

confronted, second order change (a shift in the way powerful organizational members understand the organization and its work) will not occur (Bartunek & Reid, 1992). In the three cases featured here, the informal third party went to some lengths to have conflictual issues discussed (e.g., group meetings), and disputants were assisted toward their goals. However, the actual conflicts were generally not directly confronted or understood, at least not by the higher status parties to the disputes. Therefore, second order change, which might have improved future problem solving, did not occur.

The fact that informal conflict management has rarely been the subject of systematic study has generally been attributed to problems of accessibility and lack of interest. Informal talk in the locker room or on the golf course has long been recognized for its effects on the objectives and processes of organizations (Dayton, 1959; Kanter, 1977). Perhaps there is another reason for the lack of research on informal conflict management that is related to the kinds of power these women were perceived to exercise. The power illustrated in these three cases is conceived of in a different way and goes beyond the possibility of placing a good word in the ear of the right person, or influence peddling for self-gain. These women exhibited energy, sensitivity, interpersonal insight, and the ability to facilitate and inspire the collaborative work of others.

Informal power originating from interdependence does not fit with traditional conceptions of power as domination and control (Miner & Longino, 1987) and tends to be taken for granted. Institutionalized power is often accompanied by at least the potential of dominance and violence that compels obedience (Hartsock, 1983). These women did not compel obedience, but when the organization was about to give up on the individual, or the individuals were about to give up on the organization, they were able to help them muster the strength to continue to try to work together. Reframing the issues, restructuring the situation, and furthering the dialogue generated new strength and resolve to tackle problems.

Because the benefits of informal conflict management appear to be experienced mainly by parties lower in the organizational hierarchy, those with greater formal power tend to be less cognizant of the effects of informal conflict management and may therefore be more inclined to question its value or ignore it. In the cases described, upper management was not materially affected. Although specific decisions were changed, organizational structures and practices remained largely intact. Removed from direct involvement in these disputes, the higher status parties could maintain their assumptions that conflict is best suppressed in the interests of harmony and integration. This harmony, however, was experienced only by the highest levels of management, and integration occurred only with those who could find a way to get along without sacrificing their own needs and interests.

CONCLUSION

A considerable amount of informal conflict management is done in organizations that is unacknowledged and unremunerated. In our experience much of this work is done by women whose job descriptions do not include dispute resolution. The cases discussed here suggest such work is gendered, which means there is a strong expectation that women will take on this kind of responsibility and are well suited for it. Because the women in these cases were prepared to expend considerable effort and to accept responsibility for the disputants who came to them for help, the organizational hierarchy has little incentive to alter this situation.

This analysis exposes the alternative motivations, goals, and leaderships experienced by organizational members. It suggests that when organizational norms inhibit the overt expression of conflict, upper management may lose its knowledge of and control over the processes of the organization. Management's illusion of control and harmony is upheld through extensive efforts at the informal level to address conflicts in acceptable and often disguised ways. The successful completion of work initiated by management may depend, in particular, on the existence of informal conflict managers who share the official organizational goals. If management remains unaware of key processes required to meet organizational goals, its ability to make informed strategic structural changes is reduced.

The analysis presented here supports both sides of the argument that took place after our conference presentation (Chataway, 1993). Which side depends on the desired balance between meeting individual needs and meeting collective organizational goals. People in formal conflict management roles who envision organizational change as part of their mandate are sometimes frustrated by informal work because as informal conflict managers deal with disputes they take the steam out of the mandate for change. Without a formal record of grievances, dispute resolution professionals have more difficulty convincing organizational decision makers that substantial changes in organizational structures and processes are needed. However, from the perspective of disputants, it may be safer and more immediate to request help from a person they know, a person who will keep no formal record of their dispute, and who is close to the particulars of their situation.

Both formal and informal conflict management processes will continue to exist and to influence the functioning of organizations. Our analysis suggests that as a result of gendered beliefs, relationships, and practices, women in organizations experience a burden of responsibility for informal dispute resolution work. Further research will explore how others perceive the value of this work and of the people who carry it out.

The challenge is to find ways to acknowledge informal contributions without neutralizing their influence and to develop organizational norms that allow informal and formal processes to complement each other.

REFERENCES

Abel, R. (1982). *The politics of informal justice.* New York: Academic Press.

Argyris, C. (1986, September-October). *Skilled incompetence.* Harvard Business Review, 74-79.

Bakan, D. (1966). *The duality of human existence: An essay on psychology and religion.* Chicago: Rand McNally.

Bartunek, J., Kolb, D., & Lewicki, R. (1992). Bringing conflict out from behind the scenes: Private, informal, and nonrational dimensions of conflict in organizations. In D. M. Kolb & J. M. Bartunek (Eds.), *Hidden conflict in organizations: Uncovering behind-the-scenes disputes* (pp. 209-228). Newbury Park, CA: Sage.

Bartunek J., & Reid, R. (1992). The role of conflict in a second order change attempt. In D. M. Kolb & J. M. Bartunek (Eds.), *Hidden conflict in organizations: Uncovering behind-the-scenes disputes* (pp. 116-142). Newbury Park, CA: Sage.

Bellinger, D., & Gleason, B. (1982). Sex differences in parental directives to young children. *Sex Roles, 8*(11), 1123-1139.

Black, D., & Baumgartner, M. (1983). Toward a theory of the third party. In W. O. Boyum & L. Mather (Eds.), *Empirical theories of courts* (pp. 84-114). New York: Longman.

Bray, M., Johnson, D., & Chilstrom, J. (1982). Social influence by group members with minority opinions: A comparison of Hollander and Moscovici. *Journal of Personality and Social Psychology, 43*(1), 78-88.

Bumiller, K. (1987). *The civil rights society.* Baltimore, MD: Johns Hopkins Press.

Burton, J. (1987). *Resolving deep-rooted conflict. A Handbook.* Boston: University Press of America.

Chataway, C. (1993). *Working behind the scenes: Gender and power in informal conflict management.* Paper presented at the National Conference on Peacemaking and Conflict Resolution, Portland, OR, May 30.

Collins, R. (1975). *Conflict sociology.* New York: Academic Press.

Dayton, M. (1959). *Men who manage.* New York: Wiley.

Deaux, K. (1984). From individual difference to social categories: Analysis of a decade's research on gender. *American Psychologist, 39,* 105-116.

Eagly, A. (1987). *Sex differences in social behavior: A social-role interpretation.* London: Lawrence Erlbaum.

Eisenberg, N., & Lennon, R. (1983). Sex differences in empathy and related capacities. *Psychological Bulletin, 94*(1), 100-131.

Fagot, B. (1978). The influence of sex of child on parental reactions to toddler children. *Child Development, 49*, 459-465.

Felstiner, W., Abel, R., & Sarat, A. (1981). The emergence and transformation of disputes: Naming, blaming and claiming. . . *Law and Society Review, 15*, 631-654.

Goffman, E. (1959). *The presentation of self in everyday life*. New York: Doubleday.

Greenhouse, C. (1986). *Praying for justice: Faith, order and community in an American town*. Ithaca, NY: Cornell University Press.

Hall, J. (1984). *Nonverbal sex differences: Communication accuracy and expressive style*. Baltimore, MD: Johns Hopkins University Press.

Hartsock, N. (1983). *Money, sex and power*. New York: Longman.

Hochschild, A. (1983). *The managed heart*. Berkeley: University of California Press.

Kanter, R. (1977). *Men and women of the corporation*. New York: Colophon Books.

Kimball, M. (forthcoming). The worlds we live in: Gender similarities and differences. *Canadian Psychology*.

Kolb, D. (1983). *The mediators*. Cambridge, MA: MIT Press.

Kolb, D. (1986). Who are organizational third parties and what do they do? In R.J. Lewicki, B.H. Sheppard, & M.H. Bazerman (Eds.), *Research negotiations in organizations* (Vol. 1, pp. 207-227). Greenwich, CT: JAI Press.

Kolb, D. (1987). Corporate ombudsmen and organizational conflict. *Journal of Conflict Resolution, 31*, 673-691.

Kolb, D. (1992). Women's work: Peacemaking in organizations. In D. M. Kolb & J. M. Bartunek (Eds.), *Hidden conflict in organizations: Uncovering behind-the-scenes disputes* (pp. 63-91). Newbury Park, CA: Sage.

Kolb, D., & Sheppard, B. (1985). Do managers mediate, or even arbitrate? *Negotiation Journal, 1*, 379-388.

Kunda, G. (1991). *Engineering culture: Culture and control in a high-tech organization*. Philadelphia, PA: Temple University Press.

Lawrence, P., & Lorsch, J. (1967). *Organization and environment*. Homewood, IL: Irwin.

Lazarus, R., & Folkman, S. (1984). *Stress, appraisal, and coping*. New York: Springer.

Lewicki, R., & Sheppard, B. (1985). Choosing how to intervene: Factors influencing the use of process and outcome control in third party dispute resolution. *Journal of Occupational Behavior, 6*, 49-64.

Lewin, D. (1987). Dispute resolution in the non-union firm: A theoretical and empirical analysis. *Journal of Conflict Resolution, 31,* 465-502.

Merriam, S. (1990). *Case study research in education.* San Francisco: Jossey-Bass.

Merry, S., & Silbey S. (1984). What do plaintiffs want: Re-examining the concept of dispute. *Justice System Journal, 9,* 151- 76.

Miles, R. (1980). *Macro organizational behavior.* Santa Monica, CA: Goodyear.

Miller, R., & Sarat, A. (1981). Grievances, claims, and disputes: Assessing the adversary culture. *Law and Society Review, 15,* 525-566.

Miner, V., & Longino, H. (Eds.). (1987). *Competition, a feminist taboo?* New York: The Feminist Press.

Nader, L. (1965). The anthropological study of law. *American Anthropologist, 67*(2), 3-32.

Pettigrew, A. (1973). *The politics of organizational decision-making.* London: Tavistock.

Pondy, L. (1967). Organizational conflict: Concepts and models. *Administrative Science Quarterly, 17,* 296-320.

Pondy, L. (1989). Reflections on organizational conflict. *Journal of Organizational Change Management, 2,* 94-98.

Rodriguez, N. (1988). Transcending bureaucracy: Feminist politics at a shelter for battered women. *Gender and Society, 2*(2), 214-227.

Rosenthal, R. (1988). Interpersonal expectancies, nonverbal communication, and research on negotiation. *Negotiation Journal, 4*(3), 267-279.

Rowe, M. (1987). The corporate ombudsman. *Negotiation Journal, 3*(2), 127-140.

Sarat, A. (1987). The new formalism in disputing and dispute processing. *Law and Society, 21,* 695-717.

Scott, J. (1985). *Weapons of the weak.* New Haven: Yale University Press.

Skrypnek, B., & Snyder M. (1982). On the self-perpetuating nature of stereotypes about men and women. *Journal of Experimental Social Psychology, 18*(3), 277-291.

Smith, K. (1989). The movement of conflict in organizations: The joint dynamics of splitting and triangulation. *Administration Science Quarterly, 34,* 1-21.

Walton, R., & McKersie, R. (1965). *A behavioral theory of labor negotiations.* New York: McGraw-Hill.

Wall, V. Jr., & Dewhurst, M. (1991). Mediator gender: Communication differences in resolved and unresolved mediations. *Mediation Quarterly, 9*(1), 63-85.

Weingarten, H., & Douvan, E. (1985). Male and female visions of mediation. *Negotiation Journal, 1*(4), 349-358.

Westin, A., & Feliu, A. (1988). *Resolving employment disputes without litigation.* Washington, DC: BNA.

13

Gender and the Mediation of Conflict: Communication Differences

Marcia L. Dewhurst
Ohio State University
Victor D. Wall Jr.
Cleveland State University

It has often been observed that conflict is inherent in human relations and manifests itself in a variety of forms and intensities. In most disputes, the people involved have a variety of means at their disposal to respond to, or resolve their conflict. Conflict "management" may range from violent resolution to outright avoidance. Between these extremes are several alternatives that involve utilizing third parties. The purpose of this chapter is twofold: to examine the communication used by mediators in dispute resolution and to determine whether male and female mediators differ communicatively. In both instances, we assess the effects their communication has on dispute outcomes.

Mediation

Mediation is described as the most common form of third-party intervention (Bigoness & Kesner, 1986), and its utility as a means of resolving disputes has been well documented (Kressel, Pruitt, & Associates, 1989). Sheppard (1984) uses the term for a range of intervention procedures that share a defining characteristic: the absence of enforceable decisions. Moore (1986) defines *mediation* as "the intervention into a dispute or negotiation by an acceptable, impartial, neutral third party who has no authoritative decision-making power to assist disputing parties in voluntarily reaching their own mutually acceptable settlement of issues in dispute" (p. 14). Implicit in this definition and others (Kochan & Jick, 1978; Prein, 1987) is that a mediator can perform a variety of roles ranging on a continuum from a passive mediator who uses mere presence to prevent the parties from insulting each other, to a clarifier who emphasizes rules and norms to facilitate interaction, to a prompter who interprets comments for parties to encourage coordination. For the purposes of this study, mediation is defined by its most common characteristics: the process by which a neutral third party attempts to facilitate a voluntary agreement between disputing parties.

Approximately 300 newly created neighborhood justice centers, intervening in thousands of community disputes, rely exclusively on mediation as the method for resolving disputes (Keltner, 1987; Kressel, Pruitt, & Associates, 1989). Despite its growing popularity, scholars are still in the early stages of characterizing the overall mediation process, including the behavior of mediators. No clear consensus on the performance of the mediator is evident (Kressel, 1985), and individual mediators are guided by a variety of training protocols and by trial and error. However, in the literature there is an unwarranted assumption of a unified procedure for mediation.

Research on mediation can be roughly divided studies of mediator traits (Karim & Pegnetter, 1983; Landsberger, 1960); mediation behaviors (Thibaut & Walker 1975) including contingency approaches (Bigoness & Kesner, 1986; Carnevale, 1986; Sheppard, 1984); and phasic analyses of the mediation process (Black & Joffee, 1978; Folberg & Taylor, 1984; Haynes, 1981; Jones, 1988; Kessler, 1978; Kressel, 1972; Moore, 1986). Kressel and Pruitt (1985) provided the most extensive review of the current state of mediation research. The collective implication of the research is that mediation is useful and that a typology of activities employed by mediators exists. However, in spite of the findings informing policy development and guiding the practice, "it is clear that the field of mediation research is still in its very formative stages" (Kressel et al., 1989, p. 3). Specifically, what is missing is research that specifies what actually happens in mediation. What do mediators in fact do?

A Communication Perspective

One way to describe what mediators do is with reference to the function of their talk. A major classification of communication acts has been proposed by Weiner and Goodenough (1977). "Substantive" acts, as the name implies, make up the subject matter of conversation. On the other hand, "management" or "housekeeping" acts, do not add new elements to the conversation, but provide a benchmark by which one conversational partner instructs the other how to treat what has been said, and how to proceed in subsequent talk. In essence, management acts "bracket" or "organize" sections of talk.

Of particular interest here are communication management acts that enable mediators to "reframe" (Moore, 1986), "paraphrase" (Bartunek, Benton, & Keys, 1975), or "summarize" (Walton, 1969) disputants' messages and thereby control the mediation process. As a communication act, the function that reframing, paraphrasing, or summarizing performs in a conversation is termed a *formulation* (Heritage & Watson, 1979). Formulations serve as comments on talk, providing proposed interpretations of the sense of the conversation so far (McLaughlin, 1984). Formulations have been characterized as "saying-in-so-many-words-what-we-are-doing," and they provide one instance in which achieving conversational order becomes, for the conversational parties, a topic in its own right.

Garfinkel and Sacks (1970) observe:

> A member may treat some part of the conversation as an occasion to describe the conversation, to explain it, or to characterize it, to explicate, translate, summarize, or furnish the gist of it, to note its adherence to rules, or remark on its departure from rules. In other words, a member may treat some part of the conversation to formulate the conversation. (p. 113)

Heritage and Watson (1979) observe that utterances are often subject to misinterpretation, and that understanding often comes from producing a transformation or paraphrase of the utterances. Such paraphrasing serves to preserve the relevant features of the conversation while recasting them and thus serves to preserve, delete and transform. They also propose that formulations may function to terminate topical talk in preparation to launching a new topic. Also, by placing an interpretative bracket around some part of the conversation, formulations provide a commentary on the conversational situation the communicators are in and thus help to manage roles. Ragan (1983) studied the relative use of accounts and formulations as alignment talk in 12 job interview conversations and suggested that both are used to enact and maintain the inequitable status of the interviewer and interviewee. Formulations thus create subtle social boundaries and allow parties to let each other know who they are in the conversation. Heritage and Watson suggest that formulations are commonly used in the course of unproblematic conversation as well, to demonstrate and confirm understanding.

These observations imply four characteristics of formulations that may be pertinent to mediation behavior:

1. Formulations preserve meaning, delete extraneous details, and transform information.
2. Formulations imply a decision from the recipient in the form of confirmation or disconfirmation. Confirmations are preferred.
3. Formulations function to manage topical talk.
4. Formulations function to manage roles.

Formulations in the mediation context might be more pronounced than in "everyday talk" due to the conflictual nature of the interaction. They might also play a more significant role. More specifically, their use might be critical to effective mediation. For example, the mediator's use of formulations to define the conflict and to frame the initial issues might determine both the way in which those issues are discussed and the range of resolution possibilities (Shaw, 1985, 1986). As another example, disputants' feelings of being understood might increase their satisfaction with the mediator and the process. During a review of disputants' stories, mediator formulations often highlight points of agreement as well as issues in dispute. This provides a type of "reality testing" not usually occurring in the typical negotiation situation. Also, by utilizing formulations to initiate concessions, a mediator may help parties to save face. Finally, consistency theories suggest that when disputants hear their words summarized by a mediator, reminding them of previous comments or commitments, they tend to abide by these comments or commitments.

In addition to these contributions to the mediation process, formulations could also accomplish other communication goals of mediators, including softening conflict, changing the topic, and switching talking turns. Thus, at a minimum, formulations might serve the following functions in the context of mediated conflict:

1. clarify meanings,
2. soften and/or minimize the use of harsh language,
3. change the topic,
4. switch the conversation from one speaker to the next,
5. reframe an utterance into a proposed solution,

6. force parties to look carefully at statements he or she has made,
7. emphasize points of agreement or disagreement, and
8. maintain control of the mediation process.

The purpose of this study is to analyze the use of formulations in the mediation context and to determine their contribution to mediation outcomes.

Gender and Mediation

Of equal interest to this research is the use of formulations by females and males because a number of studies have suggested that women and men talk differently (Nadler & Nadler, 1984; Rosaldo, 1974; Womack, 1987). Burrell, Donohue, and Allen (1988) suggest that gender differences in mediation behavior are more often perceived than real. They found that female mediators were perceived as less controlling even though in one of their experimental conditions, the females engaged in more controlling behaviors than males in the same condition. Males, on the other hand, were perceived as more controlling but in reality exhibited fewer actual controlling behaviors than their female counterparts. They go on to say that "even though they pursue an interventionist role with as much fervor as their male counterparts, they [females] are perceived to be less in charge of the interaction" (p. 464). These results, however, are qualified by the finding that communication behavior differences between women and men disappeared when mediators were trained to perform a specific role. The differences, they conclude, appear when the requirements of the role are less specifically articulated. Consequently, with mediation training, actual differences in gender behavior are not likely to be manifested. However, they had no basis to expect stereotypical gender-based perceptions to change.

Carnevale, Conlon, Hanisch, and Harris (1989) also report gender differences in mediation behavior. They found that female mediators were more inactive than males in that they sent fewer messages. However, female messages were more likely to be integrative than male messages. In contrast, male mediators used pressure and compensation tactics significantly more than their female counterparts. These results supported the expectations that female mediators would be more concerned than male mediators with disputants' achieving their aspirations and would therefore behave more integratively and compensatively.

Based on these findings and our earlier discussion of formulations, we anticipated differential use of formulations by mediators based on gender. Our specific expectations follow.

Research Expectations

H1. More formulations will be used in resolved mediations than in unresolved mediations.

H2. Males will use more formulations than females.

H3. Female and male mediators will use different types of formulations. Specifically, females will use more formulations of an integrative nature (e.g., clarification, emphasizing points of agreement and disagreement), and males will use formulations of a more instrumentally oriented nature (e.g., changing the topic, switching the conversation from one speaker to the next, reframing an utterance into a proposed solution, forcing a party to look carefully at statements he or she has made, and maintaining control of the mediation).

H4. Disputants in mediations that are resolved should be more satisfied with the outcome and the process than those in unresolved mediations, and will evaluate the mediator as more competent, clear, and fair.

Research Questions

Because we had no basis for predicting the effect gender would have on disputant satisfaction and compliance with the agreement, we posed the following two research questions.

Q1: What effect does gender have on disputants' compliance with the agreement, satisfaction with mediation outcome, mediation process, and disputants' evaluations of mediator competency, clarity, and fairness?

Q2: What effect does the relationship between the gender of the mediators and the gender of the disputants have on the number of formulations used, the disputants' evaluations of mediator competency, clarity, and fairness?

METHODOLOGY

Transcripts of 40 mediation sessions were used to analyze the use of formulations in the mediation context. Selection of the sample was made to include 20 resolved mediations (10 by female mediators, and 10 by male mediators) and 20 unresolved mediations (10 by female mediators and 10 by male mediators). Mediation outcomes were analyzed as a function of formulation use by male and female mediators.

Participants and Data Collection Procedures

Data for the study were collected by observing mediation proceedings at the Franklin County Municipal Court of Small Claims in Columbus, OH. Claims brought to the court are limited to civil matters. The mediations observed include a broad range of disputes: consumer issues; individuals versus individuals (personal loans, neighborhood disturbances, etc.); business disputes; landlord-tenant disputes; and various torts, including automobile damages.

Mediators for the sessions included court-appointed mediators in the daily court proceedings, and volunteer mediators for an evening mediation program offered by the court. The court-appointed mediators included third-year students in the College of Law at the Ohio State University. Volunteer mediators included individuals who have received mediation training and were typically lawyers or others involved in a community/social service profession.

The individuals in small claims court are frequently from the low end of the socioeconomic spectrum. Normally, neither the claimant nor respondent is represented by legal counsel. The types of relationships between disputing parties included family, marital, neighbor, friend, intimate, roommate, and various types of business relations (e.g., landlord-tenant, customer-vendor, and partnerships). Their ages ranged from 18 to the early 80s.

The data collection protocol required daily attendance at small claims court to await cases that the court referee directed to mediation. At that time, one of the authors would accompany the mediator and disputants to an adjacent anteroom and ask permission to sit in and audiotape the proceedings for research purposes. The disputants were told the purpose of the research was to assess how disputants reach agreement, and they were assured of anonymity. The data collection protocol was identical for the evening mediation program.

Permission for the authors to be present and tape the proceedings was granted by all but two of the mediations. During the session, the researchers would note relevant information such as date, names of disputants and mediator, issue(s) and whether an agreement was reached. At the end of the session, permission was requested to telephone the disputants at a later date to ask them some questions about the session. Again, permission was always granted (however, seven of the disputants did not have a telephone at the time of the mediation), and the disputants gave a telephone number that was recorded by the authors. The individual disputants were contacted by telephone, or personal interview, within 2 to 3 months to determine if agreements made the day of the mediation had lasted, to obtain perceptions of satisfaction and fairness with the mediation process, and to obtain perceptions about the mediator. This was done utilizing a questionnaire developed specifically for this study. Questionnaire items were developed to measure disputants' attitudes toward selected aspects of the process, the mediators, and outcomes believed to be important in mediation. The content for these items was identified through a review of the mediation literature. The questions were written as both positive and negative statements and used a standard Likert scale format with a 5-point set of responses ranging from "strongly agree" to "strongly disagree." If a disputant could not be reached by telephone, personal interviews were conducted by visiting the disputant's residence.

Concurrent with the collection of data, verbatim transcripts were made of the mediation sessions. The audiotapes of the mediation sessions were transcribed following the rules for transcription summarized in Schenkein (1978).

Coding of Transcripts

Formulations.

Drawing on an explanation by Heritage and Watson (1979), a formulation was defined as a paraphrase utterance that preserves relevant features of a prior utterance or utterances while also recasting them. Thus, preservation and transformation were central properties of the utterance. Mediator utterances that summarized, paraphrased, or reframed (transformed) a disputant's comments were defined as a formulation.

Formulation episode.

A *formulation episode*, for this study, represents the rephrased or summarized statement as well as sufficient preceding conversation to have it make sense, and/or the preceding conversation that seems to be included in the rephrased/summarized statement. The episode also included the utterances immediately after the formulation statement (confirmation, disconfirmation, or the notation of a pass). The episode was created by first identifying the formulation and then going back into the preceding conversation to determine the utterances that were formulated.

Identification of formulations.

The identification of formulation episodes was completed by the authors and one other coder (an advanced undergraduate student). Coder training consisted of discussing the descriptive information on how to identify formulations and practicing on samples of formulations in mediation transcripts not used in this study. The coders were instructed to single out the formulation, that portion of the previous conversation necessary to make sense of the mediator's formulation, and the utterances following the formulation that expressed confirmation, disconfirmation, or a pass of the formulation. After training, each coder independently identified the formulations in eight transcripts. Total agreement was reached on each of the formulation episodes, that is, in singling out the formulation, the previous utterances the mediator was summarizing or restating, and the closure to the formulation. One of the authors identified the formulations in the remaining 32 transcripts.

Categorization of Formulations

Formulations were categorized on the basis of their previously identified functions. The authors had the opportunity to observe approximately 20 small claims court mediations, during which time the prevalence and functionality of rephrasing was salient. This prompted a review of manuals and empirical studies and ultimately a review of these hypothesized categories. The original listing included two other categories: balancing power between the disputants, and stalling (i.e., rephrasing in order to have time to think what to do next). However, it was felt these two categories relied too heavily on interpreting mediator motivation. The final set of categories were as follows:

1. *Clarify meaning:* The formulation serves to ensure the mediator or the disputant has the details correct. In contrast to a question which asks for new information, clarification of information that has not been discussed, this formulation restates previously discussed information.
2. *Soften language:* This formulation serves to make previously stated comments more palatable to the other disputant. In response to comments that would not be conducive to joint problem solving, this formulation is a restatement designed to be more acceptable to the other disputant. This could include "softening" name calling and use of profane language by one of the disputants.
3. *Change topic:* The mediator's comments serve to tell the dis-

putant that the current topic has been sufficiently covered, and it is appropriate to move on to another aspect of the dispute. Paraphrasing the previous comments serves to tell the disputant that the topic is complete, and the mediator is directing the disputant to another topic.

4. *To hear other side of the story:* Although similar to changing the topic, this formulation serves to change the focus of the conversation from one disputant to the other by paraphrasing the former's comments in a manner useful to the other disputant. The topic does not change, and the formulation functions to give one disputant's perceptions to the other disputant with the intention of facilitating a response from the latter.

5. *Reframe prior utterances into a proposal:* Paraphrasing a disputant's comments by the mediator to move the process to the generation of solutions to the dispute. Reframing comments as a solution proposal permits more objective evaluation by the other disputant. For example, "so, what I hear you saying is that you would like to see the children more often."

6. *Force a party to look carefully at statements that he or she has made:* Paraphrasing the disputant's comments serves to allow the disputant to hear them again and confirm or disconfirm the content. The formulation functions to insure that the disputant means what he or she said.

7. *To emphasize points of agreement or disagreement:* Summarizing both disputants' comments, with emphasis on points of agreement or disagreement, functions to lead parties to converge, rather that diverge on the issues at hand. Thus, the formulation provides a kind of reality testing and serves to crystallize the issue(s).

8. *To maintain control of the mediation:* Implicit in all of the functions is the notion of control of the conversation during the mediation. However, at times the mediator will summarize the conversation in such a way that his or her control is made explicitly clear. This would include formulations that function as reprimands for not abiding by the ground rules, and correcting a disputant for misrepresenting comments made by the mediator. Included here also are formulations that emphasize the uncertainty of future court rulings (as a persuasive message to keep the parties in mediation and working toward an agreement).

Coding procedures.

Having identified the formulation episodes, the same set of coders were utilized to judge how the formulations functioned in the mediation dialogue. The coders had access to the full transcript. With each transcript, coders were given the defined categories and a sheet that identified each formulation episode in the transcript. For each episode, information was given to direct the coder to where the episode started (page number, person speaking, and the first few utterances), the formulation, and the response.

The authors and coder worked independently to code 33% of the transcripts. This involved 173 judgments, or 35% of the total formulations coded. A formulation was judged to be coded correctly if two of the three coders independently agreed about the function category. Unanimous coder agreement was reached on 101 judgments (58%). Agreement by two of the coders was reached in 165 judgments, which raised the percentage of properly coded formulations to 95%. Five percent required subsequent discussion in order to reach an agreement. In most cases those requiring discussion were situations in which the formulation was perceived as serving more than one function. In order to reach agreement, the coders discussed which function was best served.

The 27 remaining transcripts were coded by the authors. This involved 317 judgments, or 65% of the 490 formulations identified. Intercoder agreement (Scott's Pi) was .93.

Dependent Variables

Outcome.

At the completion of the mediation session an agreement was or was not reached by the disputants. If reached, the terms of the agreement were written up by the mediator. Outcome here, defined in the institutional sense, was either resolved or unresolved.

Satisfaction with outcome.

This was defined as the degree of satisfaction, happiness with, and fairness of the outcome and was measured by a three-item, 5-point, Likert scale ranging from "very satisfied" ("happy, fair") to "very dissatisfied" ("unhappy, unfair"). A subject's score could range from a low of 3 ("very dissatisfied, unhappy, unfair") to a high of 15 ("very satisfied, happy, fair"). Reliability, utilizing Cronbach's alpha, was .93 for this measure.

Satisfaction with process.

This was defined as the degree of satisfaction with, and perceptions of fairness of, the process and was measured by a two-item, 5-point, Likert scale ranging from "very satisfied" ("fair') to "very dissatisfied" ("unfair"). An individual's score could range from a low of 2 ("very dissatisfied, unfair") to a high of 10 ("very satisfied, fair"). Reliability estimates were .77 for this measure.

Compliance with agreement.

Disputants were asked to what extent they were doing what they had agreed to do at the time of the mediation. Their compliance with the agreement was measured by a 5-point, Likert scale which ranged from doing "everything" to doing "nothing," with varying grades of doing "some" of what was agreed. An individual's score could range from a low of 1 (indicating they were doing everything to which they agreed) to 5 (indicating they were doing nothing to which they agreed). In connection with this question, each disputant was also asked to what extent the other party is doing what was agreed to in the mediation. The same response categories were utilized.

Perceptions of the Mediator

Measures of the disputants' perception of the mediator were also included.

Fairness of the mediator.

Perceived mediator fairness was defined as the degree to which the disputant felt the mediator liked one of the parties in the mediation better than the other, to what extent the mediator was fair in his or her treatment of the disputant, and to what extent the mediator allowed the disputant enough time to say what he or she had to say. The fairness variable was measured by a three-item, 5-point, Likert scale ranging from positive to negative. Reliability was .62.

Clarity of the mediator.

Perceived clarity of the mediator was defined as the degree to which the mediator made each disputant's position clear during the mediation, and was measured by a two-item, 5-point Likert scale which ranged from a "very good job" to a "very poor job." An individual's score could range from a low of 2 (low clarity) to a high of 10 (high clarity). Reliability was .87.

Competency of the mediator.

Perceived mediator competence was defined to which the mediator was considered to be skilled, competent, and trustworthy and was measured by a three-item, 5-point, Likert scale. The scales ranged from "very skilled" ("competent, trustworthy") to "very unskilled" ("incompetent, untrustworthy"). An individual's score could range from a low of 3 (low competency) to a high of 15 (high competency). Reliability was .77.

DATA ANALYSIS AND RESULTS

To test Hypotheses 1 and 2, we compared the number of formulations that male and female mediators used in sessions with resolved and unresolved outcomes (See Table 13.1). As anticipated by Hypothesis 1, formulations were more frequent in resolved than in unresolved mediations [χ^2 = 12.12 (1), $p < .001$]. Hypothesis 2 was not supported. Male mediators did not produce significantly more formulations than female mediators [$\chi^2 = .58$ (1), $p < .05$].

To test Hypothesis 3 we compared the different types of formulations used by male and female mediators (see Table 13.2).

Chi-square indicated a relationship between the formulation categories and gender. Specific cell comparisons, using z-score transformation to assess significance of the relative proportions, indicated that female mediators used clarification formulations proportionately more than did their male counterparts, and males used formulations designed to maintain control of the mediation more than the female mediators. None of the other categories discriminated between male and female mediators, but all were directional as predicted by Hypothesis 3.

Given these results we decided to compare female and male mediators' use of different kinds of mediations in resolved and unre-

Table 13.1. Gender by Outcome: Number of Formulations

	Mediator		
	Female	*Male*	*Totals*
Resolved	139	144	283
Unresolved	94	112	206
Totals	233	256	489

solved mediations. Although analysis of the unresolved mediations failed to produce a significant χ^2 [9.25, (6), $p = .099$], its marginal significance prompted a z-score analysis of comparative proportions. In this case, use of clarification was not significantly different between genders. However, men used significantly more formulations to maintain control than women (11% to 3% respectively, $z = 2.65$, $p = < .01$). Among resolved mediations the relationship between formulation categories and gender was significant [19.63, (6), $p =< .001$]. As before, women tended to use more clarifications than men (59% to 40%, $z = 3.11$, $p = < .01$), and men tended to use more controlling formulations than women (15% to 3%, $z = 3.56$, $p = < .01$).

Further analysis of clarifications (Table 13.3) indicated these occurred more frequently in resolved than unresolved disputes regardless of whether the mediator was male ($z = 2.79$, $p = < .01$) or female ($z = 4.14$, $p = < .04$).

Table 13.2. Gender by Formulation Categories: Number of Formulations

| | Mediator | | | | |
	Female	Male	Totals	z	Sig
Clarification	119	90	209	3.55	.01
Change topic	5	7	12	.42	n/s
Hear other side	13	18	31	.66	n/s
Reframe as proposition	41	48	89	.33	n/s
Force close look at statements made	28	41	69	1.27	n/s
Emphasize agreement/ disagreement	19	14	33	1.18	n/s
Maintain control	8	38	46	4.32	.01
Totals	233	256	489		

$\chi^2 = 27.47$, df = 6, $p = < .001$.

Table 13.3. Outcome by Gender: Clarification Formulation

	Female		Male	
Resolved	79	(33.91%)	57	(22.27%)
Unresolved	40	(17.17%)	33	(12.89%)

To address our first research question on influence of mediator gender on dispute outcomes, we compared disputants' compliance with the agreement, satisfaction with the outcome, and evaluations of the mediator by mediator gender. Comparison of compliance yielded no statistically significant difference by mediator gender.

Similarly, disputants' satisfaction with the outcome did not differ by mediator gender. Mediator gender made a difference in disputant's satisfaction with the mediation process, but its effect depended on whether or not the dispute was resolved [outcome x mediator gender interactions $F(1,36) = 5.30$, $p = < .05$], As indicated in Table 13.4, when the dispute was resolved, mediator gender made no difference in satisfaction with the mediation process. When the dispute was unresolved, disputants expressed greater satisfaction when the mediator was female than male.

There were no statistically significant differences in evaluations of mediators' fairness or clarity based on gender. Mediators' gender did make a difference in evaluations of their competence, but this effect depended on whether or not the dispute was resolved [outcome x mediator gender interaction $F(1,36) = 4.32$, $p < .05$]. As indicated in Table 13.5, mediators' gender clearly made no difference in competency evaluations when the dispute was resolved. When the dispute was unresolved, male mediators received significantly higher evaluations than females ($t = 1.66$, df = 38, $p = < .05$, one-tailed).

Thus, there were no main effects of mediator gender on dispute outcomes. The two statistically significant interaction effects suggest that mediator gender made a difference only when disputes were unresolved. In these cases, female mediators appeared to generate greater satisfaction with the mediation process, whereas male mediators appeared to generate better evaluations of their competence.

Table 13.4. Process Satisfaction Means

	Female	Male
Resolved	7.90	7.80
Unresolved	7.15	6.65

Table 13.5. Mediator Competence Means

	Female	Male
Resolved	6.05	6.25
Unresolved	6.11	7.35

The final analyses addressed research Question 2 on the joint effect of disputants' and mediator's gender on the use of formulations and dispute outcomes. Comparison of formulations yielded significant differences by mediator and disputant gender [$\chi^2 = 11.81$ (2), $p = < .01$]. As indicated in Table 13.6, although male and female mediators did not differ in their use of formulations when the disputants were of mixed gender, female mediators used significantly more formulations than males when both disputants were female ($z = 2.82$, $p < .01$), and male mediators used significantly more formulations than females when both disputants were male ($z = 2.81$, $p = < .01$).

Specific types of formulations could not be compared by disputants' and mediators' gender because of small cell frequencies. Analysis of variance indicated no differences in outcome measures by disputant and mediator gender. Thus, the only interactive effect of disputant and mediator gender was that mediators used more formulations with same-sex than opposite-sex disputants.

DISCUSSION

We began our study with three expectations about mediators' use of formulations in mediated conflict. First, we expected a positive association between dispute resolution and the use of formulations. Formulations were in fact more frequently used by mediators of resolved than unresolved disputes. The apparent effect of formulations was not due to length of mediation sessions. Second, we expected male mediators to use more formulations than female mediators. This expectation was not supported. Female mediators used formulations as frequently as male mediators. Third, we expected male and female mediators to use different types of formulations. As predicted, male mediators tended to use formulations that enhanced their control of the mediation process more often than did females. Females in contrast, tended to use formulations

Table 13.6. Number of Formulations by Mediator and Disputant's Gender

	Disputants		
	Both Female (N = 6)	Mixed (N = 19)	Both Male (N = 15)
Male Mediators	29 (11.3%)	114 (44.5%)	113 (44.1%)
Female Mediators	48 (20.6%)	111 (47.6%)	74 (31.8%)

that enhanced integration between disputants by clarifying their points of agreement and disagreement more often than did males. Thus, formulations, which apparently facilitated dispute resolution, were used somewhat differently by male and female mediators.

Our analysis was also guided by questions about mediator effectiveness, that is, disputant compliance with the agreement and satisfaction with the process and outcome. Would mediator gender or mediator and disputant gender make a difference? We did not find evidence in any comparison of resolved disputes that male and female mediators differed in perceived effectiveness. Only in circumstances in which disputes remained unresolved did their effectiveness appear to differ. In these cases, disputants considered male mediators to be somewhat more competent than female mediators, but they nevertheless expressed greater satisfaction with the process when the mediator was female than male. The results are consistent with stereotypical expectations of men's and women's behavior.

Finally we wanted to know whether the gender of both mediator and disputants influenced the process or the outcome of mediation. Our analyses revealed only one difference, a tendency for mediators to use more formulations with same-sex disputants than with opposite-sex disputants. These results are important because formulations apparently facilitated dispute resolution. Thus, disputants of mixed gender would be expected to benefit equally from mediation by males or females, but same-sex disputants would be expected to benefit more from same-sex, rather than opposite-sex, mediators. Female mediators used almost three times the number of formulations when the disputants were males than did male mediators when the disputants were female. This suggests that males might be more inhibited in the use of formulations when both disputants are female than when at least one is male, which could be due to a preference for using controlling communication (e.g. formulations that control the process) with men.

IMPLICATIONS

The most immediate implication of this study is for the training of mediators. Those who train mediators will benefit from an understanding of the potential diversity of use of communication management acts by female and male mediators. For educators, this knowledge can be powerful in providing detail to the abstract instruction too often provided. To the practitioner, the knowledge of the use of formulations provides a way to focus a common communication act. Being sensitive to the tendency toward differences in use noted in this study would suggest female and male mediators should strive to utilize the full spectrum of functions of formulations. For instance, male mediators could improve their repertoire of skills by utilizing more integrative types of formulations, which might increase disputant satisfaction with both the outcome and process, and females could benefit by utilizing control formulations to a greater degree, which might increase disputant evaluation of their competence. Indeed, formulations in general should be a prime focus of mediator training, particularly those that clarify disputants' agreements and disagreements.

Males and females should most definitely be sensitized to the potential differences in the ways they communicate with all-male, all-female, or mixed-sex disputants. The data suggest that sensitization to the interaction between mediator and disputant gender may be helpful in increasing integrative outcomes, disputant satisfaction with the mediation outcome and process, and positive perceptions of the mediator.

From a theoretical standpoint, this study has several implications. First, it is important to continue to explore, at the microlevel, how women and men communicate in mediation, not just in their use of formulations. We believe a crucial point in mediation occurs when the mediator "frames" the dispute. We strongly suspect this is critical to successfully resolving disputes because it sets the "tone" for how the mediation will proceed as well as defines the conflict parameters. Our results suggest enough differences exist between female and male mediators to hypothesize that framing the dispute may be handled somewhat differently by males and females. Such information could significantly contribute to our knowledge of how mediation progresses as well as what role gender plays in that process.

Second, related questions are what else is going on, especially in how formulations relate to or integrate with other communicative acts? Are there gender differences in the use of "attending to" skills (e.g., responsive utterances such as "uh huh," "I see") that are used by many mediators to acknowledge what is being said? Are metaphors utilized differently by female and male mediators. Discovering more about the diversity of skills male and female mediators bring to the table, and what effects these have on outcomes and disputants, will provide us with invaluable information in building a theory of third-party conflict management.

Third, traditional cultural expectations of male and female behavior continue to be manifested in mediation. Women tend to orient toward others, and men tend to be more controlling. However, when mediation is successful, gender appears to be irrelevant. Further research might do well to focus on what specific behaviors tend to continue to reinforce, and what behaviors tend to counteract, these stereotypes.

Finally, it is clear that researchers have only begun to scratch the surface regarding the impact of gender in the mediation of conflict. In truth, we know very little about specific communicative differences between men and women, and we also know very little as to what is critical in successful mediation. Hopefully, this chapter will help stimulate more research into these critical issues.

REFERENCES

Bartunek, J.M., Benton, A.A., & Keys, C.B. (1975). Third party intervention and the bargaining behavior of group representatives. *Journal of Conflict Resolution, 19*(3), 532-557.

Bigoness, W.J., & Kesner, I.F. (1986). Mediation effectiveness: What can we learn from leadership research? In R.J. Lewicki, B.H. Sheppard, & M.H. Bazerman (Eds.), *Research on negotiations in organizations* (Vol. 1, pp. 229-249) Greenwich, CT: JAI Press.

Black, M., & Joffee, W. (1978). A lawyer/therapist team approach to divorce. *Conciliation Courts Review, 16*, 1-5.

Burrell, N.A., Donohue, W.A., & Allen, M. (1988). Gender-based perceptual biases in mediation. *Communication Research, 15*(4), 447-469.

Burrell, N.A., Donohue, W.A., & Allen, M. (1990). The impact of disputants' expectations on mediation: Testing an interventionist model. *Human Communication Research, 1*, 104-139.

Carnevale, P.J. (1986). Strategic choice in mediation. *Negotiation Journal, 2*, 41-56.

Carnevale, P.J., Conlon, D.E., Hanisch, K.A., & Harris, K.L. (1989). Experimental research on the strategic-choice model of mediation. In K. Kressel, D.G. Pruitt, & Associates (Eds.), *Mediation research* (pp. 344-367). San Francisco: Jossey-Bass.

Folberg, J., & Taylor, A. (1984). *Mediation: A comprehensive guide to resolving conflicts without litigation.* San Francisco: Jossey-Bass.

Garfinkel, H., & Sacks, H. (1970). On formal structures of practical actions. In J. C. McKinney & E. A. Tirayakian (Eds.) *Theoretical sociology* (pp. 337-366). New York: Appleton-Century-Crofts.

Haynes, J.M. (1981). *Divorce mediation: A practical guide for therapists and counselors.* New York: Springer.

Heritage, J.C., & Watson, D.R. (1979). Formulations as conversational objectives. In G. Psathas (Ed.), *Everyday language: Studies in ethnomethodology* (pp. 123-159). New York: Irvington.

Jones, T. (1988). Phase structures in agreement and no-agreement mediation. *Communication Research, 15*(4), 470-495.

Karim, A., & Pegnetter, R. (1983). Mediator strategies and qualities and mediation effectiveness. *Industrial Relations, 22,* 105-114.

Keltner, J. (1987). *Mediation.* Annandale, VA: Speech Communication Association.

Kessler, S. (1978). *Creative conflict resolution: Mediation.* Fountain Valley, CA: National Institute for Professional Training.

Kochan, T.A. (1980). Collective bargaining and organizational behavior research. In B.M. Shaw & L.L. Cummings (Eds.), *Research in organizational behavior* (Vol 2, pp. 129-176). Greenwich, CT: JAI Press.

Kochan, T.A., & Jick, T. (1978). The public sector mediation process: A theory and empirical examination. *Journal of Conflict Resolution, 22*(2), 209-240.

Kressel, K. (1972). *Labor mediation: An exploratory survey.* New York: Association of Labor Mediation Agencies.

Kressel, K. (1985). *The process of divorce: How professionals and couples negotiate settlement.* New York: Basic Books.

Kressel, K., Pruitt, D.G., & Associates. (1989). *Mediation research.* San Francisco, CA: Jossey-Bass.

Kressel, K. & Pruitt, D.G. (1985). Themes in the mediation of social conflict. *Journal of Social Issues, 41*(2), 179-198.

Landsberger, H.A. (1960). The behavior and personality of the labor mediator, the parties' perception of mediator behavior. *Personnel Psychology, 13,* 329-347.

McLaughlin, M.L. (1984). *Conversation: How talk is organized.* Beverly Hills, CA: Sage.

Moore, C.W. (1986). *The mediation process: Practical strategies for resolving conflict.* San Francisco, CA: Jossey-Bass.

Nadler, L.B., & Nadler, M.K. (1984, March). *Communication, gender and negotiation: Theory and findings.* Paper presented at the annual meting of Eastern Communication Association, Philadelphia, PA.

Prein, H. (1987). Strategies for third party intervention. *Human Relations, 40,* 699-720.

Ragan, S. (1983). Alignment and conversational coherence. In R.T. Craig, & K. Tracy (Eds.), *Conversational coherence: Form, structure and strategy* (pp. 157-173). Beverly Hills, CA: Sage.

Rosaldo, M.Z. (1974). Women, culture, and society: A theoretical overview. In M.Z. Rosaldo & L. Lamphere (Eds.),*Women, culture and society* (pp. 17-42). Stanford, CA: Stanford University Press.

Schenkein, J. (Ed.). (1978). *Studies in the organization of conversational interaction.* New York: Academic Press.

Shaw, M. (1985). Divorce mediation: Some keys to the process. *Mediation Quarterly, 9,* 27-34.

Shaw, M. (1986). Family mediation. *New York University Review of Law and Social Change, 14,* 765.

Sheppard, B.H. (1984). Third party conflict intervention: A procedural framework. In B.M. Shaw & L.L. Cummings (Eds.), *Research in organizational behavior* (Vol. 6, pp 141-189). Greenwich, CT: JAI Press.

Thibaut, J., & Walker, L. (1975). *Procedural justice: A psychological analysis.* Hillsdale, NJ: Lawrence Erlbaum Associates.

Walton, R.E. (1969). *Interpersonal peacemaking: Confrontations and third-party consultation.* Reading, MA: Addison-Wesley.

Weiner, S.L., & Goodenough, D.R. (1977). A move toward a psychology of conversation. In R. O. Freedle (Ed.), *Discourse production and comprehension* (pp. 213-226). Norwood, NJ: Ablex Publishing.

Womack, D.F. (1987, October). *Implications for women in organization negotiations.* Paper presented at the annual meeting of Speech Communication Association, Boston, MA.

14

Overlapping Radicalisms: Convergence and Divergence Between Feminist and Human Needs Theories in Conflict Resolution

Ingrid Sandole-Staroste
University of Virginia

About 30 years ago, scholars from different disciplines called into question the ability of the ordinary social sciences to deal with complex social problems, hence they created a new interdisciplinary field: *conflict resolution*. A new language and new concepts emerged that are now employed across disciplines to analyze, explain, and solve conflicts. A new theory evolved and from it common practices were developed.

John Burton (1990), a leading theorist in the study of conflict resolution and problem solving, advanced a theory based on a set of human needs that are believed to be universal. In this chapter, I explore his theory and examine the generic nature of human needs and the processes of conflict resolution that Burton claims can be deduced from the theory. Particularly, I examine the assertion that the theory transcends observable differences of race, class, culture, and gender. My emphasis is on gender and I explore to what extent—if at all—human needs theory and feminist theory converge.

Second-wave feminist theory evolved at about the same time as conflict theory. At that time, women had grown profoundly skeptical of all sciences. They began to question the dominant paradigms and developed numerous feminisms: liberal, Marxist, radical, psychoanalytic, socialist, existential, postmodern, cultural, and eco-feminist. Although these feminists are in some ways different from each other, each argues that the existing social system is inadequate in meeting the needs of women and does not treat women equally with men.

What is human needs-based conflict resolution theory? Does it meet the concerns about conflict raised by feminist theories? In the first part of this chapter, I examine Burton's (1990) needs theory to gain a better understanding of his claim that needs are ontological and, therefore, the very essence of a person. Burton calls into question the prevailing power paradigm that rests on the belief that the problem source is people and their nature and not the environment in which they operate.

In the second part, I explore feminist theory and examine some of the reasons feminists put forward for rejecting the prevailing power paradigm. In the third part, I examine if and where the two theories diverge and converge.

HUMAN NEEDS THEORY

Some who study the link between human needs and conflict argue that the field of conflict resolution and provention[1] should be an "adisciplinary study that cuts across all disciplines: a synthesis, a holistic approach to a problem area" (Burton & Sandole, 1986, p. 333). Indeed, Burton (1990) concludes that the field of conflict resolution and provention "knows no boundaries of thought" (p. 20). It "transcends separate compartments of knowledge . . . cannot be broken up into aspects of behavior . . . and cuts across culture" (p. 20). Burton insists that to adopt a holistic view of human conflictual behavior is politically realistic, and in no sense superficial.

Moreover, Burton (1990) argues that the only value orientation inherent in conflict resolution and provention "is the goal of resolving conflict" (p. 21). The study of conflict resolution and provention is analytical and, therefore, has no ideological orientation. Human needs theo-

---

[1]*Conflict provention* means deducing from an adequate explanation of the phenomenon of conflict, including its human dimensions, not merely the conditions that create an environment of conflict, and the structural changes required to remove it, but more importantly, the promotion of conditions that create cooperative relationships. The term *provention* was invented because *prevention* has a negative connotation (Burton, 1990, p. 3).

ry in this context is believed to have the power to explain and to "transcend observable differences in human behavior" (Burton & Sandole, 1986, p. 334).

Burton and Sandole (1986) question the dominant power paradigm that is built upon the belief that "the problem source is people and their nature, [and] not the circumstances in which they operate" (p. 334). This dominant paradigm maintains that "the function of institutions and structures is to control members of society" (p. 334). It attaches importance to the preservation of structures and institutions and rarely, if at all, sees them as the source of the problem (ibid).

The alternative paradigm advanced by Burton rejects those assumptions and makes the relations between individual and structures the center of attention. It proposes that there are limits to which the human person can be socialized or manipulated and that unless human needs are fulfilled, there can be no social stability, the availability of authoritative coercion notwithstanding (Burton, 1990, p. 23).

Needs, Burton (1990) claims, cannot be suppressed or socialized away. Accepting Burton's premise, it then follows that the roots of social conflict are to be found not in "human deformities [but] rather [in] structural and institutional deformities" (p. 32).

Human needs-based conflict resolution theory postulates that all people have certain inherent drives that are outside the control of an individual. Burton (1990) acknowledges that it is not yet clear what exactly these ontological needs are, but he has no doubt that they exist and that they are "more compelling in directing behaviors than many possible external influences" (p. 33). These drives or needs cannot "be suppressed by external socialization, threat or coercion" (p. 32). This is not to say that human beings do not respond to "opportunities of development, and . . . are malleable in this sense" (p. 32). Rather, human beings cannot be socialized to accept "denial of needs such as [identity, security, development] recognition, autonomy, dignity, and bonding" (p. 32). These basic human needs, Burton contends, are "preconditions of individual development" (p. 32). Because individuals cannot be socialized into destroying their identity, they are compelled to react against social environments that attempt to do [so] (p. 33).

Burton's proposition that individuals can be molded only to a limited extent has had an influence on the perception of the nature of conflict, its resolution, and prevention. Because individuals are compelled to pursue their needs "regardless of circumstance and consequences" (Burton, 1990, p. 33), they will seek to satisfy these needs inside or outside the legal norms of society. In other words, needs "reflect universal motivation" and "will be pursued by all means available" (p. 36). This means that "deterrence cannot deter in conditions in

which human needs are frustrated" (p. 34). The focus on needs, therefore, enhances the political power of human behavior, at all levels, for
social stability can be maintained only if human needs are met.

According to Burton, conflicts can be provented only if one
deals with their environmental origins. This involves understanding and
attending to *needs, values,* and *interests.* Although the three concepts are
linked, they are also separate. Knowledge of each will lead to distinct
conflict resolution methods.

Needs, Burton (1990) argues "are inherent drives for survival
and development" (p. 39). And even though it "is still far from clear"
what those drives are, he believes they are universal. (p. 33). Cultural
and other values are held extensively in common in any society.
Interests, in contrast, "separate society into groupings, frequently in
opposition to each other" (p. 40). Values, for Burton, exist at a different
level from needs and are not ontological. Values are "ideas, habits, customs, and beliefs" expressed by an individual or a group of individuals
(Burton, 1990, p. 37). Values concerning "linguistic, religious, class, ethnic, [and gender]" dimensions reflect cultural identities (Burton, 1990, p.
37). As such, values can unite individuals in groups, but they can also
distinguish between individuals and groups of individuals. It is through
these group associations that individuals pursue identity, security, and
development. Further, people will defend their values, if necessary in an
aggressive manner, precisely because values are linked to their need for
security and identity. This is true particularly in situations in which people feel oppressed, discriminated against, and isolated. Interests, too,
according to Burton, exist at a different level from needs, and they are
also separate from values. Interests are not an inherent part of an individual in any way; rather they refer "to the occupational, social and
political aspirations of the individual, and of identity groups of individuals within the social system" (p. 38). Interests are shared within groups
in society rather than nationally. They reflect a "high win-lose component" and are "transitory, altering with circumstances" (p. 38).

Burton (1990) argues that although individuals and groups in
conflict can negotiate and reach agreement on interests, values and needs
are nonnegotiable. To satisfy values and needs, wider social dimensions
must be taken into account: the establishment of an environment that
promotes needs satisfaction. Therefore, for example, if "valued relationships" constitute a main constraint on antisocial behavior, we need to
know what the institutional and social circumstances are that promote
valued relationships. Or, if "autonomy" means the full satisfaction of
individual human needs, we need to look at what structural and institutional conditions guarantee it. The separation of interests, values, and
needs also "marks a difference between within system conflict *manage-*

ment for some immediate gains, and conflict resolution and provention that looks to the future, and is likely to require system change" (p. 55).

In short, Burton's theory suggests that although agreements can be negotiated over interests within the existing power paradigm, conflicts over values and unsatisfied needs must be placed in a conflict resolution and provention framework because values and needs are nonnegotiable. Such an alternative framework would allow the participants in a conflict to recognize that the system, most likely characterized by traditional power relationships, has failed. Burton believes it is important to recognize that the resolution of conflicts of interests, values, and needs involves "different systems, different decision-making processes, greater decentralization, and different philosophies" (p. 115). Indeed, he argues that nothing short of abandoning the power paradigm will lead to the resolution and provention of conflicts that involve needs.

RADICAL FEMINIST THEORY

Over the past three decades the feminist movement has also searched for different systems, different decision-making processes, greater decentralization, and different philosophies. Feminists, too, have created a body of scholarly work that has drawn attention to alternative ways of organizing societies and alternative ways of solving conflicts within families, and local, national, and global communities.

Therefore, modern radical feminism is regarded by many as "a crucial human project," a political movement for social change (Dinnerstein, 1989, p. 16). Originating in the politically liberal civil rights movement of the 1950s and 1960s, and influenced by the Marxist-oriented new left, radical feminism is still evolving. It encompasses a diversity of feminists—liberal, Marxist, radical, psychoanalytic, socialist, existentialist, postmodern, cultural, and eco-feminists.[2] The theoretical frameworks these feminists advance comprise points of disagreement, but essentially they all center around the domination of women by men. Many will argue that "women's oppression is the most fundamental form of oppression." They see it as the most fundamental because it "is the most widespread, existing in virtually every known society . . . the hardest form of oppression to eradicate . . . [and] causes the most suffering to its victims" (Jagger & Rothenberg, cited in Tong, 1989, p. 710). Radical feminists also see the oppression of women as "a conceptual model for understanding all other forms of oppression" (p. 710).

[2] I am using the term *radical feminist theory* somewhat differently from how it is used by most feminist theorists who would see radical feminism as one kind of theory among many. I use the term more broadly to denote the commonalities among feminists who seek changes in the treatment of women.

In recent years, feminist women of color have criticized the elitist strain in radical feminism for not focusing sufficiently on the fact that some women participate in the oppression of other women and that white women, as a class, are not oppressed by men of color. Brock-Utne (1989) responds in part when she notes that "Not *all* women are more oppressed than all men. But generally, women are more oppressed than men of their own race, caste, or class" (p. 73). Ferguson (1989), however, points out that African-American feminists take issue with the theory that "race and class dominance is based on a prior gender dominance" (p. 17). They challenge the assumptions of "commonalities of women across race, ethnicity, and class."

Current radical feminist thinking reflects an awareness that the oppression of women of color is qualitatively different from that of white women and that class plays a role in oppression as well. However, a central tenet of radical feminism remains: The patriarchal system with its hierarchical organization in which men dominate at every level must be dismantled. Radical feminists want patriarchy abolished not only because of its hierarchical structure, but also because it divides the world into a private sphere in which women belong and a public sphere that men occupy. In this system, the female sphere is regarded as nonpolitical, consisting of "the home, children, domestic life, and sexuality (or its repression)" (Bystydzienski, 1990, p. 4). The male or public sphere is political and includes "the institutions of work, religion, government, and in general, the exercise of power and authority" (p. 4). The hierarchal organization of patriarchy guarantees that the public world not only rules the private world but that it is also regarded as more valuable.

As a result of their experience in a world that rendered them invisible and powerless, radical feminists developed the claim that the personal is political. They declared their experiences as valid and themselves, not men, as authorities on issues concerning women (Bystydzienski, 1990). This phrase—*the personal is political*—has directed attention to patriarchy or that "set of power relations which encapsulates the specific oppression of women" (Coole, 1989, p. 236). It also asserts the value of the personal and of everything patriarchy relegates to the private world.

Radical feminists assert that because female experiences have validity, basic values for society should originate from these experiences. They see the institutionalization of feminine values and feminine ways of thinking and acting as fundamental alternatives to patriarchal institutions. Radical feminists do not want more reforms; instead, they want a fundamental change of society. They hypothesize that there are direct links between "the oppression of women, the conquest of nature, and all forms of violence, including war" (Bystydzienski, 1990, p. 6). In their analyses, which took them beyond the situation of women, they discovered that the predicament of "all oppressed peoples, animals, and the destruction of [nature can be explained by the same] phenomenon—patriarchal values: aggression, competition, hierarchical relations, domination, instrumentalism, and objectification" (p. 6).

Radical feminists have no doubt that patriarchal values destroy because they are based on "power-over," which leaves no space for compassion. Patriarchal values rest on the principle of taking in order to gain. They tolerate no empathy with people's needs and feelings. Instead, they require "rules and tenets, within which [people] must mold [them]selves to fit—thus destroying so much of [the] human need to create" (Plant, 1989, p. 251).

Feminists urge both women and men to find ways to explore and transcend the patterns of power-over in their lives—this they see as a precondition for creating a peaceful environment that is conducive to problem solving and provention. Adiar and Howell (1989) suggest that "patterns of domination and submission reside not just in our institutions and political processes but within each of us. [Such patterns] limit our vision, stunt our creativity, and keep us alienated from ourselves and one another" (p. 220).

CONVERGENCE OF FEMINIST AND NEEDS THEORY

According to Rubenstein (1990), we view society and conflicts within societies through the "lenses" of theory, "whether conscious or unconscious" (p. 1). He views these as "frames of interpretation" that determine how events are perceived and analyzed. And, if the "lens" is defective or the frame is poorly constructed, both perception and analysis will be distorted. Thus, I posed the following questions: Do feminist and human needs theories provide similar lenses? Do they share common frames of interpretation? Alternatively, does each set of lenses have something to offer that can enrich the analyses and prescriptions of the other?

From the previous summaries it is clear that both radical feminist and human needs-based conflict resolution theory advocate a fundamental restructuring of society, albeit with a different focus. Burton (1990) asserts that from a human needs perspective the study of conflict resolution and provention "knows no boundaries of thought," that "it involves the whole person, the nation or identity group of the person, the political system, the physical environment" (p. 20). He claims that the study has "universal applications . . . cuts across cultures . . . cannot be broken down into 'aspects' of behaviour . . . transcends separate compartments of knowledge . . . and seeks to take a holistic view of human conflictual behaviour without being politically unrealistic or . . . superficial" (p. 20). Clark (1990) is more cautious. She argues that "human needs theory as it has so far been developed . . . has taken for its model of human nature the individual of Western thought" (p. 34). Her view seems to support the argument of feminists who carry Clark's view a step further and insist that gender is fundamental to the study of conflict. They would agree that "our [Western] culture is deeply and fundamentally structured socially, politically, ideologically, and conceptually by gender as well as by race, class, and sexuality" (Bleier, 1986, p. 2). It seems, therefore, logical that "the dominant categories of cultural experience ([Western], white, male, middle/upper class, and heterosexual) are reflected [in the study of conflict resolution and its provention]: in its structure, theories, concepts, values, ideologies, and practices" (Bleier, 1986, p. 2). Unless scholars in the field of conflict resolution and provention follow the prescription of Harding (1986) and "begin to theorize gender—to define gender as an analytic category within which humans think and organize their social activity" (p. 17), they are ignoring the magnitude to which gender meanings have permeated our belief systems, institutions, and even such apparently gender-free phenomena as *human* needs.

Thus, feminists agree with Burton and his colleagues that the traditional power paradigm has failed because of its adherence to the status quo and its preservation of outdated structures and institutions that justify the necessity of force to maintain control. But they agree for somewhat different reasons. Feminists also see an inherent identity of the traditional power paradigm (the state and all the interlocking elements of that system) with patriarchy.

Therefore, in contrast to Burton, who asserts that the roots of conflict are not to be found in individual human deformities but in structural and institutional deformities, most feminists seem more inclined to include the complexities of both. Clark (1990) supports this argument by pointing out that:

> our current fission of the concepts of "the individual" and "society" into separate, often warring, compartments blinds us to the fact that these are *one* thing. To the extent that a society is dysfunctional, then so are its individual members, for every person is inescapably a social being, formed by and forming others within his or her circle of contacts. (p. 36)

Feminists point to the field of conflict resolution as an example of how they see individuals and structures interlocked. To solve problems and to create an environment for conflict resolution and provention, therefore, requires changing both individuals as well as institutional structures. In this regard, feminists claim that generally there has been little commitment by male researchers to address issues involving gender as a variable. As feminist scholars (Boulding, 1976a, 1976b, 1992; Brock-Utne, 1989; Gilligan 1982) have shown, the traditional and not so traditional thinking and practice of scholarly disciplines have excluded women as members and justified that exclusion. Boulding (1992), for instance, notes that women played a midwifing role in peace research and that women scholars continue actively in peace studies, but that "it appears today as a very male field" (pp. 2, 11). She points out that most male researchers regard feminist research not as a contribution to the building of conflict analysis and resolution theory but rather as a special case that is primarily of interest to women.

It seems that in a field that apparently is "a synthesis that goes beyond separate disciplines . . . [and] accepts no boundaries of knowledge" (Burton, 1990, p. xi), the exclusion of feminist thought and experience suggests that the roots of conflict are to be found in both institutional and human imperfection. As mentioned above (Adiar & Howell, 1989), the "patterns of domination and submission do not reside just in our institutions and political structures but within each of us" (p. 220).

To overcome these patterns, feminists support the ideas that needs theorists advance: the necessity to create a social environment in which humans can freely express and fulfill their needs, values, and interests without fearing physical and psychological oppression. They would agree with Burton that the creation of an environment of conflict resolution and provention requires changes in which the solution to a problem is not seen as an end-product but rather as a continuing process, that is, each solution establishes new relationships that entail their own set of problems. They would further agree with Burton that such an environment would inspire "a new synthesis of knowledge, new techniques and a change in conceptualization of a problem" (p. 202). A problem would be seen as existing in a wider political, economic, and social environment that would direct the problem-solving process to look for the sources and origins of the conflict (p. 203).

However, Burton's ideas are not exactly new. Feminists point out that societies reflecting such a social environment have existed in the past (Boulding, 1976a; Eisler, 1988), thus underscoring that which feminists have always insisted on: the importance of knowing not only male but also female history. Feminists critique the "given" knowledge of Western history as largely male and argue that only knowledge of both histories will create human identity. And only when we understand human identity through time do we gain a sense of meaning, purpose, and direction that increases our autonomy of choice, particularly with regard to problem solving (Boulding, 1976a).

Thus, for example, in the past there appear to have been long periods of peace and prosperity, during which great strides were made in social, technological, and cultural developments. Eisler (1988) describes this fact as "the best kept secret[:] practically all the material and social technologies fundamental to Western civilization were developed before the imposition of a patriarchal society" (p. 66). During these periods, societies were neither patriarchies nor matriarchies (p. xvi). Indeed, they appear to have been partnership societies in which humans were able to express their needs, values, and interests freely without fearing for their physical and psychological safety. They appear to have been societies in which the perhaps most fundamental human need—social bonding—was satisfied (Clark, 1990, p. 39). Yet, "it is almost uniformly denied that prehistoric societies could have been more humane than were the civilizations that emerged between 4000 and 2000 years ago" (pp. 36-37).

Because "humans evolved with the desire to *belong*, not to *compete*" (Eisler, 1988, p. 39), Burton's (1990) idea of a social environment based on individual human needs will meet with skepticism by feminists. Burton does not spell out what needs exactly are, how we know them, how many exist, and how we separate them from values. (He regards gender, race, and class as features of values and thus considers them analytically separate from needs). He acknowledges that given the role of values in the development of identity (i.e., their importance in defending needs of identity and security), they clearly "impinge upon needs and can be confused with them" (p. 37). Needs may indeed be products of values, that is, needs may be products of gender, culture, race, and class (Avruch & Black, 1987). Therefore, to relegate gender, culture, race, and class to a less influential level denies the constitutive role these concepts play in the development of the individual (Avruch & Black, 1990, p. 227).

In light of the uncertainty of what *ontological* human needs are and whether they exist, the recommendation of the creation of a social environment based on them has to be looked at cautiously. At this point, human needs may be no more than traits common to many people in the Western, white, middle-class, male culture. Creating an environment based on human needs with no attention to how gender, race, and class identities are acquired, may not be a neutral undertaking into which women can be assimilated without loss. Such an undertaking may be a particularly masculine project, disguised as a human project. It may obscure the power structure, allowing it to go unchallenged. After all, in Western culture the central reference point is still the white, middle-class, male.

This is not to say, however, that elements of feminist and human needs theories do not intersect on essential points. Burton's concepts of "valued relationships" and "reciprocity" as preconditions for creating a social environment in which conflicts are not merely settled, but solved and provented, finds support in Gilligan's (1982) research. In her study of moral development, Gilligan found that "people have real emotional needs to be attached to something" (p. 167). She contends that the notion of rights, which is predicated on equality and centered on the understanding of fairness, is in itself not satisfying because it "fractures society and places on every person the burden of standing on his own feet" (p. 167). The notion of responsibility, on the other hand, which "relies on the concept of equity, that is, the recognition of differences in need," fulfills the emotional need for attachment. It rests on an understanding that gives rise to compassion and care, or what Burton calls "reciprocity" and "valued relationships." Clark (1990) concludes that "meaningful social bonds are an absolute need of the human organism, and rupture of these bonds is—as novelists and playwrights have been telling us for centuries —a tragedy" (p. 46).

Similarly, feminist and human needs theories recognize the importance of autonomy in creating a new social environment. From the human needs perspective, an autonomous person "has self-esteem and a sense of competence that is socially recognized" (Burton, 1990, p. 93). Feminists argue that self-esteem and a sense of competence derives from exercising real power in all areas of their lives. They do not equate power with the domination and exploitation of others "but rather the freedom and space to express [one] own desires, creativity and potential: to flourish and find '[one] place in the sun'" (Segal, 1984, cited in Coole, 1988, p. 254).

Feminists reconceptualize power as coming from within, from the attempt to reach one's fullest potential and equate it with love and responsibility. Eisler (1988) named it *actualization* power. Neither women nor men are subordinate to the other: By complementing each other, their power is doubled. This notion of power corresponds to Burton's (1990) assertion that nonmaterial needs are often fundamental to parties in conflict, and that the increase in the satisfaction of those needs for one party leads to the increase in satisfaction for the other. Conflicts, Burton argues, are very often not over scarce material resources, but over identity and security, which do not involve short supplies of resources.

CONCLUSION

In this chapter, I have explored both feminist and human needs-based conflict resolution theories to better understand why they call into question the prevailing power paradigm. I have compared some of the arguments advanced by each and discovered points of convergence as well as divergence between them. Although the "lenses" of feminist and human needs-based conflict resolution theories are not the same, they share some common vision.

I believe it is clear that the study of conflict resolution and provention would be enriched by recognizing that as "a symbol system, gender difference is the most ancient, most universal, and most powerful origin of many morally valued conceptualizations of everything else in the world around us. . . ." (Harding, 1986, p. 17). By not defining gender "as an analytic category within which humans think about and organize their social activity," conflict resolution theorists fail to "appreciate the extent to which gender meanings have suffused our belief systems, institutions, and even such apparently gender-free phenomena as [human needs]" (p. 17).

By including the experience and thinking of feminists in conflict resolution and provention theory, scholars could expand their "prevailing models of reality" and contribute to creating what Eisler (1988) has termed *partnership* societies, which tend to be much more peaceful because they are less hierarchic and authoritarian (p. xix). Such a partnership could lead feminists and needs-oriented conflict theorists to achieve more of their *common* goals than might otherwise be the case. Only by including the experience and thinking of both women and men in theory building can we fully satisfy what Clark (1990) regards as a fundamental human need: a "sense of temporal continuity between an unexperienced yet culturally present past and a never to be experienced yet personally significant future" (p. 48).

REFERENCES

Adiar, M., & Howell, S. (1989). The subjective side of power. In J. Plant (Ed.), *Healing the wounds: The promise of ecofeminism* (pp. 219-226). Philadelphia: New Society Publishers.

Avruch, K., & Black, P.W. (1987). A generic theory of conflict resolution: A critique. *Negotiation Journal, 3*(1), 87-96.

Avruch, K., & Black, P.W. (1990). Ideas of human nature in contemporary conflict resolution theory. *Negotiation Journal, 6*(3), 221-228.

Bleier, R. (1986). *Feminist approaches to science.* New York: Pergamon Press.

Boulding, E. (1976a) *The underside of history—a view of women through time.* Boulder, CO: Westview Press.

Boulding, E. (1976b). How women can build a more livable world. *Transition, 3*(1).

Boulding, E. (1992). Women in peace. In D. Spender & C. Kramarae

(Eds.), *The knowledge explosion: Feminist contributions to knowledge.* New York: Pergamon Press.

Brock-Utne, B. (1989). *Feminist perspectives on peace and peace education.* New York: Pergamon Press.

Burton, J.W. (1990). *Conflict: Resolution and provention.* New York: St. Martin's Press.

Burton, J.W., & Sandole, D.J.D. (1986). Generic theory: The basis of conflict resolution. *Negotiation Journal,* 2(4), 333-344.

Bystydzienski, J.M. (1990, July). *Connections between radical feminism, peace and ecology.* Paper presented at the 25th anniversary conference of the International Peace Research Association (IPRA), Groeningen, The Netherlands.

Clark, M. (1990). Meaningful social bonding as a universal human need. In J.W. Burton (Ed.), *Conflict: Human needs theory* (pp. 34-59). New York: St. Martin's Press.

Coole, D.H. (1988) *Women in political theory.* Brighton, Sussex (England): Wheatsheaf Books.

Dinnerstein, D. (1989) What does feminism mean? In A. Harris & Y. King (Eds.), *Rocking the ship of state* (pp. 13-23). Boulder, CO: Westview Press.

Eisler, R. (1988). *The chalice and the blade.* San Francisco: Harper & Row.

Ferguson, A. (1989). *Blood at the root.* London: Pandora Press.

Gilligan, C. (1982). *In a different voice.* Cambridge, MA: Harvard University, Press.

Harding, S. (1986). *The science question in feminism.* Ithaca, NY: Cornell University Press.

Jagger, A.M., & Rothenberg, P.S. (Eds.). (1984). *Feminist frameworks.* New York: McGraw Hill.

Plant, J. (1989). *Healing the wounds: The promise of ecofeminism.* Philadelphia: New Society Publishers.

Rubenstein, R. (1990, April) *Interpreting violent conflict: A conference for conflict analysts and journalists.* Summary of proceedings, Center for Conflict Analysis and Resolution, Fairfax, VA.

Tong, R. (1989). *Feminist thought: A comprehensive introduction.* Boulder, CO: Westview Press.

Author Index

Subject Index